CIVIL SOCIETY IN THE MUSLIM WORLD

Civil Society in the Muslim World

Contemporary Perspectives

Edited by

AMYN B. SAJOO

I.B.Tauris Publishers
LONDON • NEW YORK
in association with
The Institute of Ismaili Studies
LONDON

Published in 2002 by I.B.Tauris & Co Ltd
6 Salem Rd, London W2 4BU
175 Fifth Avenue, New York NY 10010
www.ibtauris.com

in association with The Institute of Ismaili Studies
42–44 Grosvenor Gardens, London SW1W OEB
www.iis.ac.uk

In the United States of America and in Canada distributed by
St Martin's Press, 175 Fifth Avenue, New York NY 10010

ISBN 1 86064 858 4

A full CIP record for this book is available from the British Library
A full CIP record for this book is available from the Library of Congress

Library of Congress catalog card: available

Typeset in ITC New Baskerville by Hepton Books, Oxford
Printed and bound in Great Britain by MPG Books Ltd, Bodmin

The Institute of Ismaili Studies

The Institute of Ismaili Studies was established in 1977 with the object of promoting scholarship and learning on Islam, in the historical as well as contemporary contexts, and a better understanding of its relationship with other societies and faiths.

The Institute's programmes encourage a perspective which is not confined to the theological and religious heritage of Islam, but seek to explore the relationship of religious ideas to broader dimensions of society and culture. The programmes thus encourage an interdisciplinary approach to the materials of Islamic history and thought. Particular attention is also given to issues of modernity that arise as Muslims seek to relate their heritage to the contemporary situation.

Within the Islamic tradition, the Institute's programmes promote research on those areas which have, to date, received relatively little attention from scholars. These include the intellectual and literary expressions of Shi'ism in general, and Ismailism in particular.

In the context of Islamic societies, the Institute's programmes are informed by the full range and diversity of cultures in which Islam is practised today, from the Middle East, South and Central Asia and Africa to the industrialised societies of the West, thus taking into consideration the variety of contexts which shape the ideals, beliefs and practices of the faith.

These objectives are realised through concrete programmes

and activities organised and implemented by various departments of the Institute. The Institute also collaborates periodically, on a programme-specific basis, with other institutions of learning in the United Kingdom and abroad.

The Institute's academic publications fall into a number of interrelated categories:

1. Occasional papers or essays addressing broad themes of the relationship between religion and society, with special reference to Islam.
2. Monographs exploring specific aspects of Islamic faith and culture, or the contributions of individual Muslim figures or writers.
3. Editions or translations of significant primary or secondary texts.
4. Translations of poetic or literary texts which illustrate the rich heritage of spiritual, devotional and symbolic expressions in Muslim history.
5. Works on Ismaili history and thought, and the relationship of the Ismailis to other traditions, communities and schools of thought in Islam.
6. Proceedings of conferences and seminars sponsored by the Institute.
7. Bibliographical works and catalogues which document manuscripts, printed texts and other source materials.

This book falls into category six listed above.

In facilitating these and other publications, the Institute's sole aim is to encourage original research and analysis of relevant issues. While every effort is made to ensure that the publications are of a high academic standard, there is naturally bound to be a diversity of views, ideas and interpretations. As such, the opinions expressed in these publications are to be understood as belonging to their authors alone.

Contents

Foreword

The evolving phases of what in our time is called globalisation are felt and conceived rather differently across the world. Muslim societies have begun increasingly to inquire into what culturally, religiously and socially relevant civic ideals might mean within their own highly diverse contexts. The interest and focus by Muslims on issues relevant to civil society reflect, in part, the perceived absence of sustainable institutions that respond to strongly felt needs for social and economic development, poverty reduction and proper governance in their societies. These questions also relate to the role of the state as an agent for change and as custodian of social justice.

The papers in this volume offer perspectives on many of the questions that engage the Muslim world today in the quest to delineate the form and substance of modern civil society. There is, of course, an elaborate history of discussion and debate in Muslim thought and praxis about the moral content of society, and its diverse expressions through political and legal governance. Muslim philosophers such as al-Farabi (d.950 CE) and the Ikhwan al-Safa (late 10th century CE) extensively debated an issue posed much earlier by Plato, namely the nature of the 'good society'. Building further on the Platonic and Aristotelian legacy, they underscored the necessity of 'community' and 'ethics' to reflect what in their view was a matrix where individuals pursued virtue and created an ethos of equilibrium and excellence in society. They argued for the greater good of all as a moral imperative in which the state and citizens were both engaged, because they believed that in the Muslim polity, interdependence and authority were a shared reality. This philosophical tradition not only raised universal issues of intellectual significance, but also represented for Muslim societies of the time a practical quest for consensus among several strands of thought linking intellectual, legal, theological and community concerns.

In the spirit of that deliberative tradition, the Institute of Ismaili Studies invited during the 2000–01 academic year a number of leading scholars to explore the idea of civil society in comparative Muslim contexts. Of late, the Institute has accelerated its efforts to take account of new opportunities for academic collaboration and educational activity in Central Asia. Building on its continuing interest in developments in Muslim societies in Asia, Africa, Europe and North America – and consistent with the diverse composition of its students and faculty – the Institute seeks to foster dialogue on how one might envision values of civil society that reconcile larger concerns with understanding and respect for inherited convictions, institutions, and practices.

While addressing Muslim contexts, the authors of the articles in this book have tried to avoid homogenised or reductive views of Islam and its impact on plural Muslim societies. A great deal of oversimplification about Islam, particularly in the popular media and some academic writings, has ignored the fact that the pluralistic character of Muslim societies needs to be taken seriously as a premise in analysing issues of civil society. The role of culture has also been similarly underestimated, by treating it as prescriptive or formulaic; again, the interaction of cultures within Muslim societies, as illustrated in contemporary Central Asia (and elsewhere in South and Southeast Asia) has too often been ignored in favour

of a narrowly-defined theological and deterministic definition of
Islam. In consequence, some of the attributes of Muslim society
are erroneously thought to be inhospitable to the building of civic
cultures. Religious traditions have often found extremist expression in world history, a tendency to which Muslims are no
exception. Yet there is abundant evidence of Muslim teaching,
thought and experience that has enabled moral guidance and
the building of institutions in support of the good society.

   That deep civic sensibility has pervaded the history of most
Muslim civilisations. Ethical tenets have found expression as legal
obligations, and culturally as well as intellectually as personal, social and even ecological commitment. Toshihiko Izutsu's
pioneering study of Qur'anic ethics called attention to the significant shift in the moral paradigm within Arab society upon the
advent of Islam. The late Fazlur Rahman, noted University of
Chicago scholar of Islamic thought and modernist Muslim thinker,
extended the inquiry by arguing that early Muslim society was
impelled by a keen rational and moral concern for social reform
– and that this intentionality was conceived in ways that encouraged a strong commitment to pluralist dialogue. Certainly, the
enabling elements of those historical impulses are clear enough.
The notion of the umma in the Qur'an articulates the concept of
a moral order achieved through a 'mediating community' (2:143)
which Muslims throughout history have seen as the core of the
Prophet Muhammad's mission to develop society. Such an ideal
conceived individuals as agents shaping society by investing it with
a moral underpinning based on personal and intellectual conviction. The custodial role of the community and the individual were
grounded in a perspective that saw this ideal as relevant not only
to its own members but also future generations. One institutional
reflection of this was organised philanthropy through the *awqaf*,
charitable trusts, endowed by individuals to translate the ethics of
giving into a permanent trust.

   Ethics, it has been argued, deal with values and therefore anyone contemplating acts of right and wrong, good and bad is –
consciously or unconsciously – ethically engaged. At a time of
convergence among cultures and dissonance in global affairs, the

persistence and relevance of ethical concerns become salient and universal as a cornerstone of mature citizenship. In his most recent work, *Bowling Alone,* Robert Putnam laments the prevailing uncivil trend in contemporary western society where individuals retreat into personal, private spheres, and forsake community. Communitarian perspectives have suggested that the best foundation for civil society is a shared set of values, sustained by education, embedded in strong public and civic institutions, within a pluralistic framework. Can Muslim societies build on the inherited framework of ethical and community commitment and reconcile these values with models of governance that share the common search for a moral order for themselves and others among whom they live?

Azim Nanji
Director
The Institute of Ismaili Studies

Editor's Note

This volume is the culmination of a year-long project that was highlighted by a series of seminars on civil society hosted by The Institute of Ismaili Studies, beginning in November 2000. Most of the chapters evolved from papers delivered at the seminars where participants ranged from senior academics and policy-makers to community activists, journalists and graduate students. The exceptions were the contributions by Aziz Esmail, Tair Faradov and myself, which reflected the need to address more specific aspects of the discourses on civil society within and beyond the Muslim world. As observed at several points in the volume, the implications of the events of September 11, 2001, which continue to unravel, reinforce many of our salient thematic concerns.

We have been cognizant of the need to range inclusively over the 'Muslim world', especially in view of the general tendency to focus on the Arab Middle East. Ideally, this volume would more fully evince our robust interest not only in Central Asia and the Near East, which are well represented, but also in Eastern Africa, Southeast Asia and West Africa, that lack distinct chapters simply because of acute constraints of time and resources. Nevertheless, we have sought to capture the key underlying themes that these transitional regions share in the wider canvas.

I would like to record my appreciation of the Institute's award of a visiting fellowship that facilitated this undertaking – and particularly the energetic support of Professor Azim Nanji and Dr Farhad Daftary from inception to realisation. At every stage, I benefited from Kutub Kassam's pragmatic insights and encouragement, which on more than one occasion helped keep the project on track. The task of coordinating the London seminars was made congenial by the commitment to the promotion of civic discourse by a far-flung group of guest scholars, who further had to endure my unceasing demands to incorporate fresh developments. No less committed to the success of the seminars were my Institute colleagues – notably Nadia Holmes, Julia Kolb, Rizwan Mawani, Selina Kassam, Naz Jiwa, Catherine Dove and Shahira Karmali-Kassam – together with Abdul Ismail who graciously volunteered to videotape the series.

Amid the rapid flux of political events in the course of the project, the challenge of promptly seeing this volume through to press was met only because of the editorial support of Patricia Salazar, who brought her vast experience to bear in finalising the manuscript. We were abetted in this by I.B. Tauris, the publisher, whose enthusiasm and recognition of the project's topicality were refreshing.

This list of collaborators is far from exhaustive, not least with regard to those in Central Asia who generously shared during my field-visit their experiences of living through post-Soviet transitions to putative civil society, which undoubtedly influenced the overall tenor and aspirations of this project. That is also true of the diverse graduate student body at the Institute, who engaged keenly with guest scholars and myself in sharing their perspectives, quite apart from those among them who volunteered in arranging the seminars. All in all, the foregoing collaborations are for me evidence, if it were needed, that the civic impulse remains very much alive across a plurality of communities and generations of Muslims as well as non-Muslims.

A.B.S.

About the Contributors

SHIRIN AKINER is Lecturer in Central Asian Studies at SOAS, University of London, and an Associate Fellow of the Royal Institute of International Affairs, London. She has directed British government-funded training projects in collaboration with institutions in Kazakhstan and Uzbekistan, and is a regular media consultant on Central Asia. Dr. Akiner's many books include *Tajikistan: Disintegration or Reconciliation?* (London, 2001), *The Formation of Kazakh Identity* (London, 1995) and *Minorities in a Time of Change: Prospects for Conflict, Stability and Development in Central Asia* (Minority Rights Group, London, 1997). She has also edited *Political and Economic Trends in Central Asia* (London, 1994), *Languages and Scripts of Central Asia* (with N. Sims-Williams, London, 1997); *Tajikistan: the Challenges of Independence* (with M-R Djalili and F. Grare, London, 1997), and *Sustainable Development in Central Asia* (with S. Tideman, London, 1998).

MOHAMMED ARKOUN is Emeritus Professor of Islamic Thought at the Sorbonne, Paris III, and a leading contemporary Muslim intellectual. He is the recipient of the 2002 Giorgio Levi Della Vida Award in Islamic Studies at the University of California, Los

Angeles, and delivered the 2001–02 Gifford Lectures at the University of Edinburgh on 'Islamic Reason'. Professor Arkoun is currently a Senior Research Fellow at the Institute of Ismaili Studies, London, where he also serves as a Governor. He is Chair of Islamic Studies at the United States Library of Congress and editor of the journal *Arabica*. Among his numerous writings in several languages are *L'Humanisme Arabe au IVe/Xe siècle* (Paris, 1982), *Lectures du Coran* (Paris, 1982), *L'Islam, morale et politique* (Paris, 1986), *Rethinking Islam* (Boulder, CO, 1994), and *The Unthought in Contemporary Islamic Thought* (London, 2002).

AZIZ ESMAIL is the former Dean of The Institute of Ismaili Studies, London (1988–98) and, since 1998, has served as one of its Governors. Originally trained in philosophy, literature and religion, Dr Esmail has held lecturing and research posts at various American universities, and earlier at the University of Nairobi, Kenya. He has been associated with The Committee on Social Thought at the University of Chicago, as well as Harvard University's Center for the Study of World Religions and Graduate School of Education. Dr Esmail has been a consultant to, among other institutions, the Humanities division of the Rockefeller Foundation. Besides articles in journals, his writings include *The Poetics of Religious Experience* (London, 1996) and a volume of translations of Indo-Islamic poetry, *A Scent of Sandalwood* (London, 2002).

TAIR FARADOV is a Senior Research Fellow at the International Centre for Social Research in Baku, Azerbaijan, while also affiliated with the University of Geneva's project on Reinventing Citizenship in the South Caucasus. A sociologist by training, Dr Faradov has held appointments with the American University in Baku, the University of California at Los Angeles (UCLA) Center for Near Eastern Studies, and UNICEF in Azerbaijan. His research on civic values, pluralism and Islam in post-Soviet Azerbaijan and the Caucasus has been supported by grants from the MacArthur Foundation, the Open Society Institute, and the Democracy Commission of the US Information Service. Dr Faradov has a long record of national activism on tolerance and inter-ethnic relations, and is a senior member of the Institute for Human Rights of the Azerbaijan Academy of Sciences.

ABDOU FILALI-ANSARY is Director of the Institute for the Study of Muslim Civilisations in London. He served from 1984 to 2001 as the founding director of the King Abdul-Aziz Foundation for Islamic Studies and Human Sciences in Casablanca, Morocco, having previously taught modern philosophy in the Faculty of Letters in Rabat. Professor Filali-Ansary has contributed widely to academic discourses on democratisation and civil society in the Middle East, and in 1993 co-founded the journal *Prologues: revue maghrébine du livre* (in Arabic and French). His work includes a translation into French of Ali Abderraziq's landmark book, *Islam and the Foundations of Political Power* (Paris and Casablanca, 1994), and an essay titled *Is Islam Hostile to Secularism?* (Casablanca, 1996; 1999). He serves on the advisory boards of numerous academic and cultural institutions, including the Aga Khan Award for Architecture (Geneva).

ERSIN KALAYCIOĞLU is Professor of Political Science at Sabanci University, Istanbul. He is currently engaged in a study of democratic consolidation in Turkey – while writing extensively on civil society – and previously worked on the Turkish Values component of the World Values Survey carried out by Ronald Inglehart of the University of Michigan. Professor Kalaycioğlu has authored and co-edited several books in Turkish on Comparative Political Participation, Turkish Political Life (co-edited), and Contemporary Political Science, Turkish Politics (co-edited), and co-edited in English *Turkey: Political, Social and Economic Challenges in the 1990s* (Leiden, New York, Cologne, 1995), in addition to his numerous contributions in these areas – including civil society – in English and Turkish language books and journals.

IFTIKHAR MALIK, a Fellow of the Royal Historical Society, is Senior Lecturer in History at Bath Spa University College. He was Quaid-e-Azam Fellow at St. Antony's College, Oxford (1989–94), and held postdoctoral appointments at the University of California,

Berkeley, and Columbia University, New York. Dr Malik's extensive contributions to the literature on Pakistan and Muslim politics include *State and Civil Society in Pakistan: Politics of Authority, Ideology and Ethnicity* (London, 1997) and *Islam, Nationalism and the West: Issues of Identity in Pakistan* (London, 1999) – as well as a report for the Minority Rights Group titled *Religious Minorities in Pakistan* (London, 2002). He is also a regular consultant to the media on South Asian politics.

ZIBA MIR-HOSSEINI is currently Hauser Global Law Visiting Professor at New York University. She is also a Research Associate of the Department of Social Anthropology, University of Cambridge, and of the Centre for Near and Middle Eastern Studies, SOAS, University of London. As a consultant, researcher and writer, Dr Mir-Hosseini specialises in gender, family relations, law and development in the Middle East. Her writings include *Marriage on Trial: A Study of Islamic Family Law in Iran and Morocco* (London, 1993), and *Islam and Gender: The Religious Debate in Contemporary Iran* (Princeton, NJ, 1999; London, 2000). She has also co-directed two feature-length documentary films, the multiple award-winning *Divorce Iranian Style* (1998), and *Runaway* (2001).

OLIVIER ROY is a research director in the Humanities & Social Sciences section of the Centre National pour Recherche Scientifique, Paris. He was Special Representative of the Organization for Security & Co-operation in Europe (OSCE) in Tajikistan in 1993 and 1994, and then headed the OSCE Mission to Tajikistan. Dr Roy undertook several journeys in Afghanistan during the Mujahideen resistance to the Soviet invasion of 1979, and then embarked on numerous trips inside ex-Soviet Central Asia, notably Uzbekistan and Tajikistan. He has been a consultant with the French Ministry of Foreign Affairs since 1984, and is the author of *The Failure of Political Islam* (Cambridge, MA, 1994), *Vers un Islam européen* (Paris, 1999) and *The New Central Asia: The Creation of Nations* (London, 2000) and, while also being a frequent contributor on civil society to French and English language journals and books.

AMYN B. SAJOO led the project on Civil Society in the Muslim World as a Visiting Fellow at The Institute of Ismaili Studies, London, from 2000 to 2001, which culminated in the present volume. Trained in international human rights law and policy, he was an advisor with the Canadian Human Rights Commission from 1989 to 1992, before being appointed the 1993–94 Canada-ASEAN Fellow on Pluralism at the Institute of Southeast Asian Studies in Singapore. Dr Sajoo has served as a consultant-scholar with several organisations and government agencies, including the federal departments of Justice and Foreign Affairs in Canada. He is the author of *Pluralism in Old Societies and New States* (Singapore, 1994), and is a regular contributor on international human rights, public ethics and Muslim affairs in scholarly journals and the mass media on both sides of the Atlantic.

Introduction:
Civic Quests and Bequests

Amyn B. Sajoo

'Civil society is a Western dream, a historical aspiration', claims
the eminent Turkish scholar, Şerif Mardin, and as such, 'does not
translate into Islamic terms'.[1] Civility, a 'latent' aspect of civic
culture, is a shared civilisational idea, he argues. But not civil society with its prizing of the rule of law, human agency, and the
autonomy of society and individuals from the state. While the
wellsprings of this dream can be traced to medieval Europe, Mardin – like most scholars – locates its more concrete forms in the
post-Enlightenment age where the likes of Adam Smith, John
Locke, Adam Ferguson and eventually Hegel, cast their economic,
political and spiritual aspirations in terms of *institutionalised* solidarities and liberties. The original elements of that civic journey
are felt to have survived the tides of history in the North Atlantic
community, including the currents of fascism and genocide, to
become 'the foundation … of modern democratic theory'.[2] Indeed, so successful was the quest that the term 'civil society' all
but fell into disuse, as Ernest Gellner has remarked[3] – even as
'democracy', to which it had given sustenance, became all the
rage.

In stark contrast, the Muslim dream is said to be a yearning for 'social equilibrium created under the aegis of a just prince', in which the significance of the rule of law pales against the charismatic authority of the ruler. Human agency, so critical in the emergence of Western modernity, is likewise seen as a casualty in Muslim societies. For, while it was 'filled with its own rich, humanistic content, the dream, once anchored in Islam precluded the adoption of a concept concerning the gradual perfectibility of man through man's making of his own history'.[4] The primacy of social justice in Muslim tradition becomes, in this perspective, a harking back to an imagined epoch of perfection – and worse, as Mardin sees it, a substitute for the concept of freedom that has energised liberal modernity. But what of the autonomy of religious scholars, the ulama, and of the mercantile class, who so often defied the arbitrary power of sultans and caliphs? Was this not the equivalent of the church/bourgeois resistance that fuelled the rise of civil society in the West? Not so, we are told. The defiance of despotism was not girded by an enforceable social contract, in which property and individual rights were sacrosanct under a meaningful rule of law. At best, the tenuous autonomy of merchants and scholars could be seen as 'embedded in a "lifeworld" of religious discourse', congruent with that of the medieval West before the advent of liberal civil society.[5] And there lies the rub.

Contemporary Muslim societies, it is argued, may acquire the paraphernalia of Western modernity, including the political and economic institutions of capitalist democracy. Yet the bequests of 'Islamic collective memory' and of 'post-industrial society' leave intact the fact that the Muslim dream remains different from that of the West. Civil society is inextricably bound to the latter, while the former must be understood on its own terms, in which freedom amounts at most to mystical reveries of transcendence. This is true not only of individuals but also of what Carl Petry calls 'communal transcendence', in which solidarity groups (of which the umma itself is the exemplar *par excellence*) are the upshot of inequities inflicted by arbitrary power on hapless subjects, who band together and win esteem.[6] The individual liberty that is a key condition of effective citizenship and hence of civil society remains elusive in

practice – and, in any instance, undesired in principle. Or as Gellner puts it squarely, Islam 'exemplifies a social order which seems
to lack much capacity to provide countervailing institutions or
associations, which is atomised without much individualism, and
operates effectively without intellectual pluralism'.[7]

There is enormous irony in those musings about the unique-
ness of civil society's Western dreamers. They were, after all, voiced
as part of the revival of interest among scholars, citizen activists,
policy-makers, journalists and even the general public in the subject when the former-Soviet bloc in East-Central Europe found
itself wanting to do more than dream about democratic institutions. John Keane, Gellner himself, Vaclav Havel, Jean Cohen,
Adam Seligman, and a host of others directed their post-cold war
writings at the practical and conceptual challenges of applying a
civil society paradigm where decades of communism had left only
vestiges of civic culture – without which, it was argued, mere electoral transitions were doomed to failure. Much the same thinking
was being applied, if hesitantly, to issues of democratic consolidation in Latin America, East Asia, South Africa and beyond. Then,
Robert Putnam and others directed their attention back to the
prevailing civic deficits within the developed democracies themselves, on both sides of the Atlantic, after a hiatus that had
consigned the idea to oblivion.[8]

If civil society is wedded exclusively to the particular unfolding
of North Atlantic/West European history, why the readiness to
acknowledge the prospect of Czech, Hungarian, Polish, Ruma-
nian, Slovak ... Argentine, Brazilian, Chilean, Mexican ... Chinese,
Philippine, South Korean and Vietnamese dreams of institution-
alising the legal, economic and political frameworks of civic
culture? Were not the collective memories of their publics as *sui
generis* as those of the West – and why would they not content
themselves with a commitment to civility in public life, drawing
on Buddhist, Catholic, Confucian, Orthodox Christian and other
civilisational bequests? Did those bequests treat individual freedom in the same way as did the Protestant traditions of Northern
Europe, and if not, how could they dream of modern citizenship
and its attendant cluster of political liberties?

It is not *bien pensant* academics alone who sought to apply the discourse of civil society outside its modern birthplace. So have a myriad of human rights and development activists within and beyond their national frontiers, artists and intellectuals in search of creative spaces, progressive government officials, and lenders and planners in international financial and political agencies (from the European Commission to the World Bank). What is it about the language and civic imagination of late eighteenth/early nineteenth-century Northern Europe that has come to appeal to such varied publics in our time?

It comes as no surprise – amid the burgeoning applications of the term in diverse contexts – that civil society has not quite turned from an *idée passé* to an *idée fixe*. Its usage ranges from straightforward descriptions of non-state institutions and associations that are regarded as critical to sustaining modern democratic participation, to the analytical expression of values – individual liberty, public solidarity, pluralism, nonviolence – that sustain a dynamic civic culture. A reasonably lucid core of meaning obtains across the multifarious usages, the spirit of which is captured thus by Keane:

> [T]he exercise of power is best monitored and controlled within a democratic order marked by the institutional separation of civil society and state institutions. Seen from this power-sharing perspective, state actors and institutions within a democracy are constantly forced to respect, protect and share power with civilian actors and institutions – just as civilians living within the state-protected institutions of a heterogeneous society are forced to recognize social differences and to share power among themselves. A democracy, in short, [is] ... seen as a fractured and self-reflexive system of power in which there are daily reminders to governors and governed alike that those who exercise power over others cannot do anything they want, and that (as Spinoza put it) even sovereigns are forced in practice to recognize that they cannot make a table eat grass.[9]

The appeal, then, for citizens of former totalitarian as well as authoritarian regimes of the notion of limiting the state by empowering society and subjecting both to an effective rule of law –

which would also constrain the resurgence of subversive ideologies – seems obvious. Added to this is the capacity of civil society, when successful, to accommodate ethnic and cultural nationalisms unleashed by the weakening of coercive state institutions; the flip side of which is the rash of civil conflict in the post-cold war era. Accommodation, of course, is not the same as resolution. Plural societies experience plural tensions even when, indeed especially when, genuine participatory politics are feasible. Keane rightly refers to the various forces at play as an 'ensemble ... permanently in tension with each other'.[10] The term 'ensemble' reinforces a metaphor that I have come to attach to these dynamics – that of a jazz performance in which individual improvisation is not only integral but essential to the overall effect. Why jazz in particular? Because of its free-form energy, born of a history of resistance against political, economic and social oppression.[11] Not surprisingly, jazz became a conspicuous symbol of defiance against Moscow and its satellite governments in cities like Prague, Krakow and Warsaw.[12]

That metaphor also animates another key aspect of civil society, namely the public sphere – what Jurgen Habermas calls 'a network for communicating information and points of view'.[13] He portrays it as a 'lifeworld' that harbours, but is not identical to, the more recognisable forms of institutions, organisations or social orders. Nebulous as this may appear, it is none the less the locus of citizen experience, interpretation and expression of opinion that is also the life-blood of civil society as a modern construct.[14] Put differently, it is the space where our jazz ensemble performs in relation to an engaged audience (whose members might even venture to contribute improvisational riffs on the saxophone or piano). The public sphere today can be conceived in postmodern terms as a series of 'imagined communities',[15] both within and beyond national frontiers. As such, it comprises not only the more formal webs of associations of civil society, but also its more fluid communicative actions – *outside the direct mediation of the political (that is, formal state) sphere*. It is of the essence of civil society that the public sphere stands apart from the political sphere and yet, as Charles Taylor observes, remains 'normative for power', meaning that it demands, or ought to demand, the attention of political decision-makers.[16]

Curiously, for Habermas the modern public sphere excludes the activities of the market economy, in pointed contrast to traditional Marxist analytical usage. He does not offer a coherent rationale for this insistence, given the empirical reality that it is in countries with more sophisticated market economies that civil society tends also to be most dynamic. This is not to deny some of the corrosive effects of the contemporary global economy on aspects of civic culture.[17] Rather, it is to recognise that the distinction between political and economic expressions of civic solidarity – of social capital, in the popular phrase – becomes increasingly untenable in complex societies.[18] To return to our metaphor, it is not persuasive to claim that a professional ensemble that entertains a paying audience ceases to constitute the public sphere, while the same ensemble giving a free performance does.

Where does all this leave us with respect to the claim about the West having a patented dream, so to speak, on civil society? Does the evidence support the notion that imagined communities with a desire for the rule of law, pluralism and individual freedom, fuelled and sometimes corroded by market energies, live – or can live – in the West alone? To insist that it does surely amounts to adopting a snapshot perspective on the evolution of civic culture. Writing in a context not entirely unrelated to the present, Janet Abu-Lughod has observed that '[c]ities are processes, not products', that they are subject to the tides of history rather than created by fiat.[19] The same would appear to be true of civil society: the question is whether the conditions in which it is cultivated are exclusive to the West, assuming that constructs like 'the West' (and hence its assorted counterparts) are meaningful in our time. Mardin's analysis, like Gellner's, while occasionally insightful, betrays the limits of a normative approach to the subject. If the rise of civic culture in the West was in fact the product of historical factors and choices that can inspire Eastern Europeans and Latin Americans and East Asians facing some of the same challenges of transition, then only a deterministic logic would compel the inference that they are bound to fail. Indeed, one is reduced to arguing that those other cultures and societies have 'essentials' that militate against the adoption over time of institutions like the rule of law, of the values of human rights, and of the aspirations for effective citizenship. Such pessimism does not appear to afflict the *citizens* of those societies.

Is 'Islam' Different?

We are still left with the claim, however, that 'Islam' is uniquely different in its resistance to the conditionsM or civil society, because – unlike, say, Latin America and Eastern Europe – its adherents inhabit a lifeworld that is tied inextricably to a religious discourse. Indeed, this argument has also been pressed into the service of the 'clash of civilisations' thesis championed by Samuel Huntington, in which the West is seen as somehow fated to collide with Islam because of irreconcilable differences embedded in history, culture and demography.[20] Perhaps not surprisingly, these claims have come to the fore since the events of September 11, 2001. 'Islam' is touted as the common denominator that 'explains' all manner of political militancy and violence, not least in terms of the concept of jihad that is accorded an all-encompassing primacy by its critics (as much as by religious extremists).[21] Then there is Martin Kramer's suggestion that the Middle East (except for Israel), irrespective of ethno-cultural and socio-economic variations, is undeserving of positive consideration as a locus for civil society because of prevailing authoritarian tendencies (except, in his view, for Israel) – and that American scholars of the Middle East did not anticipate the attacks of September 11 partly because they failed to recognise this reality. One of those scholars responds that Kramer might as well upbraid Harvard University's Robert Putnam for failing to anticipate Timothy McVeigh's massive terrorist bombing in Oklahoma City shortly after Putnam's work on 'bowling alone' in America earned him an invitation to the Clinton White House![22] The dystopian claims about Islamic or Middle Eastern exceptionalism imply that an affinity for Muslim values is inherently incompatible with, if not actively inimical to, modern civil society.

There are empirical as well as conceptual reasons to believe that those arguments are grounded in dubious assumptions. A common thread running through the responses offered below is that critiques like those of Mardin and Gellner fail to come to terms with the *implications* that flow from the diverse ethno-cultural, historical and political realities of the Muslim world. One recalls Edward Said's remark about the propensity in Gellner when discussing Muslim politics and culture to expend 'thousands of words without a single reference to people, periods, or events';[23] it is a tendency that extends to the apologetic literature on civil society and Islam. I propose to spell out both the scale and quality of the plural realities invoked here, including those of the recently emergent republics of ex-Soviet Central Asia and the Caucasus. In addition, the Muslim diaspora in Western Europe and North America – notably in France, Germany, Italy, the Netherlands, Portugal, Spain, the United Kingdom, Canada and the United States – today has demographic and intellectual roots that affect the evolving nature of citizenship and civil society within those countries, even as they impact emerging discourses in their ancestral lands. This trend is clearly on the upswing, yet it tends to feature more in assessments of national security than civic culture.[24] None of these characteristics taken alone is exclusive to Islam and Muslims. Their aggregate effect is to remind us that the conceptual inferences that stem from them militate against reductive references to 'Islam' as a surrogate idea or usage for unitary faith, history, or socio-economic condition. Such a conflation is no more justifiable here than it would if applied to Christian, Jewish or Hindu civilisational complexities.

Social and Economic Islam

Of the more than 1.2 billion individuals who constitute the Muslim world today,[25] the majority inhabit the four South-Asian countries of Bangladesh, India, Indonesia and Pakistan. What is generally conceived of as the 'Islamic heartland' in the Arabian peninsula is in fact home to a small minority of the umma; even within the Middle East (broadly conceived), the largest concentrations of Muslims are in Iran and Turkey, rather than the Arab world. Within the latter, the most substantial communities are in the western reaches, in Morocco – where their numbers again pale in comparison with neighbouring West Africa, notably Nigeria. Arabic, the language of the Qur'an, is not the daily tongue of most Muslims. One of colonialism's bequests is that English, French and Russian are more widely understood across the Muslim world than are either of its most ancient languages, Arabic and Persian, or any of the myriad vernaculars. This pattern is accentuated by globalisation – of media and borders – including the presence of an increasingly established Muslim diaspora within the West and the Russian Federation. Applying the traditional 'centre-periphery' configuration in this context is simply not tenable, if it is intended to capture the contemporary dynamics of the relationship among the Arab, Persian, African, Asian, European and diasporic worlds within the Muslim universe.

In terms of the quotidian realities of life within that universe, the range of standards of literacy, education, urbanisation – of the material 'quality of life' – is as varied as the geo-cultural diversity. Brunei and a handful of other oil-rich Middle Eastern states rank among the world's relatively high-income nations, with a small number of others in the middle-income category. But of the more than forty Muslim-majority countries charted in Table 1 most evince a low level of economic and social development as measured by typical quantitative indicators. This is reflected in their rankings on the increasingly sophisticated if still imperfect 'human development index' (HDI),[26] on which the higher-income Muslim countries do not perform particularly well either. Technological attainment in Malaysia, Iran and Tunisia is comparatively good, but poor elsewhere. All in all, the countries charted here share, with important exceptions, the characteristic of belonging to the cluster of states commonly referred to as the 'developing world'. The rates of literacy, life expectancy and infant mortality are typical of that cluster. Evidently, those that have recently gained independence from European colonial dominance, that is, the ex-Soviet republics of Central Asia/Caucasus (Azerbaijan, Kazakhstan, Kyrgyzstan, Tajikistan, Turkmenistan and Uzbekistan),

AMYN B. SAJOO

Table 1: Key Socio-Economic Indicators for Muslim-majority States*

Population	Urban (millions 1999)	Male Population %, 1999	Female Literacy %, 1999	GDP per Literacy %, 1999	Human capita (US$, 1999)	Technical Development (Index Rank, 2001**)	Achievement (Index Rank, 2001***)
Albania	3	41	91	77	3,189	85	-
Algeria	30	60	77	56	5,063	100	58
Azerbaijan	8	57	n/a	n/a	2,850	79	-
Bangladesh	135	24	52	29	1,483	132	-
Bahrain	0.6	92	91	82	13,688	40	-
Brunei	0.3	72	94	87	17,868	32	-
Burkina Faso	11	18	33	13	965	159	-
Chad	8	24	50	32	850	155	-
Comoros	0.7	33	66	52	1,429	124	-
Djibouti	0.6	83	75	53	2,377	137	-
Egypt	67	45	66	43	3,420	105	57
Gambia	1	32	43	29	1,580	149	-
Guinea	8	32	n/a	n/a	1,934	150	-
Indonesia	209	40	92	81	2,857	102	60
Iran	69	61	83	69	5,531	90	50
Ivory Coast	16	46	54	37	1,654	144	-
Jordan	5	74	95	83	3,955	88	-
Kazakhstan	16	56	n/a	n/a	4,951	75	-
Kuwait	2	97	84	79	17,289	43	-
Kyrgyzstan	5	34	n/a	n/a	2,573	92	-
Lebanon	3	89	92	80	4,705	65	-
Libya	5	87	90	67	7,570	59	-

Malaysia	22	57	91	83	8,209	56	30
Mali	11	29	47	33	753	153	-
Mauritania	3	56	52	31	1,609	139	-
Morocco	29	55	61	35	3,419	112	-
Niger	11	20	23	8	753	161	-
Nigeria	111	43	71	54	853	136	-
Oman	3	82	79	60	13,356	71	-
Pakistan	138	37	59	30	1,834	127	65
Qatar	0.6	92	83	80	18,789	48	-
Saudi Arabia	20	85	84	66	10,815	68	-
Senegal	9	47	46	27	1,419	145	66
Sudan	30	35	69	45	664	138	71
Syria	16	54	88	59	4,454	97	56
Tajikistan	6	28	99	99	1,031	103	-
Tunisia	9	65	80	59	5,957	89	51
Turkey	66	74	93	76	6,380	82	-
Turkmenistan	5	45	n/a	n/a	3,347	83	-
UAE	3	86	74	78	18,162	45	-
Uzbekistan	25	37	93	84	2,251	99	-
Yemen	8	25	67	24	1,464	133	-

* Afghanistan, Bosnia-Herzegovina, Iraq and Somalia have not been included for lack of adequate data.

** The Human Development Index is an annual global composite measure of the 'quality of life' by the United Nations Development Programme.

*** The Technical Achievement Index is a global composite measure of technology creation, diffusion of new and old information technologies and human skills, compiled by the UNDP.

Missing rankings for particular states reflect the lack of sufficient data.

Source: United Nations Development Programme, Human Development Report 2001 (Oxford, 2001).

do not perform better on the global HDI. However, among those countries, Tajikistan does enjoy a literacy rate of first-world standards (99 per cent), shared equally among men and women.

Despite its designation, the HDI does not purport to reflect qualitative aspects of social development like the density of non-governmental organisations, the strength of community health and education services that are not state-controlled, and the presence of independent electronic and print media. All these are part of a richer picture of networks that constitute the public sphere and other facets of civic culture. The profile of 'political life' that is offered by the compilers of the HDI – but is not part of the index itself – essentially covers electoral frequency. Still less does the HDI reflect the more subtle aspects of social solidarity that are also part of that picture, especially in traditional contexts: these include communal and neighbourhood networks (of varying formality) that often play key roles in maintaining social, economic and even legal stability where the reach of state institutions is relatively fragile.[27] But the index does convey a sense of the formal infrastructural strengths and weaknesses that underpin transitions to socio-economic modernity, and thereby of capacity-building for mature civil society.

The empirical universe of states in Table 1, in all its geo-cultural diversity and economic deprivation, hardly lends itself to generalisations of the kind tendered by civic pessimists on 'Islam'. Certainly the correlation between poverty and weak state institutions, on the one hand, and the absence of dynamic countervailing institutions on the other, cannot be ignored – as in Gellner's leap to explain deficient social orders solely in terms of religion. In oil-and-gas-dependent societies, the severe economic and social distortions to civic cultures are a well-known 'price' of prosperity?.[28] Again, the impaired individualism that Gellner posits as a cultural issue wilfully overlooks the disempowering effects of underdevelopment on effective citizenship. Indeed, the Nobel laureate Amartya Sen has shown that 'capability deprivation' across a range of basic human (and civic) potentialities is an appropriate way to define underdevelopment – and analyse social exclusion – rather than the conventional focus on income deprivation alone.[29] Or as John Kenneth Galbraith characteristically puts it, 'Nothing, it must be recognized, so comprehensively denies the liberties of the individual as a total absence of money. Or so impairs it as too little ... .'[30] Neither of these economists contends that deprivation in Muslim societies is subject to a uniquely different explanation from that in the rest of the world. When Mardin deigns to give empirical support to his argument about the controlling effects of religious discourse on civic culture, it comes in the form of an anthropological study about gender differentiation of labour in the Turkish town of Edremit in the mid-1970s; the evidence purportedly shows 'economic practices embedded in the separation of sexes structured by Islamic norms'.[31] Yet his evidence also indicates that the segregation worked to the economic advantage of the women – which fails to prompt him to ask the obvious question whether this had anything to do with their acquiescence in the division of labour. Nor does Mardin trouble to question whether such realities have much economic or social significance in Turkey's larger cities.[32]

Suffice it to observe that the sociology of diversity, poverty and demographic shifts (including migration and urbanisation) has not figured meaningfully in assertions about the 'fated' obstacles to civil society in the Muslim world. The latter shares not only 'Islam', but also the hard realities of underdevelopment and its negative impact on the conditions for civic culture. After all, explanations of the relative success of civil society in occidental contexts have routinely looked to the effects of the Industrial Revolution, the economic impulses of the 'Protestant ethic', and the impact of capitalism on the demand for a reliable rule of law framework.[33] Which is not by any means to suggest that economic factors alone can explain the dynamics of civil society.

Civic Islam

The modern concept and praxis of civil society did not spring forth wholly-formed in eighteenth-century Europe and North America any more than modern democracy or human rights could be conjured up in a single historical moment. Such ideas and practices are, of course, products of complex historical processes and convergences that – *ex post facto* – can be identified as engendering the conditions for democratic, liberal or civic 'success'. More often than not, supposedly novel creations are what historians have come to regard as the reinvention of tradition.[34] To claim that civil society is 'a Western dream' cannot amount to asserting that such a vision was immutably held at any particular historical moment: for its components would, of necessity, have to evolve with the changing conditions in which the visionaries live. There would, in other words, have to be a plurality of aspirations that converge at what we subsequently deem to be moments of shared historical significance, in reinventing shared bequests as new quests and attainments. To sustain the claim that civil society is exclusive to Western traditions, it would have to be shown that such traditions are fortresses, impermeable to any external influence in the course of history. No civilisation, while it is alive, has such a record. Moreover, it was not long ago that the political performance of southern and east-central Europe, Latin America and the Philippines might have led to the inference that Catholicism impeded democracy and civil society – before the clergy turned into a major proponent of progressive change.[35]

Orientalist readings of Muslim history have commonly posited the absence of civil society as a key issue in the failure to engender indigenous democratic institutions. Broadly, as Bryan Turner summarises it, the argument is that 'Islamic society lacked independent cities, an autonomous bourgeois, rational bureaucracy, legal reliability, personal property and the cluster of rights which embody bourgeois culture'. In an echo of the claims by Gellner and Mardin, the absence of these institutional and cultural elements is seen to have left 'nothing in Islamic civilisation to challenge the dead hand of pre-capitalist tradition'.[36] Quite apart from the questionable implication that the modern development of the West itself was on a clear trajectory of post-feudal liberal freedom arising from civil society, one must ask: what cultural or civilisational underpinnings were there for these alleged differences? What was peculiarly 'Western' about functional bureaucracies and the rule of law, or 'Islamic' about their absence or frailty? For that matter, Confucian civilisation was famous for its scholar-bureaucrats or mandarins (who were not, contrary to stereotype, expected to be blindly compliant with the Emperor's wishes),[37] while the rule of law was surely linked to the mundane demands of capitalism. By what logic can the historical contingencies of a particular region (usually, in Orientalist readings, selected Asian or Middle Eastern locales) be regarded as uniformly representative of 'Islam'?[38] This is not merely a matter of appropriate semantics, of not using the term 'Islam' or 'Islamic' loosely; it also about the essentialism that attends such analyses of history, politics and change. It is a short step thence to claim, as Huntington has done, that entire civilisations are fated by their faith or history to act in ways that conflict with contemporary notions of pluralism, respect for the rule of law and individual freedom.

As it turns out, the evidence of civic institutional and cultural *elements* in Muslim societies is substantial, even if the development of civil society as understood today has lagged in those contexts. The respective Arabic and Persian terms for civil society, *mujtama' al-madani* and *jame'eh madani* have long evoked the sense of institutions organised along civic lines (*madani* being derived from *medina* or 'city'); a more traditional reference is to *mujtama' al-ahli*, which includes a wider array of communal and religious institutions. If these notions are claimed to exist in the shadow of religious discourse, Crone and Hinds have read the corpus of religious law and practice as itself an expression of resistance to political power: 'The scholarly conception of Prophetic sunna was … a threat to caliphal authority from the moment of its appearance'.[39]

In empirical terms, Ellis Goldberg has shown that medieval societies of the Arab Mediterranean region developed a spectrum of legal and political devices, primarily in mercantile practices that ranged across frontiers, as well as urban markets and institutions, whose autonomy from state control gave them a robustly civic character.[40] Building on the work of Marshall Hodgson, Goldberg sketches a rather different picture of the status of private property, from endowments to arbitral mechanisms and debts, as well as of cities, from the standard Orientalist accounts (or that of Mardin). He rejects the claim that evidence of bourgeois autonomy is to be found only in the bargaining capacity vis-à-vis caliphs and sultans, or in their status under a sharia entirely controlled by religious discourse. Rather, a large segment of medieval law was 'a political instrument in the hands of private actors to shield themselves and others from the demands of an absolutist monarchy'. If the institutional context within which this occurred differed from that of contemporary Europe, Goldberg is adamant that the elements of civil society that prevailed then are pertinent to the creation of 'liberal (and possibly democratic) regimes'.[41] A similar argument has been advanced by Masoud Kamali with regard to 'traditional' civic culture in Iran, reposing in webs of 'communities and institutions rather than individual citizens and their associations'.[42] Typical of the former are the *bazaris* (merchants) and ulama, seen as co-existing with nascent associations of the latter kind in post-revolutionary society.

'Civic Islam' today, *qua* non-state controlled citizen action that is directly germane to modern civil society, is manifest in what Dale Eickelman and Jon Anderson have documented as 'the emerging public sphere'. Driven by the energies of new media that elude facile official regulation – from satellite television to the Internet – this public domain has already become the locus of a 'reintellectualisation of Islamic discourse', whereby the publics that participate as well as the subjects they talk about have altered radically from traditional realities.[43] The scope of the 'imagined community' (discussed earlier) in this public sphere covers subnational, national and global domains, and challenges old assumptions about gender, hierarchical authority and inclusiveness. Yet the language of exchange is frequently 'Islamic', as participants seek to redefine and re-appropriate old meanings in new contexts. The ramifications are as far-reaching for the content as they are for the mode of discourse:

> [B]y looking at the intricate multiplicity of horizontal relationships, especially among the rapidly increasing numbers of beneficiaries of mass education, new messages, and new communication media, one discovers alternative ways of thinking about Islam, acting on Islamic principles, and creating senses

of community and public space. Such a realization among large
numbers of people is a measure of the potential for a rapidly
emerging public sphere and a civil society that plays a vital role
within it.[44]

We thus have two sets of convergences: of civic and religious
dynamics, and of process and substance. The former is deeply
familiar within Muslim settings where the secular and sacred have
traditionally intertwined, in public as well as private domains. As
for the convergence of process and substance, it is clearly an inevitable outcome of citizen participation in the creation and
sustenance of the public sphere itself, where dialogical opportunity meets quotidian concerns. Indeed, both sets of convergences
are envisaged in the 'discourse ethics' that Habermas has sketched
as a vital feature of modern public spaces.[45] Practical moral issues are dealt with in such spaces through a process of dialogue
that validates (or refutes) and normatises agreement in a rational,
civil process.[46] Applied to the emerging Muslim sphere as described above, Habermas's logic is compelling in its dual emphasis
upon the individual citizen as voluntarily participant, and the so-
cial/civic process that allows such deliberative action to occur with
the safeguards of the rule of law.

What has been called the 'digital umma'[47] is patently a far cry
from stereotypes of static 'Islamic' identities, capacities and aspirations. Citizen demands for individual space, gender and minority
inclusiveness, political participation and the rule of law – but also
for ethical accountability in public life, and the freedom to redefine the 'secular' limits of the public sphere – have prompted
fundamental political change in Indonesia and Iran, along with
less radical but important transformations in Turkey, Morocco and
Jordan. And they have triggered civil conflict in Tajikistan, Nigeria, Algeria and Afghanistan, with new expectations of
accountability to society by future governments. In the diasporic
Muslim public sphere – and that of its host societies in North
America and Europe – hierarchical challenges and calls for accountability may have different targets but they have the same
impulses, abetted by easier access to the new media, as well as
more robust legal protections.[48] Nor should the diasporic context

be seen apart from those of Muslim-majority societies: the nature of the Internet and cognate media engenders fluid avenues of discourse across frontiers. The evidence is that regardless of whether it was so in the distant or the recent past, civil society has become a Muslim dream in our time. 'Historians', in any case, 'keep changing their ink', to quote Mohamed Berrada's great postmodern narrative, *The Game of Forgetting*.[49] The riffs and rhythms of the Muslim public sphere may differ from the jazz of its Euro-American counterpart, recalling instead the vernacular resonances of *gnawa*, *qawwali* and *rai* in their rich alchemy of secular and sacred; and that is testimony, surely, to the indigenisation of civil society.

Contemporary Muslim Perspectives

Depicting the full spectrum of civic life in the Muslim public sphere – or rather spheres, given the obvious complexity and stretch – is not the purport of this volume of essays, if such an undertaking were practicable. A few years ago it may have entailed, to recall our metaphor, providing a manageable listing of concerts by new and old performers on the public stage, at least within specific regional settings like the Middle East.[50] Today it would amount to the Sisyphean task of describing a plethora of ever-growing cacophonies – and happily so, for it underscores the vast multivocal and pluricultural milieus on hand. Why, then, have we chosen to take as our analytical setting the 'Muslim world', rather than regions thereof? First, because there are conceptual and empirical issues concerning the prospects for civil society in communities and societies of Muslims that need to be addressed, and not only in response to the kind of skepticism about 'Islam' that has been outlined above. Muslim scripture, thought and praxis are potential resources rich in their expressions of social solidarity, pluralism and ethics, in the wider context of advocating a this-worldly fidelity to notions of law, reason and equity. Undeniably, these bequests have too often been squandered, and continue to be in our time; but that is no reason to ignore them in appraising civic prospects among Muslims today. Several of the essays here venture beyond empiricism to looking at some of the underlying challenges of intellect and faith in the civic quest, and not by Muslims alone.

Second, we have chosen under the banner of 'the Muslim world' to range freely beyond the more traditional focus on the Arab Middle East (which also finds representation), and to look at Central Asia, the Near East and Pakistan both in regard to their indigenous socio-political realities, and the wider Islamic context just noted. Post-revolutionary Iran and Turkey offer at this time competing 'models' of civic choices for other Muslim states – not least the emerging republics of the former Soviet Union. The quotation marks around the word 'models' acknowledges the fact that both Iran and Turkey are in flux in this respect; they have the same difficult civic choices ahead as do other Muslim societies, notably on the role of religion in the public square. But they offer valuable snapshots in their respective stages of transition from the historic ruptures that they, like most of the post-colonial Muslim world, have endured

In a *tour d'horizon* of the social and intellectual terrain in which Muslims must locate their modern quests, Mohammed Arkoun warns here that the wrong approach would be to highlight the attributes and practices of Western civic cultures and apply them as tests or ideals for transitional societies of Muslims. This would lead us right past the indigenous particularities born of 'profound historical and sociological differences' that have everything to do with how civil society is actually lived. Nor will it do to embrace the reverse process, favoured by religious apologists, of singling-out specific attributes from Western societies and projecting them back onto an 'imagined Islamic Model' derived from a mythical reading of history. If civil society is about citizens taking control of their destinies, then the reality they confront is of patrimonial states – or militant groups within them – taking control of 'Islam' and tailoring it to social and political agendas that have little to do with respect for the rule of law and individual liberty. Breaking out of ideological cages, whether of nationalism or religious orthodoxy, that impede plural ways of discovering and building individual 'truths' is, for Arkoun, the precondition for civil society. The best prospects for doing so lie in the emergence of a 'global civil society' with a larger, more encompassing collective memory.

Continuing this discourse of locating civic quests in Muslim engagement with modernity, Aziz Esmail argues that it would be just as false to expect an idiosyncratic 'Islamic civil society' as it would be to neglect the 'contextual importance' of Islam in the process. He draws on Michael Sandel's critique of the 'disengaged self' in liberal thought and its conception of civil society, which fails to recognise that historical traditions – Muslim, Hindu, Buddhist, Christian – strongly shape individual ideas of self and others. For Esmail, the alternative lies in seeing the duality of the self, both as the bearer of such traditions and also as a citizen with a 'universal individualism'. He is critical of multiculturalism as an antidote to the disengaged self, for it merely privileges group identity over that of the individual; and he faults it for passively nurturing parochialism rather than civic virtues. Ultimately, liberal sentiment will need to grow from '*within* particular historical identities'. Muslim societies themselves can build on potent moral intuitions and Islamic antecedents in their pursuit of modernity, while imbibing the lessons of liberal and other humanistic traditions – including an appreciation of secularism as distinct from its Western ideological interpretation.

Some very specific civic antecedents and intuitions are spelled out in Filali-Ansary's chapter on the Maghreb, and they have less to do with limiting the power of the state (as in the West) than with providing vital social services and the regulation of social activities. This is a historical universe parallel to the mercantile one sketched by Ellis Goldberg, noted earlier, in which weak states had a monopoly of violence but not much else. The result was what Filali-Ansary calls 'proto-civil society' with a strong creed as well as robust social solidarity – and here there are striking similarities as well as differences to our own time. The state in the modern Maghreb remains relatively weak, in part because of the larger forces of economic globalisation that have limited its power, which makes it fearful of society. Associative life has again flourished, if in significant measure by default, as gaps in social services are filled by non-profit organisations and movements. Like

Arkoun, Filali-Ansary sees creed as critically contested terrain, to be taken out of the control of the clerics, the state and extremist minorities. Maghrebi civil society today, like its antecedents, is seen as a work in progress, but with external economic and social forces increasingly playing a decisive role.

By contrast, the public sphere in Iran today is very much a domestically-contested space, especially when it comes to the issues of gender and press freedom, as Ziba Mir-Hosseini shows. The poignant tussles over these issues, in which personal liberties and livelihoods are constantly at stake, go to the roots of the discourse on 'Islam' and civil society. How far can women in a patriarchal setting exercise the right to influence laws that are discriminatory in their application, yet are claimed to have sacral status? Against the wider canvas of 'reformist' and 'conservative' trends in post-revolutionary Iran, the women's press has been 'player and pawn' alike in Mir-Hosseini's extensive surveys, which have included interviews with journalists, clerics and secular intellectuals in the country. Ironically, perhaps, she generally found the Shi'i clerics more forthcoming than the intellectuals on the ethics and politics of gender equity (both groups being overwhelmingly male in Iran). In a context of limited democratic freedom, the press has tended to serve as a surrogate for political parties, and the fate of the women's press signals the overall health of emerging civil society – and the rule of law. The evidence today suggests both an inexorable movement toward a more liberal society (with reformists handily winning every single municipal and national election in recent years), as well as severe periodic setbacks for free expression and other liberties.[51]

Among the insights offered by Mir-Hosseini is the vitality of ethical claims in the Muslim public sphere, as reformist women express their critiques of sacral law in terms of sharia-grounded tenets of fairness and equality. More broadly, 'civility' as a defining component of the public sphere engages the imperatives of social ethics, the subject of my chapter. Contemporary liberalism has come to dichotomise civic and ethical norms in the public domain, preferring to privatise the latter and to give it a 'rational', amoral orientation. Although social ethics have long been a normative feature of Muslim public life, their status has tended to be subordinate to that of the sharia as a framework of law. The pattern appears to be reversing itself in some contexts, notably of transitional states where the frailty of the rule of law leaves ethical norms to play a key part in sustaining public order. 'The law is like a spiderweb', is the lament of a Tajik journalist, 'the strong simply tear through it, but weak people get caught in it'.[52] There is no substitute for the rule of law, of course; yet both strategic and moral purposes are served by anchoring civic life in the re-vival of ethical discourse, which in Muslim terms includes the norm of legal observance on the part of governors and the governed alike. Nowhere can that potential role be more critical than in relation to the issue of political violence – which since the events of September 11, 2001, has taken centre stage in public debates within and outside the Muslim world.[53] After all, appeals to reli-gious tradition already colour political militancy; engaging and reshaping that discourse is a challenge that civic actors can ill afford to ignore.

It did not, certainly, require the events of September 11 and their aftermath to evince how incompatible the conditions for civil society are with political violence. The post-independence civil war in Tajikistan (1992–94) took an enormous toll both in civilian casualties and the destruction of public and private institutions and patterns of engagement, as Shirin Akiner outlines in her contribution. Both state and society are weak, and the proliferation of non-governmental organisations is sustained at this juncture more by foreign goodwill than grassroots commitment. As in Filali-Ansary's analysis, creed is seen here as a key contested area between radical societal groups and the state (promoting its version of 'good Islam'), while the legacy of indigenous Sufi-oriented Muslim traditions is pushed to the side-lines. An exception to the overall picture is the situation of Tajikistan's eastern, autonomous region of Gorno-Badakhshan, where Akiner points to an ethos of self-help boosted by external support from the Aga Khan Development Network, in a 'unique' complementarity that has produced the makings of a bona fide civil society. Elsewhere, though acknowledging that the 'nascent pluralism' of the late-1980s could be perceived as an embryonic civic culture, she advocates an analytical focus on social ethics as a more reliable lens through which to look at contemporary Tajik society.

Within the wider context of ex-Soviet Central Asia, Olivier Roy is more sanguine about indigenous networks of solidarity – such as farm collectives (*kolkhoz*), neighbourhood associations (*mahalla*), and consultative groupings (*gap*, often among women for interest-free credit) – providing the building-blocks of modern civil society. While the Soviet ideological legacy may taint our view of such 'traditions', Roy argues that they are more substantial than the more formal, Western-type associations favoured by international aid agencies, which will only engender a 'window civil society'. Like Akiner, he is apprehensive about the impact of militant religious groups, especially in the Ferghana Valley that straddles the republics of Uzbekistan, Kyrgyzstan and Tajikistan. Which, in turn, reinforces the issue of nurturing indigenous civic institutions rather than the external prototypes that Roy sees as both ineffective and corrupting in their creation of artificial social and economic hierarchies. Nevertheless, in so far as the interface of domestic and external elements of development is intrinsic to open societies, the implications for emergent Central Asia are complex – especially when it comes to cultural vectors such as networks to promote intellectual and artistic spaces, including an independent cinema.[54]

Our picture of religiosity and civic traditions in post-Soviet Muslim societies is enriched by remarkably detailed sociological evidence gathered by Tair Faradov on Azerbaijan, a country that also experienced violent conflict since independence (over the ethnic-Armenian enclave of Karabakh). Substantial majorities of Azeris continue to desire a more religiously-grounded life, usually but not exclusively Muslim, and to reject the once-ingrained stereotypes of religiosity stemming from Soviet ideology. Yet the new adherents seldom appear to have more than a rudimentary knowledge of Islam, or take the observance of elemental rituals seriously. Faradov's survey suggests that religion at large is taken to be as much an ethical and socio-cultural commitment as a spiritual one. It therefore lends itself to constructions of Islam as linked to nationalism as well as the values of pluralism, tolerance and civic engagement, reminiscent of less successful state endeavours in this respect elsewhere in Central Asia. There appears to be strong support for official regulation of religious activism in the twin interests of national security and as part of an interpretation of Islam itself as 'handmaiden to the modern ethos of civil society', even if many citizens chafe at the more authoritarian tendencies of the present government.

Some may see in the Azerbaijani trends a receptivity to 'channels of Westernisation' en route to a 'secularised Islam';[55] but if contemporary Turkey is the exemplar, then political rather than civil religion becomes the paradigm.[56] Ersin Kalaycıoğlu's empirical analysis suggests that civic associations of the professional, entrepreneurial and certain social kind have flourished amid waves of democratisation since World War II. Yet Kemalist secularism and nationalism remain as deeply mistrustful of overt Muslim public activism as of ethno-cultural particularism (notably Kurdish and Alevi). Among other social movements, feminists who endorse the state's brand of secularism, along with environmentalists, find congenial spaces. The state is generally weak and far from effectual, contrary to the post-Ottoman stereotype. Still, society has not availed itself as robustly as might be expected of the ensuing public spaces, which Kalaycıoğlu explains in terms of low levels of trust outside traditional ties of kinship and solidarity. This appears to be changing, as shown in his intriguing account of the putative transformation of traditionalist women's demands for headscarves (*türban*) into a relatively modernist human rights movement. Old repositories of trust and solidarity, in other words, may find new avenues of associational life, including among nationalist groups that learn the language of civic rather than ethnic protest.[57]

An intense mélange of identity-politics, state suspicion of civic organisations, low levels of public trust, and sharp contests over the role of religion in public life is one face of contemporary Pakistan – but Iftikhar Malik is keen to show how resilient the other face has proven. Indigenous human rights organisations, independent media and professional civic groups remain highly visible in the public arena, along with more traditional solidarity groups. A series of authoritarian regimes masks a weak state and rule of law, while a stubbornly frail economy has undercut public institutions. Yet Malik draws attention to recent opinion surveys that reveal an enduring commitment to 'renewal of civic life', including real gender and minority equity, and a deep attachment to moderation in nationalist as well as confessional sentiment. There may be further cause for optimism on that score in the wake of Pakistan's frontline engagement in the United States-led war on the Taliban in Afghanistan, as the state is emboldened to curb the religious militancy that it often actively endorsed in the past[58] – though human rights groups will want to be vigilant about state accountability in that regard to the rule of law. Meanwhile, in post-Taliban Afghanistan, a renewed quest for civic culture has already found expression in the emergence of independent news media (including by women), with appropriate legislative guarantees,[59] and in the revival of artistic life in both traditional and modern formats.[60]

If the foregoing synopses suggest that the contributors to this volume share a particular perspective on what the salient signifiers of civil society are – much less on where exactly to locate them and whether they exist in significant measure in a given Muslim context – then the reader will quickly be disabused on perusing the texts. As Filali-Ansary bemusedly observes, when it comes to civil society there is more than the usual scholarly protestation about the elusiveness of one's topic, the limits of one's format, and the provisionality of the conclusions that can be reached in a too-rapidly changing universe. The concept and its praxis have acquired an exceptional degree of slipperiness, and when applied to Islam and the Muslim world, the challenge of delivering coherent judgements is only exacerbated.

All this has not forestalled the willingness of policy analysts and policy-makers, social scientists and human rights lawyers, political activists and their targets in and out of government, from deploying just that combination of 'civil society' and 'Islam'. The coupling has served as more than a slogan for its invokers in city squares, university campuses and hallowed conference halls from

Tehran and Sarajevo to Jerusalem, Cairo, Algiers and Lagos.
Indeed, the energetic discoursing *about* civil society in such contexts can itself be seen as contributing vitally to fostering the
associational life and intellectual autonomy of modern civic culture.[61] My own earliest exposure to debates on civil society came
not in the West but rather during field-visits to Malaysia, Indonesia and Singapore in the early 1990s. Then, as today, concerns
were raised about importing Western modes of social organisation and individualism into fundamentally different civilisational
settings. But as Arkoun points out, one can be mindful of these
differences and yet search for shared meanings, not least in an
age when national frontiers have shrinking significance. Indeed,
Etzioni has extended his communitarian vision beyond those frontiers to citizen-based 'governance without government' on the
transnational landscape.[62] This certainly holds out the congenial
prospect of extending democratic accountability, the rule of law
and civility beyond sovereign confines. Prevailing Muslim diasporic
realities, as noted earlier, accentuate these dynamics. Yet the idea
of a global civil society is only meaningful in so far as ordinary
citizens in less privileged and politically marginalised quarters par-
take of it. For the individual citizen, like civil society itself, needs
deep if adventitious roots in the everyday context – the rhythms
and resonances, the lifeworld – of local *terra firma*.

Notes

1. Ş. Mardin, 'Civil Society and Islam', in J.A. Hall, ed., *Civil Society:
Theory, History, Comparison* (Cambridge, MA and Cambridge, UK, 1995),
pp.278–300, at pp.278–9.

2. Ibid., p.285.

3. E. Gellner, *Conditions of Liberty: Civil Society and its Rivals* (London,
1994), pp.12–13. As a result, social theory today 'starts out with the assumption of an unconstrained and secular individual, unhampered by
social or theological bonds, freely choosing his aims, and reaching some
agreement concerning social order with his fellows. In this manner, Civil
Society is simply presupposed as some kind of inherent attribute of the
human condition'. (p.13)

4. Mardin, 'Civil Society and Islam', pp.285–6.

5. Ibid., p.289.

6. C.F. Perry, *The Civilian Elite in Cairo in the Late Middle Ages* (Princeton, NJ, 1981), pp.322–3; cited in 'Civil Society and Islam', p.290.

7. Gellner, *Conditions of Liberty*, p.92.

8. While there were sporadic, exploratory writings on civil society in the early 1980s, the current debate only found momentum in the mid/late 1980s and early 1990s. See, *inter alia*, V. Havel, et al., in J. Keane, ed., *The Power of the Powerless* (London, 1985); J. Keane, *Civil Society and the State: New European Perspectives* (London and New York, 1988); J. Cohen and A. Arato, *Civil Society and Political Theory* (Cambridge, MA, 1992); A. Seligman, *The Idea of Civil Society* (New York, 1992); K. Tester, *Civil Society* (London and New York, 1992); H. Koo, ed., *State and Society in Contemporary Korea* (London and Ithaca, NY, 1993); C. Taylor 'Invoking Civil Society', in *Philosophical Arguments* (Cambridge, MA and London, 1995), pp.204–24; A.R. Norton, ed., 'The Future of Civil Society in the Muslim World', special issue, *Middle East Journal*, 47, 2 (1993); R. Putnam, *Making Democracy Work: Civic Traditions in Northern Italy* (Princeton, NJ, 1993), and 'Bowling Alone: America's Declining Social Capital', *Journal of Democracy*, 6 (1995), pp.65–78; D. Wank, 'Civil Society in Communist China? Private Business and Political Alliance, 1989', in Hall, ed., *Civil Society: Theory, History, Comparison*, pp.6–79; T. Yamamoto, ed., *Emerging Civil Society in the Asia Pacific Community* (Singapore, 1995); J. Linz and A. Stepan, *Problems of Democratic Transition and Consolidation: Southern Europe, South America, and Post-Communist Europe* (Baltimore and London, 1996); M. Monshipouri, 'State Prerogatives, Civil Society, and Liberalization: The Paradoxes of the Late Twentieth Century in the Third World', *Ethics and International Affairs*, 11 (1997), pp.232–51; M. Owusu, 'Domesticating Democracy: Culture, Civil Society and Constitutionalism in Africa', *Comparative Studies in Society and History*, 39 (1997), pp.120–52; M.H. Ruffin and D.C. Waugh, ed., *Civil Society in Central Asia* (Seattle, 1999); S. Kaviraj and S. Khilnani, ed., *Civil Society: History and Possibilities* (Cambridge, UK, 2001).

9. J. Keane, *Civil Society: Old Images, New Visions* (Cambridge, UK, 1998), p.11.

10. Ibid., p.6. See also my *Pluralism in 'Old Societies and New States': Emerging ASEAN Contexts* (Singapore, 1994), pp.1–13.

11. See T. Giola, *The History of Jazz* (New York, 1997); T. Kirchner, ed., *The Oxford Companion to Jazz* (New York, 2000). Jazz also provided a metaphor for the identity of African-Americans in a heterogeneous society in *Shadow and Act* (New York, 1964), a collection of essays by one of the

United States' most celebrated writers, Ralph Ellison. See also N. Hentoff's broader explorations of the nexus between civic freedom and music in *The Nat Hentoff Reader* (New York and Cambridge, MA, 2001).

12. Among the most effective dissident groups in the Soviet bloc states was the Jazz Section of the Musicians' Union of Czechoslovakia, which came to international prominence in the early 1980s. Earlier in Europe, the Nazis in 1943 banned the very use of the word 'jazz'.

13. J. Habermas, *Between Facts and Norms: Contributions to a Discourse Theory of Law and Democracy*, tr. William Rehg (Cambridge, MA and Cambridge, UK, 1996), ch.8, at p.360.

14. Ibid., p.367.

15. As cast in Benedict Anderson's celebrated, *Imagined Communities: Reflections on the Origin and Spread of Nationalism* (London, 1991).

16. C. Taylor, 'Liberal Politics and the Public Sphere', in *Philosophical Arguments*, p.257–87, at p.266. See further my discussion of Taylor's analysis in my chapter on public ethics in the present volume.

17. R. Kuttner, *Everything is for Sale: The Virtues and Limits of Markets* (New York, 1997); J.K. Galbraith, *The Culture of Contentment* (Boston, 1992); J. Gray, *Enlightenment's Wake* (New York and London, 1995).

18. Keane expressly rejects Habermas's 'neo-Gramscian' analysis in this regard: *Civil Society: Old Images, New Visions*, pp.16–19. See also the elucidations – including the ambivalent roles of capitalism and industrialisation in fostering civil society – in J. Alexander, 'Introduction', in J.C. Alexander, ed., *Real Civil Societies: Dilemmas of Institutionalization* (London, 1998), pp.8–10; and perspectives on civically responsible capitalism in A. Giddens, ed., *The Global Third Way Debate* (Cambridge, UK, 2001).

19. J. Abu-Lughod, 'The Islamic City', *International Journal of Middle East Studies*, 19 (1987), pp.155–76, at p.172.

20. Samuel P. Huntington, *The Clash of Civilizations and the Remaking of World Order* (New York and London, 1997); and his 'A Clash of Civilizations?', *Foreign Affairs*, 72 (1993), p.22. I have discussed Huntington's thesis at some length in 'The Crescent in the Public Square', *Islam in America*, 3 (1997), pp.1–7.

21. See, for example, Bernard Lewis, 'Islam in Revolt', *The New Yorker*, 19 November 2001, pp.50–63, and his *What Went Wrong? Western Impact and Middle Eastern Response* (New York, 2002). A review of the latter by Paul Kennedy uncritically espouses the same reductive and deterministic logic: 'The Real Culture Wars', *New York Times Review of Books* (27 January 2002), p.9. Leaders of the Christian Right in the United States have repeatedly made public statements since September 11 to the effect

that Islam and Muslims are inherently prone to militancy and 'evil': see, for example, the news-report 'Islam is Violent in Nature, Pat Robertson Says', *The New York Times* (23 February 2002), p.A8; S. Sachs, 'Baptist Pastor Attacks Islam, Inciting Cries of Intolerance', *The New York Times* (15 June 2002), p.A9. Among the more sober analyses of the events of September 11 is that of F. Halliday, *Two Hours that Shook the World – September 11, 2001: Causes and Consequences* (London, 2002), and more broadly, Gilles Kepel, *Jihad: The Trail of Political Islam* (London and Cambridge, MA, 2002). See also generally, K.H. Karim, *Islamic Peril: Media and Global Violence* (Montreal, 2000), which draws attention to the role of civil society in articulating effectively the ethical and humanistic dimensions of Islam (p.180).

22. F.G. Gause III, 'Who Lost Middle Eastern Studies? The Orientalists Strike Back', *Foreign Affairs*, 81 (March/April 2002), pp.164–8, at p.167, reviewing Kramer's *Ivory Towers of Sand: The Failure of Middle Eastern Studies in America* (Washington, DC, 2001).

23. E. Said, 'Scholars, Media, and the Middle East', in G. Viswanathan, ed., *Power, Politics, and Culture: Interviews with Edward Said* (New York, 2001), p.297. See also Said's 'Impossible Histories: Why the many Islams cannot be simplified', *Harper's Magazine,* July 2002, pp. 69–74, on the continuing failure of commentators like Bernard Lewis and Paul Kennedy to come to grips with empirical complexity.

24. Some of the more egregious instances of which are noted in Halliday, *Two Hours that Shook the World,* at pp.104–13.

25. This commonly-cited global figure is in fact only a rough estimate, and probably an underestimate; it is, in any case, reflected in tabulations in the *2001 Encyclopaedia Britannica Book of the Year* (London, 2001). The authoritative guide to global Muslim ethnic and national spread remains R.V. Weekes, ed., *Muslim Peoples: A World Ethnographic Survey,* vols. 1 and 2; 2nd ed. (Westport, CT, 1984); see especially the charting of ethnic and national groups at pp.882–930.

26. On the attempts by the human development index (HDI) over the years to more accurately reflect performance beyond the traditional 'standard of living' indices, see the methodological notes in the United Nations Development Programme's annual *Human Development Report* (New York and Oxford)

27. See, for example, the discussion in the text below of civic elements in traditional Muslim society.

28. As acknowledged in connection with Freedom House's (New York) latest report on global democratic trends: see A. Karatnycky, 'The 2001

Freedom House Survey: Muslim Countries and the Democracy Gap', *Journal of Democracy*, 13 (2002), pp.99–112, at pp.95–6.

29. A. Sen, *Development as Freedom* (New York, 1999), pp.87–110.

30. J.K. Galbraith, *The Good Society: The Humane Agenda* (Boston, 1996), p.4.

31. Mardin, 'Civil Society and Islam', pp.289–90; quote at p.290.

32. It is noteworthy that the city of Istanbul at the end of the nineteenth century, then capital of the Muslim world's most powerful entity, was sufficiently cosmopolitan as to have a non-Muslim majority population: see A. Maalouf, *In the Name of Identity*, tr. B. Bray (New York, 2000), p.56.

33. See the citations in n.8, above.

34. The classic account of which is the anthology, E. Hobsbawm and T. Ranger, ed., *The Invention of Tradition* (Cambridge, UK, 1983).

35. The same could be argued until even more recently about the influence of Orthodox Christianity in Europe. See Karatnycky, 'The 2001 Freedom House Survey: Muslim Countries and the Democracy Gap', p.107.

36. B.S. Turner, 'Orientalism and the Problem of Civil Society in Islam', in A. Hussain, R. Olson and J. Qureshi, ed., *Orientalism, Islam, and Islamists* (Brattleboro, VT, 1984), pp.23–42.

37. When Confucius is approached by Zilu for advice about how to serve his prince, the reply is: 'Tell him the truth even if it offends him'. Again, while tact is deemed important, sound action enjoys primacy for Confucius: 'When the state has lost its way, act boldly and speak softly'. See *The Analects of Confucius*, tr. S. Leys (New York, 1997), pp.70, 66.

38. See H. Gerber's trenchant critique in this regard, *Islamic Law and Culture, 1600–1840* (Leiden and Boston, 1999), helpfully encapsulated at pp.144–8 ('Islamic Law, Civil Society, Capitalist Development and Democracy').

39. P. Crone and M. Hinds, *God's Caliph* (Cambridge, UK, 1986), p.94.

40. E. Goldberg, 'Private Goods, Public Wrongs and Civil Society in Some Medieval Arab Theory and Practice', in E. Goldberg, R. Kasaba and J. Migdal, ed., *Rules and Rights in the Middle East* (London and Seattle, 1993), pp.248–71.

41. Ibid., pp.249–50. See generally M. Hodgson, *The Venture of Islam: Conscience and History in a World Civilization* (Chicago and London, 1974), vols 1–3, especially his exploration of the roots of challenge to the 'absolutist tradition' in the 9th–10th centuries (vol. 1, pp.473–96).

42. M. Kamali, *Revolutionary Iran: Civil Society and the State in the Modernization Process* (Aldershot, UK, 1998), p.11.

43. D. Eickelman and J. Anderson, 'Redefining Muslim Publics', in D.E. Eickelman and J.W. Anderson, ed., *New Media in the Muslim World: The Emerging Public Sphere* (Bloomington and Indianapolis, IN, 1999), pp.1–18, at p.12.

44. Ibid., p.16. See also in the same volume, A.R. Norton, 'The New Media, Civic Pluralism, and the Slowly Retreating State', pp.19–28; J. Anderson, 'The Internet and Islam's New Interpreters', pp.41–56; and J. Bowen, 'Legal Reasoning and Public Discourse in Indonesian Islam', pp.80–105. The precise relationship between the public sphere and civil society still appears to be unsettled among scholars. Habermas refers to the 'interplay of a public sphere based in civil society' (*Between Facts and Norms*, p.371), while Taylor sees the public sphere as a 'form' of civil society ('Liberal Politics and the Public Sphere', p.259). Eickelman, on the other hand, in the quoted text, refers to civil society existing within the public sphere. I find the Habermas/Taylor view of an encompassing society more cogent, but more important perhaps is the consensus that the relationship is symbiotic.

45. J. Habermas, *Moral Consciousness and Communicative Action*, tr. C. Lenhardt and S.W. Nicholson (Cambridge, UK, 1992).

46. Ibid., especially pp.58, 68. See also V. Jabri, 'Textualising the Self: Moral Agency in Inter-Cultural Discourse, *Global Society*, 10 (1996), pp.57–68.

47. G. Bunt, *Virtually Islamic* (Cardiff, 2000), p.17.

48. See Y. Haddad, ed., *Muslims in the West: From Sojourners to Citizens* (New York, 2002); K.H. Karim, 'Muslim Encounters with New Media: Towards an Inter-Civilizational Discourse on Globality?', in A. Mohammadi, ed., *Islam Encounters Globalisation: Reaction and Adoption* (London, forthcoming). For a sample of the irreverence of the public sphere toward traditional religious/political hierarchies, across the diaspora-homeland divide, see Michael Lewis, 'The Satellite Subversives', *The New York Times Magazine* (24 February 2002), pp.30–5 (chronicling the rise of a Los Angeles-based satirical television show whose principal audience as well as political targets lie in Iran).

49. M. Berrada, *The Game of Forgetting*, tr. I.J. Boullata (Austin, TX, 1996), p.128; original titled *Lu'bat al-nisyan* (Rabat, 1987).

50. See, for example, A.R. Norton, ed., *Civil Society in the Middle East*, vol.1 (Leiden and New York, 1994) and vol.2 (Leiden and New York, 1996). Even for its time, that fine anthology fell well short of capturing

the welter of media, community and other less formal local and trans-
frontier expressions of the public sphere among the particular countries
covered.

51. According to Iran's deputy minister of culture and Islamic orientation, over 50 newspapers, including 24 dailies, have officially been shut
down since March 2000; the figure does not include the student press:
Radio Free Europe/Radio Liberty Report, vol. 2:9 (1 March 2002);
<http://www.rferl.org/mm/>. In what is perhaps a sign of the times, an
Iranian film, Smell of Camphor, Fragrance of Jasmine, has the lead character (played by the director, Bahman Farmanara) voice his frustration
at the constraints around him thus: 'When a filmmaker doesn't make
films or a writer doesn't write, that is death. I am not afraid of dying. I
am afraid of living a futile life.' Farmanara was only able to make the
film after a 22-year directorial hiatus. On the other hand, the general
vibrancy of the country's film industry is noteworthy: see R. Tapper, The
New Iranian Cinema: Politics, Representation and Identity (London,
2002). For Abdolkarim Soroush, 'One of the effects of tyranny (religious or secular) is a loss in the spirit of art. We need an art-loving God
… A mundane, superficial religion leaves little room for art; but it's quite
the reverse with mystical religion.' 'Reforming the Revolution', tr. Nilou
Mobasser, *Index on Censorship* (London), January 2002, p. 77.

52. Muhibollah Siddiqzoda, speaking in the context of legal as well as
economic and political obstacles in Central Asia's battle against narcotics trafficking across the frontier with Afghanistan: quoted in M. Orth,
'Afghanistan's Deadly Habit', *Vanity Fair*, 499 (March 2002), p.150, at
p.165.

53. An estimated 3,054 individuals of various nationalities, including
some 800 Muslims, died or are missing and presumed dead from the
attacks on that date in New York, Washington and Pennsylvania, together
with the 19 hijackers of the planes used in the attacks: see 'Dead and
Missing', *The New York Times* (4 April 2002), p.A11. Many more have
perished in the retaliatory aftermath of those attacks, centred on Afghanistan, including an indeterminate number of innocent civilians. See
generally, Halliday, *Two Hours that Shook the World – September 11, 2001*.

54. It is instructive that a leading book on the mixture of Russian,
Western and indigenous influences in the new Central Asian cinema by
the Kazakh scholar and film-critic, Gulnara Abikeyeva, is available only
in Russian: *Kino Centralnoi Azii, 1990–2001* (Almaty, 2001).

55. See L. Rzayeva, 'Azerbaijani Intellectuals during the Transition',
Central Eurasian Studies Review, 1 (2002) pp.13–14. Civil unrest in the

capital region in mid-2002 was also sparked by perceived strictures against expressions of religious orthodoxy, including the wearing of headscarves by students: Konul Khalilova, 'Government struggles to defuse discontent in Baku suburb', *Eurasia Insight*, 18 June 2002: <http://www.eurasianet.org/departments/insight/articles/eavo61302.shtml>.

56. Wherein the political order under civil religion draws comfortably upon faith-traditions, while political religion (in the Kemalist vein) sacralises the political order: see M. Erdogan, 'Islam in Turkish Politics', *Critique – Journal for Critical Studies of the Middle East*, 15 (1999), pp.25–49, at pp.43–8.

57. Ironically, the reverse holds in Middle Eastern countries where NGOs are precluded by legislation from seeking 'political gains', and therefore act under the rubric of 'religious' work such as charity and *da'wa* (missionary activity). See Q. Wiktorowicz and S. Taji-Farouki, 'Islamic NGOs and Muslim Politics: A Case from Jordan', *Third World Quarterly*, 21 (2000), pp.685–99, concluding that the practical result of this circumstance may be to promote 'Islamic values and behaviour' more effectively than formal legal codes can. See also on the situation in Egypt (where religious groups are dominant among some 14,000 NGOs), M. Huband, J. Dempsey and R. Khalaf, 'Middle Eastern NGOs strain at the bonds of authoritarian government'. *The Financial Times* (London, 10 June 1999), p.7.

58. A willingness that appears to extend to the army's entanglements with militancy beyond its borders: Douglas Jehl, 'Pakistan Cutting its Spy Unit's Ties to Some Militants', *The New York Times* (20 February 2002), p.A1. Official moves against militancy in Pakistan's madrasas or religious schools and extremist networks, had in fact begun earlier – with limited success – in apprehension over growing sectarian violence: J. Miller, 'Pakistan Outlines Plans to Curb Militant Networks', *The New York Times* (10 June 2000), p.A6. A noted Indian writer, Pankaj Mishra, remarks that Pakistani President Pervez Musharraf's government has relied on public opinion that is 'overwhelmingly' opposed to extremism – though south of the border, illiberal sentiment 'seems to be finding a home in democratic India: 'Hinduism's Political Resurgence', *The New York Times* (25 February 2002), p.A23. Mishra's comment came before an outbreak of religious violence in India that claimed over 500 (mostly Muslim) lives, stemming from the campaign to build a Hindu temple on the site of the 16th-century Babri Mosque in the northern town of Ayodhya, demolished by zealots in 1992: C.W. Dugger, 'Hindu Justifies Mass Killings Of Muslims in Reprisal Riots', *The New York Times* (5 March 2002), p.A4.

See also the lament in this regard by the Indian writer and policy analyst, Shashi Tharoor, 'India's Past Becomes a Weapon' (Op-Ed article), *The New York Times* (6 March 2002), p.A25.

59. Michael Voss, 'Afghanistan Gets New Press Law', BBC World Service Report (9 February 2002): <http://news.bbc.co.uk/hi/english/world/south_asia/newsid_1810000/1810983.stm>; Kate Clark, 'Magazine gives Afghan women new voice', BBC World Service Report, 6 February 2002: <http://news.bbc.co.uk/hi/english/world/south_asia/newsid_1804000/1804255.stm>. However, media organisations have been critical of aspects of the legislation such as those that curtail non-state-controlled reporting: see <http://www.article19.org/docimages/1321.doc>, and <http://www.article19.org/docimages/1322>.

60. Andrew Solomon, 'An Awakening After the Taliban', *The New York Times*, 10 March 2002, Section 2, pp.1, 20–1 (detailing the energetic revival of painting, music, poetry and cinema in the aftermath of both Soviet and Taliban suppression of artistic freedom, amidst the ruins of post-war Afghanistan).

61. M. Kamrava, 'The Civil Society Discourse in Iran', *British Journal of Middle Eastern Studies*, 28 (2001), pp.165–85, at p.184–5. As such, Kamrava notes, 'the civil society discourse has restored to intellectualdom the social role to which it had long aspired but had forcibly been sidetracked from, namely that of educating and informing the public through its writing and publications' (pp.184–5).

62. A. Etzioni, 'Beyond Transnational Governance', *International Journal*, 56, (2001), pp.595–610, notably at p.597. See more generally, H. Anheier, M. Glasius and M. Kaldor, ed., *Global Civil Society 2001*, (Oxford and New York, 2001); R. Falk, *Religion and Humane Global Governance* (New York and Basingstoke, UK, 2001); H. Kung, *A Global Ethic for Global Politics and Economics* (New York, 1998).

2

Locating Civil Society In Islamic Contexts

Mohammed Arkoun

'Who shall tell the concord of this discord?'
Shakespeare, *A Midsummer Night's Dream* (5:1:60)

Civil society is one of those modern concepts that is constantly debated in contemporary societies along with democracy, the rule of law, human rights, citizenship, justice and the free market. Through translation, at least when it is accurate, such ideas can be transported across cultures. But the concepts will remain abstract, cut off from their existential, cultural, historical and intellectual contexts of emergence, genesis and metamorphosis, as long as the process of conceptualisation is not rooted in or initiated by the historical experience that shapes the collective memory of each social group. There is a need also that this collective memory be expressed in the original language used throughout the historical experience of the group. This is not the case for the majority of marginalised communities, since the modern secularised languages developed in European societies from the seventeenth centuries onwards have spread across the world with colonialism – followed by the stresses of the ideologies of development, and now of globalisation with its own economic and technological constraints. In societies of what is called the Third World, the growing gaps between economic and political elites and the masses fuel a continuing process of social and cultural exclusion. The middle classes that have played critical roles since the eighteenth century in the emergence of Euro-American civil society remain, at best, a precarious entity in contemporary Muslim societies; which, in turn, forestalls them from joining the ranks of creative elites or developing solidarities with the lower classes. These sociological realities interface with authoritarian and unaccountable state institutions that negate the very idea of civil society – indeed, render elusive even the strategies for developing the rule of law and civic culture in contemporary 'Islamic' contexts.

These obstacles are rooted not only in the disintegrating forces unleashed by the industrial civilisation and their interplay with ancient indigenous histories, but also in the 'techno-scientific' system of thought imposed by hegemonic nations where the historical leaps of what we call modernity have been and continue to be initiated. If the end of the cold war opened a horizon of fleeting hopes of a shared and controlled emancipation of all societies, then the 1990 Gulf War and its aftermath inaugurated the vision captured in the 'clash of civilisations' thesis.[1] The deep, unspoken reasons for these post-colonial and post-cold war situations have yet to be adequately analysed – and indeed are too often veiled by social and political scientists whose task should be to unveil the persistent will to power, economic war and the geopolitical strategies that underlie the tensions between the dominant 'West' and 'the Rest'.

We cannot deal effectively with the issues related to civil society and the rule of law if we limit our inquiry purely to addressing formal configurations of national and international political, economic and social power as they exist today. For this kind of typology maintains the ideological frontiers between the poles of the developed and developing worlds. Scholarship must participate in the process of mapping democratic values, power, wealth and the emancipation of the human condition in assorted regimes and societies, including those that are obscurantist and disabling. In-stead, discussions about religion, secularisation, culture, governance, democracy and economy are either conducted within the traditional system of belief about the imagined, never con-cretely actualised Community (umma) and its purported 'authentic' ahistorical Islam, or within the vocabulary, definitions and forms of reasoning borrowed from European thought and arbitrarily projected on this idealised, imagined, unrealistic Islam defended as the alternative 'model' to the Western universalised paradigm. The reference to so-called 'classical Islam' (700–1400) or the Golden Age of Islamic civilisation is a rhetorical claim that overlooks, for example, the decline of the institution of the caliphate in that time. The model claimed by Islamist movements since the 1970s goes further back, to the inaugurating Time of the Revelation and the mediation of the Prophet. Concrete his-tory is still more devalued than in the discourse on the classical legacy, often with the support of 'modern' scholarship. On the other hand, defenders of the secularised model are unmindful of the concrete sociological, historical, doctrinal realities of Islam, of its laws, institutions and beliefs – so different from the secular European regimes of thought, knowledge and action.

The comparative study of these opposed models remains un-satisfactory, often irrelevant, if not aggressively ideological. The social and political *imaginary* as well as the collective memory of society's constituent groups are ignored by those who address what is sweepingly and generically called 'Islam'. Fragments arbitrarily cut from the original social discourses are reported and described rather than critically analysed to show how strong collective rep-resentations create discrepancies between the 'imaginary' and the 'rational'.[2] Modern secular societies, of course, are hardly free of mythological representations. True, they have the benefit of a robust and evolving tradition of positive law, a rationalised bu-reaucracy, productive scientific research, sophisticated technology with a potent system of economic production and exchange – all of which maintain an imaginary of 'progress'. But this does not take into account the interactions between social imaginary, col-lective memories and the role postulated for pure reason – as

Kant called it – and its capacity in turn to control the 'rationality' of all fields, at all levels of human existence. Experts, managers and engineers criss-cross frontiers to shape worldwide 'civilisation', regardless of the gaps between societies where modernity emerged and continues to expand its conceptualisation of human history, and societies where it was and still is imposed as the expression of power and dominance.

Indeed, the defenders of national interests and identities during wars of liberation have managed to live in socio-cultural enclaves within their own societies and, at the same time, to promote themselves to the enabling levels of the professional classes of former colonising societies where they choose more and more to live. This worldwide re-composition of social links, ideological alliances and visions of the future is not merely the result of the brain drain phenomenon, or the lack of political security for economic entrepreneurs. It also expresses the historical failure of nationalist regimes that emerged after the era of colonial dominance: by the exercise of individual preference, people who have not enjoyed full citizenship in their own countries show that civil society and the rule of law are basic attributes of a modern polity. Emigration to foreign countries or to enclaves inside oppressive regimes has two consequences: it delays the emergence of a civil society in more and more disabling societies, and it enhances the construction for the future of pluralist spaces for a wider citizenship in advanced, democratic regimes.

Can we identify approaches to the various types and levels of civic culture achieved in colonised, underdeveloped societies on the one hand, and those that emerged in Europe and North America with the benefit of intellectual and scientific modernity on the other? Our inquiry must begin with the debates conducted in Muslim as well as Western contexts not with a view to identifying any reliable universal model or to garnering legitimacy for the 'civil society project', but to point out failures, deviations and unfulfilled promises relating to existing models. The Euro-American experience allows us not only to identify the elements of sustainable civic culture, but also the pitfalls of purely ideological constructs that may tempt societies claiming to be 'Muslim'.

Certainly, the violent, recurrent confrontations that we are witnessing in almost all post-colonial regimes – what one could describe as politically-programmed collective tragedies – undercut the construction of a sustainable, enabling civil society. And the task of building civic culture is left to citizens under the control, legal and otherwise, of their rulers. Global debates call for priority to be accorded to building capacity for ethical reasoning and judgement – even as the capacity for ethical reasoning is weakened by the liberal/modernist privileging of managerial and pragmatic reasoning that Robert Musil warned about on the eve of World War I in *Man Without Qualities.*[3]

Yet our enquiries should avoid a posture that looks down upon, disqualifies or declares obsolete pre-modern experiences, to focus only on models offered today in Western democratic regimes. This would imply the existence of a single model for all contemporary societies regardless of their specific historical trajectories. Can societies that are not part of the industrial and techno-scientific civilisational cluster escape the triumphalist free market and its underlying liberal philosophy? That, together with the pervasive culture of disbelief, has marginalised the kind of ethical discourse that matters – or should matter – in Muslim civic contexts. What we have instead are either the idealist, apologetic sermons of religious leaders, or official calls for a secularised civic conscience – both of which circumvent the need to reactivate ethical concern with building civil societies *qua* new historical platforms for the genesis of effective spaces for citizenship, national and global alike. With these observations in mind, I propose to explore some of the contours of the landscape, away from the utopian aspirations in which one might seek to locate modern civic culture.

Beyond the Dichotomy of Religion and Secularism

This dichotomy is the outcome of the history of religions, of claims of monopoly about Truth as a whole – including the truths of belief and unbelief, of the Just Law, of the answers to questions about the universe, nature, history, societies, life and death.

Reason, imagination and memory are all associated in the articulation, the transmission and the protection of Truth from deviations and negation. Pre-modern states have adopted, supported and utilised this regime of Truth as the ultimate instance of their legitimacy. The managers of the sacred and secular share their respective responsibilities, Religion being the instance of spiritual, moral 'authority' (*hukm*), and the State, the instance of 'power' (*sulta*). Together they have sought to implement, serve and protect the Truth. This alliance between religion and politics engenders a dogmatic control on all levels of life, with the expressions of the 'subjects' submitted to the religious Law, mediated by the ruler and his delegates.

Modern revolutions have substituted their own regime of truth, which still claims full validity against contrary evidence from critical history, cultural anthropology, psychology, and the sciences at large. In human affairs, one starts with the lofty hopes and transcendental visions of the mystics – only to end up with politics and the constraining power of 'legal' violence. If we need to search for Just Governance, the *sine qua non* for the capacity to build an enabling civil society, we must also pay attention to violence as a structural force at work in each society. When modern societies speak of violence as integral to religious traditions, they overlook the anthropology of violence in all types of societies, not least the most modernised and wealthy Western societies. Violence cannot be linked exclusively with *others* – perceived, described, condemned as the barbarians, uncivilised and uneducated, ignorant of the true teachings provided solely by the religion, philosophy and objective history taught in the public schools of modern *laïc* [4] states. Upon reading French or American newspapers on the Vietnam and Algerian colonial wars, or Israeli literature on Arabs and Muslim Palestinians, not to mention Communist or Nazi writings, one recognises that the building process of any type of society involves, at some level, the Manichean split between a civilised, cultivated, peaceful, humanist *We* – radically opposed to a terrorist, fanatic, rebellious, unenlightened *Them*. This psycho-social tendency applies as well to the representation of foreign immigrants in modern societies, despite the correctives and the protection introduced by of the rule of law where it exists and functions properly. Structural violence is manifested also in the field of scientific research and education: the intellectual contest between different schools of thought is translated into political rivalries, leading to the monopoly of legal violence exercised by all types of states, academic institutions and practices, including those built on democratic majorities.

Clearly, then, religion and secularism are best dealt with as polemical concepts referring to *contingent* ideological regimes of Truth.[5] This contingency is already displayed in the founding texts of the three monotheist religions. God himself is involved in the polemical disputes and violent conflicts between the true, loyal believers and all the groups who refuse, for various reasons, to receive and hold on to the true Revelation. The polemical frame is accepted, enforced and perpetuated in the religious Law elaborated by theologians-jurists recognised as orthodox authorities in the three religions (Jewish law, Christian canon law, sharia). European revolutions endorsed the same polemical, affirmative action leading to the triumph of a *laïc*/secularised regime of Truth. The critical issue here – not cogently addressed as yet by modern historians – can be explained in the following terms. While in Muslim contexts the stakes as delineated in the paradigmatic, prophetic discourse ended with the political and cultural defeat of the philosophical, scientific regime of the Truth, in Europe – mainly Catholic and Protestant – the contrary happened. With Descartes, Spinoza, Locke, Hobbes, Rousseau, Diderot, Voltaire and others, critical reason pursued the building task of modernity as an alternative frame of thought and historical action.

In Muslim contexts, religious reason not only survived but accepted regression from the intellectual and scientific levels attained in its classical period. Muslim supporters of the reformation movement from the nineteenth century to the 1940s had an apologetic, naüve answer to this question: Muslims had deviated from the 'authentic' Islam, the Right Rule taught by God and his Messenger and betrayed by the secular civilisations of subsequent dynasties. That Right Rule could be recovered only through the intervention of learned, pious authorities. After 1945, this process

of mythologisation came to be replaced by the nationalist, secularised ideology of liberation, through to the late 1970s when the
political failure of the post-colonial 'socialist revolution' opened
the way to a fundamentalist Islamic solution.

Amid the crises faced by all regimes of truth and inherited systems of legitimating, new waves of 'believers' embrace 'the revival
of religion' as a platform of resistance to 'materialist', secularised, corrupt regimes. But they fail to rethink the status and
functions of this religion that is manipulated by activist, politically oriented 'leaders'. In European contexts, the social sciences
offer more critical approaches to the religious phenomenon, to
its traditional and contemporary expressions. The secular regime
of truth is revisited and reinterpreted within the larger perspectives
and cognitive frames offered by the discoveries of the social and
hard sciences. Evidently, though, the intellectual and philosophical explanations have not kept up with recent technological leaps
and their impact on contemporary societies and on the new human
subject: fear and anger have been generated by globalisation's
powerful, economic, technological forces. As far as Muslim
societies go, we witness physical violence in the name of a so-called
Islamic Revolution, in place of reformist discourse (*islâh*) to
reactivate the 'authentic Islam' bequeathed by the Pious sanctified
Ancestors (*al-salaf al-sâlih*). The search for a more concrete, effective, liberating interaction between thought, knowledge and
action is again delayed and distorted, if not deleted. The majority
of social actors are prevented by political, social, economic and
cultural impediments from even thinking about the possibility of
taking the initiative required to get out of their impasse.
Demographic pressure, unemployment, social marginalisation,
psychological frustrations, authoritarian governance, bureaucratic
incompetence, irrelevant systems of education, the disintegration
of cultural codes, populist religious expressions – these factors
collectively block the emergence of conditions for a modern civic
culture.

Suffice it to say at this juncture that the vaunted separation of
Mosque and State as institutional entities in the context of promoting civil society is not on the cards. Kemal Atatürk's strident

venture in that regard in eradicating Ottoman institutions can hardly be on the political agenda of any party in power today, as long as the state remains patrimonial and social mentalities are shaped by patriarchal kinship mechanisms. Gender segregation prevails in the separation of private and public spaces, in the division of daily work, in the vertical power of the father or the elder brother, in the culture transmitted by the mother to her daughters. When rural or nomadic populations are uprooted and move to slums and ghettos around overpopulated megacities, the patriarchal order breaks down and is replaced by a populist system of inner solidarity and outer hostility. A rampant secularisation permeates these new micro-societies, largely through the media. But the intellectual and cultural dimensions of what we call secularism in Western contexts are as absent and unthinkable in these micro-societies as they are among the upper classes, for whom material modernisation is too often coupled with cultural traditionalisation. In such conditions, asking for a separation of Mosque and State only amounts to imposing a foreign ideological model while the problem of increasing structural violence – reflected across the urban fabric – is addressed neither by the patrimonial state nor by the elites who must negotiate their own conditional freedom with the regime in power.

Rethinking the Trilogy of Religion, Ethics and the Rule of Law

For the majority of Muslims, Islam is simultaneously religion, state and society, the inseparable three 'ds' – *dîn, dawla, dunyâ* – of classical Islamic thought.[6] The rule of law and civil society are modern conceptualisations based on the autonomy of the religious sphere (with its specific theological speculation on spiritual and ethical values) and the political sphere (with its secular approach to governance, legitimacy, sovereignty and the separation of legislative, executive and judicial powers). In the modern frame of conceptualisation, God, Revelation and prophetic authority are no longer the source of the True knowledge, the Just Law, the ultimate spiritual and ethical values. Rather, all kinds of 'values' and 'value systems' are fated to be reassessed within the interface of political theology and philosophy – unless theology and philosophy are entirely separated to create competing frames of thought, interpretation and action. Which is exactly what transpired in the historical development of Islamic thought. After the death of Ibn Rushd (in 1198), the creative interface between theology, religious law and philosophy was interrupted; even theology as a rationalising expression of faith was to disappear after the thirteenth-fourteenth century. Schools of law ceased their *disputatio* (*munâzara*), and became isolated from each other. Ethics, which Miskawayh had elevated in the early tenth century to the rank of a key discipline in the humanist curriculum,[7] came to be disregarded as a critical endeavour to discern the positive, operative, emancipating virtues from the mass of traditional, uncriticised, unthought collective habits ritually reproduced in patriarchal societies. One cannot ignore this transformation of the intellectual scene in all Islamic contexts right until the 1850s.

The second radical transformation in all matters concerning the triple d started after 1945, and is still in progress. All so-called Muslim societies have been challenged by the modern intellectual and institutional shifts that occurred in Europe between the seventeenth and eighteenth centuries; but they were inclined to reject a historical experience introduced from the outside during colonial dominance. Indeed, the history of the colonial phenomenon needs rewriting in light of the distinction between indigenous traditional cultures of the colonised and the colonial ideological translation of intellectual modernity by Europeans themselves, including for their own peasantry and industrial workers in the nineteenth century. The colonised societies were based on the patriarchal system more than on Islamic law and ethics. Yet respected and influential Muslim personalities and leaders refer with pride and conviction to a supervening Islamic Spirituality and Ethics with no consideration of these transformations within Islamic thought on the one hand, and the challenge of modernity as a mental, historical shift on the other. Such stances contribute to the persistence of ideological and apologetic confusions.

My contention is that philosophical trends of thought and Islamic sciences, developed as competing, conflicting, differentiated systems until the eleventh-twelfth century, and the contest ended with the elimination of the philosophical trend and the triumph of religious orthodoxy to our day. The ensuing intellectual and cultural gap constrained contemporary Islamic thought from sharing in the modern debates on politics, ethics, law, history, social and economic order. Inasmuch as ethics and law generate a complex knot of problems that need to be unravelled, we cannot proclaim an Islamic rule of law with its attendant civic culture if we do not even recognise that we have inherited from classical thought complex knots of problems left aside in the stock of 'unthinkable' issues. Religion and secularism are instances of thinking and interpreting where different knots are generated – with the important difference that in a religious frame, values and juridical norms are sacralised, divinised and declared intangible, while in a secularised frame, all values and norms are doomed to change under pressure of historicity. Whether these intellectually opposed frames of reference can cohere in the nexus between the religious and political spheres in transitional Muslim contexts like that of post-revolutionary Iran, remains to be seen.

Indubitably, a rule of law with its civil society founded on specific Islamic principles, attributes and style, would be an intellectual, spiritual, ethical, juridical and institutional challenge to the 'secular model' achieved and presented in Europe as universal, or at least universalisable. Without such a challenge, the viability of an Islamic polity would at most be functional in terms of psychology, cultural expressions and chronological duration. If the challenge does ensue, the European model would be constrained to stop looking down on the traditional and contemporary experiences of Islamic social contexts – especially in facile categories like 'Oriental despotism', 'Islamic Law', and the like. More likely, however, political and juridical discourses in Islamic contexts will remain reactive, dependent on the unfolding of ideas and action within the dynamic realm of self-challenging European thought. After all, young generations of Muslims are particularly influenced by the worldwide diffusion of a global culture, inimical to the patrimonial state and patriarchal social order, and to the denial of full, effective citizenship.

We have numerous illustrations of that global culture in the struggle for freedom of thought, belief and expression in societies where an official religion is declared in the national constitution. Muslim intellectuals who dare to express critical attitudes on political or religious issues are often put on trial and eventually imprisoned in several countries. Others are obliged to practice self-censorship to avoid attacks from conservative public opinion as well as official pursuits on issues involving problems of human rights, sharia and modern law or any other proposition casting doubts on the legitimacy of states for exercising arbitrary 'legal' violence. The principle that the rule of law should protect all citizens even when they debate issues of religious law and ethics is negated, no matter that it is formally enshrined in the constitution. Moreover, the Egyptian Constitution explicitly holds that Divine Law supersedes any law elaborated on the basis of human opinion – which offers every judge the possibility of rendering supervening judgements in the name of the sharia.[8] How can a civil society ever be developed with a constitutional norm that invokes medieval mental space, where the theological regime of religious Truth presided over legal systems in Christian, Jewish and Muslim realms alike? The secular rule of law not only allows religious and ethical issues to be freely adjudicated, and studied on a scientific basis in the public space of citizenship; it also allows those issues to be kept in their orthodox expressions in private institutions of learning and practice where so desired.

Again, the divide between the public and private space in its various incarnations is open to debate in the West, but seldom in Islamic contexts where private space is the abode to which a large majority of women are still relegated. Public space is effectively monopolised by men and male activities at all levels. Yes, changes are taking place; but this old segregation continues to have deeply negative consequences for attempts to generate a civil society. The role of women is, and will increasingly be crucial for the first time in the history of Muslim polities and civic cultures. Certainly the Turkish example where a secularised state has been promoted since 1924 should be examined, to determine how far the frontier between public/private space has actually shifted over the long decades of political struggle. I am not addressing the visible social and legal frontier alone, but also the invisible motivations, needs and aspirations in such conflicting contexts, the deep fault lines that mark the relations between male and female citizens.

For modern thought, all systems of ethics are a matter for debate, research and reassessment. This task cannot be undertaken without the protection of the rule of law, and the support of a pluralist civil society where multiple traditions of thought, postures of mind and religious experiences can be confronted. As suggested earlier, the capacity of ethical reasoning and judgement is radically different, and leads to different results in every respect, when conducted in a *laïc* space of citizenship rather than under the aegis of state-imposed religion. This reflects the cognitive, philosophical and juridical frontier that divides the modern and the religious regimes of truth. Because such a frontier has existed since the seventeenth-eighteenth century in Europe, it has become one of the decisive criteria for assessing the typology of regimes and philosophies in terms of how congenial/hostile they are to an enabling, emancipating, sustainable civil society with the rule of law as its necessary partner. Like all such criteria, this one is sharply debated among 'religious' believers and secular/*laïc* believers. I speak of believers on both sides to avoid the prejudice that religious believers are not open to scientific criticism, while secularised minds are necessarily supporters of enlightening scientific knowledge. Secularism – *laïcism* – had and still has believers who are unconscious of the philosophical, social, psychological and political stakes of their belief. The Manichean division between so-called traditional, conservative believers and the modern, enlightened citizens of a modern advanced secular/*laïc* democracy, still commands the discourses of militants on both sides. Clearly, the parties must begin by debating the place and the role of belief in building the capacity for theological, ethical and other reasoning and judgement. This is not yet the case among defenders of either option, nor with scholars specialised in these matters.[9]

The fact of the matter is that the secularised/*laïc* state has generated a culture of systematic *disbelief*, rejecting religious reasoning and motivations as belonging to the obsolete past of the so-called 'dark' Middle Ages; while religion-based states continue to enforce a frozen culture, rigid rituals and contingent 'sacred' law on their subjects (who cannot appropriately be called citizens in this case). Christian readers of this last statement may protest against its arbitrary sweep. For them, I add that Catholicism continues in many places to resist the struggle of reason for autonomy, for its independence from the authority of Holy Scriptures, even as independent reason supports state-imposed proclamations about knowledge, education, and scientific interpretations on the human subject. We know how Pope John Paul II exercises his theological *Magisterium* in the wake of Vatican II. Protestant Christianity, born as one of the first claims for modern intellectual freedom, is generally linked (after Weber) with the emergence and growth of secular regimes and culture together with European capitalism. Orthodox Christianity and Judaism are in some respects closer to the instance of Islam than to the Catholic and Protestant expressions of religion and secularism. This is the historical and doctrinal platform – at least for what might be described as Societies of the Book – from which we may begin opening a new historical space to rethink inherited systems of beliefs, values and norms.[10]

What are the implications for civil society of the need to range beyond the dichotomy of religion versus secularism? A modern civil society must of necessity be pluralist. It provides individual citizens belonging to different ethnic, cultural and religious groups with all the requisite democratic freedoms; debates are multifaceted, cross-cultural, cross-disciplinary, beyond all frontiers imposed by monolithic religious, ideological communities or nation-states. Binary thinking submits to the Aristotelian tenets of the logic principles of contradiction and identity: a proposition is true or false, teaches good or evil. Pluralist logic is more flexible: there are multiple ways to articulate religious or philosophical values, to combine spiritual experiences with secularised political institutions. In such a civil society, different cultures and world visions are not juxtaposed without appropriate interactions within the same, shared space of citizenship – as is the case today in many democratic societies where multiple communities occupy specific urban spaces. Rather, interactivity is made possible, even postulated, by new modes of conceptualising both citizenship and the human subject.

The Status and Roles of 'Intellectuals'

It is far more enlightening to evaluate the reception or the rejection of intellectual interventions than to dwell, as is often done, on the eventual relevance and the substance of the contributions of intellectuals. We cannot assess the nature of the interventions in terms of shaping civil society in Muslim contexts without taking into account the social and political status, as well as the strategies of intervention of intellectuals – notably in relation to the massive audiences of the 'ulama' who command religious orthodoxy. I have placed 'intellectuals' within quotation marks above to remind us about the perennial question: what is an intellectual? In the French tradition of thought, the debate has been recurrent since the eighteenth century. Scholars and writers are not necessarily intellectuals; physicians, lawyers, journalists, politicians and managers may also be intellectuals.

I would propose the following attributes in framing the civic status and role of intellectuals in any cultural context:

The foremost condition for a claim to be regarded as an intellectual is an unceasing commitment to the critical function, apropos not only debates about cognitive and scientific activities – which are shared by scholars at large – but also wider issues of politics, religion, ethics and law stemming from the eddies and currents of daily existence, within and beyond national frontiers. For such actors (or putative actors), the quest for meaning, and the right to pursue it, must in all circumstances prevail over any ideology, no matter how wide its embrace by fellow members of one's community or nation. Moreover, in applying the critical function to concrete existential and moral debates and discourses, the very process of reasoning should itself be the subject of scepticism – much as science obliges its practitioners to question the basic methodology of their inquiry and experimentation. The intellectual is keen to generate, enrich and enlighten public debates in order to heighten awareness of the ultimate stakes; thence he makes his contribution to the building of an informed society with shared responsibility and an emancipating sense of citizenship. In consequence, every participating listener or reader ought to feel empowered, to become an informed civic actor capable of partaking and engaging in the debates and discourses of the day.

Second, the intellectual should have the cognitive and intellectual authority to elucidate complex issues in dispute among politicians, scholars, religious authorities, the judiciary and ordinary citizens. To acquire this stature, he needs to declare explicitly the epistemological postulates that command his own discourse and determine his choices as a citizen, believer, defender of a particular case. This implies a willingness to listen attentively to objections, and to seriously rethink and adjust his posture in light of the facts even when it is 'inexpedient' to do so. In the absence of such integrity, the intellectual can sustain neither his critical function nor his authority.

Finally, as a corollary, the intellectual must be prepared to constantly re-conquer his independence from any political, religious or philosophical commitment that might affect the authority of the critical function. This is not to deny the significance of loyalty and fairness to other authors, social actors and categories, rulers, communities, doctrines, cultures and states that are involved in a given debate. But the intellectual must be ready to stand entirely alone, whatever the cost. I am aware that I am presenting an ideal type; after all, intellectuals themselves need touchstones to locate their positions and initiatives in a full spectrum of values and responsibilities. We know of the reputations that accrued to Emile Zola and Marie-François Voltaire respectively by virtue of the *J'accuse* letter concerning the Dreyfus affair, and the Calas episode. We also know how luminaries like Jean-Paul Sartre, Michel Foucault and Pierre Bourdieu have squandered some of their intellectual eminence by failing to uphold scrupulously the frontier between the critical function and militant commitment to one particular political party or social/interpretive perspective.

In my *Humanisme arabe au 4e/10e siècle*,[11] I have shown to what extent the critical function was claimed, discussed and displayed among intellectuals belonging to the generation of Miskawayh (d.1029) and Tawhîdî (d.1023). The posture of mind, cognitive options and activities of those intellectuals in the Islamic city (*madîna*), may be compared with those displayed on a grander scale and with more appropriate scientific tools and social support by the European philosophers and writers of the seventeenth-eighteenth centuries. Scholars now speak of the Arab humanism of that exceptional epoch, conducive to the ephemeral emergence of a type of civil society. It was a time when many were cognisant of and aspired to the conditions for arriving at what was deemed ethically and philosophically the 'Virtuous City' (after Farabi's paradigmatic *opus*). In contrast to other periods in Muslim history, then, one observes that the role of intellectuals could either be to foster or diminish the process of building a civic culture. For attempts have been made in Islamic contexts to institutionalise a civil society, and their failure in comparison with the experience in Northern and Western Europe and America deserves careful consideration.

This brings me to the matter of intellectual responsibility, bearing in mind the socio-political contexts in which its exercise can be effective. I offer two examples to illustrate the nature of this responsibility vis-à-vis the process of building civil society – one regarding the upper reaches of authority (drawing on a Qur'anic verse), the other concerning the social status imposed on marginalised groups that lack many of the rights ostensibly guaranteed by the law to all citizens. Verse 5:44 of the Qur'an states:

> *We, indeed, did reveal the Torah wherein is guidance and light; by its norms, the prophets who bowed* [to God's Will] *judge the Jews; so do the rabbis* (rabbâniyyûn) *and the doctors of law* (ahbâr), *for having been entrusted to safeguard the revealed part of God's Book and they were its witnesses thereto. So fear not mankind, fear Me; do not sell My signs for a little gain. Whoso judges not by that God has revealed, such are disbelievers.*

The Shi'i jurist Muhammad Bâqir al-Sadr has used the verse to expound upon the constitution of an Islamic state,[12] much as the

Ayatollah Khomeini did in his book *The Rule of the Supreme Jurist* (*Vilayat-e faqîh*).[13] The verse is interpreted as a commandment to the believer's intervention in political affairs. According to Bâqir al-Sadr, the reference to *rabbâniyyûn* applies to the twelve Shi'i imams, while *ahbâr* are in effect those authorities who are qualified to fulfil the function of *marja'*, or the Supreme Jurist. Under the terms of the post-revolutionary Constitution of the Islamic Republic of Iran, the Supreme Jurist is deemed the spokesperson and the ultimate point of reference for the implementation of divine Law on earth. Hence, the doctrine espoused by al-Sadr and Khomeini and consecrated in positive law bestows upon the leadership of learned theologian-jurists a monopoly on the exercise of Qur'anic interpretation, with all that this implies for the cultivation of civic space for the citizens of Iran.

Under such circumstances, what role and status should intellectuals seek, mindful of the historical, doctrinal and juridical objections to the concept of the political supremacy of the clerical class? During the revolutionary struggle against a political regime, there is scarcely a place for intellectuals aspiring to the profile that I have sketched. Some will fully subscribe to the principles and goals of the revolution, perhaps becoming ideologues themselves. Others may keep silent, or emigrate. Of course, many intellectuals engaged in the political struggle even become active supporters of the triumphant single-party state, and rail against their fellow intellectuals who have chosen to fulfil a critical function beyond ideological constraints. Intellectual – and civic – life is always distorted and impoverished by ideology. For instance, when Algeria's FLN (National Liberation Front) enjoyed full political control, a minister of education, Mostefa Lacheraf, who was respected both as a critical thinker and a loyal activist for national independence, had to resign from office because he criticised the demagogic politics of 'arabisation'. This kind of choice is faced routinely by social actors in Muslim (and non-Muslim) transitional contexts, which only highlights the primacy of commitments to the autonomy of the self, intellectual and civic alike.

Patrimonialism and its Discontents

Not surprisingly, many Muslim intellectuals, like their fellow citizens at large, have chosen to emigrate to democratic polities in the West. In the 1960s and 1970s, this was often condemned as a betrayal of 'sacred' national (even civic) obligations. Further, renouncing one's own nationality to receive that of a former colonising state was perceived as offensive to the martyrs of liberation struggles. This kind of moral pressure frequently engendered guilty consciences, which in turn prevented many from thinking and acting as *bona fide* free citizens of either the original or adopted country. These psychological and moral dimensions and realities should not be ignored in evaluating the role of intellectuals in Muslim contexts. Today, there are those who choose to forget their ancestry and seek total integration in their adopted society; others maintain a nostalgic link to their original, imagined identity, 'waiting in the future for the past to come', to quote the Tunisian novelist Sabiha Khemir.[14] There are also some who choose to cross cultural, religious and nationalist boundaries in order to share with new visionary thinkers the humanist option for a global space of citizenship, such as through the platform of the European Union. The latter, along with Canada and the United States, have become hosts to such a diversity of peoples and cultures that a unique opportunity is afforded to Muslim intellectuals to pursue new horizons of meaning, hope and action, not only for themselves but also, in numerous instances, for their ancestral societies.

By contrast, the 'ulama' have tended not to emigrate in significant numbers. They have grown closer to the lay populace, and succeeded in perpetuating their old alliance with the patrimonial state that is content to treat society as private inherited property. This is, axiomatically, the opposite of the trend needed in pursuit of a modern civil society. In the patrimonial regime, the head of state occupies second place in a vertical line descending from God, and reaching down to the ancestor of the clan and the father of the patriarchal family. While the state monopolises power with its patrimonial logic, societies in Islamic contexts develop an

underground system of exchange and regulation, parallel to official legal codes, bureaucracies and economies. Corruption covers
complex social and economic practices (*baksheesh, trabendo*), which
are tolerated as a functional aspect of the patrimonial state, and
extend all the way to international transactions with the West. A
growing corpus of literature documents the unfolding of these
parallel worlds, including the seminal works of Luis Martinez and
Gilles Kepel.[15] The anthropological basis of the patrimonial, patriarchal system in Islamic contexts has been ably deconstructed
by Abdellah Hammoudi as well as Hicham Sharabi.[16]

Then there is the gender dimension of patrimonialism, whose
implications add to those that I adverted to earlier on the civic
status and role of women. The Moroccan sociologist Soumaya
Guessous writes in the journal *Femmes du Maroc* (June 2001) of
the brokers who provide rich urban families with teenage house-
keepers. The text merits full translation, for its depiction of a large
segment of rural society where girls are used by their own parents
as chattels displayed in the market for sale. Citizens of high social
and economic standing – from the learned, cultivated classes –
give their consent to the enslavement of young girls severed from
their families, thrown into a hostile urban environment and compelled to serve day after day in the tasks of 'housekeeping'. An
integral part of this experience is sexual harassment by young boys,
fathers and other male relatives in the host family. I am not suggesting that such practices are unique to Moroccan society. Indeed,
they are part of a worldwide phenomenon that NGOs and international institutions have been grappling with for some years as
an egregious human rights issue. But the fact remains that the
state, society, wealthy classes, religious authorities and intellectuals have all failed thus far to halt what should not only be
intolerable, but also contradicts the declared commitments of
countries like Morocco to actively promoting civil society.

It is interesting to note that the popular movements generally
described as 'fundamentalist Muslim' display an ambivalence
toward the conditions for promoting civic culture. On the pragmatic level, they certainly provide much-needed social assistance
and support to rural and urban populations that are disabled,

marginalised, excluded and exploited both by officialdom and economic elites. In a variety of transitional contexts from the Maghreb to the Near East to South-East Asia, their activism has extended to the sectors of health, transportation and education for the underprivileged; and they doubtless contribute to a sense of morality among youth deprived of traditional kinship protection. At the same time, these popular movements are anxious to promote an 'Islam' that is transformed into a refuge, and in many cases, serves as an ideological springboard to defy and replace 'corrupted-corrupting materialist, secularised' regimes. There is less of a concern on the part of these movements to promote civic bonds than communal ones, which can foster new exclusions and marginalisations, and reinforce old prejudices. This kind of ambiguity is, arguably, an integral part of the deep structural transformation now underway in all Muslim contexts.[17]

Where to From Here?

The wrong approach to the challenge of 'locating' civil society for our purposes is to outline the attributes and practices of coherent civic cultures as envisaged and realised in Western democracies, and seek to apply them in transitional Muslim contexts. This would simply fail to account for indigenous (not 'Islamic') complexities born of profound historical and sociological differences. Another approach, favoured mainly by apologist or militant Muslims, singles out ideal attributes of particular democratic cultures and projects them back on an imagined Islamic Model, usually that of Medina under the guidance of Prophet Muhammad (610–632). Hence, the contemporary Islamist or 'fundamentalist' discourse restores for the social imaginary the 'authentic' Ideal Type of mythical time and space. Meanwhile, in the cold light of contemporary history, the evidence is of patrimonial states delaying and obstructing by the politics of traditionalisation the emergence of a rule of law and civic culture. We need to subject to critical analysis the ongoing social dialectic between the elements of the common Islamic imaginary – the stubborn patrimonial political order sacralised, 'legitimised' by

the 'divine' Islamic Law – and the modern democratic culture of
the external world, brought in by international organisations and
by dint of expanding scientific, economic and technological forces.
How this dialectic unfolds in particular societies is of crucial importance in considering the prospective locus of civic culture in
Muslim contexts.

The efficacy of intellectual modernity and secularised institutions in Egypt, Morocco, Syria, Tunisia and Turkey, for example,
needs to be compared and contrasted with countries that have
different historical memories and sociological constraints, like Indonesia, Malaysia, Mali, Senegal, Tanzania and Tajikistan. As long
as the political and social sciences adhere to linear and descriptive surveys of isolated events, movements or ideologies, we will
remain ignorant of the rich web of underlying factors and
mechanisms, and of less visible social actors. Just as troubling,
theologians and the managers of the sacred continue to resist what
those in the natural and social sciences have long recognised: that
social and historical conditioning – base, materialist reality – has
everything to do with human behaviour. Perhaps the post-cold
war collapse of ideological paradigms will hasten the overdue
escape from dichotomous, binary frames of interpretation that
cast spiritual authority against political power, or ethical tenets
and virtues against relational truths and contingent law. As the
content, functions and authority of religion alter drastically under the impact of globalisation, the question arises as to whether
Muslims will resist this onslaught as many did with modernity, or
whether globalisation will be harnessed in reconstructing the nature of relations among state, society and the individual, despite
having to do so in the midst of disintegrated urban spaces, ar-
chaic organs of state, and decontextualised frames of reference
for individuals and communities.

Can the new paradigms of international relations accelerate
the shift of developing/transitional states from their patrimonial
orders to democratic cultures and commitment to the rule of law?
On the face of it, the onslaught of pluralist values and societies is
irresistible: even authoritarian states tend to present themselves
as full supporters of democratic culture, though their domestic

realities tell another story. The culture of citizenship that is essential to civil society is emerging far too slowly in most Muslim contexts, not least because governments must grapple with issues of social cohesion, tensions among heteroclite collective imaginaries, low levels of education, and profound (often growing) socio-economic inequalities. Humanist visions from above do not sit easily among populations that can no longer trust the governors – which underscores both the necessity for and the difficulty in attaining pluralist civil society. It is true that contemporary societies have many means of resistance against the ways of oppressive states. But their prospects of resistance and change would be enhanced if women citizens were fuller actors across the public spectrum, instead of being constrained in so many instances, and sometimes consigned to private domains.

More broadly, Samuel Huntington and L.E. Harrison, amongst others, have recently accorded to 'culture' a critical role not only in international relations, but also in shaping human progress.[18] Scholars from various disciplinary backgrounds suggest that there are interactive functions between types and levels of culture that prevail in each social group, and the styles and levels of economic development and human emancipation achieved. There is no doubt that culture does matter in that sense. Yet the subject is only now being tackled with proper methodologies and problematisations after decades of dogmatic socialist definitions and economic policies coming out of the ideological frameworks and clashes of developed and developing states. During the decades of the cold war, this ideological perspective generated the programmed social tragedies we are still witnessing in several Muslim contexts. As long as the required attention is not given by policy-makers and intellectuals to types and levels of culture in shaping the mentalities, structuring social imaginaries, and commanding ways of reasoning and interpreting, there can be no real success for the new proposals and initiatives to build a sustainable rule of law and civil society – not only in the developing/ transitional world but also the hegemonic one where democracy has achieved significant progress.

It is not relevant to keep inquiring – as Western media and

scholars are inclined to do – whether 'Islam' is compatible with secularism, democracy or individual rights. 'Islam' is effectively controlled by states. And robust opposition parties and movements defy this control not in order to establish secular liberal regimes, but to substitute still more 'authentic' Islamic ones. At least that has been the case in Afghanistan, Algeria, Egypt, Iran, Kyrgyzstan, Lebanon, Nigeria, Pakistan, Palestine, Sudan, Tajikistan and Uzbekistan; the list is neither exhaustive nor, one suspects, exhausted. Political regimes that monopolise the control of Islam tend, *ipso facto*, to sacrifice their legitimacy in the eyes of the managers of the sacred. Hence, such regimes will usually pay a cadre of clerics, official 'ulama', to help sustain a semblance of religious legitimacy.[19] In this regard, *'Islam' is theologically protestant and politically catholic.*

This chapter could well be re-cast under the rubric of 'Umma and Civil Society'. The idea of the umma as a spiritual Utopia was inaugurated by the prophetic discourse, and developed through diverse religious, political, ethical, social experiences, while being articulated intellectually in a large number of major works. That umma is still alive as a terrestrial and eschatological project and aspiration within the collective imaginary of millions of believers. Does that traditional, utopian umma with its specific culture and frames of thought constitute an intellectual, spiritual, ethical and/or legal obstacle to the process of building a modern, secular civil society? Conversely, does this kind of civil society, which is still an ideal type that is imagined, pursued, and partially implemented in Western Europe and North America, present ontological, spiritual, ethical and humanist perspectives for the emancipation of the human condition? And does it truly supersede in that respect the promises held dear by traditional religions and their adherents? Articulated in these terms, the problem invites a plurality of critical, comparative explorations of religious as well as secular systems of thought and action.

Have the tragic events of September 11, 2001, enough revelatory power to inspire intellectual shift and decisive cultural jumps toward not the end of history, but rather a history based on a concrete, more richly conceptualised, negotiated History – based on the solidarity of peoples regardless of their demographic size, economic development, and prevailing levels of historical development? This far, culture and systems of education have been kept out of an 'international agenda' devoted to problems of economy, trade, migration, transport regulation, and the like. Nation-states are keen to preserve sovereign control of culture and education *qua* pillars of national identity. Cultures linked to religions or ideologies tend to emancipate as well as to imprison; we need to be liberated from closed identities that deny plural ways of discovering and building 'truths'. Through the tragedies thus programmed by cultures, religions and ideologies, a new posture of reason, a more enabled imagination, an enlarged collective encompassing memory – a global civil society – appears to be emerging.

Notes

1. Triggered by Samuel P. Huntington's controversial essay, 'A Clash of Civilizations?', *Foreign Affairs*, 72 (1993), p.22; and expanded upon in his *The Clash of Civilizations and the Remaking of World Order* (New York, 1996).

2. See especially C. Castoriadis, *The Imaginary Institution of Society*, tr. K. Blamey (Cambridge, MA, 1998); and C. Castoriadis, *World in Fragments*, ed. and tr. D.A. Curtis (Palo Alto, CA, 1997).

3. For a new, two-volume English edition see Robert Musil, *Man Without Qualities* (Picador, 1995). More recently, Guy Debord's *Société du spectacle*, English tr. Donald Nicholson-Smith as *The Society of the Spectacle* (New York, 1994), revealingly sketches the shift away from personalised relationships among citizens.

4. This French notion has no ready equivalent in other European languages. It connotes the specific historical experience since the Revolution of 1789, considered by the French Republican state as the 'inaugurating moment' of a new era of Truth – just as the emergence of Christianity or Islam are the inauguration of other competing eras of Truth.

5. Consider Durkheim's reflection on this score: 'In the beginning ... everything that is social is religious; the two words are synonymous. Then, little by little, political, economic, and scientific functions free themselves from the religious function, establish themselves separately,

and take on a more and more temporal character. If one may express it this way, God, who was first present in all human relations, pulls out progressively, leaving the world to men and their conflicts. Or, if he continues to control them, he does so from on high and from afar.' Emile Durkheim, *De la Division du travail social* (4th ed., Paris, 1922), pp.143–4.

6. See my *L'Humanisme arabe au 4th/10th siècle* (Paris, 1982).

7. See my recent *Ma'ârik min ajli al-insana fi'l-siyâqât al-islâmiyya* (Beirut, 2001); French: *Combats pour l'humanisme en contextes islamiques* (Paris, 2002).

8. See the important essay by Baudouin Dupret, *Au Nom de quell droit* (Cairo, 2000).

9. The Protestant theologian Pierre Gisel and the philosopher Paul Ricoeur are notable exceptions.

10. See my *The Unthought in Contemporary Islamic Thought* (London, 2002).

11. See n.4 above.

12. See Chibli Mallat, *The Renewal of Islamic Law: Muhammad Baqer as-Sadr, Najaf and the Shi'i International* (Cambridge, 1993), pp.59–78, especially pp.62–72.

13. Ruhollah Khomeini, *Velayat-e Faqih* (Tehran, 1979); *Wilayat al-Faqih* (Arabic tr. Beirut, 1979). See also Hamid Enayat, 'Iran: Khumayni's Concept of the "Guardianship of the Juriconsult"', in James Piscatori, ed., *Islam and the Political Process* (Cambridge, 1982), pp.160–80.

14. Also the title of Khemir's powerful novel (London, 1993).

15. See Luis Martinez, *La Guerre civile en Algérie* (Paris, 1998); Gilles Kepel in *Expansion et déclin de l'islamisme* (Paris, 2000).

16. Abdellah Hammoudi, *Master and Disciple: The Cultural Foundations of Moroccan Authoritarianism* (London, 1997); Hicham Sharabi, *Neopatriarchy: A Theory of Distorted Change in Arab Society* (Oxford, 1988).

17. For a neo-Khaldunian reading of these contests for political and social ascendancy, in terms of the *bilad al-maghzin* (the orderly centre) versus the *bilad al-siba* (the dilatory hinterland), see Saad Eddin Ibrahim, 'From Taliban to Erbakan: The Case of Islam, Civil Society and Democracy', in Elisabeth Özdalga and Sune Persson, ed., *Civil Society, Democracy and the Muslim World* (Istanbul, 1997), pp.33–44.

18. See L.E. Harrison and Samuel P. Huntington, ed., *Culture Matters: How Values Shape Human Progress* (New York, 2000).

19. See Malika Zeghal, *Gardiens de l'Islam: Les oulémas d'al-Azhar dans l'Egypte contemporaine* (Paris, 1996).

3

Self, Society, Civility and Islam

Aziz Esmail

I

The single most striking fact about the concept of civil society is the extent of disagreement over it. There is, however, a peculiar quality to this disagreement. Unlike what Augustine said about time – that one knows what it is until one is asked to define it – there is broad unanimity about how civil society is to be defined. It is, we are told, made up of associations of people constituting the public sphere (as distinguished from the private) other than the sphere of the state. Indeed, intervention of the state is what civil society is precisely designed to limit or keep at bay. On the opposite side, civil society is demarcated from so-called 'primordial' units – the family, the kin-group, the neighbourhood, the tribe, the ethnic or religious community (although some of these may enter the sphere of civil interaction, and thereby be subsumed in it). Essential too is the nature of this interaction, which is expected to be inspired, fundamentally, by a commitment to democracy and tolerance of differing or competing views. From this, it is apparent that civil society has deep affinity with the ethic of a liberal democratic order in politics, and linked to it, with a market economy (with due scope for a spectrum of positions on issues of re-distributive equity).

So much, then, on the measure of agreement over what characteristics a civil society must possess to be identified as such. Beyond this, however, there is considerable debate. We may roughly classify the issues which spark controversy into the structural and the cultural. The former include, for example, the extent to which state intervention is to be tolerated; or the degree to which the economy may be regulated in the interest of the preservation of human 'dignity', defined in such terms as to preclude gross destitution. The 'cultural' concern (which is necessarily also a moral one) presses itself on attention when it is realised that the actual record of civil societies, in the economically advanced democracies of the West (for that is where this particular debate has been systematically pursued), shows an alarming rise of 'uncivil' behaviour, ranging from poor manners, disruptive self-assertiveness and hurtful competitiveness to institutional manifestations of such traits in patterns of litigation, for instance. These phenomena appear to indicate a moral deficit at the heart of modern liberal society, a failing notable, moreover, for the contrast it presents to the moral idealism of its original philosophical proponents. Some theorists, worriedly aware of this unsatisfactory state of affairs, reiterate their faith in civil society, combining their assertion of it, however, with a moral appeal to its essential, distinguishing ethic of commitment to the 'common good'. Such commitment further requires, as its necessary corollary, 'civility' of relations not only with people of one's acquaintance but, in accordance with the very notion of citizenship, with the unknown, invisible individuals who together make up the collectivity.[1] It is obvious, however, that this sense of the potential and actual failings of modern liberal society has philosophical roots as well as implications. Some theorists have sought, therefore, to trace the current malaise in modern liberal societies to their historical and philosophical foundations. One consequence of their inquiry has been a systematic critique of the differing or contrasting concepts of 'right' and 'good'; of the individual as the founding unit of society, or society as the founding matrix of individual differentiation; of a self which 'chooses' its commitments to values and ways of life, and a self which is given and formed, from the start, in such commitments.

The present essay sets out to accomplish two aims. It intends to evaluate the critique, just mentioned, of the conception of self which forms the background, and pervades the assumptions, of modern, liberal democratic societies. Secondly, affirming the importance of this and associated conceptions to the evolution of a liberal, civic order in the Muslim context (where such an order is precisely what is desired by many), it will sketch their relation to pertinent conceptions of Islam. It will be immediately obvious that this design takes a number of notions or propositions for granted. It is well at the outset to make them explicit, and perhaps, within the limited space afforded by this piece, also to explicate, if not justify them.

First, my argument assumes the intimate relevance of a cluster of fundamental conceptions – such as how one conceives of reality (and what one perceives to be 'really real'), of truth, and how one arrives at it, of the hierarchy of values deriving from these ideas, which are expected to guide one's life, and of the nature of one's identity or selfhood – to the more specifically political philosophy of liberalism. Now, many liberals dispute just this thesis of the relevance of these conceptions to the political doctrine of liberalism, a thesis which lies at the heart of the work to which I intend to refer so as to examine its argument. But, in analogy with the witticism of the Viennese satirist, Karl Kraus, about psychoanalysis, namely that it was the very disease to which it offered itself as a cure, we might say that liberalism's denial of the relevance of these conceptions is diagnostic of the very trait which accounts for its poverty as a philosophy of life. In other words, to deny this relation is to beg the question. In fact, it is not unduly hard to show (though not here) that the answers we give to the implicit question of who we are as persons, and what the world is like, have significance for what we take ourselves to be as citizens, and for our relations with one another in the public realm of modern life. This connection is denied, neglected, or else required (by what is sometimes called 'minimalist liberalism') to be bracketed out in one's public deliberations and activities. It has been asked whether such a suspension or bracketing is possible given the fundamental, identity-shaping traditions in many cultures and communities.[2] As it happens, I believe that a relative disengagement of oneself from an all-consuming commitment to such traditions is necessary in the pluralist, civic arena of modern societies. For otherwise the outcome is either unmitigated conflict or mutual incomprehension, amounting in either case to an absence of the pre-requisites of civil society. But no further argument is required to show that to say this much is already to assert the importance of a self-organisation appropriate to this necessary or desired state of affairs in public life. Similarly, to deny the relevance of philosophical ethics to the institutional order of modern liberal societies, on the grounds that this order must maintain, as one of its central principles, a position of neutrality towards the values of different groups and individuals within it, can easily be shown to be self-contradictory. That 'neutrality' is cherished as a value suffices to show that it is not the product of a 'value-neutral' attitude.

To these considerations we might add another which has importance in the present connection, namely that significant strands of opinion within many a non-Western (including Muslim) society treat the moral, religious and cultural principles derived from their historical traditions as fundamental enough to be retained integrally in the evolution of modernity in their respective contexts. At least *prima facie*, therefore, but in fact substantively, one can hardly ignore the relevance of these wider issues to the terms in which we define the structural and procedural aspects of liberal society. In effect, what these wider considerations dictate is an openness to definitions and varieties of liberalism other than the one which appears to have gained dominance in modern Western societies. To rule out such alternatives *a priori*, either expressly or by implication, would be illiberal to the utmost degree. It would be a form of fundamentalism which, despite its claim in modern secular contexts as the very antithesis of religious fundamentalism, is in fact, by this logic, no more than its mirror-image.

I assume the importance of these ideas, then, as a given. Indeed, I join to them at least one other issue which is not always linked in analyses in this particular context, namely the development of critical reason. Its importance lies not only in its relation to 'religion' (it should be apparent later why I am tempted to place this term in quotation marks here), but also in the way it comes to be undermined, as I believe, by ideologies appealing to desires and interests, whether of individuals or communities, in modern liberal society. Concepts of self and rationality are obviously interrelated; and their importance spans a wide domain of culture, ranging from psychology, through education, to public discourse and politics.

At the risk of stating the obvious, I might add a couple of caveats here to avoid misunderstanding the purport of this argument. First, being a philosophical essay, it is inevitably, in a legitimate sense of the term, speculative. I present no empirical reports, nor attribute any causal significance to conceptions of Islam, for instance, in the origin or success of civil society. At most, I view the relation between ideas and realities rather as elective affinities in the footsteps of Max Weber. Secondly, it might have been noticed that I tend here to use the concepts of civil and liberal societies more or less interchangeably. I am aware that they are not synonymous (as Marxists, for one, would maintain). However, in strictly the one aspect relevant here, namely the principle of tolerance and relative neutrality demanded in the public sphere by the pluralist composition of most modern societies, the two conceptions share an affinity which is by no means superficial or accidental. In any case, the debate to which I refer has arisen with reference to modern liberalism. Its bearing on civil society should be obvious without needing to be laboured.[3]

Taking the modern critique of liberal selfhood as a point of departure, the course of my argument may be stated in a nutshell as follows. The poverty of the liberal vision of human personality highlights the contrasting richness of selfhood as originating in communally given, historical traditions. However, democratic pluralism requires a multi-layered rather than uniformly constituted self. It implies too a traffic, *within* the self, corresponding to the traffic between the communal and civic arenas in society, between the culturally given and the critical or disengaged layers of personality. (It is my contention that the latter corresponds to the open 'space' in a democratic liberal society).[4] It corresponds, in turn, to the faculty of critical reason (celebrated in such father-figures of modern liberal thought as Immanuel Kant). It follows, furthermore, that commitment to a historical tradition such as Islam (which is, incidentally, a complex of traditions rather than a single one) can usefully be envisaged as multilayered rather than singular. However, to discuss problems of the liberal vision of society in the modern Western context and problems relating to this idea in Muslim societies in the same breath may well seem anomalous at best, and at worst, capricious. I do not believe that it is capricious to do so, though I admit that the comparison can indeed be anomalous if it is conceived in the wrong terms. A word of clarification is obviously needed, and it is to this that we turn.

II

Whether or not it is meaningful to talk about 'civil society' in the context of Islamic or Muslim societies is a question which has been pre-empted by the proliferation of literature, including the book to which this piece is a contribution on the subject. Such a topic carries underlying assumptions, and it is worth identifying these. It assumes that civil society is one phenomenon, and Muslim societies, another; and that these two may be matched against each other to ascertain whether they correspond or not. Straightaway, we ought to note an asymmetry in this desired comparison. 'Civil society', designated as such, is a generic concept signalling a set of philosophical, political and social characteristics. 'Muslim societies' is by contrast at the very least a geographical, and at most a religio-cultural concept. In fact, the religious denotation is already implied in the geographical one. For the very fact that such a territorial unit is demarcated for this purpose suggests that there is something distinct about it in relation to the rest of the world, and something common within it. This can only be Islam, and though there is an important difference between the terms 'Islamic societies' and 'Muslim societies' (the former naming groups expressing an essence called 'Islam', the latter describing groups

of people professing the faith of Islam), in discussions of civil society this distinction seems to vanish. The inference that is left is
that 'Islam' has implications for the prospects of existence, en-
richment, or a distinctive rendering – or otherwise – of constituents
of civil society. Of course, this implication can be avoided altogether by formulations such as the 'Middle East', under which
rubric the question of Islam would still need to be addressed,
though with greater freedom with which to emphasise either its
relevance or else the 'essentialism' incurred in the assumption of
its relevance. Here too, however, the issue is pre-empted by the
existence of a body of discourse, which shows no signs of abating,
of the significance of the idea of civil society to contemporary
versions as well as the historical legacy of Islam. As we shall have
occasion to note, there is a real sense in which the historical legacy
of Islam has meaning and value for the contemporary concerns
of Muslim societies.

To the anomaly resulting from the juxtaposition of socio-political and religious concepts, we must add another problem, which
is highlighted by a historical consideration. We should note that
Islam has one class of meanings when we refer to the complex of
theological, legal, psychological and cultural ideas and practices
prior to the advent of the modern state, economy and society;
and another, significantly different configuration following this
event. The tendency to conflate these – the tendency, in short,
towards ahistoricity in the treatment of Islam – is responsible for
untold distortion. It breeds chimeras, fictional entities which mask
historical realities. It is this which leads to sweeping, negative pro-
nouncements about the alleged incompatibility of Islam with
modernity. And it is this too which leads to the equation of
historical Islam with the values characteristic of liberal modern
society in Muslim modernist, apologetic interpretations.

The juxtaposition of two separate entities, 'Islam' on one hand
and 'modernity' on the other, is often based on a definition of
the former as a 'religion', and the latter as necessarily 'secular'.
What is important to note here is not only the specific
circumstances in the early modern history of the West which led
to the emergence of the modern state – namely, persecution and

inter-denominational warfare, from which the state was looked up to as a refuge, indeed as a source of secular salvation (witness such diverse thinkers as Locke and Spinoza). It is also the fact that the contradistinction of religion from politics – of the State from the Church – led to a *thematisation* of religion. 'Religion' came to be 'constructed' (to use contemporary jargon) as a category, a phenomenon unto itself. The consequences of this thematisation are to be seen everywhere in the modern landscape – in our habits of thought, where religion is distinguished from science, and in contrast to the latter, said to be concerned with such things as the 'meaning of life'; or more narrowly, in academic life, where theories (and encyclopaedias) of religion abound, and, of course, where there are flourishing 'departments of Religion'.[5]

The point of this discussion is not, of course, to claim that since Islam is a 'way of life' (as it is often said) it must rule the state. For this assertion conflates the way an earlier tradition commanded the organisation of life with the nation-state as we know it today. It is neither, as a first step, to endorse, nor to reject, a secular polity in the name of 'Islam'. For, this very distinction (reflected alike in the endorsement and rejection of institutional secularisation) is peculiarly modern. Rather, the point is to do no more, and no less, than to emphasise historicity. Concern in the Muslim world with these concepts, and with issues such as political democracy, economic freedom and human rights, is a product of modern history. Hence it is a product of comparable developments to those in the West, namely, the institutional and legal accompaniments of the modern nation-state; the practice of industrial capitalism; the type of social stratification associated with these developments; the type of personality make-up which goes with them; and the form of rationality peculiar to science on one hand, and technology on the other. Of course, there are significant historical variations. But the essential point to note is that positions taken in the Muslim world on these matters are new, modern responses – no matter how much they masquerade as old ones or as deductions from old verities.

Nevertheless, there is something specific, though not distinctive, about the positions which many Muslim authors, speaking as Muslims, adopt in relation to these issues. This is the all-too un-derstandable desire to harness the historical traditions of these societies to their contemporary concerns. Intellectual honesty requires the authors of this process to recognise that it is indeed an appropriation of the past into the present, rather than a deri-vation of the present from the past. On the other side, intellectual empathy as well as the imperatives of global understanding re-quire that others in the world appreciate the legitimacy of this exercise. In fact, at their intellectual and moral best, critiques of Western conceptions of liberalism in other parts of the world con-tain similar impulses and perceptions to critiques within the West itself. That is why these critiques must be addressed within a com-mon (rather than a departmental, 'quarantine-minded') frame of analysis.

Does all this imply that the Islamic tradition can provide no resources for a contemporary discourse on civil society? Why, we must ask, can it not do so, if philosophers in the West have ap-pealed, each in his or her own way to ancient traditions – as Hannah Arendt appealed to the Ancient Greek experience,[6] Alasdair MacIntyre to Aristotelian and Thomist conceptions,[7] and Charles Taylor, more diffusely and softly, to Judaeo-Christian the-ism[8] – to inform their critiques of modern liberal society, critiques which are interesting and substantial in their own right? How-ever, an equivalent examination of the virtues and contradictions of modern liberal society involving the resources and vocabulary of the Islamic tradition has not yet appeared. This is for reasons that cannot be explored here, though one consideration must be stated. Such a critique, if it is to emerge, cannot come out of scrip-tural reinterpretation of the type that reformist (*islahi*) authors proposed in the 'liberal age' of Islamic history.[9] No major trans-formations in human societies are ever forged by textual deduction. Scriptural reinterpretation is the product, or at most, an accompaniment, of processes of socio-cultural change. It is like the proverbial owl of Minerva, which takes to its wings only at twilight. Those who try to derive the worldview of modernity from canonical texts of the past carry out a forced exercise which is bound to mask and leave untouched, the real forces of society. This is in no way to under-estimate the enormous moral, symbolic and psychological importance of scriptural ideas in the formation of attitudes, in societies in which the 'Book' holds a sacred, paradigmatic status.[10] But this inevitably occurs after, rather than before the event – the event, that is of historical transformation.

The purpose of stressing this is to make a wider point. If fundamental critiques of modernity, of intellectual rather than rhetorical substance, were to appear in the Muslim context, they will have assimilated the resources of the Islamic traditions into them, rather than attempting to assimilate intellectual modernity into the terms of Islamic traditions. The former is genuine creativity; the latter, a reassuring appearance of continuity which skims the surface of history. It follows that the former, more radical achievement would be 'Islamic' in the sense that it will have emerged from an Islamic cultural and intellectual milieu. It will not be 'Islamic' in the sense of embodying a peculiar, generic, timeless essence divorced from the human intellectual enterprise in general. This, then, is a reason why it is false to expect an idiosyncratically Islamic civil society. But it is also a reason why it is wrong to neglect or underestimate the *contextual* importance of Islam in the process.

What is true of the Muslim context is equally true of the religio-cultural and intellectual context of other societies, including those of the West, East, and South Asia. The tendency to see Islam as a special case, an exception, a curiosity, is one of the ruling mystifications of today. If one opts to talk especially of the fate of civil society in Muslim states, it is for reasons of historical particularity. But particularity is not idiosyncrasy.

It further follows, if all this is true, that there is a fundamental set of questions about civil society – about its potential for human fulfilment, and the price exacted in its realisation – which it is wrong to regard as being of unique concern to Western theorists, and irrelevant to those working in Muslim contexts. It is intellectually misguided, and self-limiting in principle, for the latter to exclude themselves from a role of equal engagement and participation in the general debate on the merits and demerits of liberal society in the West.

III

It was Michael Sandel, in the USA, who first made a systematic connection between our conceptions of the self and the dilemmas inherent in modern liberalism.[11] Sandel's argument may in part be summarised (drastically) as follows. The treatment of justice (which includes the concept of rights) as a first virtue implies a view of ourselves as creatures of certain kind, namely as 'independent from the interests and attachments we may have at any moment, never identified by our aims but always capable of standing back to survey and assess and possibly revise them'. Closely bound up with this notion of a disengaged self is a vision of the universe which deprives it of an inherent meaning, of the type familiar to ancient Greeks as well as medieval societies. For, where 'neither nature nor cosmos supplies a meaningful order to be grasped or apprehended, it falls to human subjects to constitute meaning on their own'.[12] The type of selfhood which results from this conception is tenable only at 'great cost to those loyalties and convictions whose moral force consists partly in the fact that living by them is inseparable from understanding ourselves as the particular persons we are'.[13] The supposed freedom that this visualisation of personal identity confers is at the cost of 'moral depth'.[14] The contrast between this type of personal identity and one born of constitutive attachments (i.e., attachments which are not 'chosen' but given, which have already made oneself who one is) is reflected *par excellence* in the contrast between the classical (notably Aristotelian) notion of friendship, and the implicit notion allowed for in modern liberal society. In the latter context, no matter how 'much I might hope for the good of a friend and stand ready to advance it, only the friend himself can know what that good is'.[15] Central to these contrasting types of personhood is the extent to which one is constituted, or not so constituted, by *historical* traditions – the depth of their presence in one's very identity. These obviously include moral or ethical traditions. The crucial fact is that moral traditions on this view are not merely adhered to but constitutive of oneself. By contrast, the 'unencumbered' self in the modern liberal ethos, which is a self '*individuated in advance*, and given *prior to experience*', implies, of necessity, that

'I must regard myself as the bearer of a self distinct from my values and ends'.[16] Although Sandel does not say so in as many words, it clearly follows from this characterisation of modern liberal society that this conception of choice of the good, of moral values, reflects the model of the market. Affiliation to religious, moral or historical traditions in this outlook comes to have a very strong resemblance to consumer loyalty. (I might add that a telling linguistic sign of the extending dominance of the market model in modern culture, including its intellectual life, is to be found in the peculiar attachment of the verb 'buy' to ideas, opinions and values in contemporary usage.)

I have let Sandel speak for himself in the above summary, because his words are eloquent. His diagnosis of modern self-interpretation is, I believe, entirely correct. But the manner in which the alternative of constitutive identities is conceived by him poses, in my view, a serious impediment to civil society.

In essence, this is because the very conception of the public arena in civil society requires a partial suspension or transcendence of parochial loyalties, so that its citizens may there interact as individuals, whatever their specific historical traditions and affiliations. This calls in turn for a degree of complexity in the very identity of individuals, a multilayered inner formation in which constitutive attachments will form one layer, while a universal individualism (if one may put it thus) will form another. But Sandel's description of 'thickly' constituted, as opposed to 'thin', unencumbered identities, allows no scope (conceptually) for this co-existence of levels within the self. It does not visualise the progression or passage from one's formative associations – republican, religious or otherwise – that is, from the town hall, church, mosque, synagogue or wherever, to the civil arena. More precisely, it does not clarify the nature of the interplay which may occur in that arena between *diverse* traditions; and, not having clarified this, he does not, consequently, give it a *conceptual* foundation. Of course, liberal society as it stands today fully allows this passage back and forth. But it does so at the expense of a fundamental alteration in our inner make-up, and in our moral identities, on which Sandel has correctly laid his finger.

In recent years, however, there has been a concession on the part of liberal society to 'thickly' constituted identities. This has been done through the acceptance of multiculturalism. But the effect of multiculturalism can be pernicious, as has recently, I believe, become increasingly clear. A recognition of different cultural traditions is one thing; encouraging them to confine themselves in their respective intellectual ghettos, another. In so far as the ideology of multiculturalism treats entire communities as units, it entrenches group thinking at the expense of individuality within groups. In favouring community, it gives sanction to communalism. It extols multiple identities, but only by visualising individual identities as subsumed within group identities – thus denying the possibility of multiple affiliations *within* an individual's make-up.

The argument for multiculturalism is given succour by the type of argument advanced by Sandel. This is not, of course, intended in his text. The flaw in his conception is one of omission, not commission. It is the absence in it of a philosophical conception of how one may proceed from particular to supraordinate points of view; of how one may be both a person and a citizen; of how one might possess a fixed character on one hand, and a certain kind of openness on the other.

This same flaw exists in the later philosophy of Wittgenstein, which is predicated on a diversity of forms of life, and of language-games. But diversity as an end in itself turns out to be pointless. Plurality does not by itself lead to pluralism. Wittgenstein did not use these terms, but the problem associated with them is the same problem which inheres in his idea of 'forms of life'. That problem is absence of historicity – the fact that through interaction, forms of life absorb aspects of each other, and so grow into new forms of life.

Diversity, pluralism, freedom, openness, etc., are all values which themselves arose out of historical traditions. For this reason, it is not sufficient for liberal society to expect that if communities were to nurture their respective parochial traditions, the 'liberal' ethic would emerge automatically from their co-presence, and from the mere availability of a potential public space for them to interact.

The liberal sentiment has to grow from *within* particular historical identities. It necessarily transcends these identities, but it need
not (and must not – for Sandel is right) require their surrender
or attenuation.

   Although I cannot argue this here, the idea of complementary
forms of belonging and transcendence is related to the interplay
of subjectivity and objectivity in intellectual or educational activity. The crisis in modern education is intimately related to the
crisis in civil society, a subject which deserves study in itself. The
scientific study of 'values' divorced from moral education, is a
form of pseudo-scientism which leaves the imperatives of ethical
education unfulfilled. At the same time, the mere celebration of
moral traditions, of communal values, implies an assumption of
ethical irrationalism. It comes close to averring that values are
there to be taken or left, to be chosen, picked, or passed by; and
that they are the object of 'taste' or feeling (and a feeling only
about them, rather than about anything broader or deeper). This
trend in moral philosophy is part of a broader trend in education, whereby literary or artistic judgement, for instance, is seen
to be based on nothing more than personal taste or choice, as
opposed to rational argumentation and judgement. This subjec-
tivism elevates the self (conceived as an agent of choices and
preferences) above all objectivism. It encourages a cognitive narcissism which is probably not unrelated to its psychological or
moral counterpart. Nor is this view fundamentally altered or coun-
teracted by the emphasis on group identities. For, the celebration
of group identity is a form of group narcissism. Education at its
best is a means for the liberation of the mind from ways of thinking based on 'pre-judice' (prejudgements), views held on the basis
of inclination, habit and inertia. It is a means for the critical transcendence of these on a basis which is itself a moral foundation,
where the educational process – the quest for intellectual objectivity and progress in rational judgement – has a moral significance.
The relation of this, in turn, to existential ethics, more broadly,
must be rationalised, so that the intellectual habit becomes integrated, or at least linked, with experience of historical givens and
of the passionate springs of human existence.

It will be seen that the dynamics of education, viewed in these terms, are homologous to the dynamics of interaction between communal and civic identities. Broadly conceived, scientific education enables a disciplining, a transcendence of subjectivity in the face of the compelling realities of empirical data and logical argument and deduction. It reflects a passage from one type of self-organisation to another: from (to use Freud's terminology) the 'pleasure principle' to the 'reality principle'. This dynamic is present too in the cultivation of judgement in the arts, whose stark differentiation from science is artificial, and wrongly suggestive of the difference between 'reason' and 'feeling'. On the other hand, it is true that what Max Weber famously called 'the disenchantment of the world' resulting from the march of modernity was to a very large extent due to the replacement of magical or mystical views of the universe by those of science. Precisely for this reason, the dichotomy between science and religion, or science and the arts (in culture) and reason and feeling (in the psyche) needs to be seen as a problematic to be explored, rather than as a fact of human nature. That the dichotomy between 'sacred' and 'profane' (scientific) approaches to the world is very deeply entrenched in modern culture can be seen from the fact that even sophisticated anthropological explorations such as that of Stanley Tambiah,[17] do not quite proceed beyond a sense of the antagonistic relation between these two supposedly primary divisions in human culture.

It is worth noting that what we now call 'religions' included, in their formative histories, a great deal of rational and pragmatic manipulation of the cultural and social worlds. And as for modern science, its most eloquent exponents have always attached to the enterprise a moral evaluation which is evocative of 'enchantment' rather than the opposite. One need only recall Karl Popper's remarks on what he called the 'revolt against reason' in order to appreciate this. The fact, incidentally, that these remarks were made not in any of Popper's many works on science but in his famous political treatise, *The Open Society and its Enemies*,[18] suggests the ultimate connection between the issues of rationalism and irrationalism with the topic of liberal society. But Popper, of

course, was committed to liberalism in too wholesale a way in what
was its heyday, after all, to have come to grips with its deeper contradictions. The intimate relationship between concepts like
'reason' and 'feeling' on one hand, and politics on the other, is
more explicitly tackled by the legal philosopher, Roberto Unger.[19]
Whatever position one may take on these issues, it is important to
see that the connection between the burning questions of our
time in matters of education and the socio-political sphere is too
real to be ignored. It is hardly to be doubted that where a civil
society exists, or comes into existence, the *kind* of discourse that
occurs in it cannot be a matter of indifference. One does not need
to agree with everything in Habermas, for instance, to appreciate
the importance of what he terms 'communicative rationality' in
the public sphere. And this cannot be sought after, as an end, by
bracketing away issues of education, science, religion and indeed
ontology, from considerations of political structure and procedure.

IV

The analysis of the self presented by Sandel is an excellent example of how a critical examination of modern liberalism has
everything to gain from extending the parameters of the subject
from structural and procedural issues to issues like (in this particular case) ontology. And this specific question is far from settled.
For every student of civil society who contents himself with laud-
ing its merits and exploring its preconditions, there is another
who, while committed to its virtues, is aware of qualities, summed
up in the word 'civility', which do not always exist wherever civil
society exists. It is well to remember that civil society is required
not only as a buffer against the state, but as a corrective to self-
interested, self-seeking inclinations of the individuals and groups
included in society at large. Edward Shils, for instance, while affirming the 'virtue' of civil society, makes much of the importance
of civility. He defines it as follows: 'Civility is an appreciation of or
attachment to the institutions which constitute civil society. It is
an attitude of attachment to the whole society, to all its strata and
sections. It is an attitude of concern for the good of the entire

society. Civility is simultaneously individualistic, parochial and "holistic" '. It is 'solicitous of the well-being of the whole, or the larger interest'. More fundamentally, civility is the 'conduct of a person whose individual self-consciousness has been partly superseded by his collective self-consciousness... '.[20] Civility in this conception implies courtesy and good manners not only towards relations, colleagues or friends, but also, and especially, towards individuals whom one does not know, whose opinions or ideology one might abhor, or individuals with whom, if they are known, one may not wish to associate personally.

It does not take us intellectually very far, however, to entertain these ethical notions only though exhortation, or by way of affirming their desirability as an end. It is useful to probe further, and ask, what kind of self-organisation is favourable to the realisation of the ethic just described? What Shils' formula contains is a triple polarity: parochial commitment, holistic commitment and individualism. Although this can be stated only as a hypothesis here, it is likely that the experience of strong, primordial bonds, in family and community, which lead to the development of character (a complex phenomenon including self-expression as well as self-sacrifice), may then, other things being equal, be extended to embrace more encompassing social bonds and commitments. It is *prima facie* likely that the character-formation fostered by the kind of responsibility and obligations, the kind of social conscience and self-transcendence that primordial units like family and community require, at best, has elective affinities with the collective relatedness required in citizenship. But this link is broken, and the transfer of attachment from the former to the latter realm is actively thwarted, if the traditions of the community encourage a closed rather than open, a singular rather than multiform, identity.

On the more encompassing scale, Sandel's appeal to friendship and face-to-face relations as a model for society in a modern state breaks down. Anonymous or perfunctory relations need to be brought under a regime of ethical conduct as much as intimate or personal relationships. In some respects, indeed, 'society' and the 'common good' may be considered tautologous. The one contains the idea of the other. The way the image of 'society' is constituted in each individual consciousness will naturally determine the concrete relationship between the individual and the society. We need to understand what type of culture and self-formation is most conducive to moral sensibilities which ensure an elasticity allowing for rich relationships with those to whom one is bound in primordial ties, *as well as* those with whom one is more cursorily or partially linked. A fresh recognition of universal human dignity, hackneyed though it may sound, would seem essential. But liberalism, which was born in a recognition of this ideal, has not always lived up to it, and there seems to be much truth in the assertion that this is not only due to the difficulty of rising up to it, but also due to its inherent weaknesses. The communitarian model offers an opposite type of society, but at the price of the evils of parochial communalism.

The historian, Isaac Deutscher, speaking of Spinoza, asserted that his ethics 'were no longer Jewish ethics but the ethics of man at large'. A writer on Spinoza has taken Deutscher to task for this assertion by questioning whether the ethics of 'man at large' are not a mirage: 'Must not any religion of ethics be the ethics of someone? Liberal ethics or Marxian ethics are not the ethics of man-in-general but the ethics of liberals and Marxists'.[21]

Yet there is a strong reality, at least in theory, and a strong moral promise in the kind of universalism that Kant asserted, and that Hegel, for all his differences from Kant, endorsed in his own way: 'It is a part of education, of thinking as the consciousness of the simple in the form of universality, that the ego comes to be apprehended as a universal person .... . A man counts in virtue of his manhood alone, not because he is a Jew, Catholic, Protestant, German, Italian, etc.'[22]

It is important to understand whether and in what way this ideal was flawed, or came to be distorted, so that it could co-exist with (according to some even serve) the ravages that Europe was soon to inflict on vast areas of the rest of the world.

The paradoxical career of this ideal of 'universal human dignity' which was subverted into European ethnocentrism, is paralleled by the subversion of the Enlightenment doctrine of reason by the doctrine of the will, which is the doctrine of power. In Central Europe it led, via Nietzsche and Heidegger, to a philo-sophical outlook consonant with fascism. In the Anglo-Saxon world too there is now a subversion of reason in favour of the supremacy of will – of assertions of power – whether in the name of rights or group interests, in arenas ranging from politics to education. There is, of course, a vast difference between fascism and liberal-ism. It was the liberal democracies that saved the world from fascism. But this difference, huge as it is, does not mean that on this side of the fence of history, all is well with the human spirit.

This essay set out to explore the bearing of some of the enig-mas and contradictions of modern liberalism on the traditions of Muslim societies as they seek the liberal democratic path. It is time now to address this issue, though in terms that will remain philosophical rather then empirical.

V

There is a considerable body of writing in Muslim nations that, in addressing the topic of modern society, singles out for disapproval a set of traits like 'materialism' that are perceived to have marred human relationships in the West. There is much in this writing which may be criticised: over-generalisation; a readiness to draw sweeping conclusions from anecdotal elements; a tendency to focus on negatives at the expense of positives; a temptation to excuse failures at home by identifying failures abroad; a rhetori-cal opposition of Islamic 'spirituality' to Western materialism, and so on. But to cite these defects is scarcely to do justice to the un-derlying spirit, the moral perturbation and the quest for some form of continuity with the past, for justice and morality, and for solidity in human relationships, across as well as within the gen-erations, which is palpable in the more sincere and sober of such speeches, sermons and writings. There is a general tendency in the West, among those who listen to voices from the Islamic world, to fail to distinguish between the more rhetorical and the more earnest and questing among these voices. It is important to listen to them with an 'inner ear', so to speak, because while the style of discourse may differ from that of the West, what is said often accords with critical voices within the West itself.[23]

If the 'Islamic' element in this discourse throws Western readers or listeners off-track, it is for a twofold reason. Operating with polarities such as that between the 'religious' and the 'secular', they find the injection of what they see, without further qualification, as a theological language in a discourse on social and political issues alien or disorienting. Comprehension is made harder by the prevalent polarity between 'Islam' and 'the West' (a historically false antithesis which both ideologues of 'Westernism' and some Muslims, especially in the West, have done much to encourage). It is striking, indeed, how subtle the 'alterisation' – the generation of the idea of 'Islam' as an Other to the West – can prove to be. It is often detectable in the language, when (for instance) key Arabic terms are retained in English or other European languages without being translated, thus distancing their meaning from their more familiar counterparts at home. One notices this, for instance, in the saying that Muslims pray to 'Allah', which takes the place of saying that they pray to God. 'God' is literally what 'Allah' means. But the retention of 'Allah' in English conjures up the image of an alien, racial, or ethnic deity, which the concept is decidedly not, possessing as it does a sovereign, monotheistic, universal meaning in the Qur'an.

Likewise, the addition of the term *jihad* in the vocabulary of the West in recent times, with the Arabic term retained or translated wrongly as 'holy war' (for the Arabic equivalent of 'holy' is used much less frequently than in Christian contexts, and even so, traditionally, largely in a mystical sense), omits from Western awareness its kinship with the idea of the 'just war', invoked time and again in recent history.[24]

The point of these remarks is not to reiterate mere denunciation of the West's attitude to Islam. For I believe that this is a sterile formula which does nothing either to improve relations (if it does not worsen them) or to advance intellectual analysis by so much as a jot. The point, rather, is that the 'alterisation' of Islam in fact produces a reciprocal discourse, in which Islam is proposed as a wholly distinctive, generic essence, with wholly generic and unique answers to the problems of modernity, such that these would disappear once an Islamic 'solution' is applied. Once the discursive scales are weighted in this way, the mind is inhibited from recognising global commonalities in the dilemmas of modernity.

This is an extreme discourse which the popular mind in emotive contexts finds easier to adopt and reproduce than the many more subtle analyses of authors writing on Islam today in various Muslim societies or in the West. Once again, however, it is the *reciprocity* of Western and Muslim discourses which is meant to be emphasised here. And it is not only reciprocity at the level of overt rhetoric – employed by politicians and popular media – but the dialectic at the conceptual level that needs to be noted.

Take, for instance, the 'secular' motif. The ideological secularism that the West inherited from the Enlightenment has been rejected within its own societies, notably in the United States, where religious (Christian) fundamentalism is especially aggressive. Conversely, in the Muslim world there has been a whole spectrum of attitudes rather than a single outlook. Many thinkers from the late nineteenth century onwards, through the course of the last, have made bold, eloquent and intellectually impressive arguments against the politicisation of religion (a tradition of argument which continues today – admirably, given the dangers). The insistence on Islam as a state ideology is only one of many positions about how the past is to be harnessed to the present evolution of Muslim societies. It is, moreover, by its very logic, a modern formulation.

It is not a formulation we will find in, say, al-Shafi'i, or al-Ghazali. Of course, the culture of the day, which was Islamic, was an all-encompassing way of life. But what had not emerged then is the idea of a 'religion' which might or might not be co-extensive with the 'secular' realm. Here too, however, there are many subtleties to be borne in mind. Many Muslim scholars, from the time of the Umayyad Caliphs (661–750 AD in the central lands), from Hasan al-Basri onwards, opposed the policies of these rulers by invoking the spirit of Islamic teachings. But this 'religious' opposition as it has sometimes been called was really a complex of many elements

in which *moral* concepts such as justice and freedom were dominant. The major theological disputes of the classical period, such
as the controversy over whether human actions arose from human free will or were predetermined by God, were preoccupying
not because of the scope for casuistic reasoning they afforded but
because of their immediate, practical consequences. (Thus, if
human actions were a product of human free will, man was responsible for his deeds. This implied that one could be held
accountable for them, and this would apply, *ipso facto*, to the ruler.)
Further, the opposition of many pious men to the way of life of
the Abbasid court, including its poetry, which they found scandal-
ous, and which some interpreted as a bid to imitate or surpass the
Qur'an, was an opposition of piety to impiety, not the religious to
the secular. In short, both secularisation in the modern Western
sense, and the notion that as Islam is a complete way of life it is
entitled to rule affairs of the state, are reflective of modern realities rather than classical discourse. The dichotomy between the
religious and the secular is of modern origin; but so too is the
argument that religion must therefore command affairs of society *in toto*.

What is important, in this context, is not only to distinguish
cultural and ethical issues from religious or theological ones; it is
also essential to see that Islam as the ideology of an ostensibly or
would-be Islamic state is different, because of the historical milieu from which it arises, from the Qur'anic revelation as well as
the complex of moral, cultural, intellectual and ritual realities
that formed the context in which the classical Muslim civilisation
flourished and evolved.

But there is a different, ordinary level at which the modern
categories such as the religious and the secular happen to contra-
dict realities. The rejection of 'secularism' is often a rejection of
the ideological or fundamentalist secularism of the West. Militant
liberals are apt to conclude, from this, that the Muslim mind is
steeped in religious faith, and alien to secular reason. Of course,
there is no such thing as an abstract 'Muslim mind'. In actual fact,
those Muslims who strenuously oppose the ideology of secularism will not reflect a 'religious' point of view in everything they

think or do. Not only is there a broad spectrum of religiosity in Muslim societies, as in all others, ranging from deep, other-worldly concerns to all-too-worldly outlooks; such differentiation also exists within individuals. The modern personality is a composite or multiple phenomenon; different levels or aspects of it come to the fore in different roles or contexts. An individual Muslim may be a libertine in his sexual life; a hard worker in the old 'puritan' sense in his economic occupation; gregariously involved in kinship ties; negligent of wider social links; punctilious in his religious performances, and so on.[25] A theoretically unlimited variation in the combination of different elements may safely be assumed from one individual to another. That is the 'natural' human condition. As against this, the self-conscious representation of an individual comes into play, especially where one feels called upon to assert oneself, or defend oneself, by demarcating oneself from the Other. Demarcation in these contexts causes individuality to be submerged in group identification. But this does not mean that the entire scope of individuality can ever be subsumed in the group, or that it can be subsumed for long. The group is quantitatively larger than the individual, but the individual is qualitatively more complex than the group taken in the abstract.

It is not surprising, then, to find in practice a vigorous rejection of 'secularism' by Muslim individuals whose temperaments and life-styles may be described as 'secular', in the ordinary sense of the term. This is not necessarily self-deception. It is in part a reflection of the fact that of the many senses of the word 'secular', a single absolutist sense is likely to come to the fore. In part, it is also a reflection of the fact that under certain conditions, group identification, which is always present within an individual's make-up, becomes heightened and achieves salience. Under what conditions this salience arises is a question yet to be studied by psychologists and others.

It is safe to say that the potential for liberal culture in Muslim societies is likely to be fostered by attention to local and individual realities, and hampered by concentration on self-conscious self-definitions. The latter amount to what is nowadays called 'Islamism'. Much of what passes as Islamic thought nowadays is in fact a propagation of the *idea* of Islam. The difference is deep and radical.

'Islam' as a *theme* – as an object of thought, as opposed to the forms of thought and practice whose object was human and social issues, specific to 'Islamic' history – produces a misleading impression of homogeneity. Once this is realised, one opens the way to the co-existence of multiple elements in social culture, and multiple levels of identity, which need not add up to a singular culture or identity. Thus, the conception of selfhood we have suggested above (as a partial corrective of Sandel's view) is analogous to what we might envisage in the Muslim context. Here, as there, the liberal self (or segment in culture) must be seen as an *emergent* self or segment. It emerges in a dialectical relation to given historical traditions.

Individual judgement and critical distance from such traditions is a built-in possibility in this scheme. But the traditions themselves are not 'constructed' or 'chosen' by an individual self – a 'thin' or 'empty' one, as the critique in question shows – given in advance. This must also extend to a critique of a multiculturalism which subverts this process by encouraging a dominance of the collective or 'group' aspect of the self over all others. In this connection, it is worthwhile to note that the faith and culture of Muslim groups living in the West today are apt to take on a complexion different at once from the historically given traditions of Islam and from a liberal Islamic ethos, if they submit themselves to being defined in terms of the discourse of multiculturalism. Will Muslim groups accept being defined (and hence coming to define themselves – for these are two sides of the same coin) in terms of 'ethnic' identities? If so, will Islam come to be viewed, in Western countries, and by Muslims living in the West, as an 'Eastern religion'? Would this not be a notion quite alien to Islamic history?

We might add, in this connection, that concepts such as 'Islamophobia' have the potential for at least as much harm as good. They may have arisen as a label for the automatic, 'knee-jerk' reactions to things Islamic (blurred into an all-embracing abstraction) in modern Western societies. But labels have a way of entrenching and defining the very identities to the limitations of which they may originally have been a reaction. Both attacks on Islam, and militant or defensive reactions to them are, as far as language and mind are concerned, two sides of the same coin. They do not point to the way forward, to the culture of transcendence sketched above.

VI

Where are the materials, the mainsprings of a future body of Islamic thought to be found? They are to be found at one and the same time in historical antecedents and in contemporary realities. Starting from the contemporary situation, Muslims will be motivated to look to history. Inevitably, what will catch their eye when they do so are ideas, symbols and events that strike chords in one way or another with present-day concerns. This is not 'scientific' history in the academic sense. It is, rather, a social appropriation of history. The science of history requires the stance of a spectator. The appropriation of history engages a participant. But, if the latter is not to generate illusion, a 'false consciousness', the scientific mind must be harnessed to the task of appropriation. One must first gauge, take full stock of, the anthropological distance that separates modernity from its forebears. One must simultaneously create an intellectual distance from the environment of modernity – a critical distance, as opposed to a mind that is captive to the dogmas of modernity, apt to treat them as eternal verities. One must carry out these tasks the better, thereby, to bridge the hiatus which separates the modern enterprise of living from the wisdom of the past.

   This, at any rate, is what lies behind the insistence, among many writers in the Muslim context who are on an earnest quest for an Islamic element, or even an Islamic foundation, to a modern, democratic, tolerant, intellectually enlightened order suitable for the conditions of today. What one might take them to mean, I believe, is that they find much in modern Western society that is incompatible with their moral intuitions. They also mean to say, indeed they do so expressly, that they will not be dictated to by the West as to what form the modernity in their societies must take. They insist, and hope, that they will find the way to a humane order, beyond the violent and atavistic invocations of Islam which some of their compatriots wish to impose – an order in whose cultural arteries their historical traditions will supply the lifeblood. To those in the West who are cynical about this sentiment, or have a reflex aversion to it, they are apt to say that people with no real knowledge of or empathy for these traditions, who in fact have little empathy perhaps for the great ancient traditions that went into the formation of their own societies, since jettisoned by a modernity on the march, which applauds change for the sake of change, and consigns ancestral ideas and outgoing generations to oblivion – that people in this category have no right to dismiss this sentiment.

There can be no logical or human objection to this aspiration and this argument. But, of course, its realisation is bound to hinge on whether a truly historical consciousness arises out of it, or whether it remains at the level of nostalgia; or whether, worse still, history comes to be invoked essentially to legitimise present-day bids for control over resources and people. The task of re-appropriating the Islamic past is complicated by several factors. First, the introduction of modernity in Muslim countries was a headlong affair in which there was no attempt to co-opt age-old traditions and ways of life. These were simply marginalised; else, the new order was juxtaposed with remnants of the old. Second, and equally importantly, modernity reached the Muslim world without the long history of development which marked its career in the West, during which critiques of its consequences for society went hand in hand with the growth of its institutions. These critiques were not only philosophical but literary or artistic, with a popular appeal – names like William Blake, Charles Dickens and John Ruskin (to confine oneself to England) come readily to mind.

But there was no comparable phenomenon in Muslim societies. In sum, neither was the traditional world culturally robust enough to withstand the tide, nor was the new order culturally mature.

It is not surprising, then, that the process of re-appropriating Islamic historical traditions into the new configuration proved all but impossible. To be sure, there were the reformists: men like Jamal al-Din al-Afghani and Muhammad Abduh, Syed Ahmed Khan and Muhammad Iqbal. But the efforts of these men, in the second half of the nineteenth and the first half of the twentieth centuries, suffer from the precipitate character of the process. Their work lacked the advantage of long intellectual incubation. It likewise lacked the benefits, essential to all but the rare, solitary thinker of genius, of an institutionalised community of scholars, committed to free inquiry and to mutual collaboration and criticism, in supportive and resourced institutions of learning. Thus, with hindsight, one can see many inadequacies in their work. Abduh's knowledge of traditional sources was the most substantial among them; but his knowledge of modern philosophy or science was not deep or critical enough for an intellectually solid dialectic to emerge from their mutual engagement. Ahmad Khan's admiration for reason and science was noble; but to treat Islamic teaching as synonymous with scientific rationalism, as he was apt to do, is to preach a doctrine so removed from the popular function of religion as to appeal only to the educated bourgeoisie of the day. Then again, why expect Ahmad Khan to have had the clairvoyance to know that positivism was not synonymous with science?

But all this is only natural, in that the product of any initial encounter between cultures is always raw. More to the point perhaps, is the rationalism, the intellectualism, of these efforts, which failed to incorporate what we now call an anthropological understanding of the function of religion in popular conscious-ness. But most problematic of all is the voluntarist – the assertionist – element, which looks to Islam as a source of political power, a basis for collective identity, capable of confronting the West, which, of course, had elicited this reaction through its economic, mili-tary, or colonial dominance. One finds this reliance on Islam as something to be *willed*, something empowering to the identity, in Afghani as well as Iqbal. It is a historically understandable turn. But it is indeed a 'turn', a fundamental shift, not just in external relations, nor in rhetoric, but in self-understanding.

The work of the modernists both fed into and was superseded

by conservative traditionalism on one hand, and radical 'fundamentalism' on the other. What we now have in many Islamist
movements (though not all, for the picture is as varied as many
outsiders think it is monolithic) is this appeal to the will rather
than to the analytic or ratiocinative mind. Islam becomes, in this
subtle, transformed re-interpretation, a fuel for the will to power.
It acquires the quality of totalism, whereby every item of daily life
and conduct becomes a sign of Muslim identity or its opposite.
Everything that goes into that identity must be observed. Everything that falls outside it must be shunned. This is a different
phenomenon from the principle of traditional Islamic law, the
sharia, which was conceived in the context of the discourse of
righteous conduct in the eyes of God. No doubt this strand is also
present in modern Islamic discourse (hence the need to understand it is 'over-determined', reflecting varying motivations and
diverse traditions). However, the instruments of the modern state
afford an opportunity for what one might call 'definitional
totalism' to turn into political totalitarianism. This alters the character of the Islamic heritage beyond recognition.

Yet, as mentioned earlier, there are strong moral intuitions at
work in the desire of Muslims to develop their own version of
modernity, and their own path to a liberal, tolerant society. In
this, historical traditions – what one may call 'antecedents' – have
a crucial role to play. The Qur'an, as a revelation of God to man,
contains ideas and symbols carrying a permanent surplus of meaning, from which it is always possible to derive inspiration in the
service of a humane and humanly fulfilling order. A similar reser-
voir of inspiration is to be found in the traditions of the Prophet.
Beyond these there is the actual history of Islam. The historicity
of these ideas is of first and foremost importance. What deserves
appreciation is the human struggle, the struggle for power or recognition by contending groups, the competition of ideas reflecting
the aspirations and changing fortunes of these groups, in the
course of which many points of view were rejected and fell by the
wayside, while others were elevated to the position of 'orthodoxy',
which is the doctrinal expression of power. This history must now
be subjected to an impartial examination to see the relativity of

the various notions and institutions which emerged in its course, enjoyed prominence, or were eclipsed, eventually triumphed, or eventually atrophied, all because of the contingent circumstances of history. Many of these 'memories', properly retrieved, are such as to enrich a modern ethic of liberalism, and to give it a topical, indigenous meaning. None, however, will provide an advance, ready-made model for contemporary progress in this direction.

Complexity was the hallmark of the great, historical civilisation of Islam. Take, for example, the work of the great Hellenistic philosophers – Farabi, Avicenna and Averroes – the last of whom, in particular, helped kindle the torch of philosophy in the Latin West. In this chapter in the history of ideas in Islam, we see (to adapt a term from T.S. Eliot) an 'objective correlative', in intellectual culture, to the phenomenon of complex identity, at the individual level, to which we referred above. For these men were, if not men of all seasons, men of many parts. In someone like Avicenna, an empirically tuned, scientific temper sits side by side with visionary mysticism; an engagement with Islamic symbols rides hand in hand with commitment to a more universal, philosophical rationalism. There are, in these examples, inspiring antecedents, symbols with which contemporary engagements may find reassuring affinities. No historical ideas can provide blueprints for today. But it is very much to be doubted whether a 'today' excised from a 'yesterday' can ever furnish a rich enough form of social selfhood.

That is why the only place to which we Muslims must return (since 'returning' is a powerful symbol in contemporary discourse) is to the here and now. Starting from the realities of the present, and simultaneously foraging into the past, a new vision might yet emerge, that tackles issues of ontology, ethics, rationality, cultural creation, economic development, social morality, and psychological fulfilment, away from the current state of the art in these areas. Islamic symbols and ideas might well play a prominent part in this process, not through self-conscious contrivance, but through contact and osmosis. This may sound a hopelessly abstract and utopian portrait. It is of course abstract. Its details, even the major ones, cannot be envisaged. And there is no guarantee that anything of this will happen.

But pragmatic indeterminacy is not a reason to curb free exploration of ideas. It will be a sad day, if it comes, when intellectual discourse ceases to be tolerated except in so far as it provides the wherewithal for practical policies. Besides, it is short-sighted to underestimate the power and practical consequences of ideas. Many ideas influence the world through long, circuitous and unpredictable detours: they have something like what Hegel called the 'cunning of reason'. Others have an immediate, massive impact. We have only to think of the term 'Islam', in the current state of the world, to appreciate this fact.

I have been acutely aware, while writing this essay, of two arguments from the liberal side that could be advanced as rejoinders to what has been said here. One is the assertion that liberalism has never been opposed to ontological or religious interpretations of the universe, or to substantive doctrines of self or society. Innumerable expressions of these have in fact been produced in the freedom made possible by liberal society. It is just that a democratic liberal society seeks to ensure a space where its institutions, and the state in particular, must be impartial and disengaged from all such doctrines and points of view. The second argument, which has been made by Michael Walzer,[26] is that it goes against the very grain of the idea of civil society to favour singular conceptions of society, be they the ideals of the democratic state or republicanism, or of democratic socialism, market capitalism, or nationalism. On this view, civil society will draw upon a plurality of such doctrines, but uphold none of them, not only because it must have a free hand, but because it must abjure any exhaustive view of the good life.

Up to a point, I agree with both these arguments. Certainly, the state cannot identify with any one doctrine or ideology without undermining the freedom of expression and equality of views which are essential to a civil society. Michael Walzer's thesis is more sophisticated. I see little to disagree with in his suspicion of policies promoting one or another of the ideologies he mentions. But it is reasonable to reflect whether a philosophy of civility should not do more than recommend a free play, on a *laissez-faire* basis, to a plurality of views of life. In other words, should not such a

philosophy engage in an examination of the conceptions of human relations in society which are inherent in these different
traditions, and relate differently to the values of civil society? Must
civil society not be open to be instructed by these traditions, and
instruct them in turn?

There is a case, at any rate, for reflecting as to whether the type
of problems I have sketched above, problems of relativism, the
ideological celebration of 'choice', and the crisis of reason in
education, may not have something to do with the intrinsic nature of the dominant liberalism of our day. I have taken the view,
and others (including the authors to whom I refer) have argued
elaborately, that this is indeed the case. Whether it is so or not,
can the philosophers of liberalism and civil society shrug their
shoulders and say that these issues are not of concern to them –
that they belong to other university departments?

The point is that by excluding these issues from their central
concern, ideologues of liberalism forego, or reject, the option of
fundamental self-examination. The obverse of this is that they set
their minds *a priori* against, or at least remain inhospitable to, the
possibility that elsewhere in the world (as in the Muslim world)
there may well be the makings, at least in theory, of a version of
liberalism endorsing its fundamental values, but otherwise substantially different from what has so far been assumed as its only
or most desirable form.[27]

In the Muslim context, there are authors who recognise that
the modern democratic, liberal order is a different enough
phenomenon in history from everything that went before it to
necessitate radical revision of established conceptions of Islam –
or a radical shift in worldview generally, if this order is to be embraced. This may well be true, but the question remains: is a
re-examination of traditional Muslim concepts to be carried out
with or without a simultaneous, equally rigorous critique of
modern conceptions of man and society? If it is an exercise
confined only to the Islamic tradition, does this not carry an inherent asymmetry, whereby the concepts of modern liberalism
are taken as a given, and the others evaluated by being matched
against them?

And this brings me to a final corollary. Are 'departments of Islamic Studies' to study, say, classical Islamic philosophy, with some background reference to Plato and Aristotle, but with indifference to men like Kant and others, whose influence via the culture of modernity is present in the very lands where Muslim philosophers in their own time grappled with open minds with the Hellenistic legacy? Can Muslim cultures be studied today in any but an integrally comparative context? Are not the traditions of higher education, and the principles of its departmentalisation, then, ripe for a fundamental review?

Notes

1. Edward Shils, 'Civility and Civil Society', in Edward C. Banfield, ed., *Civility and Citizenship in Liberal Democratic Societies* (New York, 1992), pp.1–16; and 'The Virtue of Civil Society' in *Government and Opposition*, 26 (1991), pp.3–33.

2. Michael J. Sandel, *Democracy's Discontent* (Cambridge, MA, 1996), pp.18–19.

3. I should add (following Sandel on this point, in ibid., pp.4–5), that I do not use the term 'liberal' here to designate a particular political party or persuasion – the culture under criticism here is the crucible in which conservative and 'liberal' political convictions are forged alike.

4. I have advisedly said 'culturally given' so as to leave room, logically, for the possibility of diverse acculturations through the source of an individual's life, as well as for the phenomenon of religious conversion. Religious conversion is rarely, if ever, a cultural conversion, however – not, at any rate, of a total sort.

5. For a critique of religion as an object of anthropological study, and its extrapolation to Islam, see Talal Asad, *The Idea of an Anthropology of Islam* (Washington, 1986).

6. Hannah Arendt, *The Human Condition* (Chicago, 1958).

7. Alasdair MacIntyre, *After Virtue* (Notre Dame, 1981).

8. Charles Taylor, *Sources of the Self* (Cambridge, UK, 1989).

9. Albert Hourani, *Arabic Thought in the Liberal Age 1798–1939* (Oxford, 1962).

10. For the concept of 'Societies of the Book', see Mohammed Arkoun, *Pour Une Critique de la raison islamique* (Paris, 1984), pp.162–75;

and 'The Notion of Revelation: from Ahl al-Kitab to the Societies of the Book', *Die Welt des Islams*, 28 (1988), pp.62–89.

11. In his *Liberalism and the Limits of Justice* (Cambridge, UK, 1982). I draw on this first work of Sandel's rather than the more recent work cited above because the argument about self and society with which we are concerned here has not undergone any revision in the latter work, whose contribution lies instead in the explication of his earlier philosophical argument through an examination of the history of American republicanism and its displacement by a contemporary liberalism asserting the primacy of individual choice. I must also acknowledge here Charles Taylor's magisterial historical survey, *Sources of the Self*, in which he traces in detail various European traditions in the history of ideas from which our present-day assumptions about the self are derived. If I have confined myself here to referring to Sandel, it is because of the direct accessibility of his work for our purposes here.

12. *Liberalism and the Limits of Justice*, p.175.

13. Ibid., p.179.

14. Ibid.

15. Ibid., p.181.

16. Ibid., p.183.

17. Stanley Tambiah, *Magic, Science, Religion and the Scope of Rationality* (Cambridge, UK, 1990).

18. Karl Popper, *The Open Society and its Enemies* (London, 1990), vol.2, ch.24.

19. Roberto Unger, *Passion: An Essay on Personality* (New York, 1984).

20. Shils, 'The Virtue of Civil Society', pp.11–12.

21. Steven B. Smith, *Spinoza, Liberalism and the Question of Jewish Identity* (New Haven, CT, 1997), p.22.

22. G.W.F. Hegel, *Philosophy of Right*, tr. T.M. Knox (Oxford, 1967), p.134.

23. As one example of writing in the Islamic world in this mode, see Mohammed Khatami, *Islam, Dialogue and Civil Society* (Canberra, 2000).

24. I owe this insight into the failure in Western media to connect their understanding of the jihad with the concept of the 'just war' invoked by the USA and its allies in contexts like the Gulf War, to a personal conversation with Professor Arkoun.

25. Such contradictions of character are vividly portrayed in the novels of Naguib Mahfouz, especially, *Bayn al-qasrayn* (Cairo, 1960), English tr. William M. Hutchins and Olive E. Kenny as *Palace Walk* (New York and London, 1990). It is a safe generalisation to say that where ideology

suppresses individuality in favour of abstraction, literature (and the novel form in particular) suppresses abstraction in favour of individuality.

26. Michael Walzer, ed., *Toward a Global Civil Society* (Providence, RI, and Oxford, 1995).

27. Of course, the prospects for liberalism (and civil society) in a form with historical resonance in the Muslim world are undermined, to start with, by the nature of many existing regimes there. However, in our philosophical analysis of the relevant concepts, this practical reality has had to be ignored. In any case, a substantial body of work by contemporary Muslim authors, on subjects like jurisprudence and sociology (which we cannot discuss here), contains the seeds of a potential theory of liberal-civil society reflecting the principles sketched here. I must hasten to add, however, that the principles presented here are no more than (in Weber's terms) 'ideal types'.

4

Debating Women: Gender and the Public Sphere in Post-Revolutionary Iran

Ziba Mir-Hosseini

Introduction

In the third decade of the Islamic Republic, Iran is going through a transition as significant as that which ushered in the 1979 Revolution. The radical discourse of the 1980s is yielding to a more pluralistic one that is painfully trying to reconcile Islam with democracy and human rights. The turning point in this transition was the 1997 presidential election, which brought the moderate government of Mohammad Khatami into office. It also gave birth to a reformist movement and a vocal press that are paving the way, against intense and sometimes violent opposition from part of the clerical establishment, for 'democracy Iranian style'. The massive victory of reformist candidates in the municipal and parliamentary elections of 1999 and 2000, and Khatami's re-election in June 2001 with over 77 per cent of the votes, speak not only of the strength of mass support for the movement, but of the degree to which people have learned to exercise their democratic rights.

One visible outcome of this movement is the emergence of a public sphere in which different notions of Islam, modernity and citizenship are openly debated. I use the term 'public sphere' in Habermas's sense, of 'a theatre in modern societies in which political participation is enacted through the medium of talk. It is the space in which citizens deliberate about their common affairs, hence an institutionalised arena of discursive interaction'. Conceptually distinct from the state, the public sphere is 'the site of the production and circulation of discourses that can in principle be critical of the state'.[1] For almost three years between August 1997, when Khatami took office, and June 2000, when the sixth Majles (parliament) opened, the press was the main site of such discourses in Iran. Assuming the role of absent political parties, the press (though not the media at large) also became the sole platform through which the reformists could promote their agenda and their visions for a democratic system of governance.[2] In this, the press injected notions such as transparency, accountability, the rule of law and respect for the civil rights of individuals into the opaque, factional and undemocratic political culture of the Islamic Republic. All this was done under the rubric of 'Civil Society' (*jame'eh madani*).[3]

In this chapter, I examine the ways in which women have used the emergent public sphere in the Islamic Republic to debate and negotiate their rights in law and society. I do this through a discussion of the 'women's press', which continues to serve as the main site of production of discourses on gender rights. I ask two questions: To what extent is the emergent public sphere not only informed and shaped by established patriarchal views of religion, culture, society and politics, but is also challenging and transforming these views? And what do the women's press and the positions taken by their key female protagonists tell us about the potential of political reforms in creating a democratic society within the context of an Islamic Republic?

It is imperative, in my view, to address these two questions, not only because of the unequal constructions of gender rights in Islamic law but also because of the patriarchal and male-centred political culture of Iran, where discussion of gender rights is largely confined to women's magazines. A democratic society should surely address core problems of power relations, such as gender inequality. Yet male Iranian intellectuals, both secular and religious (though not clerics), have so far resisted any serious engagement with gender issues.[4] But first, let me situate the civil society debate within the currents and eddies of reformist Iran.

The Civil Society Debate in the Iranian Political Context

The notion of 'civil society' entered the official discourse of the Islamic Republic during the 1997 presidential election, becoming a kind of euphemism for a democratic system of governance. The debate has its roots, however, in a critique of the state that emerged in the late 1980s, and by the early 1990s was being aired in religious and secular intellectual journals.[5] Civil Society or *jame'eh madani* stood in opposition to Islamic Society or *jame'eh eslami* as promoted by the segment of the state that adhered to a totalitarian mode of governance and a legalistic notion of Islam (*eslam-e feqahati*). The debate was actually much older, and has been part of twentieth-century political discourses and developments in Iran. It was present during both the 1906 Constitutional Revolution and the 1979 Islamic Revolution, though in different forms.[6] Indeed, the 'Islamic Republic' was but the latest child of this debate; its constitution, as Schirazi has shown, is a compromise document, combining theocratic and democratic principles and institutions.[7] On the one hand, the constitution recognises the people's right to choose who will govern them, establishing democratic and legislative institutions such as the Majles and the presidency, both elected by direct vote. On the other hand, it subordinates the people's will to the clerical establishment, through institutions such as the *velayat-e faqih* (Rule of the Supreme Jurist or Jurisconsult) and *Shura-ye Negahban* (The Guardian Council).[8]

As long as Ayatollah Khomeini was alive, the tension between those two notions of sovereignty was relatively dormant. His personal and political charisma helped to bridge the gap between *eslamiyat* and *jomhuriyat*, Islamism and Republicanism. In the late 1980s, however, the tension was beginning to surface and the contradictions inherent in the very concept of 'Islamic Republic' were felt even by those who, a decade earlier, had argued

vehemently for the vesting of all power in the clerical establishment as guardians of the sharia.[9] The end of the war with Iraq in
1988, and Khomeini's death in 1989, brought a shift in the power
structure. With Ali Khamene'i as the new *vali-ye faqih* (Supreme
Jurist) and Ali Akbar Hashemi Rafsanjani as president, the Islamic
Republic entered a phase often referred to as 'Reconstruction'. It
was marked by increased tension between the different visions of
Islam – and between the two ruling factions, the so-called 'Rightists' and 'Leftists'. The latter were dominant under Khomeini and
enjoyed his implicit sanction, but gradually lost their hold on government ministries and the Majles, and also their influence in
the judiciary. Among the Leftists was the current president,
Mohammad Khatami, who had been minister of Islamic Guidance
and Culture since 1982; he resigned in 1992 under pressure from
the Rightists, who saw his policies as allowing a form of 'cultural
invasion'.

Marginalised and experiencing the same treatment that they
had meted out to their political rivals a decade earlier (such as
the Liberation Movement which formed the majority in the first
revolutionary government of Mehdi Bazargan), the Leftists went
through a process of rethinking. It was during this period of political retreat that some of them broke away from an absolutist
ideology, and began to argue for democratic principles and the
rule of law. During the 1997 presidential elections, this faction
re-emerged, with Khatami as its candidate and Civil Society as its
slogan. The Rightists, who now enjoyed the support of the new
vali-ye faqih, thought their hold on power complete and saw the
time as ripe for realizing their *jame'eh-eslami*, a totalitarian utopia
shaped by the mandates of Islamic law and subject to the rule of
the clerical establishment. Their triumphalism blinded them to
the potency of the *jame'eh madani* slogan as signalling the ardent
desire of most Iranians for freedom and democracy.[10]

The Politics of the Women's Press and Reforms

The women's press, as the main forum for gender debates, has
been both player and pawn in these developments on the country's

fragile political landscape. In August 1998, Fa'ezeh Hashemi –
then a member of the Fifth Majles and still in the reformist camp
– launched *Zan* (Woman), the first-ever women's daily newspaper.[11] In April 1999, it was shut down on the orders of the
Revolutionary Court. Among the charges brought against *Zan* was
'insulting Islam': the culprit was a cartoon which showed a man
holding a couple at gun-point in their house. The husband ad-
vises the robber: 'Kill her not me, her *diyeh* (blood money) is
half.'[12]

In spring 2000, when I conducted my latest field-research in
Iran, there were ten publications that could be classed as 'serious' women's magazines.[13] All but three were aligned with the
reform movement, though belonging to assorted political groups
and tendencies and adhering to varying gender perspectives. Here
I discuss them in order of their emergence, locating them within
the broader context of the reform movement – but with two
caveats.

First, rather than focusing on their content as 'texts', I consider who produces them, and whose voice and what gender
perspective they represent. I shall do this through recounting my
debates with their editors, with some of whom I had already established a dialogue in the mid-1990s.[14] To understand gender
debates in Iran (or for that matter any other debate), it is not
sufficient to examine what is said: one must appreciate who the
debaters are, and 'read between the lines'. What is not articulated (silences, omissions) can be as significant as what is.

Second, I exclude from the discussion three publications which,
in my view, have made little contribution to the gender debates in
reformist Iran. All three are aligned with the anti-reformist camp
(now referred to as the 'Conservatives') and have retained the
early gender discourse of the Islamic Republic, which is highly
ideological and has little appeal in today's ideology-fatigued Iran.
They are: *Mahjubeh* (Veiled), published in English by the Organisation for Islamic Propagation and intended for foreign readers;
Sorush-e Banovan (Women's Messenger Angel), published by the
Islamic Republic of Iran Broadcasting (IRIB); and *Zan-e Ruz*
(Women of Today), published by the Kayhan Institute. Both the

latter are aimed at a readership within Iran. *Zan-e Ruz* is Iran's oldest women's magazine, and the only one to have survived the Revolution. In its pre-revolutionary incarnation, it combined fashion with serious advocacy of women's rights. Ayatollah Motahhari's seminal text, 'Women's Rights in Islam', which framed the official gender discourse of the Islamic Republic, first appeared as a series of articles in *Zan-e Ruz* in 1966 amidst a debate between Motahhari and a pro-reform judge. After the Revolution, *Zan-e Ruz* continued its advocacy role, and helped shape and criticise the Islamic Republic's nascent discourse and policies on gender. However, by the late 1980s, it started to lose its impetus and, as we shall see, defections from *Zan-e Ruz* gave birth to three new journals. *Zan-e Ruz* has never quite been an independent voice; today, it is also more marginal than ever to gender debates.

Payam-e Hajer: The Voice of Religious-Nationalist Opposition

Payam-e Hajer (Hagar's Message) started life in 1980 as the journal of the Islamic Women's Institute of Iran (*Mo'assaseh Eslami-ye Zanan-e Iran*) headed by Azam Taleqani, a political prisoner in Pahlavi Iran and daughter of the late Ayatollah Taleqani. Shortly after the Revolution, Azam Taleqani and her associates took over the pre-revolutionary, state-sponsored Women's Organisation of Iran (*Sazman-e Zanan-e Iran*) and, to 'Islamise' and 'purify' it, purged its personnel and destroyed part of its library. But the journal's budget was axed by the Provisional Government, and disagreements developed between Taleqani and some of her allies.[15]

A veteran politician, Azam Taleqani kept the journal going and became its licence-holder, which under Iranian law means bearing the burden of responsibility for its religio-political correctness. *Payam-e Hajer* has since gone through several formats and editorial boards. In spring 2000, it appeared as a weekly, and was among the best-selling reformist journals, found in all Tehran news-stalls. It is aligned with a tendency within the reformist movement that currently has no share in the state structure of the Islamic Republic. Known as National-Religious (*melli-mazhabi*), this tendency played an active role in the Revolution, and formed the Provisional Government headed by Mehdi Bazargan. After his resignation, which followed the occupation of the United States Embassy by radical forces and the subsequent hostage-crisis, the tendency was marginalised. Although some key figures were prosecuted, it continued its political activities in the Islamic Republic as the only tolerated opposition. In the 1997 presidential election, the tendency joined the reformist forces and supported Khatami, but it again became the target of persecution. In March 2001, the head of the Revolutionary Courts ordered the arrest of 42 distinguished members of the tendency. Among them was Mohammad Bastehnegar, Azam's brother-in-law. Their arrest was clearly intended to create divisions among the reformists and to discourage participation in the coming presidential election in June, but it backfired. Not only did it provoke strong protest from the Majles and leading reformists, but it also became another argument for civil society and the rule of law – and a further incentive for people to vote for reform. In a bizarre statement issued by the Revolutionary Court (and reported by the official news agency, IRNA), the National-Religious detainees were charged with 'trying to overthrow the Islamic Republic by legal means'. Some of those arrested were released, while the rest remained in detention. The Revolutionary Court's statement speaks volumes about the inability of the anti-reform forces – for whom the judiciary is the last bastion – to come to terms with the realities of civil society activism in reformist Iran.

Taleqani and her journal are the voice of the Islamic Republic's first generation of women activists, who soon became disillusioned by its policies. Some of them with more radical views were later barred from holding public office. These women avoid any association with the term 'feminism', and their gender activism is a mixture of conformity and subversion.[16] While awaiting their ideal vision of Islam to materialise, they question and challenge the conservative forces within the clerical establishment.

Taleqani was a member of the first Majles (1980–84), but in 1992 and 1996 the Guardian Council vetoed her candidacy. She nominated herself as candidate in the 1997 presidential election, and was once again rejected. She did not remain silent but demanded an explanation. In an open letter to the Council, she asked whether she was rejected because of her gender. The Council never replied, but the episode triggered a debate on a woman's right to be president: did the phrase *rejal siasi va mazhabi* in Article 115 of the constitution mean 'political and religious personalities' irrespective of gender, or were only men envisaged, as in the literal meaning of the Arabic term *rejal* (plural of *rajul*)? The Council did not allow her to run for the February 2000 Majles elections.

From the outset, Taleqani has been bold in her critique of the Islamic Republic's gender policies; yet in her journal, factional and ideological politics have always overshadowed discussion of gender and women's rights. As Parvin Ardalan notes, whenever censorship in the country relaxes, *Payam-e Hajer*'s coverage of women's rights diminishes.[17] I asked Taleqani why. She replied, 'I believe that in our country women's problems are secondary to political ones. What our people need is a correct analysis. Women are part of society, and when its problems are solved, women's issues will be solved'. I reminded her that she had said the same thing over twenty years before; when the Revolution succeeded, she took over the Women's Organisation – only for Iranian women to lose some of the legal rights they had enjoyed under the Pahlavi regime. Taleqani protested:

> This was not my position. I wanted certain [Islamic] foundations to be consolidated, and then to move according to them; that is to say, to have rational foundations, so that we can reason with them ... That is why it is so important to have a free press, without which, of course, reforms will still go ahead; as they started without a free press. But only in a society governed by a democratic logic can one examine all shortcomings and find solutions for them. In reality, this reformist movement will transform the society's culture.

This exchange took place on 18 April 2000, when the Conservatives were striking back in full force after the landslide victory of the Reformists in the Majles elections in February. The future of the reforms hung in a delicate balance; it was not the time to re-open old wounds. Taleqani had given me an appointment at

10 p.m. that day (the only free time she could manage) in her office, which also houses *Payam-e Hajer*. On arrival, I found everyone clustered around a small television set, watching the broadcast on the national channel of an edited film of a conference held a week earlier in Berlin to discuss reform prospects in Iran. Attended by key reformists, the conference was disrupted by a group from the Iranian extremist opposition abroad – one woman performed an erotic Persian dance, another appeared in a bikini and headscarf, and a man stripped to show his torture-marks. All this was filmed by – and cynics say, staged in collaboration with – the Conservative-dominated Iranian Television (IRIB), which by broadcasting a carefully-edited version was effectively discrediting the reformists for taking part in a meeting where 'immoral acts' occurred. This logic convinced no one, but became the pretext for the judiciary's prosecution of the reformist participants. On their return to Iran, they were all summoned by the Revolutionary Court and four of them, including two women, were jailed.

A week later, in the wake of a speech by the *Vali-ye Faqih* deploring that some newspapers were infiltrated by 'enemies of the revolution', fourteen reformist newspapers and magazines were closed down by the judiciary.[18] *Payam-e Hajer* was one of them. This was not the first time that Taleqani and her journal faced the wrath of the judiciary. In 1993, after ignoring a caution to stop publishing Ayatollah Montazeri's lectures, all its printed copies were confiscated, and it remained closed for two years, after which it reappeared as a quarterly.[19] It remains to be seen when and in what format it will re-emerge.

Neda: The Voice of Women of the Elite

Neda (The Call) is a quarterly published by the Women's Society of the Islamic Republic (*Jami'at-e Zanan-e Jomhuri-ye Islami*), headed by Zahra Mostafavi, Ayatollah Khomeini's daughter. It is edited by his granddaughter, Fereshteh A'rabi. The Society was formed in 1987, as A'rabi explained to me in an interview, 'because we felt the need for a political organisation in which women could be active, and act as a political party'. Two years later, she continued, the Society launched its own journal, because 'an organisation needs to make its objectives heard and to have an audience. We did not want women as our sole audience. We believed that we could be effective for women when we reform our society. We first need to correct the views of our men – our law- and policy-makers – about women's issues'.

Like other such groups, the Women's Society makes its presence felt mainly at election time, by issuing a list of candidates and declaring support for specific positions and policies. During the 1997 presidential election, the Society supported Khatami, whose brother, Mohammad Reza, is married to another granddaughter of Khomeini. Since then, the Society has been among the moderate groups in favour of reform. In February 2000, four women on its list entered the Sixth Majles, of whom two – Soheila Jelowdarzadeh and Fatemeh Rake'i – are members of its central committee. Rake'i, who is also a poet and university lecturer, has been among the most outspoken reformist members of the Sixth Majles.[20] Jelowdarzadeh, who had been in the previous Majles, now became the first woman to be elected to the Majles Speakers Committee. Both are also among the most active members of the Women's Commission of the Majles, pushing for legislation to address gender inequalities in current laws.

Neda is the voice of the women of the power elite, demanding a share for themselves in politics. Its readership is narrow, it is rarely found at news-stands, and many women do not know of its existence. '*Neda* lacks the attraction of other women's journals, and is a bit heavy for women; most of our subscribers are men, or research and governmental institutions', its editor boasts. The 29 issues that have appeared so far (it publishes irregularly) lack a coherent gender discourse and vision. The early issues are highly ideological, featuring Ayatollah Khomeini's life, his views on women, and interviews with his family; or his two sons, Ahmed and Mostafa. Though more recent issues address women's legal rights, featuring interviews with progressive-minded clerics, they remain timid in their critique of the gender inequalities in sharia law. The journal evidently addresses the male ruling elite, not women, and is unmoved by women's increasing discontent. Rather than linking it to official gender policies, *Neda* sees this discontent as a by-product of modernity, for which there can be no immediate solution. As A'rabi put it to me: 'the situation for our grandmothers, whose lives were totally ruled by tradition, was perhaps better than ours; their situation was more or less in harmony with their expectations; in some ways we are paving the way for our daughters.'

Zanan: The Voice of Islamic Dissent

Zanan (Women) is an independent monthly and the first journal in the Islamic Republic to challenge unequal gender rights. It is part of a modernist tendency that remained dormant during the years of war with Iraq (1980–88), then re-emerged after Ayatollah Khomeini's death, which, as already mentioned, was followed by an increase in tension between different visions of Islam. Supporters of this tendency, referred to as 'New Religious Thinking' (*now-andishi-ye dini*), show a refreshing, pragmatic vigour and willingness to engage with non-religious perspectives. They no longer reject an idea simply because it is Western, nor do they see Islam as a blueprint with an in-built and fixed programme for social action.

Debates stemming from their ideas, now aired in a variety of journals and periodicals, can be traced to developments in the Kayhan Institute, following the publication of Abdolkarim Soroush's controversial articles on the historicity and relativity of religious knowledge. Known as 'Contraction and Expansion of the Sharia', these articles appeared intermittently in *Kayhan Farhangi* (Cultural Kayhan) between 1988 and 1990. Separating religion from religious knowledge, Soroush argued that while the former was sacred and immutable, the latter was human and evolved over time as a result of forces external to religion itself. The heated debate that attended their publication led to the closure of *Kayhan-e Farhangi* in June 1990 – and the departure from Kayhan Institute of a group of Muslim intellectuals sympathetic to Soroush. Two key figures among them were Shahla Sherkat, who had been editor of *Zan-e Ruz* since 1982, and Mashallah

Shamsolvaezin. Both soon became editors of new journals: Shamsolvaezin of *Kiyan* (Foundation), launched in October 1991, and Sherkat of its sister paper, *Zanan*, launched in February 1992.[21]

These two journals became a magnet for those whose ideas and writings now form the backbone of the New Religious Thinking. One might observe that in the Iran of the 1990s, they played a role similar to that of the Hosseiniyeh Ershad in the 1970s: *Kiyan* was the main forum for influential Muslim intellectuals like Soroush, just as the Hosseiniyeh had been for Ali Shariati.[22] *Zanan* ensured that women and their demands remained part of the new discourse, and set a new frame of reference in which Islam could be reconciled with feminism. It made no apologies for drawing on Western feminist sources and collaborating with Iranian secular feminists – both novel and daring in the context of the Iran of the early 1990s. Two of its regular contributors were a secularist female lawyer, Mehrangiz Kar, and a male cleric, Seyyed Mohsen Sa'idzadeh, who in their articles took issue with very premises of the official Islamic discourse on women, laying bare their inherent gender bias.

During the 1997 presidential elections, *Zanan* had a role in mobilising women's support for Khatami by depicting him as the candidate in favour of gender equality, and his opponent, Nateq-Nuri, as the one against it.[23] In autumn 1999, *Zanan* started a new section entitled 'New Religious Thinking and the Question of Women', in which leading male reformists were drawn into a conversation. This proved revealing in many ways. It not only showed that none of these men had thought about gender equality or taken the issue seriously, but also betrayed their ambivalence over the matter, especially when it came to the family domain. They repeated old clichés, or talked in broad and general terms, or displayed their reluctance to include gender rights among the priorities of the reform movement. Some stated that once their democratic ideals were realised, issues such 'women's rights' would sort themselves out; others said that women themselves should fight their own battles, and it was time for women to become producers of theories, not mere consumers. The more forthright ones said that they did not believe in gender equality and saw it as a red-herring.[24]

Zanan is the only women's magazine that is commercially viable, and is also respected by most Iranian feminists living abroad. It has survived three court trials, but lost two of its most important contributors. Sa'idzadeh was detained in June 1998 after the publication of an article in the now-closed liberal daily *Jame'eh*, in which he compared religious traditionalists in Iran to the Taliban in Afghanistan. He was released five months later but defrocked and deemed 'forbidden-pen' – deprived, in other words, of his clerical status and the capacity to have his writings published. Kar was detained in April 2000 after her return from participation in the Berlin conference; she was released two months later, and tried in November along with other reformists. Her trial and that of Shahla Lahiji, a prominent women publisher and another Berlin participant, were closed, although the trials of the others were open. Kar and Lahiji were both sentenced to four years and six months of imprisonment for 'threatening national security' and 'propaganda against the Islamic Republic'. It is expected that the sentences will be curtailed on appeal; but to judge from her recent interviews, Kar's co-operation with *Zanan* has come to an end.[25]

Shahla Sherkat, another participant in the Berlin Conference, was also charged with 'denying the necessity of the rule of *hejab*'. In her trial (which was open) in November 2000, Sherkat questioned the wisdom of the compulsory imposition of *hejab*. While stressing that she believed in the Islamic rule of *hejab* and had observed it all her life, she questioned the religious value of the dress code imposed by the Islamic Republic, calling it the 'official uniform' rather than the 'true *hejab*' mandated by Islam. She was sentenced to a six-month suspended term of imprisonment and also fined. If not overturned on appeal, this could bring about the closure of *Zanan* since, under the controversial press law of 1999 (passed in the final days of the Fifth Majles), no one with a court conviction can be the 'licence-holder' of any kind of publication.

Where is *Zanan* now headed, almost a decade after its launch? A glance at the issues so far published suggests that it has gradually moved away from its preoccupation with progressive *ijtihad* as the primary means of improving women's legal and cultural lot. Its legal section is no longer the centrepiece, and has been replaced by articles about concepts of women's rights in Islamic and feminist discourses, round-table features and discussions with reformists. One reason is the loss of two of its key collaborators, Sa'idzadeh and Kar; another is that to remain commercially viable, *Zanan* must attract readers from among middle-class women, most of whom are repelled by religiously-framed arguments. There is also Sherkat's own growing disillusionment with the politics of gender in Islam. Her open embrace of feminism puts her in a difficult situation. She receives little support from male reformists, who are reluctant to take part in gender debates, and when they are drawn in have nothing of substance to say. Her colleagues in *Kiyan* have totally ignored gender issues in their journal, which has neither featured any articles on women's rights in Islam nor made any allusion to the politics of gender in the Islamic Republic. Elite women, like those in *Neda* and in government, keep their distance: feminism is still a taboo subject in Iranian politics, and they dare not risk their political legitimacy by association. Sherkat is more or less ignored by secular women, those whose voices and organisations were suppressed soon after the Revolution, and for whom it became a political act *not* to get involved in the gender debates of the Islamic Republic. At the same time, the threat of closure hangs over *Zanan* like the sword of Damocles; Sherkat cannot afford to be more outspoken in her critique of gender inequality in Islamic law, or of the official discourse.[26] Despite all this, she is determined to continue airing women's problems in *Zanan*, which, in her own words, 'is a like a child to me, but a child that is very bothersome'.

Payam-e Zan: The Voice of Clerical Orthodoxy

Launched in March 1992, *Payam-e Zan* (Woman's Message) is published in Qom, the heart of the Iranian clerical establishment. One of the publications of the Islamic Propaganda Office of Qom Seminaries (*howzeh*),[27] its entire editorial board is made up of male clerics. Its gender discourse, which seeks to counter that of *Zanan*, is a modified version of that developed by Ayatollah Motahhari in pre-revolutionary Iran, as part of the discourse of religious opposition to the Pahlavis.[28] It rejects gender equality as a Western concept with no place in Islam, and instead puts forward the notion of complementarity of gender rights and duties. It argues that the apparent disparity in rights and duties between men and women as mandated in Islamic laws, if properly understood, is the essence of divine justice. This is so because the sharia is in harmony with the law of nature, embodying God's design for men, women and society. While admitting the injustices that are done in the name of the sharia – the plight of divorced women was widely highlighted in the 1960s by the secular women's press, as it is now by their Islamic counterparts – Motahhari then blamed them on the non-Islamic state of society and men who had abandoned Islam. *Payam-e Zan* now blames them on incorrect interpretation and implementation of the sharia.

Rather than 'woman's message' as might be understood by its name, *Payam-e Zan* is the message of clerics in Qom, intent on finding an 'Islamic solution for the Woman Question'. It is also the message of the clerical faction that adheres to Khomeini's vision of an Islamic state, the *velayat-e faqih* where the sharia, as interpreted and administered by the ruling jurist aided by the Guardian Council, reigns supreme. This doctrine holds that the sharia should regulate every aspect of life, but must be able to deal with the challenges of the new world in a realistic way. The latter consideration has been at the root of the emergence of a new 'dynamic' school of Islamic jurisprudence in Qom (*feqh-e puya*), as opposed to the 'traditional' school (*feqh-e sonnati*).

So far there has been little manifestation of the new school in *Payam-e Zan*, though a gradual shift in the tone and content of journal's articles, if not its gender perspective, can be detected. Articles in the early years are defensive and apologetic in tone and uniform in the arguments put forward to justify the sharia position; articles in recent issues are more diverse in tone, and some are indeed critical of traditional views on the nature of women's rights. This shift has become more evident since 1997.

The editor, Seyyed Zia Mortazavi, is a student of Ayatollah Yusef Sane'i, who is well known for his progressive interpretations of family law, and has come out in defence of the reformists. *Payam-e Zan* has a wide readership in Qom, and among conservative religious families who do not allow *Zanan* into their homes.

Between 1995 and 1997 I held a series of discussions with the editorial board of *Payam-e Zan*, during which we debated women's rights in Islam. Elsewhere I have written a detailed account of these meetings, in which we often talked across each other. [29] My repeated efforts to bring a sociological dimension to the discussion were in vain, as the clerics would skilfully shift ground, invoking ethical rules. When I reminded them that many of these ethical rules have never been translated into legal rulings, they would answer, 'Then that is the fault of Muslims, not Islam'. We often found ourselves in a position where, although we agreed that a particular ruling was discriminatory, they could not retract their assertion that all sharia legal rulings were the essence of justice; they saw it their duty to defend these rulings and rationalise them on religious grounds. At the same time, I could not pursue my points, as I was concerned about being accused of a lack of belief and being too 'Western' in my orientation.

My exchanges with *Payam-e Zan* were clearly conservative in content. Not surprisingly, the journal managed to keep this flavour in the way it published the transcript, giving the reader the impression that it had prevailed in our arguments, and even managed to persuade me. They changed the order in which I raised the issues. The first session, in which I sought common ground with the clerics, and was testing how far I could go in exposing my own ideas, appears in *Payam-e Zan* as though it were the concluding session. The actual final session, though amicable, was confrontational and concluded without agreement. In addition, though they carefully preserved the wording of my questions and the responses, they omitted some of my questions while expanding their responses to beyond what was in fact recorded. Both the omissions and the additions highlight *Payam-e Zan*'s own perspective.

The significance of these discussions is that it is now feasible to conduct them in clerical circles in Qom and that clerics are willing to debate with women like me (educated in the West) to seek to understand the logic of feminist critiques of the sharia rulings and to ascertain for themselves whether they contain any useful proposals for resolving basic gender problems. This is indeed new and has little precedent in the scholarly tradition of the Qom seminaries.

Farzaneh: The Voice of Pragmatism and Opportunism

If *Payam-e Zan* was the response of men in Qom to *Zanan*'s line, that of women in the political establishment in Tehran was *Farzaneh* (The Wise), launched in autumn 1993. A quarterly with academic claims, offering articles in both Persian and English, *Farzaneh* announced itself as the first women's studies journal in Iran. As with *Zanan*, its birth was related to disagreements within *Zan-e Ruz* over how women's issues should be addressed.[30] In winter 1991, soon after Shahla Sherkat's departure, four articles appeared in *Zan-e Ruz*, under the banner 'Feminism from the beginning until now'. Disparaging the stance taken by Sherkat, these articles contend that 'feminism', as a movement and consciousness, is alien and irrelevant to Muslim societies, where Islam grants women their rights. They reject feminism as a concept rooted in the West, where Judaeo-Christian religious traditions imposed such disadvantages on women that they have little choice but to organise themselves.

The writer of these articles, Mahboubeh Ommi (Abbasqolizadeh), became editor of *Farzaneh*, where she adopts a rather different stance. In 'Why *Farzaneh*?', her editorial introduction to the new journal, she argues for establishing the field of Women's Studies in Iran though rejecting organised and independent feminism. 'The women's question is a universal one that stems from the characteristics of feminine nature', she writes, even if it manifests itself differently according to context. It is futile, therefore, to address women's disadvantages in the same way as those resulting from class, race or other stratifications. Instead, she argues that the 'Women's Question' must be brought into the academic domain where it can be analysed and understood, and where suitable strategies can be planned to redress it. The solutions found can then be filtered into society at large, as 'experts' give their informed advice to policy-makers. In short, she proposes a top-down approach, a prescriptive feminism from above.[31]

Farzaneh's director, Massoumeh Ebtekar, is a veteran in political matters. She was the spokesperson of the students who occupied the United States Embassy in 1980 and seized hostages. Ebtekar was initiated into women's politics during the 1985 Women's Conference in Nairobi (Kenya), where she was a member of the Iranian delegation. For the 1995 Beijing Conference, *Farzaneh* played an active role. Both Ebtekar and Ommi organised a number of workshops in Iran to familiarise women's NGOs with the workings of United Nations' conferences, and both also participated in the international meetings at which the Conference Document was shaped.

Appointed as Khatami's deputy in the Organisation for Environmental Protection, Ebtekar became the first woman in the government since the Revolution. But her entry into government brought a halt to *Farzaneh*'s publication. The editorial in Issue 9 of spring 1998 – which appeared after more than a year's silence – speaks of a difference of opinion between the two women. Entitled 'The Red Line and Our Positions', Ommi's editorial addresses Ebtekar and criticises the government for its passive response, especially that of its female members, to the anti-women measures taken by the conservatives. She cites Iran's decision not to affirm the United Nations' Convention on the Elimination of Discrimination Against Women (1979),[32] as well as two bills introduced by conservatives in the Fifth Majles in May 1998. The first of those bills required the adaptation of medical services to religious laws, meaning that doctors could treat only patients of the same sex; the second banned press 'exploitation of images of women' and outlawed 'the creation of conflicts between men and women by propagating women's rights outside the legal and Islamic framework'. The editorial ends with a promise to devote the next issue to critical evaluation of the legacy of the last two decades' developments in the area of women's rights.

This new issue (no. 10) finally appeared in spring 2001. Meanwhile, Ommi (who now uses her maiden name

Abbasqolizadeh) runs a publishing firm that brings out books by reformist writers. In April 2000, when I asked her about the fate of *Farzaneh*, and her own current stance on gender matters, she replied, 'I need to find a new direction; I am now in the stage of deliberation'. She admitted that *Farzaneh*'s attempt to promote feminism-from-above is no longer viable, but robustly defended its involvement in the organisation of women's NGOs. She asserted that she no longer believed in the effectiveness of piecemeal solutions, and doubted whether women's rights could be achieved in the framework of the official understanding of Islam. 'I now need to "pause" and "deliberate"', mused Abbasqolizadeh.[33]

Hoquq-e Zanan and *Jens-e Dovvom*: Emerging Religious and Secular Voices

In March 1998, the cacophony of voices and ideas debating about women was joined by two other journals that approached the issues from two different angles, and framing them in varied discourses. One was Ashraf Geramizadegan's *Hoquq-e Zanan* (Women's Rights), which argues for attaining justice and women's equality within the norms of the sharia, as well as Iranian mores and culture. Geramizadegan replaced Shahla Sherkat as editor of *Zan-e Ruz* in 1991 – but resigned her post in February 1997 'to keep the respect of her pen', as she put it to me on her last day at work. She had joined *Zan-e Ruz* in 1982 as a legal advisor, and initiated a dialogue with a number of progressive clerics and women parliamentarians, which she continues in her own journal.

In *Hoquq-e Zanan* she takes these dialogues to a different level. Not only the thrust but the tone of the questions that she now poses are radically different from those in *Zan-e Ruz*. For instance, the third issue of *Hoquq-e Zanan*, which appeared in July 1998, carried a conversation with Ayatollah Musavi Bojnurdi entitled 'Islam Does Not Permit Violence Against Women', in which the idea of *tamkin* (sexual submission) as defined by Muslim jurists is questioned. According to Bojnurdi, a husband cannot compel his wife to have sex, since it constitutes an act of violence that is condemned in Islam.[34] The editorial in the same issue carries

Geramizadegan's response to those who objected to her journal's advocacy for women and condemned its feminist tone and agenda. She writes, 'Our women have made themselves the ladder for the progress of members of the family and society, without being able to achieve their own individual, social and scientific goals. Women have fewer resources than men to empower themselves, and above of all, the law has paid little attention to their situation'.[35]

So far, twenty issues of the *Hoquq-e Zanan* have appeared, similar in format, and to some extent in content, to early issues of *Zanan*.[36] There are articles on women's legal rights in Islam, on women's movements in the world and on women's political participation, which are essentially a discussion of the development of feminism and its various expressions in the West and elsewhere. But unlike Sherkat, Geramizadegan does not call herself a feminist, and has avoided even mentioning the term in her editorials. I asked her why. Her response was:

> Our problem with this term is that it is associated with radical and extreme expressions of feminism; that is, it is not been understood as women's social movement for equal rights and justice. Feminism is seen as a negative force and its positive contributions have been ignored. We consider ourselves to be advocates of women's rights, and if they call this feminism, then I must say we are feminist, but not in the radical meaning that they say. When we see inequality we want to change it in line with our culture and tradition.

Noushin Ahmadi Khorasani, the editor of *Jens-e Dovvom* (The Second Sex), on the other hand, has no qualms about using the term and placing Iranian women's issues in the context of international feminism. In her late twenties, Ahmadi Khorasani, is a writer and publisher who belongs to a generation of women that have come of age in the Islamic Republic, and whose feminist consciousness has been shaped in opposition to its policies. On the occasion of International Women's Day in 1997, she edited a special issue of *Farhang-e Towse'eh* (The Culture of Development), and then two collections of articles, entitled *Negah-e Zan* (Woman's Perspective). She applied for a licence for a women's journal, which has still not been issued by the Ministry of Islamic Guidance.

Meanwhile, she brings out *Jens-e Dovvom* as a collection of articles. It is the first women's publication to openly adhere to a secular perspective. Its very existence is a measure of the greater tolerance and openness of the policies of the Ministry of Islamic Guidance under Khatami.

The first issue of *Jens-e Dovvom* appeared in March 1998, followed by eight others marked by a leftist penchant and the conspicuous absence of any discussion of religion. There are articles on working women and women's movements, translations of well-known feminist texts, and writings by and interviews with Iranian feminist scholars abroad, like Afsaneh Najmabadi and Nayereh Tohidi. Each volume has a section containing articles on a special theme, such as Women and Modernism, Women's Organisation, Civil Society, and Democracy and Women. The theme in combined issue 6/7, Spring 2000, was the imprisonment of Mehrangiz Kar and Shahla Lahiji, the two prominent women secular activists who attended the Berlin Conference. The texts of their conference presentations were published, together with other articles about them – including one by Ahmadi Khorasani, entitled 'The Demands of Three Generations of Women in Prison'. Concluding with the demands of women of her own generation, she writes:

> Now Iranian women want to know, what is the actual 'crime' of these two women? Is 'writing' and 'speaking' on women's issues a crime? If so, you can return to sixteenth-century England, and dig out that 'damned' decree about women's chatter, and make it a law and enforce it in the twenty-first century! The reason for their arrest is a question that is whispering in the hearts of us women but does not have the power to emerge, because we don't know how to ask it without being 'trapped' ourselves. The fear of 'being trapped' is a plague that threatens our society. If the conditions are such that Iranian women today do not ask why their peers have been arrested is not because they do not care, but because of the suppressed 'fear' that the Iranian nation has been accustomed to for centuries, and despite so many things that have happened in the past two or three years the 'fear' has not left our nest.[37]

Conclusion

To recall the key questions that I posed at the outset: what do these journals and the positions that they adopt tell us about the state of civil society and gender rights in reformist Iran?

First, Iran today is going through an arduous transition from theocracy to democracy, a process that will doubtless continue for some time to come. The debate on civil society is part of this transition – an umbrella concept, a euphemism – in which different notions of Islam, and different modes of governance are juxtaposed. At one end of the spectrum are those arguing for a pluralistic and tolerant Islam at ease with human rights and democratic values. At the other are those who defend an absolutist and legalistic Islam that tolerates no dissent and makes little concession to the people's will and contemporary realities. Paradoxically, the creation of an Islamic Republic in 1979 in Iran appears to be paving the way for the de-sacralisation of the sharia and the secularisation of society. As I have argued elsewhere, this has occurred mainly through the transformation of Shi'i jurisprudence from a scholarly discipline whose relevance was confined to the seminaries, into the ideology of a state backed by a modern state apparatus.[38] The close identification of the sharia with a 'modern' state and its practice in a 'modern' world – the backbone of the project of Islamisation – has opened the door to unprecedented interpretations of notions of family, gender, society and polity in Islamic law. This is so because, once the sharia became the law of the land in Iran, not only the state but also ordinary people – whether believing or practising Muslims or not – have had to redefine their relationship with the sharia. Such a redefinition is the consequence of the state's ideological construction of the sharia; its refusal to honour the *de facto*, if not *de jure*, independence of the sharia from the state apparatus. It would perhaps be one of history's sharpest ironies if the legacy of Khomeini's doctrine of *velayat-e faqih* – intended to provide the basis for an Islamic state – opens the way for a full separation between state and religion in Iran, an eventuality that scholars like Ernest Gellner have argued was unlikely to happen in the Muslim world.[39]

Second, with the exception of *Neda* and *Payam-e Zan*, which are linked to patriarchal and clerical structures of power and put forward 'politically' and 'Islamically' acceptable gender perspectives, the other five journals discussed are independent voices that are rooted in civil society. They indicate the existence not only of 'a theatre ... in which political participation is enacted through the medium of talk',⁴⁰ but also of a diversity of voices within the reformist movement. Though they take different gender positions, all these journals appear to agree on their aims and also on their premises as far as gender relations are concerned. They all want to change the present situation, they all agree on the principle of women's rights. They differ, however, in the details of what they consider these rights to be, and the means of achieving them.

Finally, the debate on gender rights has so far been largely confined to women's magazines. If this continues, it could both ghettoise and marginalise women's rights in reformist Iran. The inherent contradiction between gender rights as constructed in Islamic law and in a democratic society, is one of the sore points on which there has been virtual silence from male participants in the debate. This silence was eloquently challenged by Mehrangiz Kar in her address to Akbar Ganji, Iran's most outspoken pro-reform journalist, editor of the weekly *Rah-e Now* (The New Way) that is now closed, and presently serving a jail sentence for his writings.⁴¹ Kar opens her address with a revealing observation about the malaise in reformist discourses when it comes to the 'women's question'. She notes that the front page of each of the first fifteen issues of *Rah-e Now* features a close-up photograph of a male intellectual, whether Islamic or secular, embellished by an impressive quotation. The editor seems to be unaware that half the population are women; neither their voices nor their issues seem to be part of this New Way for which the editor and his colleagues are agitating.

For male clerics in Iran, women's demand for equal rights has become a problem for which they are seeking an answer within the Islamic framework, though they prefer to do the thinking for women. But this is not the case with male lay intellectuals, whether secular or religious. The fact of the matter is that gender equality is a notion to which men in reformist Iran still tend not to

subscribe. Whereas secular male intellectuals are trapped in leftist discourses that can only accept feminism as part of (and
subordinate to) wider socialist goals, male religious intellectuals
have so internalised the code of sexual segregation that they have
abandoned even thinking about the issue vis-à-vis their female
counterparts in *Zanan*. The reluctance of both secular and religious intellectuals to enter any meaningful debate on gender must
be seen in this context, and their silence must be taken for what is
implied. Farideh Farhi rightly observes that as democratic feminist theorists have repeatedly reminded us, the emergence of a
democratic public sphere has never been defined solely by the
struggle against absolutism and traditional authority but has always been based on the exclusion and containment of some
people.[42] What reformists must realise is that the creation of a
democratic society entails addressing core problems of power relations – among which is that of gender inequality.

Notes

I am grateful to Richard Tapper and Farideh Farhi for reading and com-
menting upon earlier drafts of this paper; I remain solely responsible
for any shortcomings.

1. Nancy Fraser, 'Rethinking the Public Sphere: A Contribution to
the Critique of Actually Existing Democracy', in her *Justice Interruptus:
Critical Reflections on the 'Postsocialist' Condition* (London and New York,
1997), p.70.

2. Only a week before the 2000 Majles elections, the reformist press
issued a list of thirty candidates – the quota for Tehran; twenty-eight of
them were elected in first round of voting.

3. On the role of press, see Gholam Khiabany and Annabelle Sreberny,
'The Iranian Press and the Continuing Struggle over Civil Society 1998–
2000', *Gazette: International Journal for Communication Studies*, 63 (2–30),
(2001), pp.203–23. For an analysis of the mediating role of the press in
an earlier phase, see Camron Michael Amin, 'Selling and Saving "Mother
Iran": Gender and the Iranian Press in the 1940s', *International Journal of
Middle Eastern Studies*, 33 (2001), pp.335–61.

4. See Farideh Farhi, 'Religious Intellectuals, the "Woman question"
and the Struggle for the Creation of a Democratic Public Sphere in Iran',
in Ahmad Ashraf ed., *Intellectual Discourse in Post-Revolutionary Iran*, special

Issue of *International Journal of Politics, Culture and Society* (Winter 2001), pp.315–39; Ziba Mir-Hosseini, 'Religious Modernists and the "Woman Question": Challenges and Complicities', in Eric Hooglund, ed., *Iran in Transition* (forthcoming).

5. For instance, in *Kiyan* (Foundation), *Goftegu* (Dialogue), and *Jame'eh Salem* (Healthy Society). While the first is religious in perspective, the other two are secular. For an account of participation in the debate by secular as well as religious intellectuals, see Morad Saghafi, 'Crossing the Deserts: Iranian Intellectuals After the Islamic Republic', *Critique: Journal for Critical Studies of the Middle East*, 18 (2001), pp.15–46; Hamidreza Jalaeipour, 'Religious Intellectuals and Political Action in the Reform Movement', paper presented at the conference on 'Intellectual Trends in 20th-Century Iran', Princeton University (21 October 2000); available at <www.seraj.org>.

6. See Farhad Kazemi, 'Civil Society and Iranian Politics', in Augustus Richard Norton, ed., *Civil Society in the Middle East* (Leiden, 1996), vol.2, pp.119–52.

7. See Asghar Schirazi, *The Constitution of Iran: Politics and the State in the Islamic Republic,* trans. John O'Kane (London, 1998).

8. Ibid., pp.61–151.

9. Ayatollah Hossein Ali Montazeri, who was instrumental in having the *velayat-e faqih* included in the final draft of the constitution, and was until 1989 the designated successor of Ayatollah Khomeini, provides a vivid account of this tension in his memoirs, available at <www.montazeri.com>.

10. Some of them mocked the slogan by twisting it to *jame'eh Mamali* – a play on the words *madani*, meaning 'civil', and Mamal, a pet form of Khatami's first name, Mohammad.

11. On her political career, see Ziba Mir-Hosseini, 'The Rise and Fall of Fa'ezeh Hashemi: Women in the Iranian Elections', *Middle East Report* (*MERIP*) 218, (2001), pp.8–11.

12. The idea being, of course, to satirise one of the gender inequalities in sharia penal norms under which the blood money due for a murdered woman is only half as much as that for a man.

13. The research on which this paper is based was conducted in Tehran in March and April 2000, and was aided by a grant from the British Institute for Persian Studies, to whom I am most grateful. I do not discuss the few glossy beauty magazines with no gender or political agenda, such as *Banu* (Lady).

14. See Ziba Mir-Hosseini, *Islam and Gender: The Religious Debate in Contemporary Iran* (Princeton, NJ, 1999).

15. For a revealing account by Azam Talaqani, see 'Fa'aliyat-ha-ye dah saleh-ye mo'assaseh-ye eslami-ye zanan-e Iran' (Ten Years' Activities of the Islamic Institute of Iranian Women), *Daftar-e Dovvom: Masa'el-e Zanan* (Second Volume: Women's Issues) (Tehran, 1991), pp.1–10.

16. There are interesting parallels between Azam Taleqani and Zaynab al-Ghazali, the Egyptian Islamic activist. While both women live a 'feminist' style of life and have managed to free themselves from the constraints imposed on women by Islamic ideology, they continue to advocate 'Muslim values' of womanhood in their discourse. For an insightful discussion, see Miriam Cooke, 'Zaynab al-Ghazali: Saint or Subversive?' *Die Welt des Islams*, 34, 1 (1994), pp.1–20.

17. Parvin Ardalan, 'Zanan nashriyat-e zanan-ra mo'arefi mikonad: in bar *Payam-e Hajar*' (*Zanan* Introduces Women's Journals: This Time *Payam-e Hajar*), *Zanan*, 53, Khordad 1378 (June 1999), pp.16–17.

18. For the list of those closed down on 23 April, as well as others after that date, see Khiabany and Sreberny, 'The Iranian Press', pp.219–20. On the *Vali-ye Faqih*'s role in the suppression of the media and the implications for future reform, see Adam Tarock, 'The Muzzling of the Liberal Press in Iran', *Third World Quarterly*, 22:4 (2001), pp.585–602.

19. Montazeri has been more or less under house arrest in Qom since 1997 and has become an important figurehead for some of the reformists.

20. Mrs Dabbagh, the Society's most high-profile woman, three times Majles deputy, was not elected this time. She was an activist before the Revolution, and also close to Ayatollah Khomeini. See Mir-Hosseini, *Islam and Gender*, pp.105–6.

21. Shamsolvaezin later became editor of four enormously popular reformist newspapers *Jame'eh*, *Tous*, *Neshat* and *Asr-e Azadegan* (all closed in succession during 1998–2000). When *Jame'eh* was closed down in June 1998, he was imprisoned and then released without trial. In April 2000, Shamsolvaezin was sentenced by the Press Court to thirty months in prison for his part, when editor of *Neshat*, in publishing two articles criticising capital punishment. He was freed in the summer of 2001.

22. See Hamid Dabashi, *Theology of Discontent* (New York, 1993), p.127; Ali Rahnema, *An Islamic Utopian: A Political Biography of Ali Shari'ati* (London and New York, 1998), pp.226–45.

23. *Zanan*, 34 (May 1997).

24. For an incisive analysis, see Farhi, 'Religious Intellectuals'.

25. Both during the Berlin Conference and thereafter, Kar has hinted at her unwillingness to continue working with religious women. For an English text of one of her interviews, see the on-line Iranian feminist magazine <www.badjens.com> (21 November 2000) 4th ed.

26. In February 2001, *Zanan*'s brother journal *Kiyan* was suspended on the orders of the Press Court, on the grounds of 'agitating public opinion'.

27. Which differs from another outfit with a similar name, 'Organisation for Islamic Propagation', that is government-sponsored.

28. See my *Islam and Gender*, pp.24–5; and Abdulaziz Sachedina, 'Woman, Half the Man? The Crisis of Male Epistemology in Islamic Jurisprudence', in Farhad Daftary, ed., *Intellectual Traditions in Islam* (London, 2000), pp.160–78.

29. *Islam and Gender*, part 2.

30. Afsaneh Najmabadi, 'Feminism in an Islamic Republic: Years of Hardship, Years of Growth', in Yvonne Yazbeck Haddad and John L. Esposito, ed., *Islam, Gender and Social Change* (Oxford, 1998), pp.59–84.

31. *Farzaneh*, 1 (Fall 1993), pp.4–5.

32 Despite having affirmed the International Covenant on Civil and Political Rights (1966), that legally commits states to the principle of non-discrimination on the basis of gender.

33. Conversation with the author in April, 2000.

34. *Hoquq-e Zanan*, 3 (Tir 1377), pp.5–10.

35. Ibid.

36. Financial problems mean that the journal has appeared irregularly, and after the March 2001 issue Geramizadegan said that she could no longer afford to keep the publication going.

37. *Jens-e Dovvom*, 6–7 (Spring 2000), p.36.

38. Mir-Hosseini, *Islam and Gender*, ch. 1.

39. Ernest Gellner, *Conditions of Liberty: Civil Society and its Rivals* (London and Toronto, 1994), p.15; and his 'The Importance of Being Modular', in John A. Hall, ed., *Civil Society: Theory, History, Comparison* (Cambridge, UK, 1995), p.39. A leading Muslim intellectual notes that Gellner's *a priori* judgement is contradicted by the fact that Iran's triumphant revolutionaries did not establish a Shi'i Caliphate or Imamate but a republic – 'for the first time in Iran's long history … with popular elections, a constituent assembly, a parliament (where real debates take place), a president …': Sadiq al-Azm, 'Is Islam Secularizable?', in Elisabeth Özdalga and Sune Persson, ed., *Civil Society, Democracy and the Muslim World* (Istanbul, 1997), pp.17–22, at p.19.

40. Fraser, 'Rethinking the Public Sphere', p.70.

41. *'Rowshan-fekri-ye dini va mas'aleh-ye zanan'* (Religious Intellectualism and the Woman Question), *Rah-e Now*, 1 (16), 17 (Mordad 1377), pp.32–3.

42. Farhi, 'Religious Intellectuals'.

5

Soviet Legacies and Western Aid Imperatives in the New Central Asia

Olivier Roy

The prevailing discourse on civil society within the Muslim world at large is certainly relevant to the unfolding context of Central Asia, and there is no reason to search for an analytical paradigm that is specific to this region (that is the six former Soviet Muslim republics of Azerbaijan, Kazakhstan, Kyrgyzstan, Tajikistan, Turkmenistan and Uzbekistan). There is, however, a distinctive feature of the Central Asian experience that complicates the debate on civil society, namely, the legacy of seventy-odd years of Soviet rule. How does one assess the implications of that legacy with regard to the contemporary social and economic fabric – from urban cultures to collective farms – in the emergent republics of Central Asia?

Three sets of conceptualisations of civil society have been variously invoked and applied with respect to Central Asia, each drawing upon wider global definitions as well as post-Soviet realities.[1] First, there is the notion of networks of free citizens – professional associations, unions, political parties, public interest groups – that create political space as a prerequisite for building democracy and the rule of law. This view is dominant among

humanitarian workers and international organisations active in
Central Asia, including their indigenous subsidiaries or NGOs that
are internationally-funded. In essence, democracy and the rule
of law (as well as their human rights adjuncts) are cast as universal concepts in which a society is constituted of free citizens who
are not bound by any corporate or collective links, and enter freely
into associations to work for the common good. A free market is
seen as a necessary condition for such an evolution.

The problem with this conceptual approach is that it is often
perceived by local people (rightly or wrongly) as an abstract and
idealised paradigm that stems from modern Western experiences,
which have resulted from historical processes that spanned centuries. It is felt that this Western-based model is now being offered
as a mandatory, ready-made blueprint for reforms to be implemented in 'oriental' societies within the span of a single
generation.

A second conceptualisation involves traditional networks of
solidarity, based on primordial communities of kinship and patronage, that allow the population to resist the encroachments of
a strong authoritarian state, or to compensate for the weakness or
corruption of the state. It should be observed on this score that
states may simultaneously be weak and authoritarian. The majority of so-called Third World societies tend to experience either a
weak or an authoritarian type of state, or both at the same time.[2]
Without questioning the theoretical validity of this conceptual approach, the primary challenge is to determine the extent to which
there is a 'traditional society' in Central Asia. Another issue is
that such a view is intrinsically pessimistic about state-building,
for the organs of state are seen as part of the problem rather than
the solution.

Yet a third approach postulates a 'religious civil society' (the
term used by the current Iranian President, Mohammed Khatami,
and by the influential Iranian philosopher Abdolkarim Soroush),
in which a community of believers undertake to live according to
the values and ethics of their faith (in this case Islam). They envisage building a polity that will ensure the preservation of their
authentic identity and legitimacy, while resisting Western

encroachments – even in the very definition of what ought to be a 'civil society'. The values and ethics in question are seen as the basis for developing political institutions that will bypass both dictatorship and democracy based on Western values. This is the view espoused by Islamist thinkers,[3] who often (as did Khatami) refer to the Puritans' paradigm. The latter, of course, established local communities based on the free gathering of individual believers who took the political decision to live according to the true tenets of their Christian faith, with no references to traditional and primordial solidarity ties (of family, class or origin). These, in turn, metamorphosed into religious civil societies and eventually into modern polities based on open ideological and political choices.[4]

The problem here is in distinguishing between traditional society and religious society. Is such a 'Muslim civil society' a return to traditional modes of living and governance, or, to the contrary, a reconstruction of the pristine community from the time of the Prophet (with its purity blurred by subsequent political distortions and borrowings from indigenous non-Islamic cultures)? Such communities are based on virtue and ethics rather than on permanent institutions or the rule of law. What happens when the charismatic momentum, the *état de grâce*, disappears? Religious communities – from Calvinist Geneva to Puritan Boston – have tended not to endure in history as political entities. Those that have survived relatively long have done so as sects or ghettoised communities (like the Amish in Pennsylvania), not as political models.[5]

The foregoing definitions differ mostly on how to assess the nature and resiliency of traditional society. In the first conceptualisation, based on Western ideas of political and economic freedom (free elections, free markets), 'civil society' has to be created from scratch in Central Asia. This is either because there is nothing of value today upon which to build (the entire Soviet legacy being cast as negative) – or because there is no such thing as a traditional society in Central Asia, owing to the onslaught of the Soviet system on previous social structures, and the ensuing absence of anything that can be described as a Soviet *society*. Conversely, the anthropological and Muslim approaches converge on one point: that there is a danger of artificially importing values and institutions from a Western model that might be both less universal and less democratic than it claims.

However, these two approaches differ on what they see as positive historical inheritances in Central Asia. The Islamists invoke not so much the society prior to sovietisation, but rather an idealistic model of the 'true Islamic society' where social, economic and political relations would be shaped by explicit values stemming from individual faith and religious-inspired personal behaviour, at the expense of traditional clanic, parentage and patronage networks. For the anthropologists, on the other hand, those traditional collective identities are the prime safeguard against the encroachments of the state. In this sense, the Islamists accept the 'Western' notion that civil society is based on individuals and not on corporate or primordial groups, even if they consider that individuals should enter into some sort of collective community – the *jama'at* of the believers. They also criticise traditional society from which they wish to extract only that which belongs exclusively to Muslim culture (*waqfs*, or religious endowments, independent schooling systems, charity and solidarity, and so on). But what exactly do we mean by 'traditional society' in post-Soviet Central Asia? Clarifying this issue is vital in undertaking a meaningful analysis of civil society in the region, no matter what definition(s) one chooses to privilege.

Traditional Society in Central Asia

Soviet recasting of patterns of power and networking

Among the numerous international development groups and agencies operating in the republics of Central Asia, a common view is that the task of building civil society has to be undertaken from scratch, because nothing exists that can meaningfully be identified as 'civic culture' after seven decades of sovietism. The very notion of a society as distinct from the domain of the state is felt to have been eroded and ultimately destroyed. After all, the Soviet Union constituted a totalitarian system in which the state was the alpha, beta and omega of all socio-political existence. Factors like collectivisation, the assault against traditional society in the 1920s and 1930s, and the political hegemony of the Communist Party eliminated any semblance of what one would consider the warp and woof of civic life.

Accordingly, the policies of the International Monetary Fund (IMF), the World Bank and the United Nations Development Programme (UNDP) have sought to advance prompt and maximal economic privatisation, in effect aiming to remove any vestiges of the *kolkhoz* (collective farms) system.[6] Yet a closer look at the existing society shows that there is, in fact, an immense social fabric left over from the Soviet era. It comprises networks of people based on traditional patterns of solidarity groups: extended families or *awlad*, clans, neighbourhood clusters or *mahalla*, and solidarity groupings or *qawm* of varied sociological basis. These networks function at three levels: (a) organising support among citizens (for instance through the *gap* or rotating association to gather and distribute interest-free loans), (b) protecting the individual against the encroachments of an authoritarian if not despotic state, and (c) positioning the individual within the state apparatus through patron-client networks. The *kolkhoz* system has acquired an anthropological reality that goes beyond socialist ideology, because it is the expression of the *recasting* of former solidarity groups into a 'socialist' system.[7] In this sense, one should speak of 'sovietism' to characterise the anthropological reality of social life in the former Soviet Union, outside the ideological curtain.

Evidently, civic life on the basis of social networks has not been destroyed by the Soviet system, even if some groups have been physically eliminated or went into exile (as with Turkmen or Uzbek clans that fought alongside the Basmachi insurgents in the early 1920s). Rather, solidarity groups have been reincarnated within the structures of the Soviet system either through the transformation of pre-existing groups (like Turkmen clans turned into brigades in collective farms) or the fabrication of new clusters following the creation *ex nihilo* of *kolkhoz*es in depopulated or redeemed lands (like the marshes of Southern Tajikistan) – but still functioning along the patterns of traditional solidarity groups. Indeed, the internal administrative structures of the *kolkhoz* have reshaped and strengthened many of these traditional identity groups. The brigade and the *uchatska* (housing estates) often duplicate the *qawm* and *mahalla* segmentation, imparting to them an almost administrative reality which, of course, has never been expressed in official terms. Traditional endogamy tended also to strengthen the identity of the group, together with the fact that in the Soviet system work was allocated on the basis of such groupings (as may occur with privatisation today). The structure of the Communist Party also often projected these anthropological segmentations into identity groups: local leaders would come from the dominant group, and regional factions tended to fight each other or to enter into alliances on the basis of recast traditional groups of solidarity. In these latter alliances, ties were built neither on ideological nor on political common bounds, but on patronage networks based on what was perceived as a common 'primordial' identity, whether clanic or geographic.

Hence, collective farms became the new tribes of Central Asia. Neighbourhoods or *mahalla* were also institutionalised by the Soviet system, through the establishment of local bodies under the authority of the city district.[8] Socialist ideology had little to do with this complex process: identities were incarnated in the framework of Soviet bureaucratic structures, which is a form of statisation. On the other hand, the networks diverted, undermined and used state power for their own ends – facilitating benefits for the group from inputs, privileges and perks that in an over-centralised system could be obtained only by positioning one's own group within the Soviet apparatus. Such a strategy presupposes political loyalty to the system (because the group benefits from it), amid contestation among groups playing the game through political feuds and alliances inside the Communist Party, and often calling for arbitration from Moscow.

Such political contestation was hardly more than a power game: after the Stalinist purges of 1937, it never had any ideological or intellectual dimension. It was played according to traditional rules, expressed in proper Soviet terminology (a faction would be dubbed 'nationalist' by its opponents, for example). To speak of Marxist or communist/socialist ideology in this context makes very little sense. What we had was 'sovietism', a peculiar combination of bureaucracy, clanism, patronage relationships, localism and centralisation. It did not consist in a sharing of power between the centre (Moscow) and the periphery, but rather in a divide between two different spheres of concerns – one relating to strategy, security, military and state ideology that was controlled by Moscow, and another relating to appointments of local cadres, distribution of power and economic perks that was controlled by indigenous leaders. The frontier between the two spheres was constantly shifting; but during the period of the *satraps*, that is the first secretaries of the republican communist parties who were in charge roughly between 1959 and 1983, a clear distinction between these spheres of power was visible. Local rulers gave full loyalty to Moscow, avoiding intervention in strategic matters (like the definition, territorial delimitations and status of the various autonomous regions, socialist republics, and so on) – yet achieved a great deal of internal autonomy, given that Moscow was unwilling and unable to intervene at the local level because it lacked the required informants, intermediaries and cadres. Moscow had to depend on local cadres who themselves played on traditional patterns of power, networking, brokerage, and even matrimonial strategies. It did not help Moscow's cause that the local branches of the Soviet secret police (the KGB) were divided after the Second World War between high-ranking officers, most of them Europeans with a high level of turnover and no knowledge of local languages, and grass-roots permanent local officers, who were personally engaged in traditional relationships with the local population and tended to keep troubles 'inside the family.'

In other words, the local society was able with the complicity of its leaders to largely resist deep Russification and state control, while also adopting sovietism and granting lip-service to the Russian big brother. Local elites were entirely loyal to Moscow, and at the same time resisted any direct Muscovite encroachment. Only in 1983 did divorce proceedings begin between Moscow and the local elites, when the new general secretary of the Soviet Communist Party, Yuri Andropov, blamed the 'Uzbek Mafia' for the corruption of the Soviet system. In equating southern culture with corruption, Andropov sparked a nationalist backlash among the very local elites upon whose loyalty the Soviet system had relied.

It is in the above sense that I assert that a traditional sovietised society – or a Soviet re-traditionalised society – existed. The issue for us is: what to do with it? How far can it be construed as the basis for a genuine civil society? Ignoring or discarding its existence implies overlooking or bypassing the real social actors, not only at the level of the state but, more significantly, at the grass-roots level. The beneficiaries of such an approach are what may be regarded as Western-fit, isolated actors with limited leverage and influence, inefficient and non-threatening to the real actors. And the consequence is to engender what I consider to be a 'window civil society'.

The growing gap between ruling elites and grass-roots networks

With the collapse of the Soviet Union and the independence in 1991 of the Central Asian republics, the old political power games continued apace, only without the erstwhile external arbitration. It was precisely this that led to the kinds of concentration of power in the hands of a single group – whether regional, ethno-linguistic or otherwise – that were to result in the civil war in Tajikistan. The complex relationship between organs of state and groups of solidarity did not stop evolving in this post-independence period. Presidential factions in the various republics were at first based largely on regional affiliations; they have since developed into patronage networks. Leaders such as Uzbekistan's Islam Karimov and Turkmenistan's Saparmurad Nyazov played on traditional cultural values, equating 'tradition' with 'national' for food, music (*maqam* being rehabilitated by President Nyazov while opera and ballet were forbidden), ethical values and so on. In 1993, President Karimov issued a decree on *mahalla*, giving them some powers of social control (e.g. the authority to issue wedding certificates); he went as far as to create a 'President's contest for the best daughter-in-law', which duly rewarded obedience to mothers-in-law. In this context, statisation and re-traditionalisation have been occurring hand-in-hand.

But post-independence political development has had the same effect in each of the republics: the delinking of ruling elites from their rural and traditional wellsprings. In order to feed the urban populations and to elicit foreign exchange by marketing industrial crops (such as cotton) on the world market, the ruling elites have imposed production quotas on the *kolkhoz*es and farmers. Privatisation has been undertaken in favour of well-connected local apparatchik*s* (bureaucrats), usually the chairman of a former *kolkhoz*. The status of these apparatchik-farmers has been ambiguous. They used the opacity of privatisation laws, or simply ignored these laws and, through their political connections, created large farms in which ex-*kolkhozians* were hired as waged labourers. At the same time, however, they managed to appear as the new *khans* or local notables acting as middlemen between the rural population and an increasingly authoritarian state. In any case, traditional patterns of networking, solidarity and clientism do provide a safety net amidst the growing pauperisation of society, and the failure of the state to meet the basic needs of the population. One instance is the informal *gap* system in which a group of people (often women) converge to put some money together to lend to their members, who undertake to reimburse the group without having to pay interest.

Without venturing into the finer details here, it should be evident that such a traditional civil society offers a shield not only against state coercion but also against the economic ravages stemming from the collapse of Soviet social security nets. What this type of society does *not* do is provide political actors. On the contrary, its success (limited as this may be) owes precisely to the readiness of the key actors to remain aloof from politics – or to play a conservative role that does not challenge the political status quo, regardless of who the ruling elites are. Moreover, such a civil society is based not on the expression of the will of individual free citizens, but on group-oriented networks of solidarity. These networks seldom give birth to political parties, since they do not have a blueprint or vision for what should be done at the level of the nation, state or society at large. The one exception in this respect, as we shall see, is the Islamist parties. This, in any event, is the 'real' society to which two alternative models of what I consider 'ideological' civil societies have been opposed, by very different sets of actors.

The Myth of 'Islamic' Civil Society

In modern parlance, the building of a civil society entails the replacement of primordial communities and traditional networks or patronage relationships by associations based on individual, direct affiliations through civic or ideological commitment.[9] To what extent can such new affiliations contribute to creating a political sphere that would be different from the traditional social fabric, without appearing merely as a foreign import? A traditionalist Muslim (or Islamist) critique assails the concept of civil society in these terms – and is readily dismissed by Western humanitarian workers on the grounds that the Islamist activists espousing the critique have achieved little in building civil society. More broadly, the Islamists' conception of individual rights and democracy has been deemed in Western quarters (whether state or NGOs) to be inadequate and damaging.[10] Yet the insistence on 'authenticity' strikes a chord among many believers, especially the youth. One does not even have to look as far as Afghanistan under the Taliban in this regard; witness the recent breakthrough of the Hizb al-Tahrir movement in Uzbekistan (and to a lesser degree in Tajikistan and Kyrgyzstan).[11]

The Islamist movements have striven to bypass traditional affiliations by appealing to the sense of common belonging among Muslims, invoking the religious umma or community that transcends social and ethnic barriers. In Iran, as already noted, the term 'religious civil society' has been invoked at the highest levels, as well as among intellectuals. In Central Asia, the anthropologist Nazif Shahrani looked at the endeavour to build 'communities of trust' around mosques at a local level.[12] The idea here is that by returning to the true tenets of Islam, it is possible to build local communities that will eventually furnish the model for the rest of the polity, where Islamic laws and ethics would be the front for social justice and regulation. This would, prospectively, undercut the rationale for an authoritarian state.

In 1992, in the town of Namangan in Central Asia's Ferghana Valley (which straddles Uzbekistan, Kyrgyzstan and Tajikistan), a local movement calling itself Adalat (Justice) briefly took control. It imposed an 'Islamic' order, complete with sharia courts, a ban on alcohol, and so on. Other attempts were made by religious activists in the region between 1992 and 1999 – but without overt political control – to break into wedding parties to stop gender mixing, dancing and the serving of alcohol. Also, many mosques were built by self-taught *mullahs* (preachers) to function as social centres and even NGOs; they also sought to bypass traditional solidarity clusters and establish more religious communities that offered mutual assistance and education. Such endeavours to foster new types of grass-roots communities with social implications (solidarity) have yet to succeed, but one should not underestimate the potential impact of the call to create a more equitable and just society through the application of Islamic laws and values.

Why was the effectiveness of the Islamist movements so limited? Firstly, because of pervasive and fairly large-scale state repression and outright military defeat. In the instance of Tajikistan's Islamic Renaissance Party (IRP), there was defeat in the 1992 civil war, leading to exile and then a return in 1997 as a junior partner in a government coalition. The Uzbek IRP was suppressed between 1992 and 1995, while the Islamic Movement of Uzbekistan (IMU) – comprising former Adalat and IRP members – is waging an armed struggle from Afghanistan against the Uzbek government. State repression since 1999 has also curtailed more modest Islamist ventures. But there is a second reality that such ventures must contend with: nowhere, it would seem, have the Islamists been able to bypass traditional types of solidarity groups. Indeed, they have often mirrored these very networks in their activities and organization.

For despite their supranational claims, these movements have largely been shaped by national particularities. Sooner or later, they tend to express domestic regionalist alignments and interests irrespective of the ideological veneer of Islamism. This was the case with the Tajik IRP, which represented a regionalist group – the Gharmis – who entered a coalition government at least in part to stave off threats to national survival from assertive Uzbekistan. In this sense, the Islamist parties do contribute to the development of a political sphere in Central Asia (as in the Middle East). They do so by challenging authoritarian secular states, introducing ideological references, and offering models of modernist parties; but their ultimate objective is to achieve power, not civil society. Their activism at the local level is either to provide a springboard for national political contestation, or to have a local stronghold to which they can retreat after a political defeat. Whether as regionalist parties (like the IRP) or as conventional (conservative) parties, they are driven not by any blueprint for civil society but the simple will to power at the highest levels.

References to and invocations of 'Islamic' imagery and agendas have not supplied the keys to unlocking stubborn traditional affiliations. For all its 'modernity', political Islam in Central Asia has more often than not duplicated rather than reshaped old alignments and markers of identity. The same is true for more traditional forms of Islam that readily express or adapt to the fabric of traditional society. Most of the recently-built mosques, for example, expressed first of all a *mahalla* identity and are attended by members of the same traditional solidarity groups (*mahalla, qawm*, clan). During the Namangan upheaval in 1992, the *mahalla* played a key role in mobilising the people around local mosques.

It is appropriate at this juncture to consider the status of Sufi (spiritual) networks, which were a vivid facet of pre-Soviet Islam and have been able to resist sovietisation (notably in the instance of the Naqshbandi order). There appears to have been a generational crisis among the Sufi networks in the last phase of Soviet rule. Many young, 'born-again' Muslims, even when they were brought up in a Sufi milieu, were subsequently attracted by what have come to be called 'Wahhabi' ideas, an orthodoxy not necessarily linked with Saudi Arabia but to a broadly hard-line scripturalism.[13] When they became politicised in the late 1980s, these youths joined political Islamist movements: prominent examples include the Tajiks Abdullo Nuri and Akbar Turajanzade (whose father is a well-known Qaderi Sufi). There is a generation gap in the Sufi orders. Traditional affiliations in which a whole clan or tribe collectively associated with a 'holy' family seem to be on the wane. We can, however, witness since the late 1990s a Sufi revival that involves converging around a *pir* (an inspired individual) among people from varied horizons, sometimes at a distance from the place where the *pir* lives. Here, affiliations do not seem to reflect traditional identities, and may be the product of a personal spiritual quest. The issue is whether the Sufi revival will attract today's younger generation, a matter on which we lack field data. In any case, Sufi activities appear to occur at a private level, rather than to extend into the domain of public organisation of any kind (charity, teaching, social work).

A final element that merits particular consideration here is the growing influence of the Hizb al-Tahrir movement in Uzbekistan.[14] Created in 1953 as an Islamist party to contribute to the struggle to liberate Palestine, it gradually evolved after establishing its headquarters in London towards becoming a supranational movement. Its propaganda stresses two points: (a) that Muslims should revert to the true tenets of Islam in daily life and congregate in a single organisation, whatever their ethnic or national affiliations; and (b) that they should proclaim the Caliphate by ignoring present states, nations and political institutions. For them, since the umma already exists as a community in itself, it ought to be transformed into a polity. Although the movement's affiliations are rather secretive, they do not seem to duplicate traditional identity groups. Recruitment at the international level is largely among the second generation of migrant-Muslims, and its outlook is more a response to authoritarian state secularism, and to traditionalist Islam. Hizb's insistence on a personal and individual engagement makes the party a modernist organisation. Yet the defiance and disaffection vis-à-vis existing social and political structures pushes its members to behave less like a modern political grouping than a sect (even towards fellow Muslims who do not share their views).

Hizb's members are organised in small circles (*da'ira*) of five to seven persons, headed by a *mushrif*. Each group member knows only the members of his/her circle, and only the *mushrif* knows the next superior stage that members can attain. By ignoring day-to-day politics and rejecting participation in any extant political system, they contribute to spreading the notion of an alternative ideal society. In terms of their zone of influence within Central Asia, their appeal thus far has been predominantly among ethnic Uzbeks, even in Tajikistan and Kyrgyzstan. However, in August 2001, Hizb's presence in Azerbaijan prompted several arrests and some concern about the possible widening of their influence.

It is clear that there is a common interest between Western organisations and local regimes to exclude them from the debate on civil society. But however opposed the Hizb may be to pluralist, democratic values, the movement does represent a demand from the grass-roots level to resist authoritarian behaviour by state organs, and to create spaces of solidarity and autonomy, if not freedom. Even in this instance, it seems to me that ethnic, tribal and local identities cannot be kept out of the activist agenda: ideology and religion appear only to cloak those underlying realities. If the result is not quite a return to the *status quo ante*, it is still clear that ideological/religious affiliations alone are not able to generate a political civil society.

The 'Western' Model of Civil Society

As indicated at the outset, this approach has two main elements of policy: (a) the fostering of privatisation and free market economics, and (b) the protection and promotion of human rights, democracy, a free press and the status of women.[15] The World Bank, IMF, UN agencies and private NGOs and foundations are the chief proponents of this model. It is also heavily subsidised by the European Union, notably through the 'Tacis' (Technical Assistance for CIS countries) programme for rural privatisation. The two elements define a coherent policy approach, of seeking to advance civil society of free citizens in free markets. We will not discuss here the philosophical validity of such a model, but rather its practical implications.

Privatisation: the revenge of Soviet society

Under the guidelines of the IMF, privatisation aimed to create a new class of private farmers and to free peasant-cultivators from the confines of former Soviet collective affiliations and identities. At this juncture, the results fall well short of that objective. The policy has, in fact, been conducted along the very lines of Soviet society, giving further authority to local apparatchiks, who now have a proper economic basis that they lacked before. The dependency of the peasants on 'notables' has not disappeared but simply been transformed into a new relationship of economic dominance. Privatisation has not produced new actors, only new space for action for the traditional actors. All this has little to do with the content of new laws, which differ from Kazakhstan down to Tajikistan; rather, it concerns the social realities within which the laws operate, and in turn create.

A strictly legalist stance toward privatisation simply fails to take into account the formidable thrust of local practices and actors. It is also a mistake to believe that peasants who are deprived of access to private lands by arbitrary measures (no authorisation from the local governor, no access to credit) will necessarily react to such abuses of power. They may well prefer, under the circumstances, to remain in more familiar relationships of client and patron – expressed today in terms of employer/worker or land-owner/tenant relations, or in the best instance as small-scale shareholders in a co-operative headed by a club of big members.

Whatever the scope of the legislation, which can range from full privatisation of the land (Azerbaijan, Kazakhstan, Kyrgyzstan) to state ownership of the land while conceding exploitation rights to private farmers (Uzbekistan), the results tend to be similar. Large estates are created in favour of former *kolkhoz* apparatchiks (usually chairmen and their families) under two alternative forms. One is that of a 'model farm' which involves the best land and agricultural machinery for specialising in lucrative crops, while hiring former *kolkhozians* as waged labourers. The other is a kind of *latifundia* where most of the *kolkhozians*, though working independently on their own tenured land, have a crop-sharing agreement (*ijara*) with the leadership of the *kolkhoz*; this makes them more like tenants than private farmers. The process of re-concentration of land ownership, even where the land has officially been divided equally among *kolkhozians*, is possible only because the apparatchiks have access to credit and inputs (like fertilisers) – or access to the right connections to plead their case with a bureaucracy controlled by former communist party colleagues. It is a process that is well known, even if not well publicised, by the international agencies that consider it a lesser evil in managing two contradictory requirements. They wish to create, on the one hand, viable farms (far larger than the unprofitable patches that would result from equal sharing among all peasants, which usually yields 2–3 hectares), and on the other, avoid massive urban migration from the countryside because of the overly large concentration of lands among a handful of landowners. The present system entails a slow shift from collective farms to different forms of land-concentration, leaving a significant part of the rural population at a lower status; but it comes close to meeting those two requirements.

Some NGOs that are acutely aware of this distortion of privatisation have tried to directly support genuinely independent small farmers (usually dissidents from the *kolkhoz* system).[16] Yet these independent farmers generally need to be almost entirely supported by subsidies from the outside, since they lack both money and the ability to pull strings within the local bureaucracy. Whatever the free market perspective on privatisation, it clearly operates in favour of former apparatchiks who play on traditional patterns of patronage (as shown above), as well as on modern economics (using their political connections in a more or less legal way for access to credit, export licences, and so on). In a word, the modern entrepreneurs are not quite actors of the sort envisaged by the Western model of civil society: instead, they embody the transition between a bureaucratic/clanic system and a business/clanic system.

One of the outcomes is to re-cast traditional social patterns into a new model of land-tenure. We have the apparatchik-farmer, often competent, hard-working and far less corrupt than the bureaucrat, who bases his activities on the traditional networks of solidarity groups, clientelism and patronage. We also have net-works of solidarity converted into networks of patronage, where the average peasant is ever dependant on the new landowner, due to the collapse of state social security. The new notables may pro-vide some social protection against political loyalty, if not fealty. They behave neither like proudly individualistic American mid-west farmers, nor like the mafiosi among the *nouveaux riches* of the former Soviet Union. Rather, they are new *begs* and *khans*, notables looking for wealth, power and prestige, but retaining a semblance of social responsibility.[17] Their concern with status and prestige (which can involve conspicuous spending at weddings and circumcisions) contributes to maintaining networks of social protection, patronage for their children, and for tenants who seek jobs in the cities. They may also provide a counterweight to the excessive power of the bureaucracy, such as by acting as brokers for peasants; in this regard, there are rich parallels with tradi-tional Middle and Near East rural notables (*aghas* and *khans*). It is important to observe that they are not absentee landlords: they work and live in the countryside, even if some of their offspring may pursue their careers in the cities.

Hence, inasmuch as the paradigm of 'Western' civil society is fundamentally predicated on actors who are independent citizens, the beneficiaries of privatisation in Central Asia do not fit that mould. The power and effectiveness of the latter is vested in tradi-tional patterns of patronage and group identity – a reality that is not necessarily negative, for it allows the traditional-Soviet society to avert absolute collapse. It has nothing, however, to with 'mod-ern' civil society unless we recognise that it is traditional society where civic life happens.

This might explain some of the current tensions not only between apparatchik-farmers and central governments, but also between the latter and increasingly powerful urban-based entrepreneurs. After all, in the post-independence period, the expectation among ruling elites is that power and its benefits will devolve to the contending political factions, and mainly to the presidential faction. With Moscow out of the picture at least in terms of the routines of governance, who needs 'alternative' centres – economic, traditional or otherwise – as a 'counterweight'? Further, the decrease in state revenues (no more subsidies from Moscow) has 'shrunk the pie' that contending networks of patronage can hope to get a piece of. The state even tries to retake control of the more lucrative farm holdings, to impose quotas for crops, and enlarge the profits it makes from paying farmers far lower prices than their products would command in global markets.

Still more worrying is the recent trend in Uzbekistan where, in the wake of a severe drought, the central government has moved to forcibly buy food crops at low prices, and resorted to requisitions – an unsavoury reminder of the worst of the Soviet era. In response, the new apparatchik-farmers have agitated to get rid of the quotas and obtain direct access to global markets for their products, all against sharp resistance from Tashkent. In order to break personal ties between local economic actors and the bureaucracy, and to avoid new build-ups of local power, Tashkent – like authoritarian governments elsewhere in the region – ensure that local governors (*hakims*) undergo a regular turnover.

The new entrepreneurs in Central Asia have, by and large, benefited in terms of status and power from their connections with the state. But now the changing patterns of state control, amidst economic scarcity and political insecurity, have jeopardised many of those relationships. A good example of the fragility of the status of the new entrepreneurs is the regional incarnation of the 'Cola Wars', as the *Wall Street Journal* reports:

> When the cola wars came to Uzbekistan in the mid-1990s, Coca-Cola Co. emerged the big winner. Many Uzbeks and foreigners concluded that the reason was a not-so-secret weapon: a partnership with the son-in-law of President Islam Karimov. But last month, the president's 29-year-old daughter, Gulnora Karimova-Maqsudi, separated from her husband, Mansur Maqsudi, 34, president of Coke's local bottling company. And since then, the cola giant's fortunes in Uzbekistan have abruptly changed. Tax inspectors, fire inspectors, customs inspectors, and even an anti-narcotics official, have descended on Coke's main bottling plant in the Uzbek capital of Tashkent.[18]

This episode exemplifies the way the political oligarchies tend to deal with businessmen and landowners. In turn, it may prompt landowners to strengthen their local constituency in order to find a counterweight to the unpredictability of the state: they may so-licit the support of their own networks of solidarity, while trying to appear to be defending the interests of their wider constitu-ency on the premise of traditional clanic and identity ties. In other words, they may revivify traditional patterns of socialisation and grouping in response to the encroachment of the state. In this sense, the landowners and entrepreneurs are the 'real' actors of a putative civil society in the region, a buffer against the economic, political and social intrusions of the state in various forms. Once again, however, it is clear the social basis of their status lies in traditional patterns of socialisation. They have little, if any, genu-ine interest in human rights or democratic values – except, of course, when they find their own status to be threatened by offi-cial abuses of power.

A window civil society: NGOs and Westernised elites

Most Western-sponsored programmes that support the building of a civil society in Central Asia seek new local actors who are less associated with 'Soviet-traditional society'. The programmes are channelled mainly through NGOs, whether foreign or domestic (though the latter are almost always subsidised externally). Their activities span a wide spectrum, from support for battered women and the development of news media to promoting environmental awareness, democratisation, small business and English-language proficiency, to privatisation.[19]

Few of these programmes are funded exclusively by private organisations; Western governments and United Nations-related agencies are the main sources. One exception is the Soros Foun-dation, with its 'open society' programmes; but by and large, private money is partnered with more substantial governmental funds. Such funds are usually provided on a project-basis, and the projects must, of course, conform to the overall agenda of the sponsors – which is premised on the 'Western' paradigm of civil society. In practical terms, few of the sponsors actually venture into the field, or have a firm grasp of ground-level realities.[20] Accordingly, the importation of abstract visions and models is rife, parallel to what Elizabeth Faier has observed about Palestine: 'Activists contend that in order to receive foreign funds, they must design programmes and market local organisations in ways that appeal to Western agency agendas for Middle East development and peaceful relations between Jews and Arabs'.[21] I do not wish to criticise here the benevolent intentions of those promoting the entirely laudable causes of democracy or battered women. My purpose is to address the fallout from these policy ventures, beginning with the situation regarding the 'new' local actors.

In general, NGOs recruit local staff among young domestic academics and intellectuals. The reasons for this preference include language ability, 'bureaucratic' competence (they know how to prepare reports and to address audiences), and the capacity to understand what foreign NGOs want. Also, these individuals are available: they lost their positions of prestige that the Soviet system provided to academics, rarely have any business connections, and as academics today must scratch out a living at a salary of 10–20 US dollars a month. The fact that many intellectuals have few real links with networks and groups of solidarity give to their new employers the (often correct) impression that they are independent-minded.[22] But this also implies that they are not anchored in the actual, traditionally-oriented civic webs, formed of the actors discussed earlier that constitute true civil society at this juncture. Alternatively, if they do have these contacts, then their traditionalist tenor attenuates the ability of the intellectuals to spread the new gospel of freedom and citizenship. The predicament of these individuals is that they can have an impact on the traditional social context only if they play by its rules – which puts them at odds with the values and agenda of their employing institutions.[23] Frequently, they are perceived by the local population both as part of the traditional system of networks (wherein they are expected to allow their family and relatives to benefit from their position), and as profiting from Western assistance (with the huge discrepancy between their salaries and domestic ones making them appear as a sort of 'humanitarian aristocracy').

If the picture seems gloomy, we should nevertheless acknowledge the many positive effects of NGO activities in this regard. They do encourage computer literacy and the spread of Internet use, they promote the use of English (the key global language), they offer scholarships to deserving youth, and so on; all of which gives breathing space to an educated class (including many women) on a meritocratic basis. Further, by employing intellectuals whose status has been damaged by independence, NGOs neutralise the apprehension of the ruling elites that these new activists might become political actors. Their status as humanitarian activists precludes them from writing about or involving themselves directly in political life. Few governments will move against local cadres of foreign or foreign-connected NGOs. True, the Taliban did so in Afghanistan, but only after they had become the target of international sanctions. Members of the intelligentsia who come under attack by officialdom tend to be those lacking the proper foreign connections. In effect, international institutions both protect and neutralise the local actors they hire. In the process, they create 'natural reserves' for the endangered species of democratic intellectuals making the NGOs the equivalent of the World Wildlife Fund – dedicated to the protection of threatened humans – rather than the promotion of civil society. In fact, 'recycling' the cadre of local NGO employees into the domestic economy as effective members of society remains a challenge. They tend to inhabit a ghetto of sorts. In part this is because many acquire a social status that does not fit into domestic social landscapes: battered women, for example, are not considered a serious issue by any government in Central Asia. Moreover, as noted, NGO recruitment tends to foster a privileged class of employees who stand apart from the local populace.

In addition, the NGOs often contribute to a brain drain. A young intellectual who has attained a position of importance in an NGO has little opportunity to pursue a meaningful career within his country – until he becomes an expatriate. His NGO background and experience rarely provide a springboard for action domestically, where the relevant networks are tightly knit. To make a career in the NGO universe or within the United Nations, he will probably be obliged to leave town (sometimes with the benefit of a scholarship to an American or Western European university, or perhaps by marrying a foreign colleague). In other words, NGOs are less likely to create a stable new generation of future cadres than to facilitate the thinning of the intellectual class within Central Asia.

The upshot is the advancing of what I have described as 'window civil societies', constituted of isolated local intellectuals and numerous programmes with little long-term coherence. There is a mirror effect in which we help people who we believe resemble us. As noted, there are certainly many positive side-effects, from creating local employment to social centres and fuelling cyberliteracy. Yet the NGOs are able to do what they do for very specific reasons: they have money and connections, and their capacity to contribute to the employment (and real estate) market earns them friends. They are also good customers for the few local hotels and supermarkets. With rare exceptions, however, they do not impact domestic elements of power – or the deep challenges of corruption and narcotics – and therefore are not seen as a threat to the status quo. Indeed, successful NGOs function in areas where the authorities do not see any kind of challenge, a dissymmetry of interests that allows them to function without affecting the salient dynamics of state-society relations.

What Should be Done?

International institutions and NGOs both need to engage with the real actors in the region's new republics – even where they do not share exactly the same agenda. Apparatchik – farmers, entrepreneurs, local notables, even local religious figures when they have a social agenda, are the local partners who matter. Building civil society is going to be a more meaningful exercise if it is predicated on the social fabric as it exists and is evolving, rather than on abstract perceptual models derived from elsewhere of what civic culture ought to be. Reconsideration is also required of the nexus between privatisation and democracy, which is neither automatic nor compelling. In a word, international aid agencies must give up their ideological assumptions and be more attentive to the anthropological realities of Central Asian societies. This is not to deny that those realities are evolving, and the cast of actors gradually changing. Nor can one exclude the possibility of abrupt and radical political change, with all the implications that this would have for the prevailing social fabric.

Meanwhile, priority should be accorded to micro-projects, because these are usually more sensitive to the needs of indigenous communities, and hence more effective in helping to change attitudes without injuring the traditional solidarities that are sometimes the only safety net for an impoverished population. The *mahalla*, for example, ought to be regarded as a sound basic unit of social functionality and development planning – and so should the former collective farms. This can be the case even if privatisation as a long-term objective is preserved; the issue is to proceed in a manner that is compatible with maintaining key local solidarities. In this context local notables in particular need to be engaged as part of an overall strategy of reducing the dependency of grass-roots units on the control of the state bureaucracy. Indeed, the focal goal of political reform at large in post-independence Central Asia should remain the loosening of the grip of the central organs of state on society. In practical terms this means putting an end to industrial and agricultural quotas, and giving direct global access to entrepreneurs and farmers. In the final analysis, this loosening of the state's grip is an essential aspect of the evolution of modern civic culture at the national level and beyond.

Notes

1. See generally Holt Ruffin and Daniel Waugh, ed., *Civil Society in Central Asia* (Baltimore and Seattle, 1999); John Anderson, 'Creating a Framework for Civil Society in Kyrgyzstan', *Europe-Asia Studies*, 52, 1 (2000), pp.73–93; Nazif Shahrani, 'Re-building Communities of Trust in Muslim Central Asia: Past Legacies and Future Prospects', *Workshop*

for Home-grown Models of Civil Society in the Muslim World, Watson Institute for International Studies, Brown University (March 12–13, 1999).

2. See Anderson 'Creating a Framework for Civil Society', p.88; Olivier Roy, 'Kolkhoz and Civil Society in the Independent States of Central Asia', in *Civil Society in Central Asia,* above, pp.109–21. This point has been developed by other anthropologists of the Middle East: see, for example, Richard Antoun 'Civil Society, Tribal Process, and Change in Jordan', *International Journal of Middle Eastern Studies,* 32, 4 (2000), pp.441–63. In Afghanistan, the *loya jirga* or traditional assembly of elders and local notables is often presented by anthropologists as a way to built a legitimate state, as opposed to free elections that are argued to be unfeasible and inappropriate in a political culture that is based on collective identities.

3. See Shahrani, 'Re-building Communities of Trust in Muslim Central Asia'; and for another part of the Muslim world, Rachid Al Ghannouchi, 'Traditional Muslim Society is a Model of Civil Society', in 'Traditional Muslim Society is a Model of Civil Society ', in Azzam Tamimi and John Esposito, ed., *Islam and Secularism in the Middle East* (London, 2000), p.107.

4. Michael Walzer sees in the Puritans the real inventors of the modern political party: *The Revolution of the Saints* (Cambridge, MA, 1965).

5. On the difficulty of basing institutions on virtue, see Olivier Roy, *The Failure of Political Islam* (Cambridge, MA, 1994).

6. The dismantling of the collective farm system has been presented as a prerequisite for any kind of financial support for agriculture reforms; no 'third way' alternative (like a system of co-operatives) has been taken into consideration.

7. The most comprehensive anthropological study of a Soviet collective farm is that of Benedict Humphrey, *Marx Went Away but Karl Stayed Behind: Economy, Society and Religion in a Siberian Collective Farm* (Ann Arbor, MI, 1998). Although the research is not specific to a Muslim population, it does analyse how traditional segmentation has been embedded in the Soviet system.

8. See Ekaterina Makarova, 'The Mahalla, Civil Society and the Domestication of the State in Soviet and Post-Soviet Uzbekistan', *Workshop for Home-Grown Models of Civil Society in the Muslim World,* Watson Institute for International Studies, Brown University (March 12–13, 1999). See, generally, Olivier Roy, *The New Central Asia* (London, 2000), pp.85 ff.

9. Ernest Gellner, *Conditions of Liberty: Civil Society and its Rivals* (London, 1994), especially at pp.97–108.

10. See generally Anne Elizabeth Mayer, *Islam and Human Rights: Tradition and Politics* (2nd ed., London, 1995); Timothy McDaniel, 'The Strange Career of Radical Islam' in J.N. Wasserstrom, L. Hunt and M.B. Young, ed., *Human Rights and Revolutions* (Oxford, 2000), pp.211–29.

11. The Hizb al-Tahrir, now based in London, strives to recreate the Khalifa, that is a political structure uniting and leading the whole Muslim community or umma. Its *modus operandi* is to get a significant portion of the Muslim population back to the 'true tenets of Islam' through predication (*da'wa*); in this sense, the movement considers that it is through the recreation of a community of true Muslims, solely based on their faith and religious commitment, that a new polity could be created.

12. Shahrani, 'Re-building Communities of Trust in Muslim Central Asia', n.1.

13. See Bakhtyar Babadjanov 'Muhammadjan Hindustani and the Beginning of the "Great Schism" among Muslims in Uzbekistan', in Stéphane A. Dudoignon and Hisao Komatsu, ed., *Islam and Politics in Russia and Central Asia (Early 18th-Late 20th Centuries)*, (London, forthcoming).

14. On Hizb al-Tahrir, see Suha Taji-Farouki, *A Fundamental Quest, Hizb al-Tahrir and the Search for the Islamic Caliphate* (London, 1996).

15. See *Integrating Human Rights with Sustainable Human Development*, UNDP policy document, January 1998, New York.

16. As with the Agribusiness Volunteer Programs for the Citizens Network for Foreign Affairs: see *Civil Society in Central Asia*, above n.2, at p.16.

17. See Olivier Roy, 'Kolkhoz and Civil Society in the Independent States of Central Asia', above, n.2, at p.115.

18. *The Wall Street Journal* (21 August 2001), p.1.

19. For a detailed listing with regard to five of the six republics (Azerbaijan excepted), see *Civil Society in Central Asia*, n.2 above, pp.235–310.

20. Once more, the widespread and permanent presence of the Soros Foundation across the region is in contrast with that of governmental donors (with very few exceptions).

21. Elizabeth Faier, 'Making "Civil Society" in Divided Communities', *Workshop for Home-grown Models of Civil Society in the Muslim World*, above n.8.

22. For example in Tajikistan's capital of Dushanbe many local staff of foreign NGOs are 'Samarkandi', that is from families who left Samarkand in the 1920s to live in Dushanbe where they often entered academic careers. The result is that they are not linked with the local factions

(Kulabi, Gharmi) whose basis is rural and who also happen to be the wielders of both political and economic power.

23. This is still more of a problem in neighbouring Afghanistan, where it is almost impossible for a local humanitarian worker to appear as independent of traditional affiliations. Irrespective of his inclinations he will invariably have to deal with the suspicion that he is promoting the interests of his own group, or otherwise has a hidden agenda. In a society like Afghanistan, where traditional solidarity groups are in constant competition, local tribalisation tends in turn to tribalise the NGOs: most have no alternative but to work with a specific group or leader.

6

Prospects for Civil Society in Tajikistan

Shirin Akiner

Introduction

The term 'civil society' is today so overused in general parlance that it tends to be reduced to the status of a phatic utterance. One author wryly observes that 'Civil society has become a conceptual rag bag, consisting of households, religious denominations, and each and every activity that is not of the state.'[1] It is sometimes used interchangeably with 'democracy' (another term that suffers chronic overload). Both have come to be regarded as benchmarks of progress, hence societies with very different political, economic, social and cultural systems insist – as a matter of national pride – that they have acquired or are in the process of acquiring these proofs of 'maturity'. Western donor agencies have encouraged this tendency by providing generous, often uncritical, financial support for projects, however opaque and ill-defined, that are presented under the rubric of 'building civil society'. These efforts may be well meaning, but by constantly stretching the terms of reference they drain the concept of substance.

This lack of focus contrasts sharply with the copious body of contemporary theoretical literature on civil society, in which a wide range of socio-political interpretations and approaches have been postulated. Most are firmly anchored in the evolution of the relationship between state and society in the context of the European-American experience. Increasingly, however, the parameters of this discourse are being re-configured to embrace other perspectives. Elsewhere in this volume, Islamic dimensions are explored and new analytical frameworks proposed. This is helpful in that it imbues the concept of 'civil society' with greater flexibility, while retaining sufficient clarity for it to constitute a meaningful analytical category. Yet no matter how the term is defined, if it is not to be an all-embracing 'rag bag' there must be some basic boundaries. It is generally agreed that these are premised on the existence of certain conditions that include as a minimum the rule of law, political and economic stability, and a significant degree of social cohesion. It may be a truism but it is nevertheless worth emphasising that there are many parts of the globe in which these conditions do not obtain. Only missionaries or visionaries see signs of nascent civil society in these situations. This is not to exclude the possibility of change, but merely to plead that a distinction be made between what is, and what might be.

Tajikistan is a case in point. This is a society which, for over a century, has experienced incessant upheaval and trauma; currently it is only just beginning to recover from a brutal civil war. Society is still fragmented, and very largely preoccupied with questions of basic subsistence. The approach adopted in this chapter is one of 'thick description', concerned with an examination of the situation as it is, not with value judgements as to what it ought to be, still less with recommendations as to how to achieve particular goals. Much that has happened has had a profoundly disintegrative effect on society, so that 'uncivil' patterns of behaviour – crime, violence, distrust – have become ever more firmly entrenched. At the risk of seeming to devote too much space to historical digressions, the following sections (Background and Post-Conflict Tajikistan) highlight some of these experiences.[2] They do not directly address the central theme – i.e. the prospects for creating a civil society in Tajikistan – but they contextualise the issue by seeking to establish whether or not the preconditions for civil society are present.

The final section directly addresses questions relating to civil society today, and finds the prospects less than promising. Much of what passes for nascent civic culture (e.g. the appearance of non-governmental organisations and opposition political parties) is of dubious validity. A section is devoted below to the activities of the Aga Khan Development Network (AKDN), whose programmes are of particular interest because they focus on fostering the qualities that are fundamental to a civic culture. Yet these programmes are relatively new and encompass a relatively small section of the population. It is too early to judge how successful they will prove to be, still less to establish whether it will be possible to replicate them elsewhere in the country. Perhaps more encouragingly, some spontaneous signs of a re-emerging sense of social and moral responsibility are beginning to appear. As described below, these are isolated examples on a very small scale; but they do indicate that a process of societal healing, albeit slow and faltering, is under way. While this may indeed presage the emergence of some form of civil society, the situation is still too volatile to allow more definite conclusions.

Background

The Tajik nation and the Tajik state

There is a disjunction between the histories of the Tajik[3] nation (i.e. people) and the Tajik state. This has left a deep feeling of dislocation and loss – though it has also strengthened a sense of particularity, of being different from neighbouring peoples. Psychologically, this has acted as a unifying bond among the Tajik people. Yet there are also marked regional differences among the various Tajik groups, and this has created centrifugal tensions. These problems have not been fully resolved and represent a latent threat to national as well as state cohesion.

As a nation, the Tajiks represent an outpost of the Iranian world. They have been settled between the Pamir mountains and the middle reaches of the Syr Darya and the Amu Darya for more than two thousand years. From the sixth century onwards, successive waves of Turkic invaders occupied the land further to the west, thereby separating the Tajiks from the Iranian heartland. Yet by physiology, language and culture they remained very much a part of the Iranian family. However, when Iran adopted Shi'ism as the state religion in the sixteenth century, the Tajiks did not follow suit; they continued to adhere to Sunni Islam (of the Hanafi school of jurisprudence), as did the great majority of other Central Asians.

Historically, there were two main areas of Tajik settlement: on the plains (the Ferghana Valley and the basins of the Zarafshan, Syr Darya and Surkhandarya Rivers); and in the foothills and mountain valleys (the central and south-west regions). The plain-dwellers were part of the urban-based civilisation of Transoxiana. By contrast, until the Soviet era, the Tajiks of the mountains were largely cut off from outside influences. In the south-west, in the valleys and foothills of the tributaries of the Amu Darya/Panj, there are several other Iranian peoples, known collectively as 'Pamiris' or 'Mountain Tajiks'. Ethnically and linguistically, they belong to a different (eastern) branch of the Iranian family. Their languages are not mutually comprehensible with Tajik, or with each other. Together they number approximately 150,000.[4] By religion, most are Ismaili Muslims.

Modern Tajik statehood dates from the creation of the Tajik Autonomous Soviet Socialist Republic (ASSR) in 1924. This was formed as a subordinate unit within the larger administrative entity of the Uzbek Soviet Socialist Republic (SSR), likewise established in 1924. Yet an estimated 800,000 Tajiks and many traditional areas of Tajik settlement were at this time allocated to direct Uzbek jurisdiction. This demarcation divided the Tajiks of the plains from the Tajiks of the mountains. This was no accident. There were several influential Tajiks who at that time argued that the Tajiks of the cities – e.g. Samarkand, Bukhara and Khujand – were culturally closer to the Uzbeks than to the Tajiks of the mountains, whom they regarded with disdain.[5]

However, the hegemonic policies of the new Uzbek leaders angered even those Tajiks who had initially opted for incorporation into the Uzbek SSR. In 1929, a new demarcation was agreed upon, whereby the northern province of Khujand (corresponding approximately to the modern Soghd province) was transferred to Tajik jurisdiction. The status of Tajikistan was thereupon upgraded from that of an autonomous republic within Uzbekistan to that of a constituent republic of the Soviet Union. Still, over half a million Tajiks, and much of the territory that Tajiks regarded as theirs by virtue of centuries of settlement, were left within the boundaries of Uzbekistan. This remains a bitter cause of grievance.

After the physical demarcation of the territory of Tajikistan, the next task was to articulate the national identity, emphasising the features that distinguish the Tajiks from modern Iranians, and also from Uzbeks and other neighbouring Turkic peoples. One of the first priorities was the fashioning of a standardised modern literary language.[6] This was initially written in the Arabic script, but in 1930 the Latin script was compulsorily introduced, and thereafter replaced by the Cyrillic script in 1940 (still the official script today). During this period there was a rapid expansion of print and broadcast media, vital tools for bonding the population. The process was underpinned by the formation of national political, cultural and educational institutions. A vibrant community of intellectuals and creative artists emerged, who, in their various ways, gave substance and shape to the Tajik heritage. Regional divisions were never wholly overcome but were in time balanced by a palpable sense of shared national identity.[7]

On 9 September 1991 Tajikistan declared its independence from the Soviet Union. Currently it has a population of 6.3 million (2001 estimate), belonging to some 14 ethnic groups. Citizenship, subject to residency qualifications, is open to all regardless of ethnic origin. Tajiks constitute some 69 per cent of the total population, Uzbeks 25 per cent and Russians just under 3 per cent.[8] Tajiks are spread fairly evenly throughout the country, but the other ethnic groups tend to be concentrated in particular areas (e.g. there is a large Uzbek community in the Soghd province, bordering Uzbekistan). The bulk of the population is concentrated in the western half of Tajikistan.[9] The Gorno-Badakhshan autonomous province covers the entire eastern half of the country, but is very sparsely peopled, with less than 4 per cent of the total population of Tajikistan.

Statist modernisation

An understanding of the process of modernisation in Tajikstan is
crucial to any discussion of post-Soviet society. Soviet developmental policies achieved truly remarkable results in some spheres, but
in others had little impact – which produced peculiar imbalances.
Thus, while there are superficial resemblances to modernisation
processes elsewhere in the world, there are also fundamental differences. Consequently, assumptions based on assumed analogies
with the experience of other societies are often found to be invalid.
Below, the main features of the 'statist' (i.e. state imposed and
controlled) modernisation of Tajikistan are summarised.

In the early twentieth century, life in many parts of Tajikistan
was very much the same as it had been for hundreds of years. This
changed when Soviet rule was established shortly after the 1917
revolution, when a programme of far-reaching social, cultural and
economic transformation was introduced. Initially, priorities included the emancipation of women (i.e. gender equality before
the law, in education and in employment), mass literacy (free,
compulsory and universal education for children was introduced,
first to primary and later to secondary level), and better standards of health care and nutrition. Later, higher educational
facilities were developed together with advanced research institutes. The State University was founded in Dushanbe in 1948, the
Tajik Academy of Sciences in 1951. The level of scholarship in
the specialised institutes was of a high calibre. The Tajik Institute
of Medicine, for example, was one of the foremost centres of medical research in the entire Soviet Union.

In parallel to the development of education, modern state
institutions and a modern bureaucracy were established. Tajik civil
servants were trained and incorporated into the administration
at all levels of responsibility. There was also an expansion of mass
media outlets, and of cultural facilities such as museums, libraries
and art galleries. Traditional[10] art forms in music, literature, dance
and painting were neglected or deliberately eradicated. In their
place, 'modern' Soviet/Western arts such as theatre, ballet, opera
and orchestral music were introduced.[11]

In the economic sphere a programme of electrification was

introduced and new industrial complexes were established. Agriculture was transformed by the introduction of collectivisation. Collective farms (*kolkhoz*) varied in size and in range of activities. Some were very large, the equivalent of an entire administrative district; they had their own budgets and ran numerous enterprises (e.g. breweries and bakeries). They provided their members with such facilities as schools, health care centres, youth clubs, and leisure amenities; they also produced their own newspapers.[12] Other developments during this period included the creation of modern communication and transport networks. In the early 1920s, many parts of Tajikistan were accessible only by foot or on horseback. In the 1930s the state initiated the large-scale construction of railway lines and roads. Regular air links were established between Dushanbe and Tashkent, also within the republic between the capital and the main towns. Airfields and landing strips were constructed throughout Tajikistan, providing access to even the remotest parts of the country.

Soviet policies were responsible for extensive movements of population, some voluntary, some enforced. In the 1920s, the administration introduced a system of compulsory internal migration within Tajikistan, with the aim of redistributing labour resources from areas with little employment (mainly the central mountains of Tajikistan) to the newly established cotton plantations in the south.[13] No part of Tajikistan was left unmarked by this redistribution of population. Some areas were depopulated, while in the south-west (notably the Vakhsh Valley) by the 1970s, up to 90 per cent of the inhabitants were newcomers. Extended family networks generally remained together, but larger community groupings were dispersed.

There were two other migration flows which significantly altered the demographic balance in the republic. One was of Russians: in the period 1926–1979, their number rose from under 6,000 to close on 400,000. The other was of the 'punished peoples', deported here from other parts of the Soviet Union for alleged treason (in the late 1930s and early 1940s).[14] By 1959, Tajiks represented only 53 per cent of the population of Tajikistan. In the somewhat more liberal conditions of the 1980s the immigrants began to leave the republic. This trend intensified in the 1990s and eventually resulted in greater ethnic homogeneity, but at the same time caused yet more social and economic upheaval.

Soviet modernisation had several distinctive features. It was highly authoritarian, imposed by the state rather than generated from within society. Secondly, it took place in the context of a tightly controlled totalitarian system; any attempt at non-compliance was harshly suppressed. Thirdly, it was accompanied by major movements of population; this weakened traditional social structures, likewise traditional values and norms. Finally, the authorities were extremely successful in co-opting local intellectuals and community leaders, thereby facilitating the process of social transformation. Moreover, by giving the national elite a vested interest in the system, a high degree of allegiance to the regime was ensured.

The results of Soviet modernisation were uneven. Firstly, the geographic spread was not uniform: urban areas benefited most, while distant rural areas were given more cursory treatment. Secondly, although there was a rapid transformation of the public face of society, in the private domain the impact was limited. In public life, for instance, women enjoyed formal equality with men, but in the private domain they continued to occupy a subordinate position.[15] Likewise, pre-Soviet identities (tribe, region and religion) continued to be important points of self-definition. So-called 'clans' – political and economic networks based on traditional kin/tribal/regional groupings as well as newer associative bonds formed through a shared experience (e.g. in the army, at college) – dominated society.[16] Clientelism was deeply embedded in the web of social relations. It enabled ambitious individuals to 'colonise' the Soviet system by carving out private fiefdoms. This in turn often resulted in covert power struggles between high ranking officials and their cliques.

The statist nature of the modernisation process ensured that it was channelled along ideologically determined lines; deviation was not permitted. Consequently, many of the features of social development that have accompanied modernisation in other parts of the world did not emerge here. The diversification of educational and employment opportunities certainly broadened horizons and increased social mobility. Yet in attitude and outlook, society remained highly conservative. Specifically, there was virtually no political mobilisation. Insofar as there was any extension of political demands, it was a very late process (dating from the end of the 1980s) and confined to a very small group of urban intellectuals.[17]

Islamic and secular politicisation

Prior to Sovietisation, Islam was the dominant spiritual, legal and cultural vector of Central Asian society. More recently, the history of Islam in this region has been marked by persecution and conflict. This has contributed to the emergence of deeply ambivalent feelings towards the religion, and to a polarisation in attitudes regarding the role it should play in Tajik society. It is difficult to appreciate the strength of these tensions without some understanding of Soviet-era developments.

In the early Soviet period, the state authorities made a concerted effort to eradicate religion. In Tajikistan, this entailed the destruction of Muslim institutions and the use of terror ('purges') against believers. Within a generation, a high degree of secularisation had been achieved; knowledge of Islam, in so far as it survived at all, was largely confined to the mechanical repetition of prayers and rituals. Nevertheless, compared with other parts of Central Asia, Islamic traditions were slightly better preserved. The physical remoteness of the country afforded it a certain protection from external interference. Moreover, a few members of the pre-Soviet generation of Central Asian Muslim scholars had sought refuge in Tajikistan and were able to pass on their learning to clandestine circles of adepts.[18]

After the Second World War, a limited official (and strictly controlled) Islamic structure was reinstated in the Soviet Union. In Tajikistan, a few mosques were reopened for worship and a small Qaziyat (religious administration) was permitted to function. However, unofficial religious activities continued to take place. During the 1970s, a process of radicalisation occurred in this 'underground' Muslim community, coinciding with a rise in Muslim consciousness in other parts of the Soviet Union. In June 1990, an all-Union Islamic party was created. Later that year, the Islamic Rebirth Party (IRP) of Tajikistan was formed; initially a branch of the all-Union body, it soon became an independent party. It was formally registered in October 1991. Its ultimate aim was to create an Islamic state in Tajikistan.

Simultaneously, and in competition with the radicals, the most senior Muslim cleric in Tajikistan, Qazi Haji Akbar Turajonzoda,[19] launched his own campaign of Muslim regeneration. He believed that it was unrealistic to think of creating an Islamic state, since so few Tajiks had any real knowledge of the faith. Working within the framework of the existing law, he concentrated his efforts on preaching, education and the reintroduction of a Muslim discourse into public life. Yet by 1991 the political landscape was changing and the Qazi was losing influence; unable to compete successfully with the IRP, he had little option but to form a tactical alliance with them. It was a fragile coalition. The old 'establishment' and the new 'radicals' had different agendas; moreover, from the leadership down to the rank and file, personal animosities and ambitions were never far from the surface. This uneasy partnership survived the years of civil war, but once peace had been achieved, it soon fell apart (see further section on Post-Conflict Tajikistan).

Concurrent with the Islamic revival, a secular politicisation process was taking place.[20] Similar developments were to be observed elsewhere in the Soviet Union. In Tajikistan, however, to a far greater extent than in the other Central Asia republics, a real political debate began to take shape. New personalities as well as new ideas appeared on the horizon. Several (in intention at least) democratic movements were founded. Their political and economic platforms were vague, but the general thrust was political reform, economic liberalisation and re-integration with the world beyond the Soviet borders.[21] New discussion groups provided another outlet for political activists.[22] It seemed possible that out of this ferment of ideas and fledgling organisations a genuine multiparty system might develop that in turn would foster openness, pluralism and an orderly change of regime. In the event, this 'Tajik spring' was abruptly terminated by the civil war.

Civil war, fragile peace

Civil war erupted in Tajikistan less than a year after the collapse of the Soviet Union. The outbreak of hostilities on such a scale was unexpected. Yet the preconditions for conflict were already in place in the 1980s, requiring only a fateful series of triggers to escalate tensions to the point of explosion. The war is often characterised as a power struggle between 'neo-communists' on the one hand, and 'democrats' and 'Islamists' on the other. This is too simplistic. Ideological competition provided the initial impetus, but the conflict soon changed and diversified. There were already deep social tensions, in no small measure the legacy of earlier economic policies such as the transfer of manpower resources and unequal regional investments. These problems were exacerbated by the high rate of demographic growth.[23] Moreover, the institutional corruption that had long been embedded in the system was now unbridled. Law enforcement agencies as well as senior bureaucrats were heavily involved in criminal activities. The newly emergent political leaders, Islamists and 'democrats' alike, were inexperienced and impetuous; far from acting as a restraining force, they tried to exploit the situation to further their own causes. Moscow – the distant metropolis – was by this time also in a state of incipient turmoil. There were thus no institutions, no mechanisms that could prevent the slide into chaos.

Over the next few years, it often seemed as though the country would be dismembered by secessionist factions in the north and east. The very concept of a unified Tajik nation was called into question as regional allegiances assumed predominance. The active parties to the conflict were the government (from late 1992 under the leadership of Emomali Rahmonov), based in the capital, Dushanbe, and a group of opposition parties that coalesced around the Islamic Rebirth Party, which soon emerged as the dominant opposition faction. In early 1993, there was a mass exodus of anti-government forces to bases in northern Afghanistan; in 1994 this coalition assumed the umbrella designation 'United Tajik Opposition' (UTO). The conflict lasted from mid-1992 to late 1996. The most intense clashes occurred in the first 18 months of the war. Thereafter, the fighting was more localised and sporadic. Both sides suffered from internal divisions, mutinies and defections; neither was strong enough to win a decisive victory.

The peace process was initiated in early 1994, under the aegis of the United Nations and observer nations (among them Iran and Russia). It took three years, and eight rounds of negotiations, to reach a settlement. The General Agreement on the Establishment of Peace and National Accord in Tajikistan was signed on 27 June 1997[24] and registered with the Secretariat of the United Nations. In July, a further Pact on Mutual Forgiveness was signed and endorsed by the newly formed Commission for National Reconciliation. The provisions of the settlement (which included a degree of power sharing in local and national government) were implemented haltingly and imperfectly. Nevertheless, the process continued and at the time of writing the peace agreement is holding. The political parties that were outlawed at the beginning of the war were eventually allowed to re-register, among them the IRP.

During the conflict, the suffering inflicted on the civilian population was immense. The Vakhsh Valley – the 'Golden Valley' of Soviet times – was ravaged. Factories were destroyed, arable land laid waste, livestock slaughtered wholesale. By the end of the war, approximately 778,500 people had fled Tajikistan (nearly one-sixth of the population); over 60,000 sought refuge in Afghanistan, another 145,000 in the Russian Federation, and the remainder elsewhere in the Commonwealth of Independent States (CIS). Out of a Russian population numbering 388,500 in 1989, just over 88,000 remained in Tajikistan by this period. By the time hostilities ceased 35,000 houses had been destroyed. The toll of the dead and those missing without trace was estimated at 60,000. Some 55,000 children were orphaned and thousands of women widowed; 26,000 families were left without their primary breadwinners.[25]

Post-Conflict Tajikistan

Peace has brought a degree of stability to Tajikistan and this has permitted some progress to be made with economic and political reforms. However, during the 1990s the population experienced mass pauperisation. This has exacerbated the societal rifts that were already present before the civil war. Regional divisions have been re-emphasised by the conflict, and likewise by grievances over perceived disparities in the new, post-conflict economic and political balance. Regional animosities are now more apparent and often crudely expressed.[26] Since 1997 there have been serious public disturbances in the Soghd province; in part at least these were provoked by hostility to the government in Dushanbe. This raised fears in some circles that the province might be seeking secession, possibly as a prelude to reunification with Uzbekistan; such fears have harmed inter-ethnic relations. Throughout the country, the brutalising, 'uncivilising' impact of war has diminished personal security, and lowered thresholds of trust and tolerance. The situation has been exacerbated by the large numbers of former combatants, many still armed, who have not as yet been re-integrated into civilian life. The government has provided some support for rehabilitation centres, but this is insufficient to cope with the scale of the problem. Arguably, the environment today is as volatile as it was on the eve of the civil war.

Atomised society

Despite the disruptive nature of Soviet policies described above, there was a degree of stability in the private sphere that made it possible to preserve some elements of social cohesion. The events of the 1990s have had a more corrosive impact, often damaging the most intimate relationships.[27] Disintegrative factors crosscut and dissect one another, splitting society into ever smaller units. These strains have shattered traditional bonds, diminishing communal solidarity. In stable environments, the atomisation of society is often regarded as a positive development, in that it empowers individuals by liberating them from the straitjacket of enforced collectivity. As autonomous entities, they become capable of co-operative behaviour premised on privacy, equality and mutual respect. In chaotic, war-torn societies, the effect is very different. Autarkic behaviour becomes the norm, effacing concerns for the welfare of others. Armed clashes are no longer an everyday occur-rence in Tajikistan, but anxieties over basic personal security remain paramount. Society is still fragmented and disconnected, aspects of which are discussed in this section.

The family

The family used to be regarded as one of the most stable elements in Tajik society. Early marriages were the norm, especially for girls.[28] In the 1990s, however, the number of registered marriages declined sharply, falling from 10.3 per 1,000 of the population in 1991 to 3.4 per 1,000 in 1998. This was partly caused by the death toll during the war, especially among men of the younger genera-tion.[29] Also, there has been massive economic migration; each year an estimated 700,000 men (about half the male adult work-ing population) leave Tajikistan in search of casual seasonal employment in the Russian Federation and other parts of the CIS.

There are, too, other reasons for the decrease in marriages. One is economic hardship. Many men do not feel that they are in a position to support a family. Meanwhile, there has been an in-crease in multiple marriages as girls are forced, through poverty, to become second or third wives. These marriages have no legal validity, and are not registered; children born of such unions are frequently not registered, thus they are, in the most basic sense of the term, illegitimate. The girls themselves are often abandoned after a few months; shunned by their own families, they have little choice but to turn to prostitution and other forms of crime in order to survive.[30]

During the past decade there has been a noticeable fall in the social status of women. This is apparent from school age onwards, as is indicated by the decline in school attendance among girls, particularly in rural areas.[31] At work, women are increasingly to be found in menial, low paid jobs. At the same time, the incidence of abduction, rape and other forms of crime against women has increased. Violence occurs both within the family and outside the home.[32] The elderly have also experienced a sharp change in their circumstances. In the past, age commanded respect, affection and a duty of care; thus, state and society alike accorded the older generation a privileged position. Today, there are few support systems for the elderly. Pensions and welfare benefits are of little more than symbolic value. Families whose resources are already stretched to the limit cannot cope with the extra burden of providing for aged relatives and consequently shun them. Many older people are now experiencing unprecedented poverty and hardship. Children, too, often suffer severe neglect. Parents take on several parallel jobs in order to supplement the family income. This leaves them little time or energy to devote to the needs of their children.[33] Moreover, there is pressure on children in poor families to drop out of school in order to earn money in whatever way they can. Worst of all is the situation of children who have been orphaned or abandoned. There are now several thousand homeless street children who survive by begging and petty crime.[34]

Repatriants and returnees

During and after the war hundreds of thousands of refugees fled abroad. Many more people were displaced within Tajikistan. Since the signing of the peace agreement, the refugees and internally displaced people (IDPs) have been returning to their original places of residence. This is a positive development and marks the accomplishment of one of the goals of the peace settlement. Nevertheless, it has brought problems of its own. There are now many bitter disputes over property rights. Some of the homes vacated by fleeing families in 1992 were given as gifts, or simply appropriated, by local commanders. Deeds of ownership and other legal documents have often been lost, hence it is difficult for the repatriants to prove their claims. Harassment and intimidation have frequently been used to prevent them pressing their cases.

There has also been widespread destruction of property. This has left a great shortage of accommodation; some financial and material assistance for the construction of new homes has been provided by international aid agencies. Those who did not flee their homes resent the priority treatment that, as it seems to them, the refugees and IDPs are receiving. Such tensions are having a highly detrimental effect on community relations.[35] Nor is there much solidarity or mutual support among the returnees. Family or community networks often become a mechanism for exploitation, but without rendering in return the benefits of patronage. Thus, it is not unusual to find more powerful individuals colluding with the authorities in order to defraud weaker claimants (particularly women) of their rights.

Re-division of wealth

Economic disparities have further contributed to social fragmentation. There are today three economic strata: a thin layer of 'new rich'; a broader layer of impoverished, but far from destitute, urban professionals; and a very wide layer (estimated at over 80 per cent of the population) who subsist below the poverty line.[36] There is little, if any, contact between these different layers. Moreover, within each stratum there is fierce competition and rivalry. Thus, vertical as well as horizontal links within society have been weakened.

The small group of 'new rich' is very diverse in composition. Some members of this economic elite acquired their wealth legitimately, but many are involved to a greater or lesser extent in criminal activities (see section on 'Uncivil Environment' below). Several are former field commanders who, after the peace settlement, adroitly took control of major enterprises and other economic assets. They are mostly concentrated in Dushanbe and Khujand, where they maintain a lavish life style. The majority has close links to the senior figures in government (and indeed, some are members of the government). The urban professional classes and civil servants receive nugatory salaries, but most manage to retain a semblance of their old lives by supplementing their incomes in various ways. They, too, are located mainly in the capital and some of the other large towns. It is in rural areas that mass pauperisation is most acute; unemployment and underemployment are widespread.[37]

The problems of poverty and employment are exacerbated by high demographic growth. An estimated 45 per cent of the population is aged 15 years and under; the average age is 22.8 years. In the period 1989–2000, the population grew from 5.2 million to 6.1 million.[38] This rapid increase is causing relentless pressure for jobs at a time when the economy is still in crisis. In 1997, nearly 60 per cent of the 16–29 age group were unemployed; the situation had improved somewhat by 1999, but nevertheless, over half the national average of registered unemployed were still in approximately this age range.[39] The highest birth rates are in rural areas. This has changed the urban-rural balance; by 1999 the rural population accounted for 73.5 per cent of the total (as opposed to 67 per cent in 1987).[40] The closure of many industrial enterprises has led to a de-skilling of the population. This trend, coupled with falling levels of enrolment in education, is creating a situation in which a growing number of the population is equipped for nothing more than casual manual work.[41]

Uncivil Environment

Most definitions of civil society presuppose the existence of a stable environment with an established rule of law (however draconian or oppressive that might be). There is also a presumption that there will be some degree of 'civil' behaviour (e.g. respect for the law, trust, tolerance, courtesy, civic responsibility). Conditions in Tajikistan are very different. Certain types of crime were always rife. These were mainly of an economic nature (e.g. bribe taking, fraud, misappropriation of public funds) and for the most part on an institutional level. In relationships between individuals, personal morality was generally contained within perceived bounds of propriety. The incidence of casual violence (as opposed to state violence) was low. Consequently, personal safety was rarely a matter of concern.

Since the early 1990s, the situation has changed dramatically. There has been an explosion of lawless behaviour in every sphere, ranging from the activities of organised crime cartels to the abuse of office by bureaucrats, from cheating and bribe-taking in the educational system to petty theft on the street.[42] Violence and aggression have become entrenched modes of social intercourse. Each month, even on the streets of the capital, there are frequent cases of abduction, assault and murder. The victims are ordinary citizens, as well as high-profile public figures.[43] The country is still awash with arms and ammunition; attempts at a general disarmament have met with very limited success. Even those who regard themselves as peaceable, law-abiding citizens are nevertheless forced to make an accommodation with this lawless environment.

The most dangerous form of crime is drug trafficking. The main source of illegal opiates is Afghanistan.[44] In recent years the flow of drugs has increased exponentially. In 2000, opium seizures amounted to more than 4000 kg, heroin seizures to some 1,500 kg.[45] It is generally acknowledged that these amounts represent only a small percentage of the total volume. There are two main routes through Tajikistan: via Gorno-Badakhshan and via Kulyab. In both these provinces unemployment is high and poverty widespread; drug trafficking is often the only available source of income. Compared with global rates, the wholesale price for opiates in Tajikistan is low, but by local standards the profits are colossal, outweighing all the risks that the trade entails.[46]

Drug trafficking spawns money laundering, protection rackets, gang warfare and innumerable other crimes. It also impacts on the political process, providing lucrative support for unscrupulous contenders for high office. The damage to society is incalculable. One of the worst effects is the growth of drug addiction and linked to this, of illnesses related to drug abuse. The young are particularly vulnerable. No reliable statistics are available, but firsthand reports suggest that Kulyab has been more severely afflicted than elsewhere. Some 80 per cent of male adolescents, and a smaller, but growing number of females, are reportedly drug users.[47] The President of Tajikistan has shown commendable determination to combat the trade in illegal drugs; international assistance has enabled Tajikistan to move up the scale of countries that record the largest heroin seizures from twenty third position in 1998 to sixth position in 2000.[48] Yet encouraging though this is, the war on drugs is very far from being won.

It might have been supposed that Islam could act as an integrative, possibly even a 'civilising', factor in post-conflict Tajikistan. So far, however, there are no signs of this happening. This is partly because knowledge of Islam is still very weak. There is a greater observance of ritual than during the Soviet period, but familiarity with Islamic teachings remains rudimentary in the extreme. There is virtually no learned community of Islamic scholars. Such understanding as there is of Islamic precepts tends to be of a superficial, formalistic nature. Perhaps more importantly, in the wake of the civil war, religion is regarded as a potentially divisive factor. Such indications as there are of public opinion (surveys, informal discussions, etc.) suggest that the majority of Tajiks value, at least notionally, their Islamic heritage, but believe that religion should be a matter of private conscience, not a normative regulator of public behaviour.[49] They do not support the enshrining of Islamic principles in the constitution and are also firmly opposed to Islam becoming the focus of party political competition. Yet there is a minority that does seek the full implementation of Islamic law. The tension between these different visions creates an atmosphere charged with fear and prejudice. In such conditions it is virtually impossible to have any constructive public debate on the role of Islam in society.

If there were religious leaders of stature and charisma it might, nevertheless, have been possible to promote an inclusive dialogue between 'secularists' and 'Islamists', aimed at seeking common ground in the ethical teachings of Islam. There are no such figures in Tajikistan today.[50] The official Muslim hierarchy, headed by the Council of Ulama, is largely concerned with administrative questions. The IRP, the only officially registered Islamic party in Tajikistan (and indeed, in the whole of Central Asia), has also failed to present a coherent view of the role that Islam might play in post-Soviet Tajik society. Riven by internal factions, it has lost much of the following that it had in the early 1990s.[51]

The one Islamic group that is actively involved in missionary

outreach is the proscribed, radical movement Hezb-i Tahrir (Liberation Party). It appeared in Central Asia in the mid-1990s and
soon spread to Tajikistan, where it now seems to have several
hundred adherents. The popularity of Hezb-i Tahrir may be explained in part by non-religious factors. It is well funded and
reportedly distributes generous payments to its supporters. Also,
it provides a means of registering anti-government sentiment
(which may explain its success in the Soghd province). Nevertheless, the psycho-social impact of Hezb-i Tahrir should not be
overlooked. Unlike the Council of Ulama or the IRP, the movement raises fundamental questions about the role of Islam in
society.[52] The answers that they offer are, in the eyes of most orthodox Muslims, dangerously simplistic and extreme. Yet in
Tajikistan (as elsewhere in Central Asia), these are the very qualities that attract the alienated, frustrated youth.

Communications

Good communications and access to information are vital elements in social mobilisation; Tajikistan is severely handicapped
in both areas. Under Soviet rule there was tight control of the
media. In 1990, on the eve of independence, a number of the
new political movements did succeed in producing their own
publications (with or without legal registration), albeit irregularly
and in small print runs. However, this period of relative openness
came to an end with the civil war. In 1993, the government introduced a clampdown on opposition publications. Journalists who
took an independent stance frequently suffered severe physical
assault. Some fifty of them were assassinated, while many others
disappeared without trace.

After the signing of the peace agreement, the personal safety
of journalists was no longer under such threat, although harassment and intimidation were still common occurrences. Despite
some moves to establish a legal basis for independent print and
broadcasting companies, the state has continued to exercise a
stranglehold. Alleged violations of the laws on state secrets and
the 'honour and dignity of the president' often serve as pretexts

for closing or suspending independent media outlets. The result is that there is a high degree of self-imposed censorship. This ensures that controversial subjects (especially those linked to political issues) are either ignored or treated with utmost circumspection. Thus, the material that does appear is heavily biased in favour of the government

Other constraints on the media include the huge financial cost of equipment, and problems in securing basic supplies. This is a particular burden for the print media, both independent and state-owned, who often find it difficult to obtain paper. Moreover, the demand for newspapers has fallen sharply during the 1990s; this is partly because of poverty and the constant pressures of every-day living, partly, too, because there is a lack of trust in press. As a result, circulation levels are very low and most publications appear at irregular intervals. At the time of writing, there is no national daily newspaper of any political leaning in Tajikistan. Access to the Internet is restricted to a tiny, highly privileged, section of society.

The majority of the population relies on television broadcasts for news coverage. There is a state radio and television company and some independently-owned television companies operate; transmissions are in Tajik, Uzbek, Russian and, occasionally, English. It is possible to receive some foreign stations (e.g. from Russia and Iran, also the BBC World Service and the Voice of America). However, only 4.5 per cent of the population have televisions and even fewer have radios; long-distance personal contacts are limited by the fact that only 2.7 per cent have telephones (and only 2.3 per cent have motor vehicles).[53] Compared with the Soviet era, when periodical publications were cheap and plentiful (and widely read), and radio and television coverage was available to over 90 per cent of the population, this is an extraordinary shrinking of the public space, at least in terms of density of contacts.

Voluntary and Informal Associations

There are several types of informal association in Tajikistan today. The largest group is based on traditional structures, drawing on family and vicinage bonds, underpinned by client-patron relations. Political and economic 'clans' represent another important category; these include some traditional elements (e.g. kinship loyalties), but are largely self-selecting, bound together by mutually reinforcing spheres of power and social leverage. Western-style non-governmental organisations (NGOs) are a new phenomenon in Tajikistan. This form of activity first appeared here in the mid-1990s and is still very shallowly rooted. The same is true of independent political parties. At popular level, both these types of association – NGOs and independent political parties – tend to be regarded with suspicion. Finally, there are several small associations that cater for specific interests (e.g. faith communities, cultural projects and sports); most of these are informal and primarily concerned with matters of internal organisation.

Family and community institutions

In pre-Soviet times, as during the Soviet period, informal institutions played a very important role in Tajik society.[54] They included the extended family (*avlod*), the congregation of the local mosque (*jamoat*), and groups of local residents defined by such physical confines as the local town ward (*mahalla*), the neighbourhood (*guzar*), the street (*kucha*), and in later times, the apartment block. Such communities were often mono-ethnic (and members were frequently inter-related), but they could also include representatives of other backgrounds (e.g. Russians or Germans). These various bodies extended practical and moral assistance to fellow members. One of the most common activities was to organise community help (*hashar*) in such endeavours as repairing a neighbour's house, building a local facility, or helping in preparations for weddings and other large-scale celebrations and ritual events. These informal institutions helped to preserve a private space, outside the control of the authorities. They served as an important bonding mechanism, fostering communal identity and solidarity; they also reinforced social values and 'civilised' norms of behaviour, acting as both moral mentor and moral censor.

Communal links were underpinned by regular meetings known

as *gashtak* or *gap* (conversation).[55] Akin to a private dining club, its members would be drawn from particular circles of professional colleagues, social acquaintances or neighbours. These gatherings were typically a male activity, but in some places there were female circles and even mixed-sex *gashtak/gap* groups. Less structured meetings also existed, likewise centred round the communal consumption of food and drink.[56] These were all occasions that enabled people to congregate in a relaxed, intimate way, knowing that they could trust fellow guests. Members of such circles acknowledged a social obligation to assist one another whenever possible. This in turn encouraged group mobilisation as a means of self-help. Not least, these circles served as an independent channel for the dissemination and discussion of news and current affairs. The bonds created in such circles were often so powerful that they would be 'inherited' by the children of members, who would regard each other as kin and rely on each other for help.

Since independence, as discussed above, there has been a loosening of family and community bonds. Nevertheless, in most cities and towns the *mahalla* still provides local residents with some degree of moral and practical support. However, attempts by the government and by international aid organisations to use the *mahalla* organisation as a conduit for the provision of social welfare has distorted its function by giving it a semi-bureaucratic status.[57] In some areas *mahalla* officials now receive regular salaries from the state. The practice of *gashtak/gap* (and similar informal gatherings) has also declined. The sheer expense is daunting, hence such meetings are increasingly confined to more prosperous circles. Yet patronage networks based on former *gashtak/gap* ties are still strong. Indeed, they are assuming greater importance. These personal bonds, which mimic family relationships, are for many the only safety net that remains to them.

Political-economic 'clans'

The political-economic 'clans' of the Soviet period have also undergone some modification. There has been a change in elite structures, with the balance of power shifting, in geographical

terms, from the north to the south. This has brought new individuals into positions of authority and influence, and at the same
time ousted previous 'patrons'. Initially, the newcomers were accompanied by their own networks of clients. Gradually, however,
new alliances have been established, leading to the formation of
new cliques. These sometimes cut across regional boundaries,
especially in the higher echelons; likewise, they may incorporate
clients of leaders who have now lost standing, thereby acquiring
additional social breadth and depth.

These new associations are cemented by various means, including joint business ventures, marriage ties and regular socialising
(e.g. *gashtak/gap*). Such groupings act as informal, covert corporations, serving group interests without necessarily having
reference to, or acknowledging responsibility for, wider community or national interests. Actual power rests in their hands rather
than in the formal institutions of governance. Indeed, it would
not be much of an exaggeration to say that the 'state' is a jigsaw of
interlocking 'clan' perquisites, lightly clad in conventional
structures.

Non-governmental organisations

In the Soviet era, there existed a wide array of political, professional, cultural and social institutions, dominated and controlled
by the Communist Party-state apparatus. For most of this period
there were no non-governmental organisations (NGOs). In the
late 1980s, in the more liberal atmosphere of the perestroika
period, some socio-political movements did begin to appear and
a few independent parties were even granted official registration.
In Tajikistan there was a sudden blossoming of this type of activity
(see above). This development was cut short by the civil war and
it was not until the mid-1990s that NGOs began to re-appear.

The government of Tajikistan now actively encourages the formation of NGOs. A law on 'Public Associations' was adopted in
1991; at that time it covered both NGOs and political parties. In
1998, new laws were introduced that differentiated between these
activities. Public associations (defined as voluntary, non-

commercial associations set up by public initiative) now enjoy certain tax exemptions and lower registration fees.[58] In order to establish an NGO, three founder members are required, as well as a charter and supporting documentation. In the past five years, over 400 such associations have been created. The largest group (comprising approximately a fifth of the total number of NGOs) is active in fields relating to the needs of children and young people; the second largest group is devoted to gender issues, with particular emphasis on raising the status of women and supporting them in access to education and business. Other sectors that have attracted significant attention are civil society, education, health, social protection, ecology, culture, business training, mass media and science. Many NGOs cover a number of different issues. Women play an active role in these associations; approximately a third are headed by women. In recent years some NGOs have begun to participate in government social welfare programmes.[59]

These developments seem promising on paper. Yet the reality is somewhat different. The NGOs that are most active are funded by international agencies; many are staffed at least in part by foreign personnel. Local Tajik NGOs are small and lack funds; they also tend to be badly managed. Many fail to show any signs of activity after registration.[60] The motivation for establishing an NGO often has more to do with seeking paid employment rather than addressing the particular needs of the community. In Tajikistan (as elsewhere in the CIS), bright, educated individuals have become adept at understanding the predilections of foreign donors and fashioning project proposals for NGOs accordingly. Unfortunately, donor agency agendas do not always have much immediate relevance to conditions in Tajikistan. Nevertheless, this appears to matter little to prospective applicants, whose scruples as to the usefulness of a given project are easily brushed aside in the chase to secure a grant.[61] This is not to say that they obtain funding under false pretences. Most do at least attempt to fulfil the project specifications (e.g. holding the required number of seminars), but very often these are token activities that make little discernible impact on their environment.[62] This judgement may seem unduly cynical, but it is not intended as a criticism, rather as a reminder of the harsh reality of life in Tajikistan today. Jobs are scarce and in any case, hardly provide a living wage. By contrast, foreign funded NGOs seem to offer princely remuneration. It is no coincidence that women are so well represented in the NGO field: they have few alternative options for finding work. This has to some extent created the impression that NGOs are not 'serious'. The credibility of this type of activity has been further undermined by the gulf that too often exists between the stated aims of NGOs and the actual implementation of their programmes.

Political parties and movements

Signs of re-emergent pluralism are to be seen in the revival, albeit limited, of party politics. In March 1993, opposition organisations were banned, leaving the Communist Party as the only functioning party. From 1994 onwards, several pro-government parties appeared, the most influential of which was the People's Democratic Party of Tajikistan; this is now headed by President Rahmonov. In 1998, a new law 'On Political Parties' was passed. Strict criteria were introduced for official registration (a prerequisite for participation in elections). These include at least 1,000 members, drawn from all parts of Tajikistan, a written manifesto, and payment of a substantial registration fee (US$500).

By late 1999, there were some eight political parties in existence. All the previously outlawed opposition parties were granted legal registration. Several others, however, failed to secure registration (or later had registration suspended or annulled owing to false submissions). Six parties qualified for participation in the parliamentary elections held in February 2000, although only three succeeded in obtaining more than 5 per cent of the vote. These were the People's Democratic Party of Tajikistan (which won just over 57 per cent of the vote), the Communist Party (some 23 per cent) and the Islamic Rebirth Party (some 3 per cent).[63]

There are also a number of public movements. These are similar to political parties, but registration requirements are less stringent and some of their activities have a more social base. The largest by far (founded in 1997, numbering some 1.5 million members, among them the president, the prime minister, and a large number of senior bureaucrats) is the semi-official Movement for National Unity and Revival of Tajikistan. The stated aim of this organisation is the promotion of peace and social harmony. Other movements include the Congress of National Unity (founded in 1995) and the National Movement of Tajikistan (founded in 1996). They, too, aim to promote peaceful coexistence and national unity. However, the former is dominated by representatives from the north (Soghd), the latter by those from the centre-east (Garm and Darvaz); their stance sometimes suggests an element of crypto-regional opposition.

The re-appearance of a multiparty political system, however embryonic, is a welcome sign of normalisation. Arguably, Tajikistan is today one of the most open societies in Central Asia (though this must, of course be understood, in relative terms). Nevertheless, there is little sign of the popular ferment of ideas and debate that marked the 1989–1991 period. The new parties are small, under-funded and for the most part dominated by a single individual; they also tend to have a very narrow social base. They attract little support from the wider public. This is not surprising. It is in part a result of government harassment (sometimes open, sometimes covert) which makes it difficult to maintain a sustained programme of action. There is, though, another reason why these parties are not popular. Members of this new generation of activists are familiar with the principles of Western democracy and will argue passionately over the iniquities of the political system in Tajikstan, making fluent use of current academic terminology. Yet they have little knowledge, and even less interest, in the social and economic problems of their own country. Their range of vision seems not to extend far beyond their offices: the chronic stagnation of agriculture, the shattered industries, the crisis in education – problems such as these evoke scant concern.

It is difficult to escape the impression that the constituencies of these aspiring political leaders are to be found in civil liberty organisations in North America and Western Europe, not among their fellow citizens. Certainly, it could be argued that in Tajikistan

today the centralisation of power, and in particular, the accumu-
lation of power in the hands of a small ruling elite, is a serious
issue. It is thus important to draw attention to questions of democratic governance, and to contest the boundaries of political
discourse as set by the incumbent regime. Nevertheless, if such
concerns are not balanced by real engagement with the problems
that affect people in their everyday lives, it is small wonder that
these would-be politicians are regarded by many in Tajikistan as
an irrelevance.

Other voluntary associations

There are a number of associations that are linked to specific
spheres of activity. Some of these are of a religious nature. In 1998
there were 237 registered 'Friday' (large) mosques, with substantial congregations. In addition to Islam, 18 other faiths are
represented in Tajikistan. These, too, have community organisations. The largest Christian denomination is the Russian
Orthodox; its adherents are almost entirely Slav. There are also
several other Christian denominations, including a number of
Protestant evangelical sects; they have attracted a few Tajik con-
verts, but most members of these churches are from ethnic
minorities. Other religions include Bahaism and various new faiths.
The various ethnic groups also have their own associations. These
are concerned primarily with the welfare of their own communities. They have contact with designated government officials, but
have few links with the wider public, or with one another.

There is an Independent Federation of Trade Unions, with
some fifteen or so branches representing professions such as teaching and engineering, also the creative arts (architects, painters,
composers and others).[64] These developed out of the Soviet-era
professional unions (*profsoyuzy*). Their function is to protect members' rights and to negotiate the best possible working agreements.
The Youth Union, successor to the Young Communist League
(*Komsomol*), is likewise now an independent organisation; however, it has very meagre funding and consequently, is severely
restricted in its activities. There are also a few smaller bodies that

seek to promote particular cultural or intellectual initiatives. One of the most active of these groups is the Ziyadullo Shahidi International Foundation. It was founded in 1992 by Munira Shahidi in memory of her father, one of Tajikistan's most renowned composers. It conducts seminars on Tajik music and poetry, organises recitals, and holds exhibitions of works by Tajik artists. Recently it launched an academic journal devoted to music and other cultural issues. A project such as this, though quite limited in scope, nevertheless makes a significant contribution to cultural outreach not only by re-affirming the importance of the Tajik cultural heritage, but also by re-involving people in cultural activities.

A number of small local associations are devoted to sport and other leisure activities. In the context of Tajikistan today, such groups sometimes have greater significance than is immediately apparent. They help to revive a sense of community based on shared interests. They also help to foster respect for an agreed set of rules. For the younger generation, born in a time of conflict and anarchy, this is a small but important step towards the restoration of law and order. The football club in the town of Kulyab (the personal initiative of the local governor) is a positive example of an attempt to use organised sport as a means of combating the crushing *anomie* of the young.

Development Programmes: The Case of Gorno-Badakhshan

During the civil war, and in the years following the peace agreement, Tajikistan received substantial humanitarian aid from international donor agencies. Much of this took the form of food aid, particularly in the wake of the drought of 2000. More recently, the emphasis has been shifting to development aid and technical assistance, aimed at facilitating structural reforms and capacity building. The United Nations Development Programme is pursuing several long-term projects. A number of foreign NGOs are engaged in such fields as medical aid and social protection. There are also bilateral programmes in various sectors funded, amongst others, by Canadian, Japanese, Swiss and US agencies, also by the European Union and by individual EU member states.

Some of these programmes provide support for the strengthening of democratic institutions, particularly the media. This has included training for journalists, and start-up capital for independent media organisations.[65] Such undertakings are still at an early stage of development, but if they are maintained, they might eventually contribute to the creation of a more open society.

Of particular significance are the programmes of the Aga Khan Development Network (AKDN). The AKDN has been has been present in Tajikistan since the early 1990s, when it provided much-needed humanitarian relief to Gorno-Badakhshan. Its activities have since been expanded into an integrated programme of economic, social, educational and cultural development. It collaborates with the Tajik government, and a wide range of national and international partners, including the World Bank, and government agencies from Canada, Germany, Switzerland, the USA and the UK. The main geographic focus of the activities of the AKDN is Gorno-Badakhshan and the adjacent Garm region (central Tajikistan). However, some of the AKDN projects have been so successful at the micro-level that they have made a favourable impression on the central government and are gradually beginning to have an impact on national policy planning in Tajikistan. The operational work of the AKDN, and the related Aga Khan Foundation, is implemented by specialised agencies (e.g. the Mountain Societies Development and Support Programme, the Aga Khan Education Fund and the Aga Khan Humanities Project for Central Asia).

The most impressive aspect of the AKDN activities in Gorno-Badakhshan is the focus on nurturing social capital.[66] A central strategy has been the strengthening of institutional structures at village level, so as to enhance community-level participation in decision-making. A sense of shared social and ethical responsibility is encouraged by the development of community-based management of natural resources (e.g. water storage and soil conservation) and also of the construction of local infrastructure such as roads and storage facilities. These projects echo the traditional practice of *hashar* (see above), but give it a more focused and formal role. Likewise, Soviet-era skills and organisational experience have been re-directed to contribute to the development of dynamic new activities.

An important innovation has been the creation of Village Organisations. These entities are partnerships between the local communities and the Mountain Societies Development and Support Programme (MSDSP). When local communities (as represented by a significant majority of local households) enter into an agreement with the MSDSP to form a Village Organisation, they undertake to adhere to certain procedures to promote public accountability. These include the holding of regular meetings and the open election of senior officials. The Village Organisations are responsible for prioritising their own requirements; the MSDSP provides such training and support as is necessary for the implementation of these activities. The aim is to promote locally based socio-economic initiatives, thereby raising standards of living and enhancing the quality of life. By the end of June 2000, just under 400 such organisations had been established in Gorno-Badakhshan, embracing almost 37,000 members and representing some 80–90 percent of local households.[67] The needs of women receive special attention through the Women's Groups that are affiliated to the Village Organisations. A number of projects are being implemented through these Women's Groups, including micro-credit schemes for such ventures as baking and selling bread.

The ultimate goal of the AKDN programmes is to promote social cohesion, co-operative behaviour and sustainable self-sufficiency. This can only be achieved through community empowerment. Education, in the broadest and most inclusive sense, is vital to this endeavour. Accordingly, this sector has received particular attention. The education programme of the Aga Khan Foundation (AKF) was initiated in 1996. Initially, it focused on relief work for the school-aged population (numbering some 55,000 children) of Gorno-Badakhshan. More recently, there has been greater emphasis on institutional development and capacity building. This has included the training of teachers and educational administrators, as well as development of curricula and materials. In tertiary education, a central concern has been the development of a core curriculum in the humanities. This advocates an inclusive approach to the study of the history and culture of Central Asia, drawing on the diverse traditions that have contributed to the complex heritage of this region. The aim is to build bridges across cultural, religious and ethnic divides and thus to promote tolerance and greater mutual understanding.

A forward-looking venture is the founding of a new institution of higher education, the University of Central Asia. In August 2000, the Presidents of Tajikistan, Kyrgyzstan and Kazakhstan, together with the Aga Khan, entered jointly into an international treaty establishing the new university (the first private institution of higher education to be internationally chartered). The founding documents were signed at official ceremonies held in the respective capitals of the three states. Substantial funding is already in place. The main campus is to be in Khorog, capital of Gorno-Badakhshan, on land donated for this purpose by the government of Tajikstan. The construction and planning phases are expected to take some six to eight years to complete, although some academic activities are already taking place in temporary accommodation. At a later stage, centres will be established in Kyrgyzstan and Kazakhstan, likewise in other countries that may choose to join the university as participating states.

The University of Central Asia plans to offer degree programmes, research facilities and training courses. The institution will be strictly secular in character; courses on the history and ethical systems of the major world religions will be taught by specialists in those fields, but theology will not be part of the curriculum. The core mission is to serve the educational and developmental needs of peoples of the mountain regions of Central Asia. Admission is to be based on merit (supported by a programme of financial aid for those in need) and co-educational. The decision to use English as the language of instruction is a bold attempt to create an environment in which all students are equally challenged linguistically, and at the same time to provide them with the means of accessing a wider world of information and opportunity.

The activities of the AKDN in Gorno-Badakhshan have been

described here at greater length than any of the other aid and development programmes in Tajikistan because they are in many ways unique. Firstly, much time and effort is devoted to consultation with local communities; projects are designed jointly, taking into account both short term and long term needs. This gives local communities a sense of ownership of such activities. Secondly, projects are constructed in such a way as to be ultimately self-sustaining; this reinforces volunteerism and self-reliance, thereby avoiding the initiative-sapping trap of over-dependence on external aid. Thirdly, the human and material support provided by the donor is commensurate with the scale of the project; this ensures that the implementation of goals can proceed in an orderly fashion. Finally, there is a high degree of complementarity between the different aspects of the AKDN programme; this integrated approach enhances the overall impact. Most other donor agencies in Tajikistan lack the resources – and possibly the sensitivity – to engage so fully with local communities. Consequently, their efforts tend to have little lasting effect. Still worse, they sometimes inadvertently engender a cynically exploitative attitude on the part of the intended beneficiaries.

Nevertheless, while acknowledging the positive aspects of the AKDN programme, it is important to temper optimism with an awareness that several projects are still at an early stage of implementation. Initial results are encouraging, but it is difficult to predict how effective they are likely to be in the longer term – or indeed, to judge the time span that will be required for them to become firmly established. Moreover, conditions in Gorno-Badakhshan, the main focus of AKDN activities to date, are very specific. Geographically, this is a remote, isolated region. The population numbers a mere 206,000 (3.4 per cent of the total population of Tajikistan), subdivided into half a dozen or so distinct linguistic groups. Nevertheless, despite local differences, they largely share a common culture. Most are Ismailis, and thus are predisposed to accept the guidance of their Imam, His Highness the Aga Khan. This helps to promote a close identification with the objectives of the AKDN even amongst those who do not regard themselves as devout believers. Elsewhere in Tajikistan the environment may not be so receptive. The AKDN is gradually expanding its geographic reach (and is already active in the Garm region), but it is likely that many more years will be required before it encompasses the country as a whole.[68]

Prospects for Civil Society in Tajikistan

In the main body of this chapter the term 'civil society' is almost entirely absent. This is intentional. The aim was to map contemporary Tajik experiences (admittedly, as interpreted by an outsider) before attempting to draw conclusions. On the basis of the account presented in the foregoing sections, it seems clear that conditions in Tajikistan are not conducive to the emergence of civil society. This is not simply because of the lack of key institutions, but rather to the prevalent social and political culture. The theoretical discourse on civil society is rooted in political modernity. This is premised on certain attributes of the state, of society, and the nature of state-society interaction.

These assumptions are scarcely applicable to the situation in Tajikistan. Here, the boundaries between state and society are blurred – not, of course, in any Gramscian sense, but because of the highly personalised nature of power. Formal institutions, such as parliament, the judiciary, or even the state itself, are 'virtual' entities, largely devoid of genuine authority. Real power, from the village level to national government, lies in the hands of informal 'clan' networks (described above).[69] The legitimacy of the regime may be decked in the pomp of ritual elections, but the actual contest is determined by the ability of one faction or another to muster superior armed forces – and then to placate supporters and rivals alike by the discreet dispensation of patronage. Accumulated power flows to specific individuals and groups, not to the notional 'state'.

Society has been pulverised by a long sequence of violence, rupture and displacement. Social cohesion has been destroyed to such an extent that group solidarity is low and thus there is very limited scope for group mobilisation or societal self-organisation. In Tajikstan today it is not only that there is little political

participation, there is also an absence of campaigning social movements devoted to issues such as the environment, feminism and
civil rights. Networking is restricted to personal concerns and ambitions. There is scarcely a trace of an 'emerging public' that seeks
to influence official policy and to shape civic life. There are few
channels for the dissemination of news and information. Despite
some institutional attempts to create independent media outlets,
as discussed previously, there is still a high level of state control
and of self-censorship. The public response to the dearth of news
reporting is passive indifference. This may be ascribed to such
factors as a lack of trust in the media and to preoccupation with
mundane problems of subsistence. Whatever the reasons, however, the attitude is symptomatic of the wider withdrawal from the
public space.

The Tajik state today is as weak and impotent as is society as a
whole. Far from being the omnipotent monolith of the Soviet era,
it is scarcely able to discharge the basic functions that are expected
of government. Thus, its ability to regulate the economy is limited, as, too, is its ability to provide adequate social protection.
The provision for health care and education is meagre, well below the level of the Soviet era.[70] The state's powers of coercion
are puny. Bodies such as the army, security services and police
force are poorly paid, ill-equipped and of uncertain temper; currently their efforts are largely directed towards the fight to
eliminate the 'warlords' – ex-field commanders of the civil war
who still run private armies. This is a question of regime security
as much as the safety of the general public. In other spheres of
activity, state coercion is scarcely more effective than is state
protection or state regulation. In these conditions, calls to 'roll
back the state', or more grandiosely, to 'interrogate the state',
such as are raised in theoretical treatises on civil society, have little resonance.

It is possible to interpret the nascent pluralism of the late 1980s
as an embryonic form of civil society. This was the time when the
concept of civil society[71] was being discussed in intellectual circles
in Russia, the Baltic republics and in other politically active centres
in the Soviet Union, not to mention Eastern European states such

as Poland and Czechoslovakia. There was very little echo of these theoretical debates in Tajikistan (or indeed, elsewhere in Central Asia), but there was a new spirit of self-confidence, a receptiveness to new ideas, and a determination to challenge the existing order. Had there been a longer period of peace and stability, these inchoate movements might have might have become more focused, and eventually institutionalised. This did not happen. Sudden independence, followed shortly after by the outbreak of civil war, turned pluralism into anarchy. By the time peace was restored some five years later, the public had lost trust in independent, non-state voices. Opposition – dissent of any form – now tends to be regarded as a threat to the fragile peace settlement.

The appearance of NGOs has sometimes been regarded as signifying the emergence of civil society. Yet too often these are emblematic institutions, more akin to private financial enterprises than representative associational bodies that seek to impact upon public policy. There are some shining exceptions, but for the most part, the NGO sector is of peripheral significance in Tajikistan today. Independent political parties are similarly detached from society. Various reasons may be adduced to explain this delinkage. Perhaps the most significant factor is the marginalisation of the intelligentsia. Since independence, academics, creative artists and other professionals have lost social and financial status, and likewise the institutional support that was previously provided by the state. This has had a deracinating effect. Some have responded by deliberately distancing themselves, mentally if not physically, from society. Others have turned to 'business' (i.e. diverse commercial transactions), withdrawing from any on-going intellectual endeavour. A few have reoriented their interests, using their talents to 're-nationalise' the culture and the historical record in accordance with officially approved ideological tenets. Such undertakings have, in effect, turned them into state functionaries (a reprise of their roles during the Soviet era). The same strictures apply to the Muslim community: there is currently no spiritual or intellectual leadership. Some senior clerics have been co-opted by the government, while others have turned to the ubiquitous pursuit of 'business'. Most are careful not to transgress the limits of routine functions.

Given the conditions described in this paper, the civil society discourse is not a helpful lens through which to examine present-day Tajikistan. Only the most superficial similarities to any Western theoretical postulates are to be found, hence this is surely an inappropriate analytical category. Proposed Muslim approaches (as discussed elsewhere in this volume) seem equally irrelevant. To insist upon the application of such a framework merely because it enjoys cult status leads to distortion and self-delusion (calling to mind comparisons with the Cinderella's ugly sisters, who hacked off toes and heels in order to squeeze their feet into the magic slipper).

A more constructive approach to understanding civic processes in contemporary Tajikistan might be to seek signs of the re-emergence of social and ethical responsibility. There are indeed indications that this is beginning to occur. It must be stressed, however, that examples of this ethical imperative are small scale, isolated and comparatively rare. They include the case of a young couple using their own resources to teach a clutch of street children to read and write; a few friends caring for handicapped babies; a group of adults training the local sports club.[72] These efforts might seem insignificant, but they do bear witness to the beginnings of a re-engagement with society, a reviving sense of citizenship. They also reveal an encouraging degree of self-reliance in solving communal problems. These are qualities that training programmes such as those of the AKDN projects, described above, are also seeking to develop. Community empowerment, coupled with spontaneous grassroots' initiatives, could in time generate the benign momentum that would permit genuine societal healing and recovery to take place. This would allow Tajikistan to shape institutions appropriate to its needs – possibly its own version of 'civil society' – combining traditional values with Islamic teachings, the best elements of the Soviet legacy and relevant Western and international experience. This can only happen, however, if peace and stability are maintained. Regional and national security is by no means assured; in the wake of the

American-led campaign against the Taliban and their cohorts after September 11, 2001, events are still unfolding and the situation remains volatile.[73] Yet post-conflict progress towards reconstruction and development in Tajikistan, for all its shortcomings, does give modest grounds for optimism. There can be no easy or rapid solutions, but the outlook is more hopeful today than at any time in the past decade.

Notes

Note: No attempt has been made here to apply a consistent system of transliteration. If anglicised versions of Tajik names are current, they have been used in preference to strict renderings of the original forms (e.g. Bukhara not Bukhoro, Kulyab not Kulob, Leninabad not Leninobod). No differentiation has been made between the sound h (as in hat) or ch (as in loch); both are generally represented by h (unless, as in Khujand, kh has become the accepted form). The Russian term 'Gorno-Badakhshan' has been retained since it is used by the Tajik government in all non-Tajik language documents.

1. N. Chandoke, *State and Civil Society: Explorations in Political Theory* (New Delhi, 1995), p.38.

2. The account that is presented here is of necessity a very brief summary of highly complex issues. For a fuller examination, see S. Akiner, *Tajikistan: Reconciliation or Disintegration?* (London, 2001).

3. The origin of the term 'Tajik' is obscure. The most popular explanation is that it is derived from *toj* 'crown' (hence the use of this symbol on the national flag). In the medieval period it was used in the general sense of 'Persian' (as opposed to 'Turk').

4. The majority is located in Gorno-Badakhshan, though many Pamiris are now settled in other parts of Tajikistan and also elsewhere in the Commonwealth of Independent States, e.g. Kyrgyzstan. Outside Tajikistan, there are an estimated 30–40,000 Pamiris in the neighbouring mountains of Afghanistan, China and Pakistan.

5. One senior Tajik official commented: 'As an illustration, let me give you an example of the occupations of the mountain Tajiks ... they supply snow to the towns and collect brushwood which they take to the nearest bazaar'. R. Masov, *Istoriya topornogo razdeleniya* (Dushanbe, 1991), p.44.

6. It was based on the northern group of Tajik dialects; lexical and grammatical differences with standard Persian were emphasised, thereby distancing the language of Soviet Tajikistan from that of Iran.

7. For a fuller discussion of the creation of the Tajik nation and the Tajik state see *Tajikistan: Reconciliation or Disintegration?*, pp.11–18.

8. UNDP, *Tajikistan: Human Development Report 1999*, p.9.

9. Of these, 30.5 per cent are located in Soghd province in the north; 35.1 percent in Khatlon province in the south; and 31.9 per cent in the central regions (known as the 'Regions of Republican Subordination') and the capital.

10. The terms 'traditional' and 'tradition' are used in this paper to refer loosely to pre-Soviet patterns of behaviour, social organisation and culture. However, these were not static phenomena and there is no implication here that they were 'always thus' from time immemorial.

11. Tajiks proved to be immensely gifted in these new fields, producing artists of international standing (e.g. the world-famous ballet dancer Farukh Ruzimatov). The same enforced (but also successful) cultural transformation affected sport and entertainment; thus, Soviet-style circus replaced traditional juggling and acrobatic acts.

12. Some collective farms concentrated on the production of single crops (e.g. cotton), while others had a more diverse profile. The chairmen and senior officials of large collective farms were powerful individuals, regarded locally and nationally (and sometimes even at all-Union level) with great respect.

13. There were three main waves of population transfers: 1925–40, 1947–60, and 1968–70. The mountain peoples found it hard to adapt to the hot, humid climate of the plains and in the early years many children and older people died. See *Tajikistan: Reconciliation or Disintegration?*, pp.21–4; also K. Abdullaev, *Exiles of Bolshevism* (London, 2002).

14. The largest group was the German. Other deportees included Bulgarians, Koreans and even some Dutch (descendants of settlers in the Ukraine).

15. This is not to say, however, that they necessarily perceived it to be so. See S. Akiner, 'Between Tradition and Modernity: The Dilemma Facing Contemporary Central Asian Women', in Mary Buckley, ed., *Post-Soviet Women: From the Baltic to Central Asia* (Cambridge, UK, 1997), pp.261–304.

16. The closest analogy for these groupings is probably the medieval concept of an 'affinity'. See, for example, C. Given-Wilson, *The Royal*

Household and the King's Affinity: Service, Politics and Finance in England 1360–1413 (New Haven and London, 1986), esp. pp.202–4.

17. See further S. Akiner, *Central Asia: New Arc of Crisis?*, Royal United Services Institute for Defence Studies (London, 1993); 'Ethnicity, Nationality and Citizenship as Expressions of Self-determination in Central Asia' in D. Clark and R. Williamson, ed., *Self-determination: International Perspectives* (London, 1996), pp.249–74.

18. S. Akiner, 'Islam, the State and Ethnicity in Central Asia in Historical Perspective', *Religion, State and Society: The Keston Journal*, 24, 2–3 (1996), pp.91–132 (esp. pp.106–20); also M. Atkin, *The Subtlest Battle: Islam in Soviet Tajikistan*, Foreign Policy Research Institute (Philadelphia, 1989); Y. Ro'i, *Islam in the Soviet Union: From World War II to Perestroika* (London, 2000).

19. Born in 1954, he came from a line of eminent Muslim clerics. He studied at the madrasas in Bukhara and Tashkent, then went to Amman University to take a degree in Islamic law. Thereafter, he worked in the Muslim Spiritual Directorate in Tashkent until appointed head of the Tajik Qaziyat.

20. Amongst the intellectuals at this time, anti-Islamic sentiment was quite strong. As Shodmon Yusuf, founder of the Democratic Party of Tajikistan, commented in 1989: 'I feel disgusted that you should link the culture of my nation with Islam', S. Gretsky, 'Profile: Qadi Akbar Turajonzoda', *Central Asia Monitor*, 1 (1994), p.20.

21. There were three main movements: *Rastokhez* (Rebirth) National Front, the Democratic Party of Tajikistan, and *La'li- Badakhshon* (The Ruby of Badakhshan). One of the chief objectives of the programmes of *Rastokhez* and the Democratic Party was the revival of Iranian culture. *La'li-Badakhshon* supported parliamentary reform, but looked for autonomy for Badakhshan.

22. See Sh. Tadjbakhsh, 'The "Tajik Spring of 1992"', *Central Asia Monitor*, 2 (1993), pp.21–9, for a firsthand account of the political parties of this period; also S. Dudoignon, 'Political Parties and Forces in Tajikistan, 1989–1993', in M-R. Djalili, F. Grare and S. Akiner, ed., *Tajikistan: The Trials of Independence* (London, 1998), pp.52–85.

23. According to official statistics, some 60 per cent of the population was under 16 years of age. See *Naselenie SSSR 1987* (Moscow, 1988), p.140.

24. For an account of the peace process, see K. Abdullaev and C. Barnes, ed., *Politics of Compromise: The Tajikistan Peace Process*, Accord, Issue 10 (2001), Conciliation Resources (London, 2001).

25. There are no agreed statistics on war casualties. The estimates given here are based on UNDP, *Tajikistan: Human Development Report 1998*, p.35; also, *Tajikistan: Refugee Reintegration and Conflict Prevention*, Forced Migration Projects of the Open Society Institute (New York, 1998), pp.6–8.

26. The negative stereotyping that is now to be heard even in 'polite' conversation would, in most other parts of the world, be considered little short of racist. In Tajikistan today, however, it is not seen as in any way remarkable. On the contrary, it is regarded as 'objective'; yet there is no equivalent degree of self-awareness and self-criticism.

27. During the civil war there were harrowing reports of young daughters being sold into prostitution in order to acquire the sack of flour that would enable other members of the family to survive. (Communications to the author by Tajik acquaintances in 2000–2001.)

28. See further S. Akiner, *Islamic Peoples of the Soviet Union* (London, 1986) 2nd ed., p.306.

29. This is not, however, reflected in official statistics. The male/female ratio, as stated in January 2000, was almost exactly 50:50; a similar gender balance was recorded in 1970 and 1987. Cf. UNDP, *Tajikistan: Human Development Report 2000*, p.17; *Islamic Peoples*, p.306; *Naselenie SSSR 1987* (Moscow, 1988), p.46.

30. On the feminisation of crime see UNDP, *Human Development Report 2000*, p.92. Also, Sh. Tadjbakhsh, 'Women and War in Tajikistan', *Central Asia Monitor*, 1, (1994) (online supplement); and M. Aripova, 'Narcobusiness in Tajikistan – in hands of women', *Asia-Plus*, Bulletin 13 (51), 1996, <http://internews.ras.ru/Asia-Plus.htm>.

31. See UNDP, *Human Development Report 2000*, pp.33–9.

32. Colette Harris, *Control and Subversion: Gender, Islam and Socialism in Tajikistan* (Ph.D. thesis, University of Amsterdam, 2000, publication forthcoming 2002) gives the fullest account to date of this issue. See also UNDP, *Human Development Report 2000*, esp. pp.51–2.

33. UNDP, *Human Development Report 1998*, esp. pp.32–46.

34. There are no exact statistics, but numbers certainly run into the thousands. A UNHCR programme provides care for 2,000 such children. See UNDP, *Human Development Report 1998*, p.48; also *Human Development Report 2000*, p.35.

35. *Refugee Reintegration*, pp.48–54. Also personal communications by foreign aid workers with field experience in Tajikistan.

36. According to official estimates, some 33 per cent of the population is 'very poor', and almost 20 per cent are 'destitute' (i.e. with a per

diem income of below $1.075 at PPP). See UNDP, *Human Development Report 2000*, p.61; also P. Foroughi, *1998 Socio-Economic Survey of Household, Farms and Bazaars in Tajikistan* (USAID-funded, unpublished). Poverty exists not only in terms of income, but also in access to resources.

37. Official statistics consistently under-report the level of joblessness. When hidden unemployment and temporary unemployment are taken into account, the real level of unemployment is probably as high as 30 per cent. It should be noted, however, that there is considerable regional variation (UNDP, *Human Development Report 2000*, p.19).

38. However, there is considerable under-reporting of data on births, owing to social factors (e.g. illegitimacy), as well as to the high registration fee (UNDP, *Human Development Report 2000*, p.17).

39. Cf. UNDP, *Human Development Report 1998*, p.81; *Human Development Report 2000*, p.19.

40. UNDP, *Human Development Report 2000*, p.109.

41. During the Soviet period virtually all school-aged children were in full-time education. However, drop-out rates in primary schools rose from 6 per cent to 20 per cent in 1989–1997 (Aga Khan Foundation's Education Programme in Gorno-Badakhshan, briefing notes, 9 March 2001).

42. 'Heinous' offences accounted for almost two thirds of the crimes committed in 1999. There has also been a distinct upward trend in economic crimes, e.g. the theft of state property. For a break-down of numbers and types of crimes committed in the period 1992–2000, see UNDP, *Human Development Report 2000*, pp.91–3.

43. In 2001, victims included the deputy minister of the interior, the foreign affairs advisor to the president and the minister of culture.

44. In 1999, Afghanistan accounted for 79 per cent (5,674 tonnes) of global production of opium. In 2001, following a Taliban ban on the cultivation of opium poppies the previous year, there was a sharp decline in the harvest (estimated at 1,600 tonnes). However, this had little effect on the flow of narcotics into Tajikistan, since there were large stockpiles along the border.

45. Data from United Nations Office for Drug Control and Crime Prevention, regional office, Tashkent, December 2001. See also Martha B. Olcott and N. Udalova, *Drug Trafficking on the Great Silk Road: The Security Environment in Central Asia*, Working Papers, Carnegie Endowment for International Peace, 11 March 2000.

46. In early 2001, the wholesale price of 1 kg of heroin in Tajikistan was US$981, but even in neighbouring Kazakhstan it was US$9,667, almost ten times higher (ibid.).

47 Personal communication by teachers from Kulyab University, Dushanbe, April 2000. See also UNDP, *Human Development Report 2000*, pp.94–6.

48. Data from United Nations Office for Drug Control and Crime Prevention, regional office, Tashkent, December 2001.

49. See, for example, results of surveys carried out by *Opinion Analysis*, Office of Research Department of State, Washington DC, 6 July 2000.

50. The Soviet-era Qazi, Akbar Turajonzoda, might have been able to achieve this (reviving the mission of regeneration that he was pursuing before the civil war). However, in recent years he has become embroiled in political manoeuvrings and has devoted little time to spiritual matters.

51. For a discussion of the Islamist spectrum in Tajikistan see *Tajikistan: Reconciliation or Disintegration?*, pp.66–70.

52. The Tajik authorities have recently increased their efforts to combat unregistered Muslim clerics (presumably mainly Hezb-i Tahrir supporters). Local officials now have the right to close down unregistered mosques, on the grounds that they might become 'centres of extremism'. In Dushanbe, it is claimed, the number of such mosques far exceeds the registered mosques (*Keston Institute News Service*, 23 November 2001).

53. UNDP, *Human Development Report 2000*, pp.31, 109; data cited in this source are provided by the Tajik State Statistical Agency. Some Tajiks find it scarcely credible that the communication profile of the country should have suffered such massive deterioration. However, official data, as recorded in the annual UNDP *Human Development Reports*, published from 1995 onwards, show a fairly consistent pattern of decline.

54. This section is based on S. Akiner, 'Social and Political Reorganisation in Central Asia: Transition from Pre-Colonial to Post-Colonial Society', in T. Atabaki and J. O'Kane, ed., *Post-Soviet Central Asia* (London, 1998), n.53, p.33. The author is grateful for additional information provided in autumn 2001 by Tajik friends, especially Kamol Abdullaev, Fatima Akhmedova, Sarfaroz Niyozov and Safar Tabari, who also read the entire paper and made valuable comments and suggestions.

55. In some areas both terms are used, elsewhere one or the other predominates.

56. E.g. *tabaq* (literally, 'large platter', i.e. the practice of eating together from a common bowl), *chaq-chaq* (chat), *suhbat* (dialogue), *yak piola choi* (a cup of tea) and *tashkili* (party).

57. UNDP, *Human Development Report 2000*, p.57.

58. Fees for registration of public associations (i.e. NGOs) are as follows: international – US$780; republican – US$240; local – US$165. NGOs with a focus on youth and women pay only half these amounts, while registration for NGOs that are concerned with children's issues is free of charge. See further UNDP, *Human Development Report 1999*, pp.33–4.

59. UNDP, *Human Development Report 1999*, pp.33–5.

60. By 1999, only about 200 NGOs (half the registered number) were actively functioning. UNDP, *Human Development Report 2000*, p.31.

61. The calculated pursuit of project funding is wittily parodied in a playlet by Iskandar Ruas, entitled *Lyubov' moya demokratiya!* (Dushanbe, 2000).

62. It should also be noted that the majority of these projects are located in the capital and in Soghd province, not in rural areas where deprivation is greatest. See UNDP, *Human Development Report 1999*, p.35

63. For a full report on the parliamentary elections of 27 February 2000, see the *Final Report*, Office for Democratic Institutions and Human Rights, Organisation for Security and Cooperation in Europe, Warsaw, 17 May 2000 <http:/www.osce.org/odihr/election/tajioo-1-final.htm>.

64. For numbers of mosques, professional unions etc., see UNDP, *Human Development Report 1999*, p.33.

65. See report by A. Loersch, and M. Grigorian, *Report on the Media Situation in Tajikistan*, CIMERA (Switzerland), October 2000.

66. The views expressed in this section are based upon personal interviews carried out by the author in Tajikistan in 2000–2001, supplemented by informational briefings published by the Aga Khan Development Network.

67. A similar scheme is being introduced in the Garm region, but is currently at a very early stage of implementation.

68. For more information on the AKDN, see <http://www.akdn.org/about.html>.

69. The author is indebted to Oleg Bilyy, of the Institute of Philosophy, Ukrainian National Academy, Deputy Editor-in-Chief of the journal *Political Thought/Politychna Dumka*, for an illuminating discussion on the nature of 'virtual' and 'real' institutions in the post-Soviet space (University of California, Berkeley, October 2001).

70. Available statistics of the Soviet and post-Soviet periods are not easily comparable, but practical observation reveals the scale of the decline in social welfare provision. Some idea of the present level of social

investment can be gained from the following allocations of public expenditures as a percentage of GDP in 1999: 2.1 per cent on education, 1 per cent on health, 2 per cent on social protection, 0.1 per cent on science, 0.35 per cent on culture (UNDP, *Human Development Report 2000*, p.70). GDP per capita at PPP was US$330 (ibid., p.9).

71. In the late 1980s, Mikhail Gorbachev amongst others, frequently spoke of the need for 'civil society', using the term as a synonym for 'law-based society'. See F. Starr in M. Holt Ruffin and Daniel Waugh, ed., *Civil Society in Central Asia* (Seattle and London, 1999), p.28.

72. Random examples personally known to the author, encountered on visits to Tajikistan in 2000–2001.

73. See further *Tajikistan: Reconciliation or Disintegration?*, pp.63–85.

7

Religiosity and Civic Culture in Post-Soviet Azerbaijan: A Sociological Perspective

Tair Faradov

In the aftermath of the collapse of the communist system in Azerbaijan, a plethora of social and ideological trends have filled the vacuum in mass consciousness. The search for new identities and affinities to replace the ascriptive ones of the past is as poignant as anywhere among the former Soviet republics of Central Asia and the Caucasus. At this juncture, the outcomes of sharp citizen-contentions about the country's political and cultural orientation are far from clear. Yet the upshot is that Azerbaijanis in the current transitional phase enjoy a fair degree of political and cultural pluralism, even if this is rather more by default (relatively weak state control capability, uncertainty among socio-political elites about future directions) than by design.

The loosening of Soviet-era control over the public sphere has, in particular, unleashed a fresh dynamism in cultural and religious life. Doctrines of 'scientific atheism' and general state intolerance of religious practice – even of spirituality – have fallen by the wayside. Freedom of religion is guaranteed by Azerbaijan's constitution,[1] and taken at face value by all concerned. Public interest in Islam has deep historical and cultural roots and robust spiritual traditions in the country,[2] and has rapidly increased in recent years, especially among the youth and intellectual class. For many, religious norms and values are becoming a major factor in, if not the principal determinant of, identity, worldview and day-to-day conduct.

Of late, numerous mosques have been built and restored, along with Orthodox churches, Jewish synagogues and other temples. Programmes in religious education are gradually being set up, and an abundance of literature on Islam and other faiths is being published; television and radio broadcasts on religious affairs have proliferated. A multitude of public associations and communities are dedicated to religious activity, as are new scientific and cultural centres. An estimated 2000 religiously-oriented groups are in existence, ranging from officially registered associations to the far more numerous ad hoc mosque-based communities.[3] This state of affairs raises a number of theoretical and practical issues. Certainly, a systematic investigation of the emergent religiosity of Azerbaijan's population – and the ensuing impact on the country's putative development of civic culture as the basis for democratic consolidation – is overdue. In so far as the efficacy of such consolidation depends on the support and participation of ordinary citizens and the empowering effect of social change, the presence and cultivation of values such as tolerance, equality, respect for the rule of law and engaged citizenship is of primary significance.

Among the salient questions that underlie the investigative survey that informs the present analysis are the following: What are the principal tendencies and peculiarities in the development of religious processes in post-Soviet Azerbaijan? What specific factors condition the trend in growing religiosity among citizens? How does religion influence the tenor of public and individual life? Is public opinion inclined more toward secular or religious preferences in terms of social organisation? Are there conditioning factors that may lead to the politicisation of Islam in the future? There is currently a serious lack of reliable empirical data on all these matters in post-Soviet space, and it is this deficit that I have sought to address in the sociological survey at hand.[4]

The Dynamics of Religiosity

A key objective of this survey has been to identify typologies of religiosity relevant to the prevailing phase in Azerbaijan's civic life. The empirical questions mentioned above serve as a logical starting point in preparing such a typology. Respondents were asked about their attitude toward religion, in which regard each respondent could attribute himself only to one of the main typological categories; degrees of religiosity were hence 'fixed'. On the basis of this confessional self-identification, the survey found that 'believers' constituted 62.7 per cent of all respondents; 6.4 per cent said they were 'firm believers'. Those hesitating between belief and non-belief made up 10.6 per cent, while 7.4 per cent considered themselves 'non-believers'. Only 9 per cent were indifferent, and 3.8 per cent regarded themselves to be 'firm atheists'.

Evidently, 'believers' and 'hesitant' are the dominant religious categories; sharing as they do the element of some belief, they may be regarded as the 'religious population' of 79.7 per cent of the population. Another approach would be to divide the populace into three relatively large groups – of believers (69 per cent), hesitant/indifferent (about 20 per cent) and non-believers (11 per cent). Of course, there is a rich diversity of attitudes and positions about religion that the typologies simplify, and sub-categories of belief and non-belief within each of the major categories. Back in the Soviet period, it might be recalled, all non-believers were automatically considered atheists.

What religions do respondents follow? Muslims make up 94.4 per cent of the overall population of 8 million, Orthodox Christians 3.5 per cent, and Jews 1.1 per cent. Representatives of other confessions (such as Lutherans, Baptists and Catholics) form 1 per cent.

A rather complex picture of attitudes toward religion emerged, in terms of continuity and change. Some two-thirds of respondents have remained constant in their views of religion. Just over half indicated that 'they were and still are believers', while nearly 13 per cent maintained that they 'have never believed before and do not believe now either'. A third of respondents have changed their views in the direction of increasing religiosity, of whom 8.7 per cent indicated that 'they never believed before, but have become believers now'. Every fourth respondent 'believed before, but has become more religious now'. A very small proportion have 'estranged themselves from religion' (1.5 per cent), or 'have changed their religion' (1.0 per cent).

Among respondents whose views have changed in the direction of enhanced religiosity, the widest representation is among the 31–40 and 51–60 age groups. For those who had never believed before but have started now, 16–18 year-olds as well as those over 60 are the dominant categories. The rural population is strongly represented among who 'were and still are believers' (73 per cent); among urban dwellers, particularly in Baku, this category makes up only 48 per cent. However, over a recent period, residents of the cities of Gandja (29.7 per cent) and Sumgait (33.5 per cent) profess to have become 'more religious'. Refugees and internally displaced persons have grown drastically in number in the past decade; the proportion that 'believed earlier, but have become more religious' stands at 72 per cent.

Overall, the degree of religiosity in Azerbaijan appears to be on the rise, albeit with the usual peaks and troughs. The first wave of rising religiosity occurred in the phase attending the country's independence; thereafter, the peaks have been lower within a continuum that remains upward. A broad spectrum of motives and reasons for religiosity can be discerned, which are in turn influenced by a several conditioning factors. First, there are the social and psycho-social considerations, in which the family/immediate kin play a vital role. Thus, 14.8 per cent of respondents indicated that their religious affiliation is explained 'by their family traditions, because this has been accepted in the family'. Slightly over 15 per cent stated that they 'have been nurtured in a religious spirit since childhood and received a religious upbringing at home'. For another segment of respondents, ethnic and cultural identity and acts of national self-consciousness were the determining elements. One in seven respondents have adopted religion because 'this meets their national customs and traditions'; one in five explain their adherence to Islam by the fact that 'we are a Muslim nation and our entire nation is Muslim'.

Among individual and personal reasons and stimuli in adopting religion, the most frequently encountered were: 'this helps moral self-perfection' (19.4 per cent); 'it is easier for me to live this way, it has created an interest and meaning in life' (8.9 per cent); 'this has become my inner need' (6.3 per cent); 'it has been caused by my personal life circumstances, personal hardship and difficulties' (2.3 per cent). Lesser factors included 'tribute to fashion, prestige' (0.9 per cent) and 'ordinary human curiosity' (0.4 per cent). Among the motives that impelled respondents to abandon religion were 'deep disappointment with its help'. 'circumstances of personal life'. and 'helplessness'.

For both men and women, as indicated in the table below, moral self-improvement is the prime motivation expressed for religious affiliation. Family traditions weigh more strongly among men, while considerations of national identification sway women more than men.

Table 1

Motives and Reasons for Following Religion, by Gender (%)

		Men	Women
1.	Family traditions	17.0	12.6
2.	Religious nurturing at home	15.4	15.4
3.	Moral self-perfection	19.7	19.1
4.	It is fashionable now	0.3	1.5
5.	National customs and traditions	14.7	12.3
6.	We are a Muslim nation	18.3	18.7
7.	Interest and meaning in life	7.4	10.4
8.	Circumstances of personal life	2.2	2.4
9.	Inner need	5.0	7.6

For the youth, religious attitudes were found to relate first to moral self-perfection and family upbringing – as they do for the middle aged, along with national identity. For the older generation, family traditions, upbringing, moral self-perfection and national identity are all vital. But adopting belief 'out of fashion and accepted standards' is also commonest among the youth. For refugees and displaced persons, 'national customs and traditions', 'ethnic identification', 'hard living conditions and difficulties' and 'domestic upbringing' are all significant motives. Clearly, the process of adopting religion in most cases involves complex, multiple motivations (is polymotivated), even as each social group has its own specific motivations for religiosity.

The role of religion in the lives of a tenth of all respondents is 'very important'; for a quarter of those polled, it occupies 'an important enough place in his/her life'. This role is regarded as 'moderate' for 41 per cent, and 'insignificant' for about 12 per cent of respondents; a tenth indicated that religion 'does not play any role at all for them'. For a strong majority, then, religion plays some part in their lives. Men attach somewhat greater importance to religion than women: 40.2 per cent versus 22.8 per cent respectively considering religion to be important or important enough in their lives. But the share of men for whom religion does not play any role (11.4 per cent) exceeds that of women (9.5 per cent). Older generations accord a higher role to religion in their lives: most of those who regard it as 'very important and considerable' are over 50 years of age. The largest share of those who felt that 'religion does not play any role' belongs to the 16–25 age group.

A relatively higher assessment of the role of religion is characteristic of the rural population. For instance, the share of those considering this role to be 'important enough' (50.2 per cent) is twice as large as among residents of Baku (20.7 per cent) and Gandja (26.4 per cent). There were no respondents in the countryside who 'do not attach any importance to religion at all'. It is noteworthy that refugees generally did not rate this role very highly – as many as 59.3 per cent considered it 'moderate' and only 32 per cent as 'important enough'.

Religion, in the opinion of most respondents, promotes the formation and nurturing of several social and individual features – from 'high moral standing' (52.5 per cent) and 'tolerance/patience' (36 per cent), to 'attentive attitude towards people' (33.4 per cent) and 'kindness' (39.6 per cent). Also referred to were qualities such as 'respect for the elderly', 'modesty and unpretentiousness', 'service to the nation and society', 'sense of social responsibility', 'love for parents and motherland', 'absence of pride, selfishness and greediness', 'industriousness', 'aesthetic thinking' and 'self-esteem'. In mass consciousness, therefore, religion is most frequently identified with ethics/morality in the private as well as social spheres. By and large, cognitive interest in religious issues is quite high (68 per cent) – relating to pertinent developments in Azerbaijani society, informing oneself of religious matters and participating in rituals/religious practices. Some non-believers also professed to having such interests.

A significant part of religious consciousness is the level of one's knowledge/awareness of doctrinal matters, and respondents were asked to judge their own competence in this respect. A third had 'some idea of the subject', 38 per cent could 'maintain a conversation on the subject, but would like to know more', just over 7 per cent had 'good enough level of knowledge' – with 0.4 per cent having 'undergone professional training'. Only 7.5 per cent felt they had 'extremely low level of knowledge and understanding', while 13 per cent asserted that it was 'hard to evaluate one's own knowledge'. Apparently, a considerable proportion consider themselves reasonably versed in religion, though the share of those finding their knowledge inadequate and wishing to correct this is not insignificant. Perhaps not surprisingly, awareness of religious issues is higher among the educated members of society, though they also tend to be more critical in assessing their own knowledge/competence in this respect.

Further, those with lower educational attainment are more interested in the practical and customary-ritual aspects, whereas the better educated tend to be engaged by the more esoteric facets, including religious literature. There is also an intellectual class that takes an acute and even professional interest in these issues.

Adherence to Islamic beliefs presumes some familiarisation with the sharia (corpus of formal religious norms). The survey indicated that 57 per cent 'have a certain idea' ('have heard about it') of what that corpus entails, and about 15 per cent know it 'quite well'. Some 23 per cent are 'absolutely unfamiliar with the sharia' – while 5 per cent know the principles 'very well'. Respondents were also asked about their understanding of fundamental doctrinal ideas (*iman, 'ibadat, islam*); it turned out that very few have a real grasp of such terms/ideas. When it came to desiring familiarity with these doctrines – and those of other religions – the overwhelming majority of respondents (71 per cent) replied in the affirmative about Islam, and a significant portion about other faiths (43.6 per cent).

Observance of religious commandments and norms in everyday life is an important indicator of religiosity. Just over 6 per cent of respondents professed to fulfilling such commandments/norms in all life situations, some 14 per cent sought to fulfil them as much as possible, and 19 per cent felt that they fulfilled them partially. A robust majority of 60.4 per cent did not fulfil them at all. There were no particular gender differences in observance. The middle-aged generation was the most observant, while the youth was the least so – and declining in this regard. Reasons and motives for religious observance varied from respondents considering it their (Muslim) duty (31.7 per cent), their conviction (21.7 per cent), and national tradition (22 per cent), to the notion that it helped them in their lives/imparted confidence (11.4 per cent). Social or domestic conformity generally weighed as minor factors. Again, gender differences were not significant, though national tradition weighed more heavily with observant women than men. Women were also more likely to gain a sense of well-being from observance.

What particular religious observances tend to be followed? The *salat* or *namaz* (daily ritual prayer) was observed by only 16.3 per cent of believers. About 27 per cent observed the ritual fast, though some admitted to incomplete fasting. In general, an increase among older Azerbaijanis performing the *salat* and fasting was evinced, and rural residents tended to be more active on both.

Among the refugee population, a third of respondents said they performed the *salat* and two-fifths observed the fast. Did respondents read the Qur'an, and if so, how often? Half had never read it, while about 20 per cent 'haven't yet, but were going to'. Some 10.4 per cent read it 'rarely', another 10 per cent read it regularly, 5.6 per cent had recently started reading it, and 4.6 per cent read and also studied it. Did respondents attend mosques, and if so, how often? A quarter 'visited from time to time', 39 per cent did not attend at all, and 26.3 per cent 'only on holidays and special occasions'. Just over 6 per cent attended regularly, and about 3 per cent on Fridays. Older respondents were more regular, and those in the 16–25 age group the least so.

More broadly, 26 per cent of all respondents engaged in charitable activities and providing help to others. For some respondents, charity had no religious colouring and was motivated simply by a sense of compassion and the aspiration to do good. Others were influenced by their perceived religious obligations, notably with respect to *zakat* (almsgiving). However, many respondents were reluctant to answer this question, and were embarrassed to discuss their own acts of charity. When it comes to the *hajj* or Muslim pilgrimage to Mecca, over two-thirds responded that they had not undertaken it, nearly 16 per cent said they would like to, and about 9 per cent that they 'haven't thought about it'. Just under 1 per cent had performed the *hajj*. The survey found that sharia prohibitions were generally observed, though in varying degrees: on 'gambling' by 71.6 per cent, on 'eating pork' by 62.6 per cent, and on 'drinking alcoholic beverages' by 49.3 per cent. A small number of Muslim respondents also cited proscriptions on smoking, adultery, dancing at wedding parties, modest dressing, lying, and 'avoiding everything that contradicts the sharia'. Members of other religions mentioned avarice, gluttony and adultery.

Involvement with the activities of religious communities, associations and organisations is also an indicator of religiosity. Only 3.4 per cent of respondents said they were members of religious organisations and communities and participated in their activities. Women and men were equally active on this score. About a tenth of respondents had encountered difficulties or obstacles in observing their perceived religious duties or commitments. Women and girls referred to disrespect toward the wearing of the *hijab* or headscarf, problems concerning modest attire, working with men, and difficulty in finding a 'believer' spouse. Among the most frequently mentioned challenges for all respondents were the shortage of suitable religious literature ('the existing literature is too difficult', 'no suitable source for familiarisation'), the lack of time for observance of rituals, poor understanding within the family, the atheistic views of members of the older generation, and the absence of prayer-breaks in the workplace.

Perceptions of Religion in Public Life

The survey invited respondents to opine about how religion has in their experience affected the nature of Azerbaijani society in recent years, in a variety of public contexts. Well over half believed the role of religion has been 'on the increase'; that it has 'started playing a more noticeable role in the society'. Nearly 40 per cent felt the role of religion in society 'remains unchanged'. It is noteworthy that these opinions were expressed by believers and non-believers, and by Muslims and non-Muslims alike.

For a strong majority of respondents (60.3 per cent), the impact of religion was an entirely 'positive phenomenon', because in their view it 'improves moral values and leads to spiritual revival', 'teaches how to live and constrains wrong-doing', 'helps overcome difficulties', 'promotes national unity and consolidation', 'invigorates the family' and 'revives Islam'. While a third of respondents welcomed the growing religious influence in terms of aiding a 'return to ethnic-religious historic roots', 'people acquiring new knowledge' and the like, they were also concerned about preserving a secular state. A few respondents expressed the wish that such influence 'not reach the level of fanaticism', fearing that 'under certain circumstances this may grow into a dictatorship over how to behave and dress'. Only a few (2.6 per cent) felt that prevailing levels of religiosity 'have not led to improved moral values yet', or that 'there are some progressive changes, but extremely insignificant as yet'. At the same time, 6.5

per cent of respondents considered the growing impact of religion as 'a negative phenomenon', including the concern that 'religion is being politicized'.

Respondents were also asked about the role of Islam in the historical and cultural development of the Azerbaijani nation. The majority, 64 per cent, found the impact to be entirely positive, most frequently invoking the following sentiments: 'Islam gave impetus to the development of national culture, science, philosophy, art', 'Islam has taught us to tolerate', 'we owe Islam all our merits'. However, some 25.3 per cent saw this role as both positive and negative, while 2.2 per cent found it entirely negative. These results reflect the opinions of believers and non-believers, and of Muslims and non-Muslims. A significant majority of respondents (over 90 per cent) thought that religion should lead to 'upgrading and supporting morale', 'spiritual revival, 'struggle against negative phenomena like drug addiction and alcoholism, and 'preserving national culture, customs and traditions'. Considerable importance was attached to the creative and mobilising function of religion in addressing social and national tasks such as 'attitude to national history', 'struggle for sovereignty', and 'strengthening patriotism and dignity'. The peacemaking potential of religion as a resource for building 'accord and civil peace' was stressed. Next to its national impact, religion was seen as aiding the family, as well as the education and upbringing of children – followed by its role in enhancing inter-personal relations in society.

Opinions about whether teaching the basics of Islam in schools is necessary and important have noticeably polarised. Those believing that 'this is important' (48.2 per cent) explained themselves mainly as follows: 'one must know and respect one's religion, one's spiritual roots', 'this is important for the formation of moral personality', 'this is important from an educational standpoint', and 'this will help them in their lives'. The arguments of respondents who were opposed (43 per cent) were based chiefly on their concern about preserving the secular orientation of society, in accordance with the constitution; there was also the apprehension that 'schools will not be able to teach the subject well'.

Again, attitudes about the extensive construction and reconstruction of mosques and temples in recent years varied considerably. More than half (51 per cent) regarded this as important, for reasons of 'justice', 'as an indicator of respect for the feelings of believers' and 'for improving spirituality'. But every fifth respondent felt it was better to spend money on other needs – including 'assistance to the destitute, handicapped and orphans', 'increase pensions and allowances', 'income generation' and 'medicine'. About 5 per cent expressed indifference to the question, and nearly a quarter would say nothing specific in this regard.

Respondents were asked to cite spheres of social life that, in their opinion, ought to function according to religious norms and customs. As evinced in Table 2 below, the main areas of such dependence – whether partial or full – were identified as 'public morality, ethics' (85.3 per cent), 'culture' (65.9 per cent) and 'family' (70.2 per cent). For the vast majority, religion was not considered to be important in the economic/commercial life or political life of society. The assumption at the level of mass consciousness appears to be that 'religion' is predominantly a moral phenomenon, with ethical content, that affects quotidian individual and communal affairs – but does not have a direct role in the larger secular affairs of the nation.

Table 2

Views on the Spheres of Social Life Dependent upon Religion (%)

	Entirely depends	Partially depends	Does not depend
1. Family	27.3	43.0	29.8
2. Morality, ethics	36.2	49.1	14.8
3. Economics, trade	7.1	17.6	75.4
4. Culture	17.8	48.1	34.1
5. Politics	3.1	5.4	91.6

Since Azerbaijan has long been home to a plurality of confessional groups and communities, tolerance in religious affairs is a key social issue, not least in the current 'transitional' period. The survey first asked respondents to assess the general situation in inter-confessional relations in the country. The majority of respondents (65.5 per cent) held the view that the situation is unchanged from the Soviet era. Every fourth respondent believed that the situation has in fact improved, in that citizens have become more tolerant; only 8.5 per cent felt that the situation had worsened. When asked more specifically about inter-confessional relations directly in the residential areas surveyed, an overwhelming majority (67.2 per cent) of respondents of all denominations were of the view that the situations had remained 'normal' or 'calm'. More positively, such relations were perceived as 'friendly' or 'mutually respectful' by 16.5 per cent – and negative, as involving 'rivalry' by 11.4 per cent. Only 3.4 per cent thought these relations involve 'mutual mistrust' or 'dislike'. Rural respondents professed not to have any negative views or experiences at all in this respect.

In terms of attitudes toward citizens of other faiths, the dominant sentiments were of 'neutrality' (32.1 per cent), 'respect' (19 per cent), 'interest' (13.7 per cent), 'understanding' (12 per cent) and 'amiability' (10.7 per cent). Intolerant attitudes (dislike, censoriousness, superiority) were encountered among only 8.6 per cent of respondents. Between 'believers' and 'non-believers', a third felt that belief was one's right and personal choice, while 15.3 per cent saw the matter as 'neutral, not my business'. Some 18 per cent would actively try persuading non-believers to acquire religious belief; only 4.5 per cent were condemnatory toward non-believers. As for non-believers' attitudes, 50.6 per cent felt the matter was one of personal choice, and nearly 30 per cent that it was not their business; only 3 per cent were condemnatory of religious belief. When respondents were asked whether they had encountered disrespect toward religiosity, 90 per cent answered in the negative. For those who had encountered disrespect, it tended to harken back to the Soviet period, often in connection with hiring for a job.

However, there was a palpable sense of mistrust and suspicion directed at groups like Jehovah's Witnesses, Adventists, and 'Word of Life' Pentecostals, seen as proselytising under the pretext of teaching English, and also as exploiting local economic hardship. More broadly, such evangelical groups are often perceived as impacting negatively on the relationship between Muslims and Orthodox Christians, who tend to favour limits on missionary activity. Further tensions have also ensued from the proselytising against military service by some missionary groups operating among ethnic minority youths. Nevertheless, all this must be seen within the context of a generally high level of mutual tolerance in matters of faith.

Religion, Democratisation and Civil Society

A salient goal of the survey was to determine whether there is a correlation between the 'religious' and socio-political views of citizens, and thence to draw appropriate conclusions about their correlation (if any) in Azerbaijan's quest for civil society. Part of the background in this regard is the armed territorial conflict with neighbouring Armenia over the enclave of Karabakh. Respondents were asked to list what they considered to be issues of primary concern for their society today. In what was an extensive enumeration, the main issues singled out were 'the economic situation/living standards of the population' (90 per cent), 'resolution of the Karabakh conflict/return of the occupied territories' (89 per cent), 'unemployment' (62 per cent), 'strengthening of statehood' (56 per cent), and 'achievement of civil peace and nation-wide accord' (30 per cent). Lower down on the list were 'democratisation of public life' (21.6 per cent), 'religious education' (16.7 per cent)', and 'improvement of moral standing' (12.7 per cent).

When asked about their attitudes to building a democratic and civil society, nearly a third considered this a very important national task, while a quarter rated it as a priority issue; another 15 per cent felt that it mattered for Azerbaijan's international image. Some 16 per cent believed there were other more important priorities, and 7 per cent felt that it was of no importance at all. Nearly two-thirds of respondents did not think that the pace of democratic reform was rapid enough, and 22.3 per cent expressed complete dissatisfaction ('reforms are not progressing at all'). Only 7 per cent believed 'reforms are progressing fast enough'.

In probing attitudes to democratic values and norms, the survey found that the greatest weight was given to 'human rights' (69 per cent), 'rule of law' (66.8 per cent), 'peace, stability and public order' (57 per cent) and 'social responsibility' (40.2 per cent). Also important were 'credible, legitimate authorities' (33 per cent), 'pluralism and freedom of opinions' (27 per cent) and 'personal freedom' (23.4 per cent). Every sixth respondent found 'freedom of consciousness and creed' to be important; only 6.3 per cent mentioned guarantees of religious minority rights. In demographic terms, youths gave particular weight to 'individual, personal freedom', and older respondents to 'stability and order' and 'rule of law'. Members of all confessional backgrounds attached equal value to 'stability' and 'non-violence'. There were, however, some differences: non-Muslim respondents were three times as likely to want guarantees of minority rights, while Muslims were almost three times as likely to call for 'social responsibility of everyone'.

There did not appear to be a significant statistical link between religiosity and democratic preference in general, either among respondents of different confessions or between believers and non-believers. One exception was in the attitude to 'pluralism and freedom of opinion': this was of greatest importance to those indifferent to religion (45.8 per cent), and least important to non-believers (21.6 per cent). There was no evidence, however, to support the stereotype of an 'oriental' (that is Muslim) disposition against modern liberal ideological and political values.

What model of socio-political development did Azerbaijanis most favour? A robust majority (over 91 per cent) wanted a secular polity, among whom the preference was for 'Western-style democracy'. A minority of 2 per cent wanted a Muslim theocracy, with sharia law – some of whom called for a moderate-theocratic model, and others for a more orthodox religious one. A third group of respondents (no more than 7 per cent) favoured authoritarian/ totalitarian values, expressing nostalgia for the communist past;

they condemned both democratic and religious-oriented change. It should be underlined that for over 96 per cent of respondents, both 'aggressive nationalism, ethnic intolerance' and 'religious fanaticism-intolerance' were not acceptable, representing serious threats to stability and public order.

How, in the opinion of the experts surveyed, should the issue of 'Islam and democracy' be addressed in Azerbaijan? A majority (72 per cent) felt that Islam and democracy were compatible, on the bases that Muslim social values as well as scripture favoured humanistic and participatory politics. Some respondents opined that Islam had deeper roots in Azerbaijan than democracy, and therefore it was vital to use religious values to further democratisation. Some thought it essential to expressly correct popular perceptions about Islam as linked with extremism. Only 6 per cent of experts viewed Islam and democracy as incompatible; some felt that democracy was connected with Christianity, and Islam therefore needed to borrow from the former in this respect. While there is no hard data yet on the influence in this regard of secular Turkey, as compared with the impact of the Iranian Revolution, the contesting approaches to the polity among these two powerful neighbours are undoubtedly influencing Azeris. By and large, the republic's historic and cultural orientation has been Turkic (including in terms of language and ethnicity), though there are also important ethno-cultural ties in southern Azerbaijan to Shi'i Iran. At this stage, apprehension among Azeri elites over religious radicalism is already impelling them to strongly oppose any prospect of theocratisation of politics, whether along Iranian or Saudi (Wahhabi) lines.

Among the experts polled in the present survey, nearly half cautioned that poverty, social and political dissatisfaction, and declining educational levels – together with democratic deficits – could all provide conditions for religious radicalism. Certainly, evidence of pockets of foreign Islamist movements in Azerbaijan has recently become incontrovertible. Many experts felt, however, that indigenous mass consciousness in Azerbaijan is resistant at this time to any kind of religious extremism. Again, the kind of East-West polarisation embraced by radical Islamists has limited appeal in this post-Soviet transition, where spiritual values rather than ideological ones tend to be sought after by the vast majority of citizens.

Conclusions

A clear empirical picture is discernible of rising religiosity – often characterised by strong and dynamic expressions of faith – in Azerbaijani society since independence from the Soviet Union. The demographic basis of this trend has encompassed the youth, intellectuals and women, rather than being confined to the narrow 'religious' segments associated with the Soviet period; yet the strength of religiosity among the rural population represents continuity rather than change. Religious affinities are also conspicuous among refugees and displaced persons. However, a significant minority retains the atheistic orientation favoured by the communist system that dominated Azerbaijan for much of the twentieth century. Transitions to religiosity from desacralising communist cultures involve complex processes of redefining and re-appropriating individual and social identities, and attendant changes in value-systems on the part of citizens, families, communities and entire societies. While the key trends in Azerbaijan that favour a secular polity, tolerance and religiously-inspired social ethics are reassuring, the stakes in terms of 'which Islam' (or rather 'Islams') will ultimately be embraced remain high.

Most experts surveyed were of the view that the Azeris' 'coming to Islam' is less an ideological commitment or response than a long-term 'return' to the freedom to pursue quests for spiritual, cultural and social values. An 'evolutionary development' of Islam, and of society, was seen by a majority as a probable prospect: in this perspective, 'strengthening Islam' was a route to consolidating the civic values that underpin national solidarity and individual freedom alike. A small minority expressed the concern that growing religiosity would lead to less liberal political trends and perhaps to a theocratic public culture. Others felt that such outcomes had less to do with religiosity than socio-economic factors, including poverty, social exclusion and democratic participation.

For the majority of ordinary Azeris, religious affinities appear to imply a commitment to norms and customs that guide daily behaviour, and provide a benchmark for social and personal judgements. Religiosity in the more traditional sense of adherence to rituals and rules, much less active membership in religious organisations, is noticeably weak. In part, this might be accounted for by the paucity of learning resources, despite the sharp increase in access to such materials in recent years – including the educational role of mass media. None the less, the openness with regard to religious affiliation has engendered a widening of spaces in which the individual can both express personal identity – most commonly, but certainly not exclusively, as a Muslim – and also engage in a variety of communal activities with an overtly religious purpose (like mosque-building). The civic implications of these trends are manifold.

In the perceived linkage of Islam with national identity and civic virtues, women more than men tend to see religiosity in terms of national consciousness. Despite occasional outbursts of intolerance toward non-Muslims (mainly directed at non-traditional and evangelical sects than at Orthodox Christians or Jews), the overall climate of opinion among non-Muslims does not reflect serious concern about the role of religion in public life. Yet, actual knowledge among ordinary Muslim citizens about Islam in terms of its theological and historical heritage is generally poor. How the gaps in knowledge and understanding are filled in years to come is obviously a matter of vital importance to the country: across ex-Soviet Central Asia and the Caucasus, as in the Near East at large, contestation on 'what and which Islam' will prevail is an ongoing reality.

Consonant with the secular ideal of church-state separation, the government generally does not intrude into religious affairs. At the same time, the state does play a regulatory role of sorts in seeking to maintain a de-politicised religious sphere through the registration of associations and certain types of activities. Beyond that, there is an obvious element of state promotion of 'good Islam': this ranges from the desired public image of government figures and civic respect for religious holidays, to actively discouraging extremist groups and aggressive proselytising, as well as reiterating the underlying principle of institutional religious-state separation.

The experts in this survey were generally inclined to support state regulation both in terms of drawing upon the civic dimensions of Islam as a handmaiden to the modern ethos of civil society, and also in safeguarding national security. Nor was there any serious hesitation on the part of most in recommending that legal tenets with respect to religious freedom be observed as assiduously as the control of funding and socio-religious activities of the growing body of religious groups, and indeed 'ideological and material support to Islam on the state level'. In the wake of the events of September 11, 2001, this need for a balanced approach is likely to be underscored. The Establishment response to such acts of political violence has been that they only discredit the Islam that Azeris know (in effect, that 'extremist Muslims are not Muslims at all'). There is also the recognition that public education in support of Muslim civic values requires resources that will need to be developed anew, in competition with the flood of books and programmes that propagandise hard-line religious orthodoxy. The scope for further sociological research on this score is as abundant as it is urgent.

Notes

I gratefully acknowledge the assistance of the Research Support Scheme of the Open Society Foundation, grant number 110/1999, that facilitated this survey.

1. According to the constitution adopted on 12 November 1995, Azerbaijan is a 'secular and unitary republic' (Article 7), where 'religion is separated from state', and 'all religions/faiths are equal before the law' (Article 18). Under Article 48, all are guaranteed 'freedom of conscience', and all 'have a right to freely express their attitude towards religion, on their own or together with others', or to 'not profess any religion'; religious rituals must 'not infringe public order or public morality'.

2. See A.S. Pasha-zade, *Islam in the Caucasus* (Baku, 1991); A. Geyushev, 'Peculiarities of the Process of Revival of Islam in Azerbaijan', *Pole*, 1 (9) (March, 2000), pp.32–7; N. Tohidi, 'Soviet in Public, Azeri in Private: Gender, Islam, and Nationalism in Soviet and Post-Soviet Azerbaijan', Hoover Institution Working Paper, Stanford University, (Stanford, CA, 1995); A. Maleshenko and M.B. Olcott, ed., *Islam in the Post-Soviet Newly Independent States: The View from Within*, (New York, 2001).

3. According to figures cited by the State Committee for Work with Religious Organisations and Associations, reported in the newspaper *Echo*, 11 (August 2001), 132.

4. The main purpose of this survey was to elicit a comprehensive sociological snapshot of the peculiarities, dynamics and basic tendencies of religiosity in post-Soviet Azerbaijan. The research explores the characteristics and parameters of mass awareness and behaviour of Azerbaijan's population, and considers the social, political and psychological vectors and circumstances affecting religious change in a transitional period. It also assesses the role religion plays in public and individual life, and in inter-group and interpersonal relations. Uncovering the correlation between 'Western-democratic', 'Islamic', and 'totalitarian' sets of values was an important objective. The sampling was conducted from September 1999 to February 2000, and from September 2000 to February 2001, in five regions of Azerbaijan: 1) the capital, Baku, and its suburbs; 2) Sumgait and its suburbs; 3) Gandja and suburbs; 4) Guba and nearby villages; 5) Sabirabad and its nearby villages and 2 refugee camps. The total number of individual respondents interviewed was 2000, and the sample was representative of across social and demographic groups. Structured and formalised face-to-face interviews were conducted by trained individuals under the author's supervision, with confidentiality strictly guaranteed of the interviewees' identity. The expert survey component was conducted by the author among 200 ranking individuals in the academic, socio-cultural, political and religious life of Azerbaijan.

8

Ethics in the Civitas

Amyn B. Sajoo

Prevailing liberal discourse on civil society accords a less than conspicuous place to ethical tenets – if it allows them into the civitas
or public square at all. The secular mind once saw in civil society
the ethical edifice of human relations; but it has learned to mistrust public and collective virtues as coercive and ideological,
evidence of which is today felt to lie in the civic frailty of theocratic states.[1] Hence, public ethics find segregated expression in
talk of the Good Society – while Civil Society is invoked in analyses of improvements upon or transitions to democratic values and
practice. To be sure, this dichotomy has been lamented of late,
notably in critiques of liberal citizenship both in the West and the
emerging democracies of East-Central Europe. When applied to
the Muslim world, its implications are only exacerbated: the very
idea of civil society tends to be seen as running into profound, if
not *sui generis*, barriers of history, ideology and religion. Among
the most intractable of those barriers is thought to be Islam's
merging of the categories of secular, sacred and state (*dunya, din,
dawla*), as well as the concept of umma as a transcendent community. For these are seen as inherently problematic ideas and
practices in a liberal discourse on civil society, premised on the

existence of a pluralist and secular public sphere in which the individual freely associates with others outside the control of the state.

If impetus were required for fresh thinking in that regard (especially but hardly exclusively by Muslims), it appears to have been furnished by the events of September 11, 2001, and their aftermath.[2] The public arena on every continent has since been convulsed in debate over the implications with regard to so-called 'Islamic' political culture. One must here resist prejudging the full scope of legal responsibility for the wantonly destructive acts of that date, on which actual evidence at the time of this writing remains inconclusive.[3] Moreover, the ensuing debate has all too frequently degenerated into polemics that merely stoke cultural prejudice, and often wilfully deny the socio-economic and political roots of 'religious extremism', in which the West itself is frequently complicit.[4] But this cannot be allowed to detract from the pressing need to examine the role of ethical values in the contemporary public culture of the Muslim world, most notably with regard to accountability to the rule of law and to the citizenry in all its diversity, as well as political violence in the wider context of civility.

Contrary to the mainstream liberal view, ethical affinities – at the personal and communal levels – remain a hallmark of Muslim conceptions of social being. Historically, this perspective can be traced to the founding tenets of Muhammad's Medina, through al-Farabi's celebrated tenth-century work, *The Virtuous City* (*al-Madina al-fadila*), and down to modern conceptions of the ideal polity.[5] Can such a perspective be reconciled with the modern conception of the public sphere, the secular civic space that is considered essential to civil society?[6] Or should that quest be undertaken on its own terms, and the ethical affinities of old consigned by and large to the private sphere? Is it not sufficient to ground issues of accountability, pluralism and non-violence in a secular ethos of human rights? There are compelling reasons, in my view, for embracing the ethical option, even if it entails a reconception of the nature of the public sphere in light of indigenous Muslim experiences.

I sketch here first what appear to be the salient contours of the liberal discourse that leads to a dichotomy between norms of 'civic' and 'ethical' conduct, as an integral part of the privileging of secular, individual rights. It is this rift that prompts my use of 'civitas' in the title of this paper, recalling the original Latin idea of citizenship within the democratic context of the modern polity, and its nexus with the ethos of civility. A Muslim critique is applied to that unfolding discourse – before both are finally brought to bear upon prevailing social and political realities in the Muslim world. I hasten to add that at this juncture, the nature of the analysis is necessarily preliminary, and certainly does not purport to do justice to every facet of the complex discursive relationships on hand (including the ethical implications stemming from socio-economic globalisation, and from the spate of new biomedical procedures and technologies). An exhaustive critique awaits manifold contributions – Muslim as well as non-Muslim – across disciplinary lines, and drawing upon a more extensive body of sociological data than is available at this time.

II

For contemporary liberalism, a minimal consensus on moral and ethical precepts[7] is part of the *quid pro quo* for a maximal consensus on the rules and mores of coexistence amid diversity. 'The ethic central to a liberal society is an ethic of the right rather than the good', Charles Taylor has observed; hence, 'its basic principles concern how society should respond to arbitrate the competing demands of individuals'.[8] In consequence and effect, 'society must be neutral on the question of the good life' – that is, on what most of us would deem the core question of personal and social ethics.[9] Indeed, even the classical, Aristotelian definition of the 'good' in ethical context arguably amounted to just such a perspective in its pragmatic stress on what is appropriate (rather than morally correct), from a situational as well as personal stance.[10] Again, the powerful impetus to the emergence of modern civil society imparted by the Scottish Enlightenment also celebrated virtue – but as 'private mores rather than public commitments'.[11] The individuated self trumped the social in a trend that also became the hallmark of Anglo-American jurisprudence. At its most emphatic, this has culminated in what Richard Rorty considers a compromise of higher amorality: the many, competing quests for Truth have all been discredited anyway, so democratic pragmatism favours moral indifference.[12]

Another way of framing this central liberal 'bargain', in terms closer to the conceptual and policy concerns of civil society, is that the more a state is committed to a minimal agenda of upholding negative liberties (that is, freedoms from abusive intrusions against the sanctity of the individual and his choices), the greater the prospect of maximising the plural goals that citizens and communities wish to pursue – and the less the danger of utopian engineering of the kind required in pursuit of particular virtues or ideologies that forestall the openness of civic culture. It is no surprise that this perspective, which is associated with the writings of Isaiah Berlin and Karl Popper,[13] emerged from the mid-twentieth century European experience that culminated in key international human rights agreements.[14] Nor that it should have found deep resonance in post-cold war eastern and central Europe where the current discourse on civil society experienced its strongest rebirth, through the writings (and activism) of Vaclav Havel, John Keane, Ernest Gellner, George Soros and others.[15] In both of those European contexts, nothing could be perceived as more threatening to the vibrancy of civic culture than ideology emanating from an authoritarian state, the church or fascist social movements.

The upshot is that much of liberal discourse seeks to privatise ethics and morality – or at least the moral dimension of ethics. There can hardly be a total severing of ties between the tenets of social ethics and those of civic culture, given the shared preoccupation with upholding 'appropriate' behaviour (in regard to public order, accountable governance and participatory politics, the integrity of the environment, and other fundamental values). However, ethics *qua* hard judgements about right and wrong is generally outside the parameters of the public sphere; indeed for some, such judgements fall outside the realm of ethics itself. In the most widely discussed recent work on civic culture in Western perspective, Robert Putnam's *Bowling Alone*,[16] there is not a single direct reference to ethics. Putnam, whose 1996 essay of the same title triggered an enormous academic and policy debate, does invoke individual moral values like altruism, philanthropy, trust and honesty as well as religious participation.[17] But nowhere in the book are ethics *per se* deemed worthy of consideration either as a conceptual or a pragmatic facet of the public sphere where civic engagement happens.

Still more recently, John Ralston Saul, a leading Canadian public intellectual, has argued that neither public nor private ethics should be 'confused with morality', since 'ethics is not about good intentions'.[18] Saul is right to warn that moral certainty can quickly transmute into political evil. But if the road to Hell is paved with good intentions, can an amoral ethics get us to Heaven? The answer on the other side of the Atlantic, in Joan Smith's *Moralities*,[19] appears to be in the affirmative. She assails the notion that social ethics can embrace judgements about right and wrong without encountering a fatal scepticism. For Smith, Judaeo-Christian ethics have been discredited by the behaviour (and 'Victorian' sensibilities) of proponents who have fed a hypocritical disjuncture between precept and practice.[20] Hence, public morality rests in the more pluralist culture of human rights.[21]

Given that a secular landscape is felt to be the proper locus for modern civic culture,[22] perhaps this rejection is predictable, though certainly not inevitable. A robust occidental critique of that liberal posture has emerged in the past decade, spearheaded by the 'communitarian movement' that draws upon liberal values like the rule of law and pluralism, coupled with the civic republican tenets of social trust, self-help and community-building. Among the leading trans-Atlantic proponents of communitarianism are Amitai Etzioni, Anthony Giddens, John Gray, Gertrude Himmelfarb, Robert Kuttner, Robert Putnam and Michael Sandel, a broad church with varying political affiliations but joined by their primary concern about the corrosive effects of liberal individualism on civic solidarity and engaged citizenship.[23] For Himmelfarb and others on the more conservative end of the communitarian spectrum, the traditional morality dismissed by Smith is a condition *sine qua non* to advance civil society; any other brand of 'social ethics' simply lacks substance and undermines the desired civic ethos. For Giddens, Kuttner and other more liberal communitarians, it is chiefly economic/free market individualism that undercuts social solidarity. To counter this tendency, public policy must draw upon a shared ethos of civic patriotism. Both conservative and liberal tendencies appear to decry the sharp dichotomy between private and public ethics that is the staple of mainstream liberalism and its conception of civil society.

Yet the communitarian critique has also been seized upon by those with a less pluralist commitment, and pressed into the service of a cultural patriotism that privileges a particular view of the Judaeo-Christian ethic. In the influential writings of Samuel P. Huntington on the 'clash of civilisations', for example, what is seen as a decline in fealty to traditional values (including respect for education, family integrity and the rule of law) is treated as a root cause of growing Euro-American political and economic weakness in relation to other cultural zones or civilisations, most notably that of Islam.[24] As I have noted elsewhere, Huntington sees no contradiction in issuing a summons on behalf of 'Western' ethical values that pointedly degrades the multicultural components (and citizenry) of Euro-American polities.[25] At the same time, he is oblivious of the new realities of global citizenship and culture that enlarge civic membership beyond traditional frontiers of nationality and geography. Huntington's thesis also lends itself to a validation of a closed view of society in response to the incursion of non-Western values and people[26] – which would, one is inclined to think, be antithetical to the open society envisaged by most theorists as vital to a mature civic culture.

The communitarian movement and other critiques of the 'radical secularity' (after Taylor) of occidental civil society tend to find themselves defending, at best, a marginal nexus between morally-based social ethics and the modern public sphere. In this vein, Etzioni asserts that the moral revivalists among his fellow communitarians are really in pursuit of the Good Society rather than Civil

Society,[27] implying that social virtues need to be siphoned-off from civic values.[28] Inasmuch as the rationale here is a concern for civil liberties and the rule of law (as opposed to the emphasis on individual responsibilities by moral revivalists), it seems to reaffirm the primacy of an individualist ethos in the civic calculus.[29] It also brings us full circle to Gellner's stance that modern man must choose between being 'modular' – that is, 'individualist and egalitarian, while nevertheless capable of cohesion against the state'[30] – or being 'communalist' in his resistance to bonds outside of kinship, religion and tribe.[31] This captures the essence of a liberal definition of civil society that is mistrustful of serious ethical affinities. The corollary for Muslim and other 'segmentary' communities, as Gellner sees it, is a choice between the traditional bonds of the umma, and the strictly secular bonds of pluralist civic modernity.[32]

There is much that Gellner and other mainstream theorists can be challenged about in the sweeping assumptions about Islam, the umma and what constitutes 'civic culture'.[33] Apart from the Orientalist overtones of some of those assumptions, the notion that the social capital generated by communal bonds is vitiated by a uniform resistance to freely moving in and out of such associations is surely anchored in a limited understanding of how fluid those bonds often are – as Dale Eickelman, John Esposito and others have documented.[34] One recalls, too, the paradigm of 'discourse ethics' as a vital aspect of the ideal public sphere that has been sketched by Habermas.[35] Our paramount concern here, however, is specifically with the unfolding nexus between social ethics and civil society in mainstream liberal and, in the rest of this analysis, transitional Muslim contexts. I say 'transitional' in recognition of the quest for democratic modernity and its attendant civic culture that marks the contemporary reality of those societies and communities, whether or not this is shared by the governments of the day. Muslim intellectual and activist critiques – unlike those of their Western counterparts – are directed less at existing indigenous 'models' than at putative/emerging ones, even if they are acutely mindful of particular approaches (like the opposing ones of Iran and Turkey). The stakes range far beyond mere theory, to the realm of competing choices with far-reaching social and political implications.

III

Before venturing into the rationales for an ethically-oriented Muslim approach to civic culture, it is necessary to delineate the elements that define the latter, *dehors* the bounds of liberal, conservative or other political ideology. Most theorists and activists would concur that any modern conception of civil society must include three requisite elements: the rule of law, equal citizenship and participatory politics with state accountability to the civic sphere. These primary elements in turn favour the organic separation of state and society, the independence of the judiciary as well as of the media, and guarantees of free association and thought. Only then is it meaningful to invoke a public sphere in which civic interaction can occur.[36] Yet no matter how desirable the existence of this civic culture in a secure and legitimate public space, it is value-neutral in the sense of commanding no allegiance to specific moral principles. There are certainly moral dimensions to human rights that uphold the integrity of individual and communal life, belief and equality; but appeals to secular law are sufficient to safeguard these entitlements.

The value-neutral nature of these elements also accounts for how a rigorous critic of liberal ideology like E.P. Thompson could be effusive about an institution often associated with economic and social inequity: 'the rule of law itself, the imposing of effective inhibitions upon power and the defence of the citizen from power's all-intrusive claims, seems to me to be an unqualified human good'.[37] Thompson's recognition of the *instrumental* value of the rule of law in limiting state power and safeguarding individual liberties had nothing to do with ethical or moral value; his praise could be rephrased as 'an unqualified civic good'. Likewise, writing of the revival of the rule of law as a cornerstone of democratic transitions since the end of the cold war, Thomas Carothers singles out as its defining traits public knowledge, transparency and equal application to all, including the government.[38]

While those traits may be seen as necessary conditions for a liberal ethos, Carothers notes their embrace across ideological lines.

The same is true of the other defining elements above, from equal citizenship to the freedom of worship: each is cherished instrumentally *qua* civic good in this 'procedural liberal' perspective. Indeed, the logic extends to the institutional basis of secular culture – the separation of church and state – that accompanies the autonomy of state and civic spheres in civil society. True, there is much to contest even in a nuanced appreciation of what secularism means. But secular culture as an institutional facet of civil society is here taken to be value-neutral, without the anti-religious resonance that often attaches to it in other contexts.[39]

Admittedly, the liberal characterisation of civil society as – ideally – a zone of freedom, tolerance and politico-economic choice that can face down the despotism of states and even the atomisation of communities,[40] comes close to a conception of civic virtue rather than as only a neutral set of civic values. Fed by the historical streams of Western European contests among monarchical and church institutions and the emerging bourgeoisie, and the more recent east/central European contests between totalitarian state institutions and the *volk*, a powerful wave of Civic Truth has swept contemporary discourse. The State is effectively seen as bad, and Society as good. Hence human rights tend to be defined narrowly as limits on the power of the state (negative liberties), and only reluctantly as involving fundamental socio-economic obligations and individual responsibility.[41] In this characterisation, the quality of the public square is a function of society's autonomy from the state. From this perspective, it is but a short step to the generalisation that *all* civil societies must be thus defined, irrespective of the diversity of historical and cultural realities. Or as Keane puts it, such idealisations wrongly suppose that 'civil societies are largely unencumbered by self-paralysing contradictions and dilemmas' - which in turn calls for the need to constantly develop new images.[42]

In that regard, Keane argues that in transitional states that lack civic traditions to enable peaceful democratisation, a common recourse is to seek refuge in nationalism or other certitudes of

cultural and religious identity; these are as perilous as the certitudes embraced in established democracies, like individualism or
the notion of rational public argumentation. For they lapse into a
reductive 'foundationalist' understanding of civil society, at odds
with the pluralism of purpose and commitment that the members of society actually have.[43] In effect, 'the meaning and ethical
significance of civil society at any given time and place can be
asserted and/or contested as such only within a socio-political
framework marked by the separation of civil and state institutions,
whose power to shape the lives of citizens is subject permanently
to mechanisms that enable disputation, accountability and representation'.[44] This, for Keane, is a preference that must override
other organising options, contrary (as seen earlier) to Rorty's willingness to treat civil society as merely one (however desirable)
among alternative choices. Otherwise, relativism takes over and
undercuts pluralism, in precept and practice.

The modern public sphere, in other words, may encompass
ethical or ideological frameworks but not the other way round: its
boundaries are determined by civic elements alone. That is the
only available recipe for serving contemporary diversities of ethnicity, culture, religion, politics and individual purpose – *a fortiori*
amid the growing impact of economic and political globalisation,
which has spawned a transnational, if still inchoate, civic culture.
What has yet to be addressed, whether by theorists or activists, is
the nature of the relationship between an ethical framework such
as Islam's to the kind of public sphere outlined above that is central to modern civil society, while recognising that varying national
and cultural contexts make for varying dynamics on the ground.
This takes the discourse beyond the usual question about whether
'Islam' is 'compatible' with democracy or civil society: that line of
inquiry simply normatises Islam – a faith shared by over a billion
Muslims around the world – and occludes the complexity of *changing* Muslim intellectual and social life in favour of stock models
and images. Rather, the key questions here are about why and
how an ethical framework matters in a post-foundationalist (after
Keane) understanding of the public sphere. Many of the issues
on hand have been grappled with by Muslim thinkers and activists

like Abdolkarim Soroush, Mohamed Abed Jabri, Fazlur Rahman, Rachid al-Ghannouchi, Sadiq Jalal al-Azm, Nurcolish Madjid, Chandra Muzzafar, Mohammed Arkoun, Abdullahi An-Na'im and Bassam Tibi, some of whose works are drawn upon in the remainder of this paper.[45]

IV

There is rich irony in today having to negotiate the nexus between ethics and civic culture past the currents and eddies of 'secularism' and 'religion', and not only in the Cartesian context of Western societies where this dualism has long prevailed amid the ascendancy of the secular. In the *weltanschauung* of Islam, where the sacred and secular (*din* and *dunya*) are merged – and in which some are inclined to subsume the state (*dawla*) – there is a different challenge. Bernard Lewis is among those who conflate the *weltanschauung* with the *institutional* arrangements of the polity, claiming that church and state are not 'separable' in Islam.[46] This would imply, wrongly, that civic life cannot accommodate a deep regard for the sacred amid such legal/political separation. The real problem has to do with the continuing pervasiveness in Muslim discourses of what Arkoun calls a 'moral totality validated entirely by divine teaching', which is given further public momentum by an attentive media.[47] This tendency in the discourse has less to do with the exercise of moral reasoning that is vital to social ethics, than with nourishing the 'social imaginary'.

What is ironic is that in the classical age of Islam when the leading ethical texts were authored, drawing inspiration both from scripture and the philosophical heritage of the Mediterranean world at large, a moral critique of politics was not seen as a profaning of sacred norms. The pragmatic rationale for the *Virtuous City* of al-Farabi (d.950) is the interdependence of human beings in pursuit of self-sufficiency and fulfilment, a *voluntary* quest that ultimately requires the social and spiritual aid of Islamic tenets.[48] Moral traits (*akhlaq*) and habits (*adab*) were individual acquisitions with a social purpose, transcending the public-private divide. *Adab* as a code of dignity and social refinement had ancient roots in the Near and Middle East, which Islam infused with a conscious moral dimension.[49] The upshot was a flowering in the work of, among others, Miskawayh (d.1030) in *The Cultivation of Morals* (*Tahdhib al-akhlaq*)[50], and its Persian-Shi'i counterpart, *The Nasirid Ethics* (*Akhlaq-e Nasiri*) of Tusi (d.1274),[51] which drew conspicuously on Aristotle and neo-Platonist sources.[52]

Indeed, Muslim writings on ethics caught fire after the translation by Ibn Hunanyn (d.911) of the *Nicomachean Ethics*, on which al-Farabi was the first scholarly commentator in Arabic.[53] The ethos of the Greek *polis* was subsumed into a new universe where integrity, courage, temperance, charity, justice and reason were virtues that made for individual happiness and the ideal umma. For al-Ghazali (d.1111) in the *Criterion of Moral Action* (*Mizan al-amal*), they find expression as more than a set of social and personal rules about right and wrong (*ma'ruf wa munkar*); they become part of the process of moral reasoning.[54]

Yet that aspect of ethics, as furnishing a critique of political and individual conduct, was in contestation with the role of the enacted sharia, itself derived from the moral framework of the Qur'an and the hadith. While al-Ghazali was able to bring his considerable authority to bear in casting a sceptical eye on what he perceived as the ethical deficits of those wielding the enacted sharia, the overarching historical trend was of the latter's dominion.[55] The reasons ranged from the need for an authoritative corpus of law over a rapidly expanding Muslim empire, to the political conservatism of Arabia from around the eleventh century that led many jurists to affirm the 'closure of the gate of *ijtihad*' (independent legal reasoning).[56] The decline of *ijtihad* was accompanied by a pattern of compartmentalising law and politics, so that the latter – *siyasa* – became the domain of the caliph or sultan, as an exercise in kingship. The law, in all its potent civic and religious if not intellectual authority, was the domain of the ulama or religio-jurists.

Hence the die was cast for the ruler to seek the collaboration of the ulama in an expedient arrangement: the former in pursuit of 'religious' legitimacy, the latter for enhanced political influence.[57] Although this did not preclude *ad hoc* ethical judgements by communities and individuals about the conduct of civic affairs through to the modern era, the sacralisation of the law inevitably curtailed the scope, potency and systematisation of such a critique. The potential of ethico-legal principles as *rationes legis* – generalised tenets that lent themselves to application in particular cases – was overshadowed by the spirit of *taqlid,* an imitative compliance with a set of specific rules extracted from the manuals of various legal schools.

Since the sacralisation of law enhances the legitimacy of political establishments that can invoke it for the exercise of their authority, the tension with those seeking civic accountability is obvious. The hallowed phrase *siyasa shari'a* refers formally to the political and administrative facets of the law; but it also signals attempts at sacralising political power.[58] In post-Revolutionary Iran, for example, the constitutional tenet of *velayat-e faqih* (rule of the juriconsult) confers supra-democratic authority on the un-elected 'supreme religious leader' and renders the clergy and their courts as 'guardians' of the political process, including control over the media.[59] On an even more pervasive level, civic life in Saudi Arabia has been stifled by conservative, intertwining princely and clerical institutions that claim religious legitimacy – and, ironically, face a still more conservative challenge on those very grounds of legitimacy.[60] Elsewhere, the primacy of the sharia – as interpreted by traditionalist establishments – operates to trump secular law and effectively circumscribe civic discourse, as witness recent developments in societies as diverse as Egypt and Pakistan with regard to strictures on blasphemy, apostasy and gender equality.[61]

All of which underscores the need to separate the institutions of state, religion and society, as a shared modern democratic and ethical imperative. That proposition was famously advanced in the 1920s by the Egyptians Ibn al-Jawzi and Ali Abd al-Raziq, only to run into a wall of orthodox opposition.[62] Yet far from violating Islam's *weltanschauung,* this institutional separation is a means of advancing its civic spirit in practice. Secular culture in this respect is an ally rather than an antagonist of religious well-being, with social ethics serving as a bridge between the two in the public sphere. It is in this sense that Abdolkarim Soroush advocates the secularisation of ethics en route to modernity,[63] abjuring the 'ethics of the Gods' for 'concrete and accessible rules' that admit of human frailty.[64] Judging by the results of successive Iranian elections since the mid-1990s, in which ordinary citizens have repeatedly and overwhelmingly endorsed the most anti-clerical choices available, it is obvious that Soroush (a key supporter of the 1979 Revolution) speaks to a deep disenchantment with theocratic claims over the public sphere. 'Having freed themselves from the cordon of previously luminous ideologies', notes one observer, 'many of Iran's intellectuals are now busy articulating serious and sophisticated criticisms of ... authoritarianism, censorship, clientilism, cult of personality, etatism, fanaticism, influence peddling, partisanship, and violence'.[65]

Moreover, sacralising the law provides no guarantee of the primacy of the rule of law as an institution, identified earlier as a vital element of civil society. Indeed, the argument can be made that sacralisation actually undermines the rule of law, since both the content and the implementing institutions *ipso facto* operate outside the framework of democratic/civic accountability in all its contemporary pluralist complexity. It is tantamount to a foundationalist approach of the type explicitly rejected in the preceding segment. The more general problem of the weakness of the rule of law shared by emerging democracies – especially those in post-civil conflict transitions (like Algeria, Azerbaijan, Bosnia, Indonesia, Iraq, Lebanon, Somalia, Sudan and Tajikistan) – only reinforces the 'ethical imperative'. That is, public respect for social ethics acquires the burden not merely of supporting the rule of law, but of actively filling a normative as well as practical gap in the latter's absence or enfeebled condition.

Reliable sociological data on citizen perceptions of civic life in Muslim-majority contexts are relatively scarce, but not entirely lacking. A seminal survey on Azerbaijan, discussed in this volume by Tair Faradov, is instructive about attitudes in transition both from Soviet rule and territorial conflict (with neighbouring Armenia) – conditions not atypical of post-colonial experience in much of the Muslim world. Over 90 per cent of Azerbaijanis opined that religion should not influence politics, but was an important determinant of 'public morality' (84 per cent) and 'culture' (70.6 per cent); this in a country where the majority did not consider themselves observant Muslims.[66] The institutional division of church and state written into the country's secular constitution enjoys widespread endorsement, with 'Islam' perceived foremost as an affirmation of personal spiritual and ethical values.

In neighbouring Turkey, according to another recent survey, majorities of 78 to 85 per cent oppose amending the civil code to accommodate sharia norms concerning women – yet robust majorities favour social practices like prohibiting the sale of alcohol during Ramadan, allowing exclusively religious marriages, and modest public dressing by women.[67] In both instances, and likely across much of post-Soviet Central Asia and beyond, support for secular culture and religiously-inspired social ethics is perceived not only as compatible but also as desirable – a trend likely to be accentuated by the events of September 11, 2001, and their aftermath. More broadly, it bears observing that a symbiotic nexus between law and social ethics is integral to the evolution of modern legal systems, and that a seminal principle of Muslim ethics is respect for the rule of law.

Again, if transitional societies often draw upon their ethical heritage to compensate for the weakness of the rule of law, they may also need to do so in terms of solidarity and self-organisation – the social capital of civic culture – that are especially necessary when states are weak. Social capital is customarily seen as stemming from engaged citizenship, an elusive expectation in pre-democratic states. Legacies of authoritarian or communist regimes tend to vitiate citizen trust in public organisations and curtail associational life, at least among those who recall the experience of that past.[68] On the other hand, social traditions relating to charitable endowments (*waqfs*), direct and institutional aid through religious tithes (*zakat*) for the disadvantaged, and community-based schools (*madrasas*) have deep roots in Muslim praxis. Regional variants of these include the *mahalla* (neighborhood organisations) and *gap* (consultative groupings that include interest-free loan associations among women), as well as other indigenous networks whose critical role in post-Soviet Central Asia has been well documented.[69] The potency of these ethical affinities becomes all the more evident in times of crises, when official institutions prove inadequate. This occurred rather conspicuously during the massive Turkish earthquake of August 1999, when mosque-based self-help initiatives were often the principal source of aid for thousands in need of food and shelter in several towns and cities; a militantly secular *devlet baba* (paternal state) was abruptly challenged by the civic efficiencies of 'Islam'. That, at any rate, was the view from official Ankara, which has long viewed religious solidarity groups with the suspicion directed at those demanding equity for Turkey's Kurdish minority.[70]

In comparison with most transitional states in the Muslim world, the Turkish state is relatively strong and Islamist movements in the country do not at this juncture pose a significant threat to the Kemalist Republican status quo. What is discomfiting about religiously-inspired ethical critiques from a statist perspective, of course, is their capacity to appeal to sources of legitimacy beyond the democratic framework of the modern polity – especially in transitional contexts when the state's democratic credentials have yet to be fully established. Freedom of the media, judicial independence, clean elections and the probity of public finances, along with secessionist movements and the role of the military, are issues that can profoundly undercut claims to democratic legitimacy. In these circumstances, political accountability may be elicited through appeals to the sharia, as has occurred in Afghanistan, Algeria, Iran, Sudan and, to a degree, in Nigeria. The results for individual liberty and civil society have been disastrous, not least because of the sundering of the sharia from its ethical roots.

Yet as evinced by the surveys from Azerbaijan and Turkey, even a 'secular' citizenry is cognizant of the civic value of Muslim ethical precepts, including normative expectations of financial probity and consultative policy-making.[71] Hence, to the value of social ethics as a compensatory buffer against the frailty of the rule of law and of formal citizenship in transitional states, can be added its prospective role in fostering public accountability and participatory politics. In states where the primacy of the sharia curtails democratic avenues of accountability and participation, an ethical critique may effectively be the *only* available means to challenge the clerical establishment. This has typically been the case at various stages in post-revolutionary Iran, notably with regard to the contest between reformists and conservatives on the status of women. By grounding challenges to male-dominated readings of the sharia in wider Muslim notions of social equity and solidarity, Iranian intellectuals and activists have acquired a platform with a competing claim to legitimacy.[72] Thence, such platforms can bridge appeals to more universal norms of human rights and pluralism that would not otherwise get a hearing in such theocratic contexts. Iranian women, for instance, have been actively engaged in United Nations conferences on gender equality – and not merely to influence the latter in favour of conservative interpretations of international human rights law. Rather, progressive global agendas can find expression in otherwise hostile territory through legitimate indigenous actors.

V

If social ethics have an empowering role to play for assorted Muslim publics, they can offer crucial restraints, not only as proto-rule-of-law but also as a compass for appropriate *means* to respond to and foster change. After all, the very notion of a 'civil' society is grounded in opposition to *uncivil* conduct, involving not only disrespect for the rule of law but also the absence of comity and non-violence. Indeed, democratic orders alone offer no assurance of civility, as instanced by the violent twentieth-century histories of both eastern and Western European states. Taming the impulses of incivility is, in effect, a precondition for civil society – and a task that enjoys '*distinct* ethical status':

> Modern societies are able to function because of some reliable expectation of civil treatment among their participants, and this expectation is a normative one. It is what ought to happen: a society is better, more like what it ought to be, if there is a high degree of civility, and such civility is a form of trust and mutual respect or recognition ... Persons *are* entitled to respect

as 'moral ends in themselves,' to use Kant's well-known language.'[73]

Within a Muslim ethos, this expectation is not merely pragmatic or functional but also, in the Kantian sense, moral. Applied in the context of transitions to democracy, amidst the pressures of new global economic and political forces, change rather than continuity is the norm for the majority of Muslim societies. The pace and radical quality of that change may be perceived as a deliberate assault on indigenous values. On occasion, the assault is physical, when politico-economic establishments use the security apparatus of the state to stifle dissent and protest, or to deny the exercise of the right to collective self-determination. The responses by citizens and groups are often also violent, with the rationales drawing on a religious vocabulary.[74] 'Islam' is readily harnessed as a legitimating discourse and ideology that privileges opposition to social, political and economic injustice – while its clear proscriptions against violent reaction are simply discarded. In self-reinforcing cycles of militancy – epitomised by the tragic recent histories of Algeria, Afghanistan and Palestine – the result is to profoundly debilitate the public sphere.

It is but a small step thence to export such militancy beyond national frontiers by proclaiming jihad (reduced to the notion of a 'holy war') against 'collaborating' foreign establishments or societies. The events of September 11, 2001, and their fallout are only the most graphic contemporary instance of such patterns. Normative frameworks like those of international human rights that outlaw the use of violence to advance claims of justice,[75] can be dismissed as ideologies of the same Western establishments that collaborate with oppressive governments in the Muslim world. A *fortiori* with regard to transnational criminal law directed at terrorism.

Hence, invoking ethical injunctions against violence becomes imperative. I am not, of course, suggesting that such injunctions should be a substitute for the rule of law as a *cordon sanitaire* for civic culture. Rather, the latter must be an integral part of the revival of dialogical, non-violent politics as the prevailing ethos. And there is no dearth of Islamic tradition and authority in this regard. 'Whoever slays an innocent soul … it is as though he slays all of humanity', is an oft-quoted Qur'anic verse (5:32). Muslims are forbidden from initiating hostilities, and warned when taking up arms in self-defence to 'not transgress limits'. (Qur'an 2:190). The rationale for jihad was to *limit* the legitimacy of warfare to preserving the loftiest moral values (Qur'an 4:75; 22:40), not to provide an alibi for the discontented.[76] Those moral values could never, for example, include forced conversion: 'There must be no coercion in matters of faith!' (Qur'an 2:256). Ideologues who claim that Muslims are enjoined to 'slay [enemies] wherever you find them!' (Qur'an 4:89) tend to overlook not only the defensive context,[77] but also the fact that the same verses insist that if the enemy ceases hostilities, 'God does not allow you to harm them' (Qur'an 4:90). Repeatedly, Muslims are urged to abjure revenge (Qur'an 5:45; 2:192, 193), and to iterate 'Peace' when provoked by the ignorant (25:63). Prophetic traditions or hadith cherish an even disposition, as in the sentiment, 'The most worthy of you is one who controls himself in anger!'[78]

Muhammad invoked in one of his last public sermons the pluralist tenor of the faith, epitomised in the Qur'anic verse, 'O people! We have formed you into nations and tribes so that you may know one another' (49:13). Indeed, the social ethos of inclusiveness, compassion and reason is captured in the concept of *hilm*, (derived from *al-Halim*, the Forbearing, one of God's Qur'anic 'names' and attributes) which several eminent non-Muslim scholars also see as a prime feature of the Qur'anic text:

> In a certain sense the Koran as a whole is dominated by the very spirit of *hilm*. The constant exhortation to kindness (*ihsan*) in human relations, the emphasis laid on justice (*'adl*), the forbidding of wrongful violence (*zulm*), the bidding of abstinence and control of passions, the criticism of groundless pride and arrogance – all are concrete manifestations of this spirit of *hilm*.[79]

In this vein, there ensues a convergence of individual and communal, private and public notions of rectitude. The idea of the umma becomes the embodiment of ethical affinity, bridging the sacred and the secular: 'Oh my community, my dear community,

Thus cries Muhammad', was Yunus Emre's fourteenth-century expression of that sentiment.[80] The ethos at hand is one of principled embrace of civility (as befits a religiously-motivated outlook), which is to be distinguished from a mere tactical adoption of non-violence (guided by expedient judgement that an adversary can be more effectively dealt with by such means). The importance of that distinction has been underscored by Richard Falk in contexts ranging from post-Revolutionary Iran to Eastern Europe and the Philippines: it is ultimately a principled opposition to violence that is required to sustain the civic culture.[81] Such a grounding amounts in our time to a global ethic, extending across religio-cultural frontiers. Precisely because that moment so clearly presses itself upon us, argues Falk, it provokes 'widespread fear, foreboding, and a disposition to retreat into the closed and rigid structures of the past, both a traditionalist past and a blinkered secularism that represents a degeneration of the modern impulse toward freedom, reason, and autonomy.'[82]

Certainly that goes some way toward explaining the claims of those who resort to self-serving, decontextualised quotation from scripture and prophetic tradition in support of political agendas whose legitimacy beggars the sanction of reason, revelation or civilisation. That such claims appeal to the socially and politically disenchanted is testimony to their ability to integrate themselves into the framework of cultural identities of Muslim societies. This is endemic to post-cold war 'discourses of origin' in which multiple affinities are reduced to a single dominant identity, which is felt to encompass a community 'whose unity is constructed upon an imagined nation'.[83] Yet frameworks of identity cannot be meaningful if they are not also *integrative*, capable of absorbing new ideas and evolving along the way.[84] Which brings us full circle to the need to conceive of ethics as moral reasoning, not normative rule-making and compliance – or the slave of an 'instrumental reason' that denies the sacred on the basis of an ideological construction of rationality.[85] The burden of such a revival must fall ultimately on the intelligentsia – whose need for spaces of freedom underscores, in turn, the primacy of a civil society safeguarded rather than coerced by the powers of the state.

VI

In sum, the polarity between Muslim and liberal approaches to the public sphere is paralleled by the acute opposition within liberal discourse on human rights between state and society, which reinforces the marginalisation of ethics in the civitas. Liberal praxis has come to privilege an amoral rationality in which ethical norms function as surrogates either for 'appropriate conduct' (denying any judgement on the basis of the good), or 'rational conduct' (denying any role for the sacred). In effect, this not only privatises the moral content of ethics but also subordinates it to 'self-fulfilment'. The practical consequence in our time is a veritable cottage industry of ethical talk that has more to do with 'professionalism' and 'transparency' – deemed key public values – than with commitments to acting rightly rather than wrongly. Contending voices like those of Himmelfarb and Seligman remain in the wings, and are even seized upon by the 'clash of civilisation' warriors on behalf of a patriotism that undercuts pluralism.

For Muslim societies in transition to modern polities, mobilising social ethics in the service of civic culture has strategic as well as intrinsic value. The weakness of the rule of law in these polities lends obvious pragmatic weight to a functional ethical framework, for state and society alike. Equally, the inchoate institutionalisation of democratic accountability and participatory mechanisms leaves a serious vacuum in the public sphere, which can be ameliorated by recognised ethical tenets. That recognition is linked to the legitimacy that principles of social solidarity, self-help and integrity command *qua* Muslim ethics. Those principles enjoy legitimacy even among citizens who regard themselves as firmly secular or nominally Muslim. Which underscores that there is more than instrumental value in espousing social ethics that have a religious grounding: there is also the critical dimension of moral capital, for all the seeming dissonance in the secular liberal mind.

The world's 1.2 billion Muslims are diverse in their cultures and understandings of Islam. But they share a *weltanschauung* in which *din* and *dunya* (but not the modern *dawla*) are merged, so that both secular and sacred resonate in the public domain. Far from precluding the institutional separation of Mosque and State, this perspective takes no ideological position in that regard: the umma can thrive in a plurality of political arrangements. In other words, the occidental liberal conception of civil society is not inimical to Muslim traditions simply because it is wedded to secular space. On the contrary, the primacy of the rule of law, participatory politics and the integrity of individual membership in a pluralist community are values cherished by both traditions. However, a radical secularity that banishes social ethics from the public sphere is patently inimical to Muslim society, for the moral orientation of individual and umma alike are privileged as public as well as private goals. Such a banishment also amounts to squandering potential social capital in the form of citizen-public trust, which enables associational life and civic culture to flourish.

There are, it must be admitted, pitfalls in that ethical privileging in the context of civil society. Pluralism – of culture, thought and life-goals – as well as the capacity of modern states to abuse power, suggest that ethical frameworks should be post-foundational, bounded by principles of democratic and civic commitments, including human rights. Tibi has cogently observed that the underlying challenge is about relocating civic life from a jealously-guarded 'religious' domain to a cultural-political one that accommodates the warp and woof of modernity.[86] For all the cultural anomie (after Durkheim) that is said to afflict Muslim elites in this Age of Anxiety, the prospects for civic life are unlikely to be enhanced by theologically-led invocations of political or social authority. There is abundant evidence on this score from the contemporary histories of several transitional states, including the poignancy of Afghanistan's post-1995 experience under the Taliban regime.

As well, the rigidities of traditionalism that can reduce ethics to the minutiae of law must be resisted. If Muslim ethics are to occupy a salient position in the civitas, then they must tap into the veins of moral reasoning beyond mere scriptural citation to support one or other political act or ideology. Indeed, this resonates deeply with Habermas's 'discourse ethics' in his ideal model of the public sphere, wherein capable citizens engage dialogically in a communal process of reasoned deliberation on quotidian moral issues. It is on this basis, surely, that the pressing issue of political violence must be confronted: for it goes to the core of what is acceptable conduct, even in response to grave injustice, when the result is a rupturing of the civility and social order in which the umma has its being. Ultimately, the interdependence of individuals and societies alike leads to a social ethics whose frontiers are transnational, calling for integrative quests in the civitas. But a welcome ecumenical globalism in matters of ethics, as on civil society at large, cannot dispense with the persistent need to draw upon and evolve indigenous cultural-religious traditions. For the latter impart incision and substance to the ever-thinning identities and ethical frames of reference of our postmodern age.

Notes

Author's Note: An earlier version of this paper appeared in the online journal *Polylog*, 2 (2001), 1–35 (<www.polylog.org/them/2/asp4-en.htm>); I am grateful for the many edifying responses thereto. However, the present text departs in many respects from that earlier one in response to the particular thematic concerns of this volume, and is also less constrained by the acute space-limitations of the earlier format.

1. See A. Seligman, *The Idea of Civil Society* (New York, 1992). The opposition of 'secular' and 'religious' is of growing importance in emerging Muslim discourses, and has been addressed elsewhere in this volume. Real and imagined polarities on this score are also finely sketched in B. Tibi, *Islam between Culture and Politics* (New York, 2001), pp.106–15; A. Filali-Ansary, 'The Challenge of Secularization', *Journal of Democracy*, 7 (1996), pp.76–80; and J. Keane, 'The limits of secularism', *The Times Literary Supplement*, 9 January 1998, pp.12–13.

2. See generally F. Halliday, *Two Hours That Shook the World – September 11, 2001: Causes and Consequences* (London, 2002).

3. Serious concerns have been raised by independent observers about disregard for the rule of law on the part of governments in their pursuit of alleged terrorists who happen to be Muslims, and the implications this will have for human rights in the long-run, not least in the Muslim world. A key suspect in Britain – Lotfi Raissi, alleged to have been the 'lead trainer' of the hijackers – was found by the courts to have had no

connection at all to the events: A. Cowell, 'Case tying Algerian to September 11 Collapses in Britain', *The New York Times* (13 February 2002), p.A1. On some of the longer-term implications, see 'War on terror "curbing human rights"', *BBC World Service Report* (16 January 2002) citing concerns expressed by the New York-based Human Rights Watch: <http://news.bbc.co.uk/hi/english/world/americas/newsid_1763000/ 1763641.stm>; M. Ignatieff, 'Is the Human Rights Era Ending?' (Op-ed article), *The New York Times* (5 February 2002), p.A29; and Statement by the UN Human Rights Commissioner, Mary Robinson, opening the Commission's 58th Session, Geneva, 18 March 2002, warning that 'we need to respond to terrorism not only by legislative and security measures but with the armory of common values, common standards and common commitments on universal rights that define us as one global community and which enable us to reach beyond our differences'.

4. See my cautionary comment on this score, 'Muslims Beware' (Op-ed article), *The Guardian* (London) (14 September 2001), p.22; and also prior to the events of September 11, with regard to the use of religious rhetoric in political conflicts, 'No ticket to paradise' (Op-ed article), *The Guardian* (4 September 2001), p.16.

5. On the 'Constitution of Medina', see R.N. Bellah, ed., *Beyond Belief: Essays on Religion in a Post-Traditionalist World* (Berkeley, CA, 1991), especially at pp.150–1; on al-Farabi and the ethical heritage in Islam, see R. Walzer, *Al-Farabi on the Perfect State* (Oxford, 1985); M. Fakhry, *Ethical Theories in Islam* (Leiden, 1994); *Ethics in Islam*, ed. R.G. Hovannisian (Malibu, CA, 1985).

6. See J. Habermas, 'Civil Society and the Political Public Sphere', *Between Facts and Norms: Contributions to a Discourse Theory of Law and Democracy*, tr. W. Rehg (Cambridge, MA and Cambridge, UK, 1996), pp.329–87; Charles Taylor, 'The Public Sphere', *Philosophical Arguments* (Cambridge, MA and London, 1995), pp.257–87. Both are discussed in my comments on the public sphere in the Introduction to this volume.

7. 'Ethics' and 'morals' tend to be used interchangeably in contemporary parlance, scholarly and otherwise (though see text accompanying note 18 below). Both terms are rooted in the Greek/Latin for 'customs', viz. *ethikos* and *mores*. For present purposes, I shall refer to ethics as the set of rules that purport to guide the behaviour of a society. Morals are referred to more specifically as judgements about right and wrong – which is not to say that ethics and morals are mutually exclusive, least of all in Muslim perspective (whether classical or contemporary). See generally

P.Singer, 'Introduction', in P. Singer, ed., *Ethics* (New York and Oxford, 1994), at pp.4–5.

8. C. Taylor, 'Cross-Purposes: The Liberal-Communitarian Debate', in *Philosophical Arguments*, at p.186. See also his *The Ethics of Authenticity* (Cambridge, MA, 1992), in which the collective and individual good are seen as casualties of the liberal quest for 'authentic self-fulfiment' and most recently, his *Varieties of Religion Today* (London and Cambridge, MA, 2002), on the frame of 'expressive individualism' that even shapes non-secular quests within the public sphere (ch. 3).

9. Ibid., at p.194, in the vein of the legal-political philosphy of John Rawls and Ronald Dworkin, among others. Taylor observes that in a broad sense, the 'right' may include 'the shared good'. But strictly speaking, a liberal consensus among citizens in increasingly pluralist societies is about such shared goods as individual dignity and sanctity, and respect for the rule of law, in other words, values that maintain social harmony. See also his *The Ethics of Authenticity* (Cambridge, MA, 1992), in which the collective and individual good are seen as casualties of the liberal quest for 'authentic' self-fulfilment.

10. Hence 'virtue' is 'human excellence', which requires man to 'perform his function well': *The Ethics of Aristotle: The Nicomachean Ethics*, trans. J.A.K. Thompson (London, 1976), p.99–100; and Jonathan Barnes's introduction in the same volume, especially pp.29–36.

11. A.B. Seligman, 'Animadversions upon Civil Society and Civic Virtue in the Last Decade of the Twentieth Century', in J.A. Hall, ed., *Civil Society: Theory, History, Comparison* (Cambridge, MA and Cambridge, UK, 1995), pp.200–23, at p.206.

12. R. Rorty, 'The Priority of Democracy to Philosophy', in *Objectivity, Relativism, and Truth: Philosophical Papers* (Cambridge, 1991), vol.1, at p.176. He therefore advocates working for a 'post-Philosophical culture' in the name of civic pluralism. See further the critical analysis of Rorty in J. Keane, ed., *Civil Society and the State: New European Perspectives* (New York and London, 1988) at pp.57–63.

13. See Isaiah Berlin, *Four Essays on Liberty* (London, 1969), and *The Sense of Reality: Studies in Ideas and their History* (London, 1996); Karl Popper, *The Open Society and Its Enemies*, vol.1 (London, 1945; repr., London, 1999).

14. Notably the 'international bill of rights' that comprises the Universal Declaration of Human Rights of 1948, and the ensuing United Nations covenants on Civil and Political Rights, and on Social, Economic and Cultural Rights. See generally C. Hesse and R. Post, ed., *Human*

Rights and Political Transitions: Gettysburg to Bosnia (New York, 1999); P. Sieghart, *The Lawful Rights of Mankind: An Introduction to the International Legal Code of Human Rights* (Oxford and London, 1985); Charles Taylor, *Sources of the Self: The Making of Modern Identity* (Cambridge, MA, 1989).

15. See V. Havel, *The Power of the Powerless: Citizens against the State in Central-Eastern Europe*, ed. J. Keane (New York, 1985), and *Summer Meditations* (New York, 1992); John Keane, ed. *Civil Society and the State: New European Perspectives* (New York and London, 1988); E. Gellner, *Conditions of Liberty: Civil Society and its Rivals* (London, 1994). Popper's influence on Soros is reflected in the latter's flagship Open Society Institute, which has offices across eastern and central Europe to fund civic projects.

16. R.D. Putnam, *Bowling Alone: The Collapse and Revival of American Community* (New York, 2000). The transition from essay to book is narrated at pp.505–13. See also M. Barone's review of the book, 'Doing Your Own Thing By Yourself', *Times Literary Supplement*, 23 February 2001, p.5.

17. *Bowling Alone*, chapters 4, 7 and 8.

18. J.R. Saul, *On Equilibrium* (Toronto, New York, London, 2001), p.86. Interestingly, this does not prevent him from invoking Solon, one of Athenian democracy's founding fathers, who warned of the 'public evil' that 'enters the house of each man', past courtyards and high walls. This leads Saul to conclude that 'ethics is a public matter' (pp.65–7) – yet he appears to see no contradiction in opposing public evil with an amoral public ethics. It is also noteworthy that 'public reason', as conceived by one of the twentieth century's leading political philosophers, John Rawls, is premised on liberal foundations that begrudge a morality linked to religious faith: see P. Berkowitz, 'John Rawls and the Liberal Faith', *The Wilson Quarterly*, Spring 2002, pp.60–9 (arguing that the Kantian basis of liberalism warrants a more generous acknowledgement of the intertwining of secular and sacred).

19. J. Smith, *Moralities: Sex, Money and Power in the Twenty-first Century* (London, 2001).

20. Ibid., pp.67–148.

21. Ibid., pp.149–86.

22. See Taylor, 'The Public Sphere', at pp.266–71; Gellner, *Conditions of Liberty*, pp.44–52. Richard John Neuhaus famously decried this state of affairs in *The Naked Public Square: Religion and Democracy in America* (Grand Rapids, MI, 1984); see also R. Thiemann, *Religion in Public Life: A Dilemma for Democracy* (Washington, DC, 1996); S. Carter, *Civility* (New

York and London, 1999); and *The Culture of Disbelief: How American Law and Politics Trivializes Religious Devotion* (New York, 1993).

23. See, *inter alia*, A. Etzioni, *The Spirit of Community* (New York, 1994), and 'Law in Civil Society, Good Society, and the Prescriptive State', *Chicago-Kent Law Review*, 75 (2000), p.355; A. Giddens, ed., *The Global Third Way Debate* (Cambridge, 2001); J. Gray, *Enlightenment's Wake* (New York and London, 1995); G. Himmelfarb, *The De-Moralization of Society: From Victorian Virtues to Modern Values* (New York, 1995); R. Kuttner, *Everything is for Sale: The Virtues and Limits of Markets* (New York, 1997); M. Sandel, *Liberalism and the Limits of Justice* (Cambridge, 1998).

24. *The Clash of Civilizations and the Remaking of World Order* (New York, 1996). Huntington's deterministic views about Islam and other civilisations in the context of contemporary politics are not unique: see, for example, L. Pye, *Asian Power and Politics: The Cultural Dimensions of Authority* (Cambridge, MA, 1985).

25. I have critiqued these views in 'The Crescent in the Public Square', *Islam in America*, 3 (1997), p.1; and 'The Islamic Ethos and the Spirit of Humanism', *International Journal of Politics, Culture and Society*, 8 (1995), p.579. See further B.S. Turner, *Orientalism, Post-modernism and Globalism* (London and New York, 1994), especially at pp.20–35; S-E Ibrahim, 'Civil Society and Prospects of Democratization in the Arab World', in *Civil Society in the Middle East*, ed. A.R. Norton (Leiden and New York, 1995), vol.1, p.27.

26. See, for example, J. Clark, 'Americans are blind to barbarians at their gates' (Op-ed), *The Times* (London), 15 September 2001, 18. (Clark, who is Hall Professor of History at the University of Kansas, invokes Huntington in support of an all out 'jihad' against terrorism in the wake of the September events). I drew attention to Huntington's new fan club in this context in 'Muslims Beware', cited at n.4, above; see also Edward Said, 'Islam and the West are inadequate banners', *The Observer* (London, 16 September 2001), <http://www.observer.co.uk/comment/story/0,6903,552764,00.html>.
Ironically, Huntington was challenged in this context by Francis Fukuyama, who insisted that the global liberal convergence envisaged in his 'end of history' paradigm remains valid – that the 'paroxysms of anger and violence' among Muslims did not alter the fact that there was no 'viable political program for Muslim societies to follow' outside Western liberalism: 'The West has Won', *The Guardian* (11 October 2001), p.21.

27. Etzioni, 'Law in Civil Society'. See also McClain and Fleming, 'Some Questions for Civil Society-Revivalists', especially at pp.302–9. On the

idea of the good society, see R. Dagger, *Civic Virtues: Rights, Citizenship, and Republican Liberalism* (Oxford and New York, 1997); R.N. Bellah, R. Madsen and W.M. Sullivan, *The Good Society* (repr., New York, 1992).

28. For an eloquent exposition on this parting of the ways in liberal discourse, see Seligman, 'Civil Society and Civic Virtue'; and his *The Idea of Civil Society* (New York, 1992).

29. Indeed, the communitarian movement has been accused of creating self-contained, exclusivist groups whose adherents have 'a long tradition of self-reliance and individualism' and undercut civic capital: see Eva Cox, *A Truly Civil Society* (Sydney, 2001), pp.29–37 (quote at p.36). For Mary Ann Glendon, the virtue-value dichotomy and the primacy of individual liberties have eroded the 'seedbeds of virtue' in which the entire civil society project must be grounded: 'Introduction: Forgotten Questions', in *Seedbeds of Virtue: Sources of Competence, Character, and Citizenship in American Society*, M. Glendon and D. Blankenhorn, ed., (Lanham, MD, 1995), p.1, especially at p.12.

30. *Conditions of Liberty*, p.102.

31. Ibid., pp.98–9.

32. Ibid., pp.26–9. Segmentary communities may avoid central/authoritarian tyranny, Gellner argues, but in their failure to shake off the tyranny of ritual and kinship they cannot qualify as civil societies.

33. See my review of *Conditions of Liberty* in *Canadian Journal of Law and Society*, 11 (1996), p.307.

34. See D. Eickelman, 'Inside the Islamic Reformation', *Wilson Quarterly*, 22 (1998), p.80; J.L. Esposito and J.O. Voll, *Islam and Democracy* (New York and Oxford, 1996); E. Özdalga, 'Civil Society and Its Enemies', in E. Özdalga and S. Persson, ed. *Civil Society, Democracy and the Muslim World* (Istanbul, 1997), p.73.

35. J. Habermas, *Moral Consciousness and Communicative Action*, tr. C. Lenhardt and S.W. Nicholson (Cambridge, UK, 1992), discussed in my remarks in the introduction to this volume.

36. See n.6 above.

37. Quoted in D.H. Cole, 'An Unqualified Human Good: E.P.Thompson and the Rule of Law', *Journal of Law and Society*, 28:2 (2001), pp.177–203, at p.182. Cole shows that Thompson's 'minimal conception' of the rule of law – a functional view that contrasts with more elaborate, ideology-ridden definitions – allowed him to be derisive about the workings of the law and yet laud it as an institution.

38. T. Carothers, 'The Rule of Law Revival', *Foreign Affairs*, 77 (1998), pp.95–106, at p.96.

39. See, for example, K. Armstrong, *The Battle for God* (London, 2000); C.G.A. Bryant, 'Civic Nation, Civil Society, Civil Religion', in J.A. Hall, ed., *Civil Society: Theory, History, Comparison*, pp.136–57; R. Coles, *The Secular Mind* (Princeton, NJ, 1999); and citations at notes 1 and 22 above.

40. Gellner, *Conditions of Liberty*, at p.5.

41. While this conceptual opposition was accentuated by the ideological clashes of the cold war, so that Soviet bloc states favoured socio-economic rights as against the civil-political rights espoused by Western states, the roots of the conflict can be traced within the liberal tradition itself. Taylor has shown this persuasively in outlining the competing 'Lockean' and 'civic humanist' approaches to civil society: 'Cross-Purposes: The Liberal-Communitarian Debate', pp.197–203.

42. John Keane, *Civil Society: Old Images New Visions* (Cambridge, UK), p.80.

43. Ibid., pp.52–7, 79–89. Keane tends to use 'virtue' and 'value' loosely and interchangeably here. It is prudent for purposes of clarity to avoid such overlapping usage.

44. Ibid., p.56.

45. See, *inter alia*, A. An-Na'im, 'The Synergy and Interdependence of Human Rights, Religion and Secularism', *Polylog*, 2 (2001), pp.1–43. <www.polylog.org/them/2.1/fcs7-en.htm>; and An-Na'im's 'Human Rights in the Muslim World: Socio-Political Conditions and Scriptural Imperatives', *Harvard Human Rights Journal*, 3 (1990), p.13; Mohammed Arkoun, 'The Ideal Community', 'The Person', and 'Ethics and Politics', in Robert.D. Lee, ed. and tr., *Rethinking Islam: Common Questions, Uncommon Answers* (Boulder, Colorado and Oxford, 1994); S.J. Al-Azm, 'Is Islam Secularizable?' in *Civil Society, Democracy and the Muslim World*, pp.17–22; A. Filali-Ansari, 'Can Modern Rationality Shape a New Religiosity? Mohamed Abed Jabri and the Paradox of Islam and Modernity', in J. Cooper et al., ed., *Islam and Modernity* (London and New York, 1998), pp.156–71; N. Madjid, 'Potential Islamic Doctrinal Resources for the Establishment and Appreciation of the Modern Concept of Civil Society', in N. Mitsuo et al., ed., *Islam and Civil Society in Southeast Asia* (Singapore, 2001), pp.149–63; C. Muzaffar, 'Ethnicity, Ethnic Conflict and Human Rights in Malaysia', in C.E. Welch and V.A. Leary, ed., *Asian Perspectives on Human Rights* (Boulder, CO, 1990), pp.107–41; Rahman, 'Law and Ethics in Islam', in *Ethics in Islam*, pp.3–15; M. Sadri and A. Sadri, ed. *Reason, Freedom, and Democracy in Islam: Essential Writings of 'Abdolkarim Soroush* (Oxford, 2000), ch. 3 and 7; R. Wright, 'Two Visions

of Reformation' (on Soroush and Ghannouchi), *Journal of Democracy*, 7 (1996), pp.64–75; B. Tibi, *Islam between Culture and Politics*.

46. B. Lewis, *The Multiple Identities of the Middle East* (New York, 2001), pp.28–9.

47. Arkoun, 'Ethics and Politics', at p.117. See further his, *The Unthought in Contemporary Islamic Thought* (London and New York, 2002), chapter 2, especially at pp.77–9.

48. Walzer, *Al-Farabi on the Perfect State*, at pp.229–59.

49. See M. Hodgson, *The Venture of Islam: Conscience and History in a World Civilization* (Chicago and London, 1974), vol.1, pp.444–95.

50. Miskawayh, *The Refinement of Character*, tr. C.K. Zurayk (Beirut, 1968).

51. Nasir ad-Din Tusi, *The Nasirean Ethics*, tr. G.M. Wickens (London, 1964).

52. See Fakhry, *Ethical Theories in Islam*, pp.61–99.

53. Ibid., pp.78–92.

54. Ibid., pp.193–206; Arkoun, *Rethinking Islam*, p.118. See generally, M.A. Quasem, *The Ethics of al-Ghazali: A Composite Ethics in Islam* (Petaling Jaya, Malaysia, 1976).

55. Rahman, 'Ethics in Islam', especially at p.4.

56. See M. Iqbal, *The Reconstruction of Religious Thought in Islam* (Lahore, 1962), especially at p.178. While *ijtihad* was more curtailed in the Sunni than Shi'i tradition, where imams and ayatollahs continued to exercise it, the innovative impulses of the early years were certainly attenuated even in the latter. See generally B. Weiss, 'Interpretation in Islamic Law: The Process of Ijtihad', *American Journal of Comparative Law*, 26 (1978), p.199.

57. There were exceptions, such as Iran's Shi'i ulama who held out against pre-Revolutionary despotisms through much of the twentieth century, and likewise al-Azhar's Sunni ulama in Cairo. But such resistance became, by and large, symbols less of ethical authority and autonomy than of rigid traditionalism in the face of 'secular modernity.'

58. In which al-Ghazali himself, for all his theological stature, played an important part amid the Turko-Arabian tensions of the Seljuk period in the late eleventh century: see G. Makdisi, 'The Marriage of Tughril Beg', *International Journal of Middle East Studies* (1970), pp.259–75.

59. F. Kazemi, 'Civil Society and Iranian Politics', in *Civil Society in the Middle East*, ed. A.R. Norton (Leiden, New York, 1996), vol.2, p.119, at pp.123–6; A. Banuazizi, 'Faltering Legitimacy: The Ruling Clerics and Civil Society in Contemporary Iran', *International Journal of Politics, Culture*

and Society, 8 (1995), p.563; R. Wright, *The Last Great Revolution: Turmoil and Transformation in Iran* (New York, 2000), pp.32–76, 243–88. The validity of the *velayat-e-faqih* notion in Shi'i theology and praxis is disputed; for its critics, it is simply an ideological tool to preserve clerical political dominance. See Soroush, *Reason, Freedom and Democracy in Islam*, pp.63–4.

60. See M. Fandy, *Saudi Arabia and the Politics of Dissent* (New York, 2001); J. Teitelbaum, *Holier than Thou: Saudi Arabia's Islamic Opposition* (Washington, DC, 2000).

61. See A.S. Moussali, 'Modern Islamic Fundamentalist Discourses on Civil Society, Pluralism and Democracy', in *Civil Society in the Middle East*, vol.1, p.79; T. McDaniel, 'The Strange Career of Radical Islam', in J.N. Wasserstrom et al., ed., *Human Rights and Revolutions* (Oxford and New York, 2000), pp.211–29; Human Rights Watch, *World Report 2002* (New York and London, 2002); Z. Hussain, '"Blasphemy" Doctor is Sentenced to Death', *The Times* (21 August 2001, London), p.11 (on a verdict against a medical professor, Younus Shaikh, under Pakistan's blasphemy law).

62. Ibn al-Jawzi, *Talbis Iblis* (Cairo, 1928); A. Abdelraziq, *al-Islam wa usul al-hukm* (Cairo, 1925). See the discussion on this issue in Tibi, *Islam between Culture and Politics*, pp.128, 163–4.

63. *Reason, Freedom, and Democracy in Islam*, pp.39–53.

64. Ibid., at pp.105–21 (quote at p.120).

65. M. Boroujerdi, 'The Paradoxes of Politics in Postrevolutionary Iran', in J.L. Esposito and R.K. Ramazani, ed., *Iran at the Crossroads* (New York, 2001), pp.13–27, at p.24. See also M. Kamrava, 'The Civil Society Discourse in Iran', *British Journal of Middle Eastern Studies*, 28 (2001), pp.165–85, remarking on today's 'more measured and less ebullient' quality of a reborn intellectual life (at p.184).

66. Although 63.4 per cent of respondents identified themselves as 'believers', 57.6 per cent said they did not observe any of the basic religious obligations, and 82.3 per cent said they did not pray formally.

67 A. Carkoglu, 'Religion and Public Policy in Turkey', *Institute for the Study of Islam in the Modern World (ISIM) Newsletter*, 8 (September 2001), p.29 (report on the 'Political Islam in Turkey' project).

68. See, for instance, M.M. Howard, 'The Weakness of Postcommunist Civil Society', *Journal of Democracy*, 13 (2002), pp.157–69.

69. See D. Kandiyoti, 'Rural livelihoods and Social Networks in Uzbekistan', *Central Asian Survey*, 17 (1998), pp.561–78; O. Roy, 'Kolkhoz and Civil Society in the Independent States of Central Asia', in M.H.

Ruffin and D. Waugh, ed., *Civil Society in Central Asia* (Seattle and London 1999), p.109; and S. Akiner's chapter in the present volume.

70. See E. Kalaycıoğlu, 'Civil Society in Turkey: Continuity and Change?' in B.W. Beeley, ed., *Turkish Transformation – New Century, New Challenges* (Walkington, UK, 2002); N. Gole, 'Authoritarian Secularism and Islamist Politics: The Case of Turkey', in *Civil Society in the Middle East*, vol.2, p.17.

71. Fiduciary obligations on the part of private and public custodians of wealth are a well-known facet of Islamic tradition, as is the *shura* principle of decision-making by consultation with those will be affected.

72. See Z. Mir-Hosseini, *Islam and Gender: The Religious Debate in Contemporary Iran* (London, 2000), especially pp.103–4, 128–43, 241–6 (conversation with Abdolkarim Soroush, on the limits of the law). See also Wright, *The Last Great Revolution*, pp.133–87.

73. R.B. Pippin, 'The Ethical Status of Civility?', in L.S. Rouner, ed., *Civility* (Notre Dame, Indiana, 2000), pp.103–17, at p.106.

74. See Halliday, *Two Hours that Shook the World*, pp.51–68, 193–211; Armstrong, *The Battle for God*, Part 2 ('Fundamentalism').

75. The premier international human rights activist group, Amnesty International, does not campaign on behalf of individuals as 'prisoners of conscience' if they have used violence to further their ends. At the same time, it should be recognised that the large-scale mobilisation of political violence by 'radical Islamists' is hardly the growing trend that it is often portrayed to be today, as Gilles Kepel persuasively shows in *Jihad: The Trail of Political Islam* (London and Cambridge, MA, 2002).

76. Typically, a widely-quoted hadith or prophetic tradition has Muhammad saying to his companions on returning from battle that they were now headed for 'the greater jihad' – of expunging wrongdoing from one's self and community.

77. Parallel to those that underpin far stronger exhortations in the Bible: 'Kill every breathing thing in the city', says the Book of Joshua, for example. In this context, the late, much-revered activist and scholar, Mahmoud Mohamed Taha, postulated a distinction between the Qur'an's Meccan verses with their universalist articulation of ideals, and the subsequent Medinan verses that reflected the hard realities of resistance to the Prophet's mission. For Taha, and his best-known disciple, Abduallahi an-Na'im, non-violence is to be grounded in the universalism of the Meccan revelation. For a succinct exposition, see D.L. Smith-Christopher, "That was Then ... ": Debating Nonviolence within the Textual Traditions of Judaism, Christianity, and Islam', in J. Runzo and N.M.

Martin, ed., *Ethics in the World Religions* (New York and Oxford, 2001), pp.256–9.

78. D.M. Donaldson, *Studies in Muslim Ethics* (London, 1953), p.70.

79. T. Izutsu, *God and Man in the Koran: Semantics of the Koranic Weltanschauung* (Tokyo, 1964), at p.216. On the shared views of Ignatius Goldziher and Charles Pellat, see F. Denny, 'Ethics and the Qur'an: Community and World View', in R.G. Hovannisian, ed., *Ethics in Islam* (Malibu, CA, 1985), pp.114–15. See also Nasr Abu Zaid, 'The Qur'anic Concept of Justice', *Polylog*, Vol. 2 (2001), 1–43 (<www.polylog.org/them/2/fcs8-en.htm>).

80. Signifying the timeless intercession of the Prophet on behalf of the community, in versification much favoured by Turkish dervishes: *Divan*, tr. A. Golpinarlı (Istanbul, 1943), p.559, no.229.

81. R. Falk, *Religion and Humane Governance* (New York and Basingstoke, UK, 2001), pp.143–56. In the Iranian instance, Falk observes that initial restraint on the part of the ulama opposing the Shah was tactical, and soon gave way to the systematic use of political violence in maintaining the new regime. However, he does not consider the possibility that the initial opposition was in fact principled – on the part of a different set of leaders from those who eventually came to control the regime.

82. Ibid., at p.3.

83. V. Jabri, *Discourses on Violence: Conflict Analysis Reconsidered* (New York, 1996), p.120, building on Benedict Anderson's much-quoted *Imagined Communities: Reflections on the Origin and Spread of Nationalism* (London, 1991). See also the novelist Amin Maalouf's elegant essay, *In the Name of Identity: Violence and the Need to Belong*, tr. B. Bray (New York, 2000), especially pp.96–7, 100.

84. I. Serageldin, 'Mirrors and Windows: Redefining the Boundaries of the Mind', *American Journal of Islamic Social Sciences*, 11 (1994), pp.79–107, at pp.88–9. Serageldin argues that society's felt need to preserve cohesion, especially in a time of rapid change, strengthens the influence of the quotidian on the collective ethos – at the expense of deeper commitments that might filter and shape quotidian elements.

85. See Taylor, *The Ethics of Authenticity*, especially pp.4–11; Saul, *On Equilibrium*, pp.297–308 (drawing on Taylor).

86. *Islam between Culture and Politics*, especially at pp.69–81.

9

State and Civil Society in Turkey: Democracy, Development and Protest

Ersin Kalaycıoğlu

Introduction

Turkish politics has, since the end of the Second World War, been under the influence of rapid democratisation as well as social mobilisation. Although there need not be any causal linkage between the two, Turkish efforts at democratisation instituted multiparty politics and introduced popular influence on political decision-making – which also precipitated the delivery of services to the neglected periphery of society. Roads that were built to connect the remotest settlements to the cities seem to have facilitated a major exodus from the countryside. Hence, urbanisation appears to have been the most important outcome of the democratisation process. The growth of industry, private business and commerce in the budding capitalist economy of the 1950s also fuelled rapid social mobilisation, which gained pace by the late 1950s and further escalated through to the 1980s. Although it has slowed down from the late 1990s, social mobilisation robustly continues. In any event, the relationship between the periphery and the centre of Turkish society has changed once and for all:

the country has increasingly become urban, industrial and democratic.

In the meantime, the one-party rule of the Republican People's Party (CHP), which had been established before the proclamation of the Turkish Republic in 1923, ended in 1945. New political parties were established to enter the electoral contest, among them the Democrat Party (DP) that won the general elections in 1950. Electoral races since the 1950s among the political parties representing various ideological positions across the left-right spectrum – and the periphery versus the centre – eventually produced an overwhelming preponderance of the periphery, and simultaneously of the right and even far right ideologies in Turkish politics. Eleven of the fourteen elections held since 1946 were won by political parties representing the periphery, and various combinations of right-wing ideologies and perspectives like conservatism, liberalism, traditionalism, chauvinism, and religious-reactionism (a yearning to return to a Golden Age, *Asr-ı Saadet*). A sharp cultural divide, inherited from the Ottoman era, dominated the early Republican period of 1923–1946: a coherent, modernising, 'progressivist' centre that comprised elites who believed in an Image of Good Society built around 'science and reason', versus a culturally heterogeneous periphery whose masses believed in a contrasting 'Image of Good Society' built around tradition as represented at its core by religion (mainly Sunni Islam).[1] In the aftermath of democratisation and rapid social mobilisation of the last half century, the division persists of Turkish society into two *kulturkampf*s.[2] However, the cultural cleavage in question has become less pronounced in that period.

Thanks to democratisation, many members of the periphery gained political power and social recognition by serving in such capacities as deputies of the Turkish Grand National Assembly (TBMM), cabinet ministers, public prosecutors, judges, under-secretaries of the cabinet ministries, and general managers of the State Economic Enterprises (SEE). Rapid social mobilisation also provided more opportunities for the agents of the periphery. They had better opportunities of attending school and of being employed as professionals in the urban centres of Turkey. Social mobilisation also precipitated upward mobility, which was un-checked by any social class system that efficiently and effectively kept the lower classes at bay. The centre was gradually penetrated by the forces of the periphery, which obviously led to the former slimming down. Currently, a state elite that specialises in security, defence, foreign relations and finance still seems to evince signs of being affiliated with the older image of the centre. The rest of the state apparatus – cabinet ministries, the SEE, and various state agencies – are mostly subdued and taken over by agents of the periphery. The heterogeneous culture of the periphery now seems to be replicated in the formerly homogeneous centre.

The overall outcome of this transformation appears to be a larger but sluggish state bureaucracy which has in part become subservient to the new political patrons from the periphery. Thus, the predisposition of the state bureaucracy to control the periphery has been effectively curtailed by the new political elites representing the periphery. The taming of the centre by the agents of the periphery also resulted in the establishment of new rela-tionships between those who wield political power in the name of the 'State', and those who do not. The ideology of the governing parties that emphasised the application of liberal economic poli-cies in a capitalist economy contributed to the emergence of an economic space for private entrepreneurial initiative. Democrati-sation also paved the way for the establishment of a multitude of social and political associations and a variety of political parties. Hence, it became possible, since the 1950s, for individuals to take civic and political initiative in establishing associations with other like-minded individuals. A burgeoning civil society emerged with the drive to democratise the political system. But this process was neither easy nor smooth. Civil society in Turkey has gone through phases of severe relapse and rapid rebound. This paper appraises state-civil society relations in a cultural environment shaped by a rift between centre and periphery, and a socio-political environ-ment of rapid change, volatility and turbulence.

250 ERSIN KALAYCIOĞLU

The State: Traditional Strength or its Illusion?

Turkish political culture is replete with references to the 'omnipotent state' that functions as an eternal force, shaping and moulding
the political system and society alike. This transcendental percep-
tion of the state by the public as well as the elites precipitated a
scholarly tendency to depict Turkey as having a robust state tradition, inherited in part from the Ottoman Empire.[3] There appears
to be a visible statist orientation (*étatism*) in Turkey that stresses
community over the individual, uniformity over diversity, and an
understanding of law that privileges collective reason.[4] Such an
orientation toward the state lends itself to an understanding of
politics as leadership and education of the 'ignorant' masses
through the intervention of state or bureaucratic elites.[5] Those
tendencies went together with a centre that assumed that its functions legitimately included the goal of dominance over every nook
and cranny of social life, through its control of the state. Indeed,
the centre viewed the periphery as a launch pad of seditious activity, and hence acted to forestall or suppress every dissenting
opinion and movement.[6]

Under those circumstances a popular image developed of the
state as an omnipotent control mechanism. It was not necessarily
an image of a Leviathan that harasses society, but rather of a fear-
some tool in the hands of the centre. As such, it was to be avoided
at most times, yet also assumed to have infinite resources and
means at its disposal that could be distributed to the subjects of
the state through benign largesse. This is an ambivalent image,
both punishing and rewarding. It is small wonder that the Turkish state has come popularly to be referred to as the 'Papa State'
(*Baba Devlet*).[7] When challenged, it turns into a nasty and cruel
(*ceberrut*) mechanism of suppression; but when socio-political
forces co-operate with it, there is much to be gained from its benevolence.[8]

However, it is not the popular image of the state alone that
results in a style of rule detrimental to the development of civil
society in Turkey. It is also the attitude of the bureaucrats serving
in the state mechanism and dealing with the periphery. Too often
that attitude has been patronising and humiliating, with the

periphery too harassed to develop 'a public interest and emerge as 'civil-society-as-public'.[9] Under these circumstances, one does not expect to find much evidence of the roots of civic initiative, of the voluntary activism necessary to engage and re-shape the state. It is small wonder, then, that the state tradition in Turkey does not sit well with civil society. But such a 'genetic' explanation of state-civil society relations, which is deeply rooted in history and culture, does not necessarily do justice to the potential for change in the political system, or indeed within society itself. What I mean by this is that though traditions matter, political structures and behaviour tend to alter over time. Second, although the state tradition is depicted as strong, the very strength of the state itself is, at best, a matter of debate. Indeed, if a strong state is assumed to be one that possesses high capability to regulate the behaviour of those under its jurisdiction, to extract and distribute resources effectively and efficiently from the society and territory over which it is presumed to have power, and to create and declare symbols that elicit awe and deference,[10] then the state does not seem to have much strength in Turkey.[11] Third, the Turkish political regime has veered toward democracy since the 1940s. However imperfect that drive, election campaigns and electoral contests among different political parties have had their impact on state-civil society relations. The periphery has found ample opportunity to make its impact on the state through the processes and institutions of the democratic regime, which rolled the state back and provided for greater breathing space for the periphery as well as civil society.

Civil Society: Voluntary Action and State Reaction

Civil society refers to a social context that is determined by structures, processes and institutions which, in turn, stem from the voluntary, private actions of individual citizens. Hence, civil society connotes the lack of intrusion of the state or centralised national power in the affairs of private citizens. It is the autonomous, consenting and self-initiated actions of each individual that determine the gist of the matter that constitutes civil society. The overall emphasis of such a definition is on the free will, local decision-making and social contract undisturbed by the state. Seligman refers to Daniel Bell to define civil society as emphasising 'voluntary association ... (so) that decisions are made locally and should not be controlled by the state and its bureaucracies'.[12]

A context of social and political tolerance, and an environment of interpersonal trust, are often considered necessary for the vigour and sustainability of civic or associational activism.[13] Concomitantly, Hann defines civil society with reference to problems of accountability and cooperation that all groups face.[14] Consonant with what is implied by these definitions, associability should be considered as a core component of civil society. If the vigour and plenitude of voluntary associations are the most critical components of civil society, then it is appropriate to closely examine associability in the Turkish context. Associability occurs in an environment of interpersonal trust and social tolerance of dissent. Consequently, we should expect to find ample evidence not only of associability but also interpersonal trust and social tolerance of dissent in consolidated civil societies. Similarly, we should be able to observe a vigorous associational life. In consolidated civil societies not only do we observe a myriad of voluntary associations but also a high level of membership in such organisations. The extent to which associability and associational membership exist, and the extent to which interpersonal trust and social tolerance of dissent are internalised by the population, should provide a measure of the existence and quality of civil society. In what follows in this section, I will primarily examine the variety and the number of voluntary associations in Turkey and, secondly, consider the relationship between associability, on the one hand, and interpersonal trust and social tolerance of dissent, on the other.

In a recent publication, Toprak argues that the total number of voluntary associations in Turkey is 54,987;[15] Pusch quotes a higher figure of 61,000.[16] An article by Hikmet Yavuzyiğit in *Mülkiyeliler Birliği* (Alumni Association of the Faculty of Political Science of Ankara University, which is extremely well connected with the public bureaucracy of the central government) puts the number at 112,000 in the mid-1990s.[17] Reporting on that article, the daily newspaper *Radikal* (28 November 1998) cited the General Directorate of Security, Desk of Associations (*Emniyet Genel Mudulugu, Dernekler Masasi*) as the source for Yavuzyiğit's data, though he cites no source in the article. However, even that figure does not include all unions and co-operatives, which are registered with the Ministry of Industry and Commerce, and the Ministry of Agriculture and Forestry. Co-operatives are also voluntarily established associations, which aim to mobilise civic and local financial resources without state involvement. As of 24 March 2000, the total number of active co-operatives in the country is reported to be 59,236 by the aforementioned ministries.[18] If the last two figures are correct, there should be no less than 170,000 officially registered voluntary associations in Turkey, as of Spring 2000.

But not all of the 112,000 associations cited above were active at the time. About half were reported to be inactive in Yavuzyiğit's article.[19] So an approximate figure of 56,000 active voluntary organisations, and 59,000 co-operatives, yields an aggregate of about 115,000 active voluntary associations as a plausible estimate for the late 1990s. There appears to be one voluntary association per 540 or so citizens in Turkey by that count, a relatively low figure in comparison to post-industrial liberal democracies. Still, the Turkish performance does not seem to be dismal (see Table 1). Table 1 indicates that the average membership size of voluntary associations in consolidated democracies tends to be smaller, indicating the plenitude of voluntary associations there. Among the countries included, the United States hosts the highest number of voluntary associations and Turkey the lowest. If one examines the overall trend of growth of the number of voluntary associations in Turkey, the difference between Turkey and the post-industrial liberal democracies may indeed be narrowing. As of 1938, there were only 205 officially registered voluntary associations in Turkey.[20] In 1950, that figure rose to 2011, and by the mid-1950s there were about 11,000 legally registered voluntary associations – increasing to some 36,000 in the mid-1960s, to 38,000 in the mid-1970s and to 53,657 by 1981.[21] Finally, as already mentioned, the voluntary associations officially registered with the Directorate of General Security rose to 112,000 by the mid-1990s. Co-operatives established in the urban areas also seemed to have followed a similar pattern.

Table 1
Associability in Comparative Perspective

Country	Number of Citizens per Voluntary Association
Canada	429
France	84
Sweden	44
United Kingdom	436
United States	172
Turkey	**543**

Sources: <http://ncss.urban.org>; <www.etwelfare.com/analmri.htm>; <www.ccp.ca>

About half of the voluntary associations in Turkey are co-operatives and unions, about 12 per cent are religious associations, (the majority of which are associations for mosque construction), about 13 per cent are regional or local solidarity associations, approximately 12 per cent are educational, and 9 per cent are sports associations.[22] Environmental, self-help, recreational, human rights, welfare and charity associations are much fewer in number. Interestingly, it appears that most of the voluntary associations cited here were established in the last two decades. Most notably, associability seems to be closely related to urbanisation in Turkey. Major metropolitan areas host most of the voluntary associations. The megapolis of Istanbul tops the list with 12,733 associations, followed by the second most populous city, Ankara, hosting 8,541, and Izmir with 5,235 associations; among the least populous provinces, Ardahan hosts 88, Batman 210, Bartin 218, and Hakkari only 52 voluntary associations.[23]

While the number of voluntary associations does not seem to indicate a frail civic culture, this information alone is not enough to determine whether civil society is a vigorous and effective part

Table 2

Membership in Voluntary Associations in Comparative Perspective (%)

	Type of Voluntary Association								
	Religious	Sports	Culture/Art	Trade Union	Political Parties	Environmental	Professional	Welfare/Charity	Overall*
Turkey	**3.7**	**5.7**	**3.1**	**4.8**	**9.7**	**1.9**	**8.6**	**4.1**	**7.0**
World									
Mean=	15.5	16.8	11.3	19.8	9.1	4.7	8.8	6.2	
Median=	11.2	15.7	9.3	14.0	7.4	2.9	6.2	5.8	
S.Dev.=	14.5	10.3	7.6	18.1	6.8	4.7	5.9	3.7	

Notes: Table entries for Turkey are percentages of the sample of respondents representing the voting age population who registered that they were members of corresponding voluntary associations at the time of the interview in 1997. Table entries for the World are the arithmetic means, median and standard deviation of the corresponding percentages per type of organisation reported across those countries included in the World Values Survey 1989–1990. 'Mean' refers to the average percentage for the countries included in the Survey, 'median', is the middle value of the countries included therein; together they indicate the central tendency of each type of associability for the entire group of countries included in the Survey, except for Turkey.

*Percentage of the respondents representing the voting age population in Turkey who reported that they were members of a voluntary association in Autumn 1900.

Sources: Turkish Values Survey 1990, and 1997; and World Values Survey 1989/90.

of the Turkish body politic. In order to establish how active and effective civil society is in Turkey, we need to know how active the rank-and-file members of those associations are, and how large their membership is. Finally, we need to ascertain whether they wield any power and influence vis-à-vis the state.

The overall rate of membership in voluntary associations appears to be quite low, hovering around 7 per cent of the population for all associations, except for the co-operatives (see Table 2). Co-operatives have more active members, who constitute around 11 per cent of the population.[24] There should be some overlap in those two figures, for there must be multiple memberships; but the extent of such memberships is impossible to determine. An informed estimate is that one of every seven or eight citizens belongs to some kind of voluntary association in Turkey (see Table 2). Membership in various types of associations in Turkey – except for political parties – is relatively low.

It is also not certain what proportion of the members pay their dues regularly or take part in the activities of those organisations. If the responses given in the surveys to whether the interviewees belong to voluntary associations are taken as an indication of reporting for active members only, that figure seems to be around 7–8 per cent of the adult population. Indeed, Yavuzyiğit also argues that 'most associations are either established for reasons other than their declared goals, or they fail to attract members and support from the masses'.[25] Under those circumstances, I am inclined to argue that membership in voluntary associations does not extend to much of society, let alone the majority of the Turkish population. Active membership seems to be a scant commodity in Turkey. Consequently, there seem to be a large number of small organisations, with even smaller critical masses of active members, that vie for the attention of the masses and the political elites alike.

The lack of enthusiasm to join voluntary associations may partly be accounted for by a culture deeply penetrated by a sense of interpersonal distrust. In fact, survey after survey seems to indicate that more than 90 per cent of the Turkish voting age population declares that fellow human beings cannot be trusted.[26]

When compared with the findings of the World Values Survey, Turkish interpersonal trust rates rank at the bottom of a list of 43 countries, with Brazil.[27] Lack of interpersonal trust undermines any effort at establishing and sustaining partnerships, whether they are economic, political or cultural.[28] The development of associability and mass membership in associations is an obvious casualty of this culture of distrust.

Turkish culture also appears to be characterised by lack of social tolerance of dissent.[29] Values surveys indicate that most respondents do not express tolerance of neighbours who seem to have a lifestyle that deviates from their own.[30] Such shallow social tolerance induces voluntary associations to function with few members, who 'look and act alike'. A plenitude of voluntary associations emerges with low participation and a proclivity for viewing the rest of society as untrustworthy, and intolerable. Nor do voluntary associations evince an eagerness to engage with other voluntary associations, deliberate issues with them or co-operate and co-ordinate their activities to promote their goals.

Although the result is a highly fragmented and curtailed civil society, active participants of voluntary associations may still be effective in their interactions with the state. In fact, values surveys indicate that feelings of political efficacy are rather strong and widely distributed in Turkey.[31] Feelings of political efficacy are based on perceptions, which may of course be accurate or otherwise. The effectiveness of participants is dependent upon the extent of their control over political resources, and their capacity to co-operate and co-ordinate with other associations in dealing with the state. There is, however, little evidence that voluntary associations have much control over such political resources as votes, wealth and information. The few that do have some control appear to lack the capability, interest, and/or the will to cooperate with others to influence the state.[32]

Some effective associations, like the Turkish Businessmen and Industrialists Association (TÜSIAD), the Confederation of Turkish Trade Unions (Türk-Is), and the Turkish Union of Chambers and Stock Exchanges (TOBB) often benefit from their co-operation with the state, rather than co-operation with other voluntary associations to pressure the state. What Turkey is experiencing is not only a fragmented civil society, but one consisting of voluntary associations that are better at rivalry than mutual co-operation. As a rule, voluntary associations do not seem to consider the state as an adversary, but rather an ally to be mobilised against their competitors. So voluntary associations tend to campaign for state attention, subsidies, and assistance, while seeking to eliminate or eclipse their closest rivals. For example, TOBB would rather link up in a corporatist manner with the state and be treated as the sole representative of the organised economic interests in the country. It is not surprising to hear declarations by TOBB calling for TÜSIAD and other voluntary associations to be muffled – for TOBB believes that the others represent the 'special interests' of their members, while TOBB itself represents 'the public interest of all business and commercial classes' of the country.[33] Other types of associations have been more difficult to monitor; yet there is hardly any evidence that they act collaboratively with perceived competitors to promote common interests vis-à-vis the state. A mutually rewarding relationship of symbiosis seems to emerge only between the state and relatively resourceful associations.

There is no scarcity of protest movements and advocacy associations – like the Human Rights Association (IHD) and the religious *Mazlum Der* (literally 'Association of the Oppressed') – that systematically confront the Turkish state. Although such movements achieve remarkable media attention and publicity, it is doubtful that they have any significant impact on political decisions – or that they get any of their demands met by the political authorities.[34] Recent surveys indicate that a vast majority of the voting-age population in Turkey believes that protest behaviour is the least effective means of influencing political decisions.[35] Not surprisingly, then, protest movements, campaigns of civil disobedience and advocacy activities seem to elicit little mass support. The political authorities tend to view them with utter suspicion, as potential acts of conspiracy to undermine the Republican political system; and the security forces give no quarter to advocacy associations that challenge the political establishment. However, clashes between such associations and the security forces receive wide coverage in the national and international media, and thus contribute to an image of state-civil society relations marked by ill-will, distrust and a lack of tolerance.

It is true that are a myriad of well-organised economic, solidarity, religious, charity, sports and self-help groups that are recognised as legitimate, non-governmental organisations by the state and the public alike. There is little evidence that local or regional self-help and solidarity associations (*Yardımlaşma Derneği*, or *Kayserililer Derneği*), or Mosque Building Societies (*Cami Yaptırma Cemiyeti*) are ever treated by the state as conspiracies. But those religious and ethnic groups that launch protest campaigns and advocate a change of political regime or the Republican system itself do not enjoy legitimacy in the eyes of either the political elite or the majority of the people. Hence, the relationship between the state and civil society is two-pronged: on the one hand, there are co-operative attitudes and symbiotic linkages, at times culminating in corporatist relationships.[36] On the other, there are conflict-ridden, confrontational relationships culminating in clashes between the advocacy groups and the security forces.[37] Protests by advocacy groups that fail to mobilise mass support or sympathy trigger harsh and suppressive reactions from the state – which generally seeks to control and if necessary suppress protest movements, seen as manifestations of civil disobedience and even sedition. How, then, may we best understand state-civil society relations in Turkey?

State-Civil Society Relations

What we have so far unearthed indicates that there is an established associational life in Turkey, which functions as the core of civil society. Associations that demonstrate a large variety of social, economic, cultural, recreational and political interests, with varying capacities to organise and command political resources, exist in Turkey. Active social involvement in this multiplicity of associations is still confined to a relatively small number of citizens. Most associations remain deeply influenced by primordial bonds which are established around religious affinities, blood ties, local and regional solidarity (i.e., *hemşehrilik*), as well as economic interests.

The state is not reflexively or monolithically opposed to any specific forms of association in Turkish society. Indeed, state agencies have not only tolerated but also, as during the catastrophic earthquakes of 1999, extended support to self-help organisations mobilised in response to public needs. Local and regional solidarity associations and religious organisations tend likewise to elicit the support of the state. Nor is there evidence that such international organisations as the Lions or Rotary Clubs are treated unfavourably. Business and commercial associations, foundations, co-operatives and conference groups are tolerated or even encouraged by the political establishment. Such overtly political organisations as the right wing Marmara, and left wing Taksim groups have shown remarkable continuity in their deliberative meetings over the years. They have been meeting regularly for the last two to three decades. They invite guest speakers and deliberate on the political issues of the day. All major political figures – from presidents and prime ministers to deputies of the Grand National Assembly (GNA) – have sought to take part in their activities. Taksim, Marmara and other similar groups managed to preserve an environment of free debate and deliberation about the overtly political issues of the country without any meddling from the state.

However, we also observed that the state demonstrates an entirely different posture toward associations that advocate drastic change in the Republican system or the political regime. Human rights organisations that propagate an end to the unitary state and adoption of a federal system, claims to special rights by ethnic groups like the Kurds, or women who cover their heads in the *türban* on religious grounds (discussed below), elicit little sympathy or tolerance from the state.

As I have argued elsewhere,[38] it is not the strength but the relative weakness of the Turkish state that impedes the full development of civil society. The weakness leads to a lack of regulatory, extractive and distributive capacity on the part of the state, which renders the elite (centre) vulnerable and fearful about the discontent of the masses (periphery). There is also a relatively long history of mutual suspicion between the centre and periphery in Turkey that further complicates and corroborates this perspective. The political authorities seek to use executive power in a relatively arbitrary manner to establish a punitive capacity to suppress actual or potential challenges to the establishment. The promulgation of the 1982 constitution, which reinforced and consolidated executive supremacy as the core value of the political regime, was designed to extend legality if not legitimacy to such a style of rule. The use of arbitrary executive power renders civil society somewhat fragile by intimidating many who would otherwise consider civic activism.

A recently-developed framework suggests that the relations between the state and society can be classified along two dimensions: inclusiveness versus the exclusiveness of the state, and activism versus passivity of the state.[39] Using this framework Sunar suggests that Turkey seems to demonstrate the outlook of a 'passive-exclusive state', defined as a state that 'resists the entry of disadvantaged groups in the official domain of the state regime but neither combats nor promotes civil society'.[40] He further argues that the passive-exclusive state does not have the same attitude toward all groups in civil society. For instance, the Turkish state allows the organisation of economic groups, or associations based on gender; but it is watchful of religious associations and actively resists associability on the basis of cultural ethnicity.[41] The passive-exclusive nature of the state reinforces its relative weakness. A weak state extends its resources and boosts its capacity by ignoring large swathes of civil society, which it is not, in any case, able to regulate and control. Accordingly, only those associations that are perceived as bent on sedition and radical conspiracy, and hence deemed to be security risks, are seriously monitored, prosecuted or suppressed. The rest are either simply left alone or co-operatively engaged.

Evidently, a problem emerges for ethnic and religious nonconformists who would like to have recognition, respect and representation within the political system. The problem is that they want these on their own terms, without adapting to the rules

of the political game. The Kurdish nationalists, for example, demand a political voice and recognition in the fullest sense.
Religious radicals demand representation and respect in all institutions of the political system, however much they contest and
condemn the rules and regulations that the institutions operate
under. The state, on the other hand, demands that the 'nonconformists' first accept and fully internalise the principles of the
Republican system, the constitution and the laws, and the related
rules of the political game. So there ensues a crisis in political
participation to which a compromise solution is nowhere in sight.
But there is an interesting precedent in this regard, which may
point the way to how relations between advocacy groups and the
state could evolve.

Conjectures

The relationship between women's advocacy groups and the state
has shown remarkable change over time, and deserves to be closely
examined. Women's associations were faced with an exclusivist
and even suppressive attitude in the 1980s when they first became
active.[42] Over the years, friction and confrontation between these
associations and the state became more inclusive and passive. The
attitudes of some local governments toward the associations provided a chance for them to realise some of their goals through
co-operation with the municipalities. For example, shelters for
women were established by city administrations, and enabled
women experiencing marital problems and maltreatment to take
refuge there.[43] Women's groups were able to establish themselves
in Bar Associations and other legal organisations and work with
them to change the civil code and improve the record of wom-
en's rights. International pressures and treaties signed by Turkey
also resulted in a shift of state policies and practices. By the early
1990s, a cabinet-level ministry was established with the specific
task of looking after the affairs and rights of women. Confrontation between women's associations and the state evolved into
dialogue, negotiation, and eventually co-operation. Currently,
there is scant evidence that women's associations are, for the most

part, still considered as seditious groups by the institutions of the state.[44]

Could relations between ethnic and religious associations and the state follow a pattern similar to the secular women's and feminist associations? Religious or religiously motivated associations may be divided into three categories on the basis of their relationship with the state. Associations that engage in such self-help projects as mosque building, running soup kitchens for the poor, providing scholarships to students, and so on are usually deemed legitimate civic actors by the Turkish state. Religiously motivated economic associations, such as Islamic banking, or the conservative Businessmen and Industrialists Association (MÜSIAD), which are established with the approval of the state, tend to have ambivalent standing. Some high-level politicians support or even promote such economic interests; but there are also those who vehemently oppose economic activism. The state's wavering attitude to such associations depends on the socio-political climate that in turn determines which of these two opposing political attitudes achieves the upper hand in government. The third category of Islamic groups are protest movements that confront the state and often clash with its agents. Such groups have established publications, conduct protest campaigns and organise rallies and meetings. They include associations that promote the rights of individuals imprisoned from among the ranks of Islamic advocacy groups (*Mazlum-Der*), or promote and propagate an issue with the intent of changing government or state policy.

One such issue – that of women wearing the *türban* (the headscarf in a certain style so as to cover the hair, neck and shoulders) – has, since the 1980s, come to occupy a prominent part in Turkish politics and has engulfed both universities and lower-level educational institutions. Like the abortion issue in the United States, the *türban* has become an all but irresolvable cultural-political problem.

Historically, this confrontation arose when secondary and college students argued that their religious beliefs require that the *türban* be worn at all times and in all places. The conflict between educational administrators and the teaching staff on the one hand,

and the students on the other, came to a head when students demanded that they be allowed to cover their heads and parts of
their faces in diploma photographs. They also insisted on retaining their scarves in surgical theatres, and while examining male
cadavers in schools of medicine and nursing. The administrators
and instructors resisted these demands. Eventually, such students
began to fail their courses, and appealed to administrative courts
to lift what they considered to be undue restrictions on their educational rights. The request was turned down, prompting appeals
to higher administrative courts, and eventually the Constitutional
Court, all in vain. The Constitutional Court decided that 'the relationship between religious beliefs and the kind of dress one wears
was completely severed' by an act of the Turkish Grand National
Assembly (TBMM) in 1925.[45] The Constitutional Court further
ruled that donning religious dress in lay academic institutions is a
breach of articles 3 and 14 of the 1982 constitution, which defines the state system as a *laicist* parliamentary democracy. Since
these articles and the principle of *laicism* cannot be amended,
nor any group of deputies of the TBMM table a motion of amendment of the articles, the TBMM was unable to legislate on the
matter. Having utilised all legal avenues within Turkey, the disgruntled students turned to the European Court of Human Rights,
which in May 1993 also turned down their application.

   With all legal mechanisms for appeal exhausted, the students
turned to politics. They organised protest marches, rallies and
meetings and attempted to demonstrate to the public and the
political elites of Turkey the wrongs alleged to have been committed against them. In the meantime, the National Security Council's
proposal to extend the length of mandatory elementary education to eight years – which was initially accepted and adopted by
then-prime minister Necmettin Erbakan and his coalition government, and implemented by succeeding prime minister Mesut
Yilmaz's coalition government – added fresh fuel to the *türban*
conflict. The conservative and radical right argued that it would
not be possible to provide 'proper' religious education to students
after eight years of elementary school education. The political
rallies, demonstrations, and protests gained momentum in the

summer of 1997. Coincidentally, the Higher Educational Council (YÖK, which is in charge of all universities in the country), decided that secondary school graduates who take the university entrance examinations would earn higher scores if they applied to college programmes that coincide with their secondary school branches. This meant that graduates of *Imam Hatip Lycées* (secondary schools that educate prayer leaders) would be accorded higher scores in the university entrance examinations only if they were to apply to Schools of Theology (*Ilahiyat Fakülteleri*). Previously, the graduates of such schools were treated no differently from other secondary school graduates and they managed to enrol in such programmes as law, medicine, social and natural sciences. As a result, the *türban*-wearing girls became further restricted in their career goals.

The two educational policies thus converged to fuel political protests against the political centre. Clashes between the protestors and the police became daily incidents by summer 1997; they continued until February 1999, when the capture of Abdullah Öcalan, head of the radical Kurdish organisation, PKK, precipitated a marked change in the political agenda. Nevertheless there is some evidence that the outcome of the 1999 general elections was influenced by the *türban* issue, and related educational issues concerning the status of the *Imam-Hatip Lyceés*.[46]

Currently, all secondary schools and universities ban the wearing of the *türban* on their campuses. While some students still demand that they be permitted to enter the educational institutions in their *türban*, many cover their heads by other means (even hats), and participate fully in academic activities. Although the issue still remains unsolved, its importance seems to have been eclipsed in Turkish politics. As argued by Özdalga, cases of moderate pragmatism have become more common among the students. As confrontation loses its effectiveness and media attention, greater flexibility and less militancy seems to be emerging.[47] A number of activists in the *türban* movement also seem to have changed their outlook on society and begun to appreciate diversity and tolerance for diverse interests and opinions.[48] Likewise, the motives and goals of the girls who participate in the campaign

vary greatly. For some, it amounts to no more than social conformity, while for others it is a way of adjusting to a modern, urban
lifestyle; yet others see it as a way of demonstrating their credentials as a 'lady' (*hanım*), or of being the only appropriate public
attire according to their understanding of Islam. Nor is it only the
girls and women who are eager to protect what they consider to
be their religious entitlement; many men are also involved in the
same 'struggle'. Hence, a political movement with its own
structures and publications has mushroomed.[49] As Pusch has
shown, although the Sunni conservative women's organisations
seem to espouse human rights and democracy in their propaganda, they do not generally espouse values like gender equality
or respect for a majoritarian form of democratic rule.[50] They instead seem eager to change society to what they regard as a
conservative-religious community, while holding an authoritarian
image of the state.[51] Such a proclivity leads to conflict with the
secular feminist organisations, which in turn perceive their religious counterparts as a threat to their own feminist ideology.[52]

While the rigid stance of the state (centre) on the ban of the
türban in educational institutions and for public employees (*kadın
memur*) has frustrated conservative-traditional Sunni women and
their associations, it has also provoked soul-searching on their part.
A more sophisticated understanding of 'the Other', whether secular women and men, or non-Sunni Muslims (mainly the Alevis in
the Turkish context) seems to be emerging.[53] The contestation
and confrontation levelled at the Turkish political regime by the
türban movement have lost their allure, and are metamorphosing
into a regular civic movement seeking a voice and participation
in the country's political process. The 'absolutist' claim that there
is a single dress code for Muslim women – to which all women,
whether Sunni, Alevi or secular must conform – seems no longer
to be voiced. Hence, the demand of the *türban* movement has
become one of 'democratic and human rights' for conservative
Sunni women, asserted not only within Turkey, but also apropos
of what some of them had earlier deemed the 'infidel', 'imperial-
ist' European Union and its Human Rights Court. A protest
movement that was once determined to press its demands by any

avenue, legal or otherwise, now increasingly appeals to legalistic arguments and contexts to further its interests. Consequently, the *türban* movement today offers a new associational example in the development of Turkish civil society.

What is interesting about the *türban* movement is that it has become less dogmatic over time, leaving behind the claim of a 'non-negotiable' religious right that every 'Islamic' authority must accept and impose. In becoming a human rights claim adjudicated under the democratic aegis of the Turkish system, it has itself engendered a secularisation of the movement. If those who presented the human rights argument about the *türban* in the Turkish and European Human Rights courts did not, at the outset, quite subscribe to the democratic regimes of Turkey and the European Union, they certainly engaged with them. Concomitantly, the 'dogma' diminished in importance as the girls involved in the process began inquiring about 'democracy', 'human rights', the rights of 'others' and tolerance. Göle has observed with regard to an earlier phase that

> ... contemporary Islamist movements (in Turkey) thus appeared at the 'center' not only in the geographical sense of urban spaces, but also in the cultural and political sense of participation in the production of the symbols and values, and in the course of change. Their action was inscribed not in the production of a logic of refusal of the system, but instead a logic of participation.[54]

Similarly, the *türban* movement was embroiled in 'secular issues' and became less militant and more 'conventional' in its demands for participation in politics. If it is yet early to argue that the movement has been firmly converted into another set of voluntary associations in a secular democracy, we may none the less conjecture that its less dogmatic and monolithic character may be consolidated if prevailing trends in state relations with civil society continue into the future.

I believe that this example illustrates the significant variability of state-civil society dynamics over time. What are conflict-ridden relations at a given moment can metamorphose into co-operative arrangements. Today, Kurdish nationalist and religious radical

associations seem frequently to be treated as seditious conspiracies, constantly monitored, regulated and occasionally prosecuted
by the state. The trend has hardened in many respects since the
events of September 11, 2001, and their aftermath in Central Asia.
Yet if these advocacy groups develop a non-threatening view of
themselves and of the ideas they promote – as occurred with the
women's associations – it is likely that the tenor of their relations
with the state will improve, to their mutual benefit.

Conclusion

Associability and civil society seem to have flourished in Turkey
with democratisation and rapid social mobilisation in the aftermath of World War II. Urbanisation, industrialisation and the
democratisation of society and polity led to the establishment of a
multitude of voluntary associations. In particular, economic associations, such as TOBB and TÜSIAD, and trade unions and
co-operatives mushroomed in the 1970s and 1980s. Religious associations, local and regional solidarity groups, civic and cultural
initiatives were already becoming part of Turkish society by the
1950s. However, mass participation has not matched the burgeoning growth in the number of such associations. A relatively small
minority of Turkish society appears to be committed to organising and mobilising, while the overwhelming majority fail to do so
at all.

The attitude of the state to civil society in Turkey is one of
aloofness and disinterest so long as civic activism avoids regime-
contesting protests which are readily considered to be conspiracies
against the *raison d'être* of the Republic. In the latter instance, the
security forces and judiciary have acted effectively to control, regulate and even suppress such activity. Ethnic and religious
associations that are organised to challenge Republican tenets and
laws are perceived as the most threatening to the status quo and
are therefore vehemently resisted, prosecuted and suppressed by
the state. Other solidarity, economic, patronage, self-help, charity and recreational associations are generally neither supported
nor discouraged – though civic activism in response to natural

disasters (like the 1999 earthquakes) is strongly supported by the state. Hence, a rather complicated image has developed of benevolence and intimidation on the part of the state in its relations with voluntary associations.

Associational life in Turkey is still influenced by blood ties (*akrabalık*), marital relations (*hısımlık*), and local or regional solidarity (*hemşehrilik*) bonds created among men in military service (*askerlik*) and through religious orders (*tarikat*). Successful partnerships appear mostly to stem from such primordial or traditional ties. Moreover, effective linkages to institutions of political power are still activated through ties of this kind. Urbanisation and social mobilisation have eroded some of those primordial/traditional ties – yet their presence is noticeable in every inquiry into political corruption, where links fostering underhand deals between powerful politicians and their family members, religious brothers, and local/regional affiliates (*hemşehri*) are often unearthed.

Finally, the lack of mass support, or of the capacity to mobilise large-scale popular participation, often debilitates voluntary associations in their relations with the state. Only a few associations have such capacities, or access to sizeable political resources like votes, wealth or information. The vast majority are too small and under-resourced to matter to most political parties and elites. Their principal opportunity to exert influence depends on the willingness to form enduring coalitions with other voluntary associations, and thereby enhance their access to political resources (from finance to public participation in civic initiatives and elections). However, this brings us to another debilitating hurdle: civil society seems to be made up of fragmented and fractionalised voluntary associations involved in constant rivalry among themselves. This allows the state to have a passive-exclusive attitude towards the associations. In response, some voluntary associations express their demands for recognition and representation through protest behaviour aimed at effecting serious systemic change. Under these circumstances, the Turkish state abandons its passivity and benign neglect turns, with the collaboration of the security and judicial organs, to aggressive exclusion.

Notes

1. Şerif Mardin, 'Center-Periphery Relations: A Key to Turkish Politics?' in Engin Akarlı and Gabriel Ben-Dor, ed., *Political Participation in Turkey: Historical Background and Present Problems* (Istanbul, 1975), pp.15–32.

2. For a discussion of this term see Nur Yalman, 'Some Observations on Secularism in Islam: The Cultural Revolution in Turkey', *Daedalus*, 102 (1973), pp.139–67.

3. Mardin, 'Center-Periphery Relations', pp.7–32; Engin D. Akarlı, 'The State as a Socio-Cultural Phenomenon and Political Participation in Turkey' in *Political Participation in Turkey*, pp.135–55; Metin Heper, *The State Tradition in Turkey* (Walkington, UK, 1985), *passim*; Ali Kazancıgil, 'The Deviant Case in Comparative Analysis: High Stateness in a Muslim Society: The Case of Turkey' in Mattei Dogan and Ali Kazancıgil, ed., *Comparing Nations: Concepts, Strategies, Substance* (Oxford, 1994), pp.213–38.

4. Heper, *The State Tradition in Turkey*, pp.8, 50–66.

5. Ibid., pp.50–97.

6. Mardin, 'Center-Periphery Relations', pp.10, 22–3.

7. Heper, *The State Tradition in Turkey*, pp.102–3.

8. Ibid., p.103.

9. Ibid.

10. Joel S. Migdal, *Strong Societies and Weak States: State-Society Relations and State Capabilities in the Third World* (Princeton, NJ, 1988), pp.19–22; and G.A. Almond and G. Bingham Powell, Jr., *Comparative Politics: System, Process, and Policy* (2nd ed., Boston and Toronto, 1978), pp.286–9.

11. Ersin Kalaycıoğlu, 'Civil Society in Turkey: Continuity and Change?' in Brian W. Beely, ed., *Turkish Transformations: New Century, New Challenges* (Walkington, UK, forthcoming).

12 Daniel Bell, 'American Exceptionalism Revisited: The Role of Civil Society', *The Public Interest*, 95 (1989), pp.38–56; cf. Adam B. Seligman, *The Idea of Civil Society* (Princeton NJ, 1992), p.2.

13. Francis Fukuyama, *Trust: The Social Virtues and the Creation of Prosperity* (London and New York, 1995), pp.49–57.

14. Chris Hann, 'Political Society and Civil Anthropology', in C. Hann and E. Dunn, ed., *Civil Society: Challenging Western Models* (London and New York, 1996), p.20.

15 Binnaz Toprak, 'Civil Society in Turkey', in A.R. Norton, ed., *Civil Society in the Middle East* (Leiden and New York, 1996), p.104.

16. Barbara Pusch, 'Stepping into the Public Sphere: The Rise of

Islamist and Religious-Conservative Women's Non-Governmental Organizations' in Stefanos Yerasimos et al., ed., *Civil Society in the Grip of Nationalism: Studies on Political Culture in Contemporary Turkey* (Istanbul, 2000), p.478.

17. Hikmet Yavuzyiğit, 'Derneklerin Demokratik Toplumsal Yapıya Katkısı' *Mülkiyeliler Birliği Dergisi*, 22 (1998), no.210–12, p.64; and *Radikal* (daily newspaper) (28 November 1998).

18. See <www.turkiyemillikoop.org.tr /istatsi/istatis4.htm, 2001>.

19. Yavuzyiğit, 'Derneklerin Demokratik Toplumsal Yapıya Katkısı', p.64.

20. Ibid., p.64.

21. Ibid., p.67.

22. Ibid., p.64.

23. Ibid., p.68. Ultimately, it is clear that there is a Pearson's product-moment correlation of 0.93 (statistically significant at 0.01 level) between the population size of the provinces and the officially registered voluntary associations they host – which is a good indication of the closeness of the urbanisation-associability nexus in Turkey.

24. See <www.turkiyemillikoop.org.tr/istatsi/istatis4.htm, 2001>.

25. Yavuzyiğit, 'Derneklerin Demokratik Toplumsal Yapıya Katkısı', p.64.

26. Ersin Kalaycıoğlu, 'Türkiye'de Siyasal Kültür ve Demokrasi' in E. Özbudun et al., ed., *Türkiye'de Demokratik Siyasal Kültür* (Ankara, 1995), p.57; and Yılmaz Esmer, *Devrim, Evrim ve Statüko: Türkiye'de Sosyal, Siyasal, Ekonomik Değerler* (Istanbul, 1999), p.33.

27. Ronald Inglehart, *Modernization and Postmodernization: Cultural, Economic, and Political Change in 43 Countries* (Princeton, NJ, 1997), p.174.

28. Fukuyama, *Trust: The Social Virtues and the Creation of Prosperity*, pp.149–281.

29. Kalaycıoğlu, 'Türkiye'de Siyasal', pp.52–6.

30. Yılmaz Esmer, *Devrim, Evrim ve Statüko* (Istanbul, 1999), pp.87–90.

31. Kalaycıoğlu, 'Türkiye'de Siyasal', pp.61–3.

32. Gottfried Plagemann, 'Human Rights Organizations: Defending the Particular or the Universal?' in *Civil Society in the Grip of Nationalism*, n.16 above, p.479.

33. See the declaration of Fuat Miras, the Chairman of the TOBB, *Hürriyet* (daily newspaper), (22 February 2001), p.3.

34. Plagemann, 'Human Rights Organizations', pp.433–71.

35. Fikret Adaman and Ali Çarkoğlu, *Türkiye'de Yerel Yönetimlerde*

272 ERSIN KALAYCIOĞLU

Hizmetlerden Tatmin, Patronaj İlişkileri ve Reform (Istanbul, 2000), pp.66–8.

36. İlkay Sunar, 'Politics of Citizenship in the Middle East: An Agenda for Research' in *Suna Kili'ye Armagan: Cumhuriyet'e Adanan bir Yaşam* (Istanbul, 1998), pp.367–8.

37. Ibid., pp.367–8.

38. Kalaycıoğlu, 'Civil Society in Turkey', n.11 above.

39. John Dryzek, 'Political Inclusion and the Dynamics of Democratization' *American Political Science Review*, 90, no.1, (September 1996), cf. Sunar, 'Politics of Citizenship in the Middle East', p.366.

40. Sunar 'Politics of Citizenship in the Middle East', p.369.

41. Ibid., p.370.

42. Yeşim Arat, 'Feminist Institutions and Democratic Aspirations: The Case of the Purple Roof Women's Shelter Foundation', in Z.F. Arat, ed., *Deconstructing Images of 'The Turkish Women'* (New York, NY, 1999), pp.295–309.

43. Ibid., p.298.

44. For a major treatment of the subject see Yeşim Arat, 'Feminist Institutions and Democratic Aspirations', pp.295–309.

45. *Journal of Constitutional Court Decisions* (AMKD) no.25, (7 March 1989), p.156.

46. Ersin Kalaycıoğlu, 'The Shaping of Party Preferences in Turkey: Coping with the Post-Cold War Era', *New Perspectives on Turkey*, 20 (Spring, 1999), pp.47–76.

47. Elisabeth Özdalga, 'Civil Society and Its Enemies', in E. Özdalga and S. Persson, ed., *Civil Society, Democracy, and the Muslim World* (Istanbul, 1997), pp.81–2.

48. Ibid., p.81.

49. Pusch, 'Stepping into the Public Sphere', pp.489–502.

50. Ibid., p.501.

51. Ibid.

52. Ibid.

53. Özdalga, 'Civil Society and Its Enemies', pp.81–2.

54. Nilüfer Göle, 'Authoritarian Secularism and Islamist Politics: The Case of Turkey', in *Civil Society in the Middle East*, pp.38–9.

10

Between Identity-Politics and Authoritarianism in Pakistan

Iftikhar H. Malik

The challenges of governance, uneven development, ethno-sectarian conflicts and sheer authoritarianism in the post-colonial and specifically post-cold war world have led academics and public interest groups to focus on the issue of civil society. It is widely agreed that many of these problems can be mitigated or resolved through the empowerment of civic actors and institutions, and by redefining their symbiotic relationship with organs of the state. State-led unilateralism, without it being moderated and humanised through civic forces, has spawned intra- as well as inter-state schisms. Weak civil societies and unrestrained official hierarchies underpin the identity crises faced by many transitional states. Before one can address the urgency of a new and positive equilibrium among these crucial trajectories, one needs to respond to various academic and even not-so-academic queries. They include questions such as: Is civil society a Western construct alien to Muslim polities? How do we define it in its historical as well as current perspective in reference to societies such as Pakistan? Is it possible to expect an essentially 'Muslim' civil society without raising serious questions about long-held social traditions? Evidently, in the existing models in the Muslim world – from secular to theo-cratic polities, from one-party governments to military regimes – the issues of national identity and civic culture remain dilemmatic.[1]

This paper first considers civil society in broad reference to Islam, secularism and pluralism in South Asia, before turning to a particular context – Pakistan. It explores the changing relation-ship between Islam and the state in South Asia and Pakistan over the years within the context of the politics of pressure groups. It also takes into account public opinion across the board over vital social policy issues, where the state appears lacking in resolve and initiative. To a significant degree, Pakistan can deal with her iden-tity crisis, minimise the economic disparities and counter a fundamentalist threat – *talibanisation* – by taking aboard this societal consensus.

'Landscaping' Civil Society

'Civil society' involves various mediating institutions seeking a redefinition of state-society interdependence, as well as intra-societal equilibrium. It comprises institutions that are rooted among the populace and operate as a bulwark against infringe-ment of individual as well as communal spaces and liberties. Human rights groups, women's and minority constellations, au-tonomous think-tanks, groups with reformist agendas on ecology, the rule of law, social justice and equality, regional peace and the media, typically make for a vibrant civil society. In addition, inde-pendent intellectuals, lawyers, artists and the like resisting authoritarianism or unilateralism are vital pillars of an alert civil society – one that upholds a public sphere *not* dedicated to poli-tics as *raison d'etat*. Thus, an ideal polity would have a vocal and engaged civic culture that effectively constrains official unilater-alism, while offering healthier alternatives of governance and pluralist participation. In effect, civil society constitutes democra-cy's lifeline, nourishing free debate, tolerant policies and administrative accountability.[2] In any authoritarian set-up, civil society will remain bruised and suspect, and subordinate to political society; in the process, the populace is likely to become hostage to the whims of a sectional or ideological particularism. Communities with weaker or non-existent civil societies tend frequently to fall victim to authoritarianism.

An empowered public sphere and a responsive state will pursue mutually supportive agendas even while contesting public policy. 'Civil society relates to the state', notes a leading theorist, 'but it does not aim to win formal power or office in the state'.[3] Hence, organisations or movements that seek to 'monopolize a functional or political space in society' are inimical to the pluralist ethos of civic culture.[4] Indeed, authoritarian tendencies may stem not only from statist institutions, but also from ethno-sectarian groups that seek dominance over society – as part of the wider *imaginaire social* in which all kinds of utopian visions are embedded.[5] Factors such as the economy, religion, regional politics and ethno-nationalism may also deeply impact the composition and orientation of civic forces. While continued economic stratification or dependence upon foreign sources can damage the social fabric, the superimposition of religious or any ethnic uniformity can take place only by disavowing diversity and pluralism. In the same vein, regional peace and cooperation offer multiple benefits, and through a substantial 'de-othering' of neighbours, domestic inter-communal coexistence and harmony can also be achieved. Ethnic nationalism can, of course, undermine pluralism and unleash severe instability – though it may also have the salutary effect of engendering decentralisation.[6]

The concept of civil society is neither new nor region-specific, despite the tendency in mainstream literature to trace its origins to eighteenth-century Western Europe. An alternative perspective would reject this Euro-centricity, arguing that non-European societies trying to reinvent themselves at different stages in their past offer their own civic narratives and discourses. The roles of Sufis, *bhagats* and other such elements even in patriarchal societies aimed at empowering or protecting the underprivileged sectors is part of such an indigenous narrative in South Asia. But since all these societies were parochial even during the imperial era, the civil societies functioned in a localist milieu, drawing sustenance from a defined morality. Religion, in other words, stood as a major component right through the emergence of modern territorial statehood. The relocation of power in the West from state – monarchical or otherwise – to the echelons of society took centuries to happen, and such trajectories may have significant variations in non-Western communities. In this context, Muslim societies may be seen as sharing aspects of a common civic trajectory, in which there is a priorisation of a certain perspective of human rights (*huquq al-'ibad*).

The prophet Muhammad's own early life in Mecca as an orphan closely associated with the downtrodden in society, his employment under a woman whom he married through her initiative (despite her seniority by fifteen years), and his teachings celebrating humanity, all offered a fresh personal and ideological model of social justice. This 'theology of rupture' was to evolve into a 'theology of community' – as Maurice Causse aptly terms it – in Medina.[7] For the city-state that Muhammad created there was among the earliest societies formally to uphold tenets of solidarity and equity, challenging the primacy of kinship ties *qua* operative social bond, in an intricate nexus between religion and politics.[8] Old hierarchies and vested interests were thrown into question by ordinary Muslims, by Sufis, and even by many ulama, engendering social capital and a nascent public sphere.

Islam accorded new respect to the rights of women and oppressed minorities – though the subsequent appropriation of this progressive ethos by feudal and clerical oligarchies, and the eventual onslaught of colonialism, belie a legacy far removed from the conservatism and statism that became the norm. The traditions of *ijtihad* (legal interpretation and innovation) gave way to *taqlid* (imitation) and in the process, numerically/militarily weaker Muslim groups suffered marginalisation. Islam's encounters with modernity unleashed several complex responses, including severe introversion as well as efforts to reinterpret Muslim heritage. In the meantime, the issues of poverty, health and illiteracy aggravated the situation, making reform a monumental task. The colonial/nationalist era was characterised by an ideological polarity between modernists and conformists, which in the post-colonial era re-emerged with greater intensity due to a grow-ing disillusionment with ruling elites (as commented upon at some length by Mohammed Arkoun and others elsewhere in this vol-ume). In other words, from a civil society perspective, the post-foundational Muslim experience has done justice neither to Muhammad's theology of rupture nor to that of community.

Islam in South-Asian Historiography

While addressing the quest for identity in diverse Muslim regions and communities in recent centuries, the contemporary historio-graphical debate in South Asia has tended to centre on 'High Islam',[9] allocating to it a kind of monolithic and overarching es-sentialism. The missionary, colonial, Orientalist, nationalist and even proto- or post-nationalist schools either remain confined to these parameters, or simply dwell on the inevitability of respec-tive nation-states (Pakistan, India and Bangladesh). Partition has left an indelible imprint on this discourse, as the reductionist typologies of secularism/modernism and traditionalism/ commu-nalism remain ascendant. The role of religion and politics, and of diverse communitarian manifestations in reference to class, gender or identity formation, have yet to be fully investigated. Islam in South Asia has been perceived through narrow prisms, succumbing in most instances to nationalist prerogatives. The hostilities between India and Pakistan have not helped a com-parative discourse either. Anyone speaking of Islam in post-1947 India tends to be derided as a communalist or a Pakistani agent, something that many secular Muslim writers in India have not resisted. Thus, the studies on Islam in South Asia began to focus on Pakistan only – which Pakistani historians themselves readily accepted. This squeeze of Islam into a territorial envelope did not let critical scholarship flourish, while in India a Muslim scholar writing on Islam would either be apologetic or end up supporting Indian secularism. The disowning of Islam by many Indian Mus-lims at the expense of their own identity so as not to appear communal is quite obvious.

Both Islam and Pakistan have, unfortunately, become

problematic for Indian secularists, though it hardly need be so. Indian nationalism induces such disavowal even as the class-based interests of some Muslim elites underwrite these negative attitudes. The rise of the Bharatiya Janata Party (BJP) and other movements espousing Hindutva,[10] should have made it easier for scholars experiencing self-denial in this regard to revisit Islam. The identification of secularism with India and of Islam with a communal interpretation of Pakistan, should now surely be seen as simplistic; one hopes for a fresher perspective, though the damage to Indo-Muslim culture has already been done to a great extent. An Indo-Pakistan normalisation may also help recast Islam within a wider historical and cross-regional perspective. The imperial, nationalist, secular and leftist schools of historiography have found 'Islam' problematic and have generally avoided researching its impact, precepts and prospective. Even an eminent historian like Ayesha Jalal, while writing on Muslim politics, chose to concentrate on a few major personalities, ignoring cultural, ideological or class-based realities within Muslim India.[11] The tradition of intellectual history as pioneered by Aziz Ahmad still remains weak, despite the valuable contributions of Rafiuddin Ahmed, Farzana Shaikh and Taj Hashmi – though Mushirul Hasan's otherwise passionate study ends up falling into the usual trap of India-Pakistan nationalist subjectivity.[12] The debate on Muslim identity needs to be located in the nascent civil society of the colonial era. Pakistan may not have been the perfect solution to the Indian Muslim predicament, but to see its evolution as a mere incident of history is surely unwarranted. After all, most post-colonial states, including India, could simplistically be characterised as mere artefacts. A mature discourse on Islam in South Asia must move away from these pillar-posts of separatism and syncretism that merely generate emotive subjectivities.

During late-Mughal times, civil society took on a regional and proto-national character. Sultan Hyder Ali, Tipu Sultan,[13] the Jihad movement, the Faraizis, peasant and tribal constellations, and individuals like Ahmed Khan Kharal, resisted the British East India Company's expansionism and attitudes of racial superiority.[14] The protagonists and the antagonists vacillated in their respective strategies, though South Asian Islam – in Sufi and scriptural forms alike – remained uncomfortable with this historic dislocation: the loss of political power, combined with the Western mercantile-missionary enterprise had bleakly exposed Muslim vulnerabilities in India. The construction of Occidentalism – as a counterpoise to Orientalism – owed itself to the Muslim elite, including Mir Abu Talib Khan, Muhammad Husain, Itisam al-Din and others who had a close experience of working with Sir William Jones and other administrator-scholars.[15]

It was after the Revolt of 1857, a debilitating development for Muslims in particular, that the *ashraf* – combining Islamic and Western learning – initiated regenerative efforts that, despite their multiple strands, converged on the need for Muslim revitalisation. Regionalism as well as an emergent trans-regionalism became the key characteristics of such efforts. Syed Ahmed Khan's programme, and those of the Deobandis, Brelvis, Nadwis and of the Tablighis, are well known and can be described as trans-regional; efforts by the regional *tanzims* (organisations) and *anjumans* (associations) still remain relatively under-researched. The *tanzims* operated within the praxis of an Islamic discourse co-optive of Western educational and scientific precepts. This educational and cultural dimension eventually led to a political discourse seeking to define the place of the Muslim community in a plural and changing India. Schemes like those for a separate state, or a composite nationalism or regional pluralism, were being put forth amongst the trans-regional groups long before Partition.[16]

Governance and Civil Society in Pakistan

The post-independence division of an India-wide Muslim community in 1947, and the consolidation of its principal segment in a nation-state (Pakistan), were events that radically altered the civic life of regional Islam. The historic trans-regionality of the community was dissipated and a sizeable minority in India was left rudderless after the exodus of the bourgeoisie and elites. In Pakistan, after the demise in 1948 of Muhammad Ali Jinnah, its founder, the concepts of security and nation-building became conjoined with a growing militarism at the expense of a nascent civil society. The relative openness and tolerance of the 1950s, despite weak democratic institutions, eroded before a statist uni-lateralism and societal emphasis on a rather exclusivist Islam.[17] The state, which had originally sought to pursue a pragmatic and secular public policy, came to seek refuge in a religious symbol-ism that eventually turned into obscurantism, especially under martial law regimes. Over the last twenty-five years or so, official authoritarianism in varying degrees has cohabited with a social nihilism, even as regional geo-politics and wider misperceptions of Islam have fuelled religious extremism – and the growing in-fluence of intelligence agencies with their invidious agendas in domestic and international politics. Fragile economic institutions have compounded the nation's plight, not least in terms of social inequality and political insecurity.

All of which has left human rights groups, journalists, women activists, and other civic elements in a precarious situation. Even under the weak democratic regimes of the 1990s – the second major phase in the evolution of civil society – the state was wary of those elements. The harassment of progressive media and civic actors has been commonplace, within and outside the ambit of the law, as attested by a stream of critical reports from independ-ent organisations like Human Rights Watch (New York), Amnesty International (London), and the Human Rights Commission of Pakistan (Lahore). This, in turn, can be better understood in the broader context of structures of governance that fail to privilege public accountability, probity and the rule of law. Which is not surprising when one recognises that successive governments in Pakistan have maintained the structural fundamentals of the co-lonial era, wherein *administration* took precedence over governance. Typical of this approach are the politics of patron-age by a high-handed executive, the low priority accorded to social and political reform (as compared with 'national security'), and the resistance to effective devolution of powers to the regions. Any real interface between official and civic agendas and actors is at best an elusive goal – and at worst, a matter to be actively mini-mised by the state.

In a country that has endured martial law for more than half its independent existence, the lack of respect for constitutionalism and the rule of law is not helped by judicial institutions that have largely failed to resist the power of the state. The prospective role of an independent judiciary – and of access to justice – in upholding the autonomy and integrity of civic spaces and actors is axiomatic. In transitional societies where legal institutions must struggle to establish their own independence against the intrusions of state power or of politico-economic elites, one looks to the upper echelons of the judiciary for effective leadership – as, for example, has occurred in India or South Africa. But when in May 2001, the Supreme Court of Pakistan was invited to rule on the validity of the military coup of October 1999, it not only decided in favour of the military regime but also allowed the amendment of the constitution to legitimise the status quo. The judgement invoked the hallowed 'law of necessity', which has frequently served to validate martial law; allowing the constitution to be amended only added salt to the wounds to legalism.[18] All in all, Pakistan's courts are overworked, and the low morale of the judiciary over the years has fed a propensity to corruption.[19]

The failure of governance is abetted by the feudal nature of the national economy, where bureaucrats and politicians operate as latter-day *mai-bap* (parents) dispensing largesse and *ad hoc* doses of administrative and land reform.[20] Pakistan's drift through a longstanding series of financial crises, heavy expenditure on defence, and the burdens of accumulated external and internal borrowings with low accountability, are among the traits of a cold war-era political economy. Further, there are only half a million taxpayers in a population of 135 million; the landed classes (*zamindar*s) are notorious tax-dodgers, with the tacit if not active collaboration of the state (some of the *zamindar*s having been among the country's civilian prime ministers). This is over and above the tax exemptions granted to the military, judges and other members of the political class. Such institutional patterns have led to the 'privatisation' of politics and the economy, generating a web of networks – mafias – that operate parallel to rather than within the official bounds of the state. Ironically, many Pakistanis hope for salvation each time a military coup rides the wave of popular discontent with promises of radical change – only to find that the 'system' has been reinforced and civic life further subverted. In the process, the middle class, which is conventionally perceived as the backbone of a nation's civil society, has itself grown dependent on the state's conduct of political economy as a vehicle for the manipulation of linguistic and ethno-religious factors through various channels.

Pakistan's armed forces have attracted a vast historiography, a central theme of which is their extra-professional role in the life of the nation.[21] Critics see the army as a state within a state, seeking a pliant oligarchy of weaker politicians as its 'civilian partner'. Often, the generals are seen as following their 'khaki' predecessors by attempting to depoliticise the country in order to prolong their stay at the helm, such as through the invocation of 'emergency' measures against threats that may or may not be real. Civilian leaders who defy the trend can quickly find themselves on the losing side: at the moment, former prime ministers Benazir Bhutto and Nawaz Sharif, along with Altaf Hussain who heads the third main political party, are all in exile. Still, some observers insist that while the army may be praetorian and neo-colonial, it remains the only effective institution to save Pakistan from total collapse.[22] These claims are surely discredited by the Hamoodur Rahman Commission Report of August 2000, which highlighted the graft, professional incompetence and brutality that are rampant in the military.[23] The Report, which Islamabad had earlier suppressed, called for legal redress as well as structural reform within the armed forces. Neither trials nor reforms have occurred, and there is no indication that they will. Meanwhile, the expectation appears to persist that the burden of defence spending, endemic to Pakistan's non-development expenditure, will be met by more indirect taxation in a country where official poverty has increased from 25 to 40 per cent of the population. Senior military officials, however, are well insulated from the country's economic malaise: they remain a privileged class who enjoy generous allotments of land, retirement benefits and high civilian appointments after leaving the army.[24]

It is testimony to the prevailing politics of identity that the military brass still attracts the support of many civilians from ethnic groups like the Punjabis and Pashtuns, whose martial traditions have made them a stalwart pool of talent for recruitment into the army. Whatever the lessons about identity-politics that may have been imbibed during the violent break-up of Pakistan and the emergence of Bangladesh in 1971 – with its traumatic impact on the national psyche – those lessons appear to have quickly dissipated. Ethnic dreams have remained as potent, if not more so, than those of the 'imagined nation' of 1947,[25] amid a weak culture of citizenship. How this contest between ethno-cultural particularism and national/global affinities unfolds will surely have much to do with the fate of civil society-building in Pakistan, and within South Asia at large.

A Vision Deferred ...

With the movement for a Pakistan aimed at ameliorating Muslim underdevelopment in British India's Muslim-majority provinces, Islam became a rallying point for economic, religious and political ideals. One might have thought that a state whose population was more than 90 per cent Muslim would have few apprehensions over its identity. Yet in a diverse society without a sustained participatory system, expressions of political and economic disenchantment came to be aired through a religious idiom that itself became divisive, even for Muslims. Again, the steady dominance of Punjab over civil and military sectors, and the failure of the Westernised elite in offering tangible solutions to problems of basic economic needs, pushed huge sections of the populace toward a rhetorical Islamic ethos. In the cold war era and its aftermath, disgruntled youth in particular have seen a reductionist form of Islam to be the antidote to all their problems. Muslim agonies in Bosnia, Kashmir, Palestine, Afghanistan and elsewhere conveyed to them a picture of a world arrayed against them. The Afghan jihad in the 1980s offered free training to a whole generation exposed to traditional madrasas, and with the rise of the Taliban it is no surprise that some of the discontented perceived in that regime a model for the entire Muslim world. The failure of state sector education and growing poverty have pushed many youths toward these madrasas which, through their own well-organised networks and occasional support from the military, have been involved in various regional adventures.

Populist Islam is, in a real sense, a rebuke to elitism and a superficial Westernism as represented by the ruling classes. At the same time, it is a strategy by several religio-political parties to mount 'street power', to compensate for their poor performance in elections. It is often argued that since such parties barely enjoy 5 per cent electoral support in Pakistan, the risk of being radicalised is marginal. This ignores the potency of street power as an instrument of economic and political subversion, and the further damage that would ensue to civic forces. Jinnah's vision of a tolerant, progressive and egalitarian society remains a point of consensus. He, of course, desired a Muslim state without ever espousing a theocratic culture. Jinnah's Islam was foremost an ethical code that extended to minority entitlements, as he observed on 11 August 1947: 'You are free; you are free to go to our temples, you are free to go to your mosques or any other place of worship in this state of Pakistan. You may belong to any religion or caste or creed – that has nothing to do with the business of the state'.[26]

But the harrowing question of political legitimacy faced by various non-representative regimes eventually brought hard-line clerical groups across the Rubicon and into the mainstream arena. The imposition of separate electorates for minorities under Zia-ul-Haq not only severely eroded their civil liberties, but also emboldened extremist religious elements. The demands for sharia law persistently put forth by many of the ulama received impetus from Zia; thereafter, both Nawaz Sharif and Benazir Bhutto kowtowed to them. Movements like the Jamiat-Ulama-i-Islam (JUI) with both its factions (led by Fazlur Rahman and Sami ul-Haq, respectively), Ahl-i-Hadith, Tehreek-i-Shariat of Maulana Soofi in Malakand and Malik Akram Awan's al-Ikhwan in the Salt Range, share mutual rivalries yet demand the imposition of an unexplained sharia. Without an outright ban on private militias, together with far-reaching reform of the educational system and the fostering of a culture of shared citizenship, the country will endlessly remain a battleground for an assortment of fuzzy yet incendiary agendas.[27]

There is encouragement to be drawn, however, from the orientation of opinion among ordinary Pakistanis on a host of core public policy issues. As will be seen, the results counter the thrust of anti-democratic culture unleashed on the populace for the better part of Pakistan's national history. And those results bear directly upon the prospects of fostering a culture of common citizenship and social solidarity in a country often perceived (in common with South Asia at large) as riven by fault-lines of regionalism and ethnicity. Pakistanis were surveyed in 1997 on some fifty critical issues facing the nation, at domestic, regional and global levels.[28] Taken together, the formal and informal surveys suggest a remarkable degree of agreement across divisions of region, class and gender on the way ahead. For Pakistan's would-be reformers in the civil society sector and among progressive elements in the state apparatus, the need to harness and cultivate popular sentiments of this kind is self-evident.

A majority 67 per cent firmly rejected legal and policy constraints on women of the kind imposed by the Taliban, while 63 per cent favoured complete gender equality before the law. This is an implicit rejection of the evidentiary rule adopted under the regime of Zia-ul-Haq that accorded to a woman's testimony half the weight of a man's. Among men, 59 per cent endorsed the equal right of a woman to divorce. In a society with deep rural roots, 74 per cent were in support of family planning. More broadly on equality, 74 per cent wanted joint electorates for all Pakistanis, including minority citizens.

On the matter of political integrity, Pakistanis were certainly not ambivalent. A majority of 76 per cent considered the country's generals to be corrupt – while 95 per cent had the same opinion about their politicians. Another 55 per cent felt that Pakistanis would never have true political accountability. Martial laws were considered by 52 per cent of those polled to have damaged the country, and 51 per cent wanted cuts in the military budget. A high proportion – 59 per cent – desired better relations with India.

Some two-thirds opined in favour of Kashmir joining Pakistan, as against 34 per cent who favoured an independent Kashmir. Most of those polled – 82 per cent – had a positive view of their country, and wanted to remain there permanently. A clear majority – 75 per cent – demanded a ban on the religio-sectarian parties that spawn hatred and violence, and a similar proportion favoured restrictions on political sermons in the mosques. An overwhelming majority expected the state to improve standards of health and education. Overall, 58 per cent of Pakistanis felt that the Muslims of South Asia were better off in the 1990s than during the pre-partition era. While this was the viewpoint of Pakistanis, one suspects that a wider regional survey among Bangladeshis, Indians, Nepalis and Sri Lankans would yield a congruent picture of civilian aspirations.

Admittedly, the results reveal a high level of politicisation on the status of women, minority rights, democracy, corruption, Islam, relations with India, Kashmir and religious fundamentalism. But they also show that the public generally shares a clearer view than many of their leaders about the policies that could ultimately move their country toward the Jinnahist vision that Pakistan's military and civilian elites alike profess to cherish. Evidently, ordinary Pakistanis see a future in democratisation and privileging of the social sector over competing ideological agendas – and remain a largely tolerant society supportive of equal rights for women and minorities. And they appear to harbour little animosity toward India despite the continuing legacy of bloody conflict.

Concluding Reflections

It is tempting to conclude that the overbearing forces of state and ethno-sectarianism leave Pakistan with dim prospects for civil society in the foreseeable future. Yet the fact remains that civic forces have weathered rougher times than the present. The media, print and electronic alike, show greater self-confidence than ever, and the Internet surely offers abundant promise for community development in the long term. There is a wider acceptance of NGOs, notably after the laudable civic record of, among others, the Edhi Foundation, Orangi Pilot Project, Citizens Schools Foundation, the Aga Khan Foundation, the Human Rights Commission of Pakistan, and Imran Khan's Shaukat Khanam Hospital.[29] In addition, there is the work of Asma Jahangir's shelter project for battered women, the conservationists of the National College of Arts, and the Indus Valley School of Art and Architecture. True, there are numerous stories of corruption among NGOs, often involving former bureaucrats who have reportedly pocketed donations intended as development funding.[30] The NGOs also face strong resistance from fundamentalist religious groups, not least because the former consider them to be working for foreign interests and yielding national secrets to the latter. This is not, of course, a peculiarly Pakistani phenomenon; NGOs in India, Bangladesh and beyond have similar problems of transparency and acceptance.

There are numerous ways to fight the malaise. First, the NGOs must urgently develop an in-built accountability mechanism that reduces the possibility of corruption, or the misappropriation of funds or information at any level. Funding and assistance from abroad, in particular, should be totally transparent and subject to a rigorous audit. This would be consonant with current trends among civil society groups and institutions in transitional as well as developed states, pursuant to robust critiques about the accountability of the 'third sector' to its various constituencies. Second, and again mindful of wider NGO practice, the non-governmental sector should seek greater autonomy, both from the government and Western donors. Their reliance upon the latter compromises their integrity in domestic contexts of opinion and politics while raising serious questions about the legitimacy of such civic institutions as genuine home-grown products. This is not to deny the collaborative role of international and national partnerships in promoting civic culture; rather, it is to recognise the sensitivities inherent in such partnerships. Relatedly, NGOs must 'indigenise' themselves in their orientation.[31] It is noteworthy that the Western-supported NGOs tend to be the main targets of local criticism. Their life-styles, language, class background and closer associations with the power elite often alienate them from the locals. Finally, the NGOs need to foster a culture of networking: from conducting seminars and teach-ins to co-ordinating complementary efforts and educating the public on their shared goals and strategies. Such webs of interconnectedness are of the essence of civic culture, if NGOs are not themselves to become exclusivist, perhaps even elitist elements in transitional societies. Indeed, effective networking may also be a countervailing force against 'divisive politicisation' – the tendency of interest groups to undermine civic solidarities through single-issue politics, just when such solidarities are strongly required in transitional settings.[32]

There is abundant scope for the civil society sector to work through an independent and supportive media on defining and promoting the goals of Pakistani society, notably on the tangible benefits of democratisation and pluralism. The development of art and culture through greater popular participation can go a long way toward thickening the webs of 'civic kinship', with the added potential for cultural partnerships across regional frontiers within and beyond the country. Civic actors will have to recognise that rather than duelling against religion as 'inherently regressive' – a tendency that Western civic activists have historically tended to embrace but often question today – they must seek a reconstructive discourse of engagement that incorporates the most positive aspects of both secular and religious cultures. The governance crisis engendered by an opportunistic elitism and a diehard militarism exposes the limitations of a middle class-centred, Euro-centric definition of civil society. It also reflects poorly on an obscurantist vision of Islam where pluralism is scoffed at. With both statist and societal regimentation on the offensive, civil society in Pakistan has entered another difficult phase in its history.

Nor will Pakistan's economic debilitation, thanks to an ever-escalating, massive non-development expenditure, narrow tax base and pervasive corruption, readily facilitate politico-economic empowerment of the masses. In other words, the battlefront stretches from domestic issues to pressure group politics and from regional discord to the diverse domains of political economy. But there is a wellspring of optimism that can be drawn upon in the trends in mass public opinion, with a high degree of grassroots consensus on key aspects of social policy that can feed the renewal of civic life, including the country's relations with its neighbours. It is Pakistan's regimes and official structures that have failed the wisdom of the populace.

Notes

1. For a discussion of the Turkish model, whose embrace of secularism has at best produced mixed results for civic life, see my 'Turkey at the Crossroads: Encountering Modernity and Tradition', *Journal of South Asian and Middle Eastern Studies*, 24 (Winter 2001), p.2.

2. See further my *State and Civil Society in Pakistan: Politics of Authority, Ideology and Ethnicity* (Oxford, 1997), pp.4–11.

3. Larry Diamond, 'Rethinking Civil Society: Toward Democratic Consolidation', *Journal of Democracy*, 5 (1994), p.5.

4. Ibid., pp.6–7.

5. See Nilüfer Göle, 'Toward an Autonomization of Politics and Civil Society in Turkey', in Metin Heper and Ahmet Evin, ed., *Politics in the Third Turkish Republic* (Oxford, 1994), pp.213–22.

6. Within the South-Asian context there are various forms of ethno-regionalism. Some movements are simply secessionist, some are separatist, a few seek equal empowerment, while others are nativist. The Muhajir/Muttahida Qaumi Movement (MQM) vacillates between separatism and sheer anarchy. Concurrently, some Sindhi *nationalists* may be perceived as nativist forces reasserting their cultural nationalism. Pushtun nationalism – sometimes referred to as *Pushtoonistan* – has subsided largely due to the integration of Pushtuns within Pakistan and also the decimation of Afghan regimes that often propped up such elements. The Baloch and Pushtun elements in Balochistan appear to be striving towards a more equal and parallel participation in regional affairs rather than seeking secession. For a useful overview, see Subrata Mitra, ed., *Sub-national Movements in South Asia* (Boulder and Oxford, 1996).

7. 'Theologie de rupture et theologie de la communaute', *Revue d'histoire et de philosophie religieuse*, 44 (1964), pp.60–80.

8. Maxime Rodinson has further elaborated this view in *Mohammed* (London, 1993).

9. This implies focusing on elites rather than investigating broad societal trajectories. The emphasis would remain on a few seminaries or groups whose views would be seen as typical of the entire Muslim population. For example, an emphasis on the Deobandis, Brelwis,

Tablighis or Jama'at-i-Islami alone can hardly reflect the diverse lives of Muslim communities and individuals at large.

10. The ultra-right ideology prevalent among certain middle class Hindus, to whom secularism amounts to appeasement of minorities and is divorced from Indian socio-cultural realities. It is often cast as a 'New Hindu' movement.

11. Her *The Sole Spokesman* (Cambridge, 1995), despite its significance, echoes the perspective of the 'Cambridge school' of South-Asian history with its emphasis on imperial/high history interpretation, though her later works have ranged over a somewhat wider spectrum of issues.

12. Aziz Ahmad, *Islamic Modernism in India and Pakistan, 1857–1947* (Oxford, 1967); Rafiuddin Ahmed, *The Bengal Muslims, 1871–1906: A Quest for Identity* (Delhi, 1981); Farzana Shaikh, *Community and Consensus in Islam: Muslim Representation in Colonial India, 1860–1947* (Cambridge, 1989); and, Taj-ul-Islam Hashmi, *Pakistan as a Peasant Utopia: the Communalization of Class Politics in East Bengal* (Boulder, CO, 1992). Mushirul Hasan ends up denigrating Pakistan as an historical accident and a harbinger of problems for Indian Muslims: *Legacy of a Divided Nation: India's Muslims Since Independence* (London, 1997). For a review of various interpretive strands in recent South-Asian historiography, see my *Islam, Nationalism and the West: Issues of Identity in Pakistan* (Oxford, 1999).

13. Both the Muslim rulers of Mysore, a predominantly Hindu state, resisted the European incursions into India. Tipu Sultan, the son of Hyder Ali, and a hero of the Indo-Pakistani nationalist and folk traditions, died fighting the British East India Company in 1799 at Seringapatam.

14. These movements, mostly occurring in northern India, were based on a sustained concept of resistance to the British (*feringi*) rule. Except for Kharral in Punjab the rest were largely inspired by a religious ideology.

15. For a useful commentary on these early Muslim observers of the West, see Gulfishan Khan, *Indian Muslim Perceptions of the West during the Eighteenth Century* (Karachi, 1998).

16. Indian Muslims were not unique in this respect. Their cultural nationalism eventually matured into political nationalism, even if it remained polarised between traditional elites and their Westernised counterparts. Similar processes can be seen at work among Sikhs and Hindus in India today, where revivalism and reform contest the same spaces.

17. For an early analysis, see Leonard Binder, *Religion and Politics in Pakistan* (Berkeley, CA, 1961). Several important studies have since appeared by, among others, Louis Hayes, Khalid B. Sayeed, Anwar Syed,

Charles Kennedy, Ishtiaq Ahmed, Lawrence Ziring, S. Vali Reza Nasr and Ian Talbot.

18. It all began in 1953–54 with the dissolution of the first Constituent assembly when the Governor-General, Gholam Muhammad, dismissed the elected house as it was becoming more vocal on the legislative front. The petition against the dismissal was heard first by the provincial court in Sindh, which declared the executive decision to be unconstitutional; but the Supreme Court upheld the governor's order on the basis of a dictum of 'law of necessity'. It rationalised such a decision on the basis of special and critical circumstances affecting national security. The decision became a precedent for all future such dissolutions by Ayub, Yahya, Zia and Ghulam Ishaq Khan. See generally Paula Newberg, *Judging the State: Courts and Constitutional Politics in Pakistan* (Cambridge, 1995).

19. To cite but one recent instance, a senior judge of the Punjab High Court, Malik Abdul Qayyum, made headlines in the national and international media in April 2001, when it was revealed that while hearing petitions against former premier Benazir Bhutto, he had allowed himself to be influenced by ministers from Nawaz Sharif's cabinet in 1998–9. His secretly-recorded tapes (now available on the Internet), show Malik seeking guidelines on the case from one of Sharif's colleagues. Judge Malik resigned under public pressure in June 2001.

20. See generally *State and Civil Society in Pakistan*, n.2, pp.81–93.

21. See, for example, Stephen Cohen, *The Pakistan Army* (Karachi, 1994); Hasan Askari-Rizvi, *Military and Politics in Pakistan* (Karachi, 1998); and Brian Cloughley, *The Pakistan Army* (Karachi, 1999).

22. Not surprisingly, such apologetics have tended to come from retired generals like Gul Hasan, Farman Ali, A.K. Niazi, K.M. Arif, Jahandad Khan, Sher Ali and Faiz Chishti.

23. *The Nation* (14 August 2000), Internet edition.

24. Other than their separate hospitals and schools, these officials are routinely given, on retirement, agricultural lands in Sindh and its border regions – to the consternation of the local inhabitants. Appointments to governorships, cabinet, ministries, embassies and quasi-autonomous corporations are also commonplace. The present government has appointed retired generals as vice-chancellors of academic institutions as well.

25. See Tazeen Murshid, 'Nations Imagined and Fragmented: Bengali Ethnicity and the Break-up of Pakistan', in W. van Schendel and E.J. Zurcher, ed., *Identity Politics in Central Asia and the Muslim World:*

Nationalism, Ethnicity and Labour in the Twentieth Century, (London, 2001),
pp.85–105.

26. Quoted in Liaquat H. Merchant, ed., *The Jinnah Anthology* (Karachi,
1999), p.11, reinforcing his statement of 14 July 1947, p.22, in which
Jinnah offered this assurance: 'Minorities, to whichever community they
may belong, will be safeguarded. Their religion or faith or belief will be
secure. There will be no interference of any kind with their freedom of
worship. They will have their protection with regard to their religion,
faith, their life, their culture.'

27. This appears to be occurring in the wake of the events of September 11, 2001, though not without considerable resistance of course. See
Anatol Lieven, 'The Pressures on Pakistan', *Foreign Affairs*, 18 (2002),
pp.106–18, at 108–10. More generally on the range of hard-line religious groups in regional context, see M.E. Ahrari, *Jihadi Groups, Nuclear
Pakistan, and the New Great Game* (Carlisle, PA, 2001).

28. The surveys were conducted across Pakistan, using formal and informal methods: 'Fifty Years, Fifty Questions', *The Herald* (Karachi), 28,
1 (January 1997), pp.139–92; 'Fifty Years Later', *India Today* (New Delhi),
22, 21 (18 August 1997), pp.66–71.

29. A 'modest estimate' puts the number of NGOs in the country at
some 10,000, 'at least 5,000 of them active'; their most common activities relate to charity, relief and welfare-oriented provision of services in
health, education and financial support for the underprivileged and disabled: Irfan Mufti, 'Policy and Legal Framework for NGOs in Pakistan',
paper presented at the Enabling Environment Seminar – Legal Dimensions (The Hague, Netherlands, 2–3 October 2000), cited in *International
Journal of Not-for-Profit Law* (online), 3, 1, Country Reports: South Asia
<http://www.icnl.org/journal/vol3iss3/>.

30. See Khawar Mumtaz, 'NGOs in Pakistan: An Overview' in Tariq
Banuri, et al. ed., *Just Development: Beyond Adjustment with a Human Face*
(Karachi, 1997), pp.171–90.

31. The message was underscored by a recent conference on Indigenous Philanthropy in Islamabad, Pakistan (16–17 October 2000),
attended by 250 delegates from all sectors of Pakistani society. The Report
of the proceedings notes that against the 'grim realities' of the country's
economic and social indicators, Pakistanis gave the equivalent of 70 billion Pakistan rupees in monetary donations, volunteer time and
gifts-in-kind during 1998' – and 'over 100 intermediary organisations
provide vital social services through a network of grassroots groups:
Online   Report,   <http://www.akdn.org/agencypublications/

ingphilINTRO.html>, at pp.2–3'. The initiative for the Conference stemmed from an NGO, viz., The Aga Khan Foundation.

32. See Olle Tornquist, 'Civil Society and Divisive Politicisation: Experiences from Popular Democratisation in Indonesia', in Elisabeth Özdalga and Sune Persson, ed., *Civil Society, Democracy and the Muslim World* (Istanbul, 1996), pp.119–40, especially at pp.136–7.

11

State, Society and Creed: Reflections on the Maghreb

Abdou Filali-Ansary

It is quite remarkable how most studies dedicated to civil society today begin by complaining about the elusiveness, fuzziness and other such defects perceived in the concept. There is more to this, surely, than the usual declarations by which scholars tend to open their presentations by pointing to the breadth and complexity of their subjects, to the limits of the approaches they are obliged to adopt, and to the provisional character of their conclusions. For the idea of civil society, reintroduced of late in studies and debates about contemporary societal transformations, seems especially resistant to attempts at dispelling ambiguity and mastering (or at least ordering) the strands of its manifold usages or at conveying a concrete idea of its objects.

Current usage of the term shares the idea of an 'intermediate associational realm between state and family populated by organisations which are separate from the state, enjoy autonomy in relation to the state and are formed voluntarily by members of society to protect or extend their interests or values.'[1] However, the prevailing impression among most scholars is captured in the observation that, given the history of ambiguity in Western political theory about the idea, it is unclear 'to what extent it provides a useful point of departure for theoretically grounded empirical work', which in turn 'has reinforced a picture of an ideological rather than an analytical construct'.[2] This leads, in a sense, to a paradoxical situation.

On the one hand, the term is widely embraced within scholarly and activist circles, giving the impression that it introduces a real turn in the understanding of key events and processes. At the same time, there is the quasi-unanimous sense about the difficulties in deploying it to grasp and analyse the processes going on within contemporary societies. Does all this amount to a bowing by its users to intellectual fashion – or does it indicate a *bona fide* receptivity in academe and elsewhere to new waves of discourse in our time?

It is a fact that the concept of 'civil society' has been re-discovered recently and has, in a very short period, invaded the field of human and social sciences, and of numerous political and activist discourses. Its uses, from the start, strike by the breadth of their variety. In some instances, it is adopted as a tool that helps analyse with supposedly greater accuracy and pertinence some processes within modern societies. In other cases, it is thought to refer to forms of social organisation that have only emerged recently. It has also become, in still other cases, following Ernest Gellner, a *slogan* that mobilises social actors and defines a new 'horizon of hope' within some social environments.[3] Hence, we find ourselves in a complex situation where a concept comes from theory (where it already has numerous connotations) and informs practice – even defining new attitudes among various social actors.

When it is applied to societies different from those where it originated and to which it was originally applied, especially the societies of the 'South' in general and of Muslims in particular, the aforementioned difficulties are accentuated. This need not lead us to the kind of polarity that 'essentialist' theories draw between 'Western' and 'Muslim' societies. The concept, in its initial uses at least, has definite historical referents. It points to processes and events that occurred in European history, and maintains its original connotations – while adding new and different issues and interrogations. Thus it operates as a shell, a conventional (community imposed?) category for expressing and thinking about current issues related to the emancipation (real or otherwise) of contemporary clusters of society.

What can be observed in the recent literature is that civil society is invoked at the same time as a *normative* and as a *descriptive* category. It is, in the words of Gellner again, a slogan and an analytical tool, and it is probable that the malaise generated by its usage stems precisely from the constant and uncontrolled, often not even explicitly formulated, movement between the two uses.

When we venture beyond this initial 'dualism', there emerges another (and important) divergence among those who use the concept of civil society as an *analytical tool*. Some social scientists invoke it as a category that helps understand key historical processes within different societies, and to reach the 'foundations' of specific types of social order. Others use it with rather more limited ambitions, as a concept that helps analyse prevailing social and political change. As illustrations of the first approach, we will discuss the conclusions proposed by Gellner and Wajih Kawtharani in their recent works. As an example of the latter approach, we will review salient observations offered by contemporary social scientists. For both approaches, the Maghreb is taken as a case-study and a starting point for comments that are intended to be of general import, of some pertinence at least, for 'Muslim' environments at large.

'Civil Society' as a Key to the Foundations of the Social Order

Whether in its recent or more 'remote' phases, the historical experience of the Maghreb can shed useful light on relations between social actors and institutions – on the prospects for civil society within, and perhaps beyond, the region. The exercise may lead us to question some patterns of traditional scholarship, most notably in relation to such questions as: 'Is Islam compatible with modernity?', and 'Could Islam accommodate democracy?'. These queries presume the existence of homogeneous 'blocs' of Islam, and the concept opposed to it. The exercise may lead us also to question some of the prevailing usages of civil society and clarify our understandings.

As a primary observation, one should recall that the Maghreb was incorporated into the Muslim world very early. It was not part of the founding moments of the Islamic community that included the *khilafa rashida* as a political system (and later as a paradigm within the majority Sunni fold), and the elaboration of the fundamental theological and judicial systems. But the Maghreb was integral to that community in the era of what Marshall Hodgson called the *Islamicate* social system,[4] when it lived within the conceptions and regulations which ordered traditional Muslim societies. It gave birth, at the height of this period, to one of the finest observers of that kind of society, Abdul Rahman Ibn Khaldun, whose work gives us among the most vivid descriptions of the social interactions that prevailed within it.

If, as noted earlier, invoking civil society across socio-historical contexts raises particular challenges, then the instance of the Maghreb richly complicates the analyses – as evinced by some of the diametrically opposed readings of its experience. Among the many approaches to the subject, we can begin with two interpretations that were formulated during recent decades, one by an 'external' observer interested in a comparative (or 'horizontal') perspective, and the other by an historian keen on grasping long-term historical trends (a 'vertical' perspective).

For one of the most eminent theorists of civil society, the late Ernest Gellner, there was a sharp contrast between a social order defined by the lively presence of civil society, and environments where the ideal of umma was instilled and is alive and influential. 'Umma' is taken here to be a paradigm that helps understand a peculiar societal type. It is, in effect, a charismatic community, and like such polities, tends to make virtue the prime object of government. Gellner also evokes other, non-Muslim, contexts where similar ideals have taken hold and shaped social and political structures – as with regimes under communism.

So we have, on the one hand, civil society, defined as 'a set of diverse non-government institutions which is strong enough to counterbalance the state and, while not preventing the state from fulfilling its role of keeper of the peace and arbitrator between major interests, can nevertheless prevent it from dominating and atomising the rest of society.'[5] In contrast, we have societies shaped by the umma model. Gellner argues that the latter could not develop historically strong sets of non-governmental institutions and, 'in the end, society seems to possess no cement other than the faith on one hand and the loyalty, once upon a time of clan and now of clientele, on the other'.[6] The reason for this absence is found in Islam, a faith that permeates these societies and defines all its institutions: 'Islam ... exemplifies a social order which seems to lack much capacity to provide political countervailing institutions or associations, which is atomised without much individualism, and operates effectively without intellectual pluralism'.[7]

The future of societies where Islam prevailed in the past is therefore predetermined by this given situation, and by the paradigm or system imposed by this religion: they are fated to impose an umma wherein Islam benefits from the conditions of industrialisation. Why? Because the circumstances of 'scripturalism, pervasive rule-orientation and Puritanism, the regulation though not sacralisation of economic life, the monotheism, restrained ritualism and religious though not political individualism, have somehow produced a world religion which, at any rate so far, is secularisation-resistant, and tends increasingly to dominate the polities within which it has a majority'.[8] We have, then, a sort of mechanical process through which a faith provides the only counterweight to primitive loyalties (clan and clientele) and directs some societies towards forms and institutions different from those built by their 'Western' counterparts. The process and the ways through which it keeps and even strengthens its hold on these societies is further developed along the lines of agrarian authoritarianism, in which Islam is in fact disembodied from political life:

> [I]t can live on without the state, and sit in judgement on it. It is no longer linked to and permanently controlled by any one political authority, being incarnated in a transcendent law preserved in writing instead and in the keeping of a trans-polity and trans-ethnic class, which, if the law is defied, can in alliance

with communal forces on/at the edge of society restore the moral order. So in a sense faith dominates the state while remaining independent of it, even though the state is authoritarian and normally brooks no rivals in the sphere of coercion, in the territory it actually controls. Though specialists on the law may be individually or even collectively powerless, yet the ethos they transmit dominates society and imposes itself even on the state. Political authority can neither change it nor even manipulate it to any great extent. This solution to the question of how to run society worked well in the traditional agrarian world, and contrary to expectation is working even better now: Islam has grown stronger and purer in the last hundred years. It would be foolish to be dogmatic about whether this will continue. If indeed it does, then Islam will constitute a permanent and serious alternative to sceptical Civil Society, and we shall have this option of a fully industrial, computerized *Umma*.[9]

From this series of syllogism-like inferences, Gellner presumes that civil society cannot thrive in environments where Islam predominates. In such settings, religious truth is taken to be absolute, it cannot be openly challenged, and pluralism, diversity, critical attitudes are not allowed. It is rather believed that an entrenched constitution or 'meta constitution' has been given by God eternally to society, and defines forever all norms and forms of collective behaviour.

Returning to actual historical data, Gellner accepts that civil society was born accidentally, in a particular place and time, and has managed to survive and to eliminate its rivals, not in consequence of the work of a necessary historical reason but 'only' by practical performance. Hence its birth is an historical fact that can be described and analysed. In a second stage, it has been conceptualised by thinkers and became lately a slogan, since the alternatives which were opposed to it (its 'rivals') did not create societies that performed as well as it did – in other words, did not 'deliver' what they promised in terms of prosperity and freedom.

This product of accidental birth has come to check the power of the state that is potent and endowed with important economic resources. Civil society lives because no creed is absolutised, because no power is capable of atomising and subjugating society.

What Gellner holds, in sum, is that civil society prospers in (or is the emblem of) conditions where there is a *strong* state, a *strong* society and a *weak* creed. Through its institutions, a fragile but lasting equilibrium is put in place.

The sharp oppositions drawn by Gellner have already stirred waves of criticism.[10] Ilkay Sunar has pointed to an important ambiguity that prevails in Gellner's reasoning, leading to an oversimplification of grave consequence – indeed, a confusion between two models which have inspired public behaviours in Muslim societies:

> Gellner does not spell it out clearly, but there were actually two variants of urban, High Islam: the lax ('not properly practised') one, and the enthusiastic, zealous kind. The lax, relaxed Islam grew in the commercial and civilized soil of urban centers and was incapable of governing itself. The enthusiastic one was engendered by the combination of tribal *asabiyya* and the normative ideals of High Islam and provided governance of the lax, atomized urban residents enfeebled by commerce and influence.[11]

Two paradigms, not one, have guided Muslims in their quest for conformity with Islamic principles in public undertakings. That one or the other prevailed at specific moments should be understood by reference to political configurations that were not enforced by the 'eternal norms' of Islam. Why, in contexts where society is favoured and community undermined, the 'fundamentalist, enthusiastic version' should gain ascendancy over the 'relaxed version of High Islam' (when both are conducive to industrialisation), is not obvious. It would, Sunar, argues, be more rewarding to address 'the kinds of power balances that exist in the contemporary Muslim world between the relaxed and enthusiastic, and the "caliphal" and "imperial" variants of High Islam'.[12]

If these configurations are hostile to civil society, it is in fact for other considerations that are linked to the strength that they gave to specific forms of communalism.

> Within the 'sultanic/imperial' tradition, then, Islam is not unfriendly to the separation of state and religion. Neither is it unfriendly to pluralism; on the contrary, the Ottoman millet

system was *pluralism* par excellence. To put it in Gellner's terms, the problem of 'imperial' Islam vis-à-vis civil society does not lie in its fusion of faith, power and society but in the kind of countervailing pluralism that underwrites society, the kind of 'stifling communalism' in which identities are not freely chosen, social ties are not flexible and instrumental but constrained and hampered by religious-moral bonds. This is the problem-area of the imperial variant of High Islam, not the ideocratic fusion of state, religion and society.[13]

If both the 'caliphal' model – where the circle of faith, power and society were intact – and the 'imperial' model – in which the nexus of faith and power was broken, but that between faith and society remained – each presents problems for civil society, it is for different reasons that should not be conflated. Gellner has confused norms with fact, slogans proposed by some activists with processes at work in the real world. 'In Gellner's account', notes Sunar, 'history is ultimately the handmaiden of the Original Norm not only in the case of Islam but of Christianity as well: History serves all without discrimination on the basis of faith: each to his own Norm'.[14]

In opposition to the line of reasoning adopted by Gellner, we are alerted by Kawtharani to the reality that the history of Muslim societies is not yet appropriately and adequately known. The *'sultanian'* state – which is considered to be the principal institution, encapsulating the essential features of Islamicate societies – is but one feature of the story. It is the visible cover of a complex system within which spontaneous, free and powerful social institutions played an extremely significant role. The *sultanian* state was accepted formally as *legal*, but never as fully *legitimate*. In order to limit the hold of this state on society, the law was founded on religious precepts and therefore sacralised. Local customs were linked to God-given commands, in wide encompassing systems that integrated large spans of social life, and were designed in a way to preserve the main functions of social regulation from the intervention of political power. What for Gellner is the supremacy of an 'ethos' is viewed by Kawtharani as a

configuration of legal and political power that preserved the autonomy (or means of autonomy) of a social order.

Sacralisation of the law was a means of achieving and defending this autonomy. Some regulations were taken from sacred texts,
but layers of purely social, sometimes strictly local, regulations
were added in order to build coherent and total systems. Direct
management of social activities by communal institutions such as
traditional corporations and endowments, gave to society a kind
of autonomy from, and protection against, the 'sultan'. Thus society had designed, and maintained in the face of diverse and
changing political masters, a working and substantial social order. This was made possible by a kind of 'proto-civil society' that
Kawtharani calls 'communal or clanic society' (*mujtama' ahli*).[15]
Instead of defining this society by 'clusters of absences',[16]
Kawtharani uses the concept of civil society as a parameter, an
empty structure, for which he finds comparable (but not identical) forms in certain pre-modern societies. Although adopting a
'vertical' approach that highlights specific systems of social organisation, he does not end up claiming an irreducible
particularity for the societies at hand.

Among social scientists who recognise the value of this particular historical process and the attendant conceptualisation, Inga
Brandell offers an interesting view of Muslim societies today. Although she restricts too narrowly the meaning of the word *ahl* in
the expression *al-mujtama' al-ahli*, holding that it refers to 'family
society' instead of 'communal' or 'clanic' society, she attempts to
develop to the full the consequences that flow from contemporary transformations of traditional societies:

> [I]n precolonial society there existed what is termed *al-mujtama'
> al-ahli*, family society, to be contrasted with the modern con-
> cept *al-mujtama' al-madani* (*ahl*=family, *madina*=city). This 'family
> society' constituted a public sphere linked to the state but which
> also had a certain autonomy, and was divided into several parts:
> the group of religiously and legally learned men, the ulama
> (the religion 'doctors'), the merchants, the religious Sufi or-
> ders, the professional corporations, and perhaps the peasants
> and the tribes. Economic functions and social services formed

an essential part of this 'family society', although the state controlled certain services. The ulama in turn, through their
legitimacy as the interpreters of the law, put limits on the power
of the state and could – and did – represent the rest of the
'family society'. Other authors add to the preceding groups *al-
ashraf*, notables with religious legitimacy stemming from their
descent from the Prophet. Suffice here to point to the use of
the concepts, and the following problematization of the equiva-
lence instituted in modern civil society discussion between the
family and the private sphere. Here, quite evidently, we have to
do with a different concept of the family, in fact one which does
not at all coincide with the private one of the family in modern
Western understanding. There was, no doubt, a private sphere
in those societies, but it was not 'the family'. The regional debate has not pursued this line of reasoning ... .[17]

Returning to the case of the Maghreb, we can concur with
Kawtharani that the state was in fact much weaker than it seemed
to be. Historians have remarked that the sultan 'had his throne
on the back of his horse', that he was forced to fight continuously
in order to maintain his power. Often the state took the form of a
mhalla, (military camp), a group of tribes travelling across the
country in endless military campaigns, or that of a *makhzen* (forti-
fied depot or storage of grain designed to withstand long sieges),
the name given to the traditional state by Moroccans. In both
cases, the state was linked with or reduced to a military adventure.
In fact, the state consisted more or less of a large band of political
and military adventurers who constantly fought to retain power
of sorts – restricted to minimal functions (order maintenance and
defence against other 'predators'), and whose main feature was
what Khaldun called the 'monopoly of legitimate injustice'.[18]

Hence in so far as civil society is about a web of institutions that
maintain social functions independently of the state, it has a precedent in Muslim contexts. This configuration was reached after a
long and complex evolution during which new political and religious attitudes came to the fore. Its initial impetus lies in the
political disenchantment that prevailed among Muslims with the
failure to create and sustain durable legitimate states (the *khilalfa
rashida* for the Sunnis, the infallible Imamate for the Shi'a).

Muslims found themselves in situations where they had to submit to illegitimate systems of power, mostly to dynasties founded by political and military adventurers who could mobilise sufficient tribal military segments to impose their rule – and who 'confiscated' even the religious discourse. The 'compromise' that was found between an imposed reality and entrenched principles was to concede formal legal status to these *de facto* regimes but to withhold full legitimacy and the legislative power from them – and to entrust both to scholars notionally independent from the political establishment, and relying exclusively on religious truths in building their views and attitudes. Muslims were hence led to devise particular patterns, where the state was a kind of external layer added to existing and autonomous social structures, where state and society functioned as external bodies, largely independent from each other.

The formulation here would be: proto-civil society born in a pre-modern setting with a *strong* creed, a (relatively) *strong* society and a *weak* state. This kind of 'civil society' was not intended to resist or limit the power of the state, but to manage basic public functions in the absence of an effective public authority. It did not protect society fully and efficiently against the violence of the *makhzen.* But it was the minimum that could be done, and this was often quite substantial in terms of social functions and services, indeed the regulation of most collective acts. It is true that this was linked to what Mohamed Abed Jabri has described as the 'practice of politics within religion', by which he refers to the fact that political competition among opposed actors was conducted and expressed through theological controversies, political battles fought in the name of religious doctrines.[19] Politics as such, as a field by itself, was not recognised and did not form an independent sphere. We arrive, then, to another limitation of the possible use of the concept of civil society.

'Civil Society' as a Tool for Analysing Contemporary Changes

During the twentieth century, modern states have replaced sultanian states virtually everywhere in societies of Muslims. This was a major change not only because institutional forms were different but, as the historical conditions within which the change occurred were 'special', the impact was profoundly disturbing for Muslims in their institutional configurations and in their moral consciousness. New relationships with the historical 'Other' (Europe) were built, and profound revisions of traditional world views undertaken under the influence (or against the challenge) of modern philosophical and political theories. On the one hand, the institutions of modern states were imposed from the outside: the complex processes through which modern nation states emerged in Europe had not been directly experienced by Muslims. The 'imported' state, as it was called, had to accommodate existing patterns of governance, traditional views of legitimacy and, at the same time, modern expectations. Thus the modern state was supposed not only to control effectively the whole territory and the whole population, but to transform the territory, the population, the economy and the prevailing culture. It was also to define new relationships with former colonising powers. We are confronted here with the notion of a 'modernising', not merely a 'modern', state. It was not only different in nature from traditional states, but emerged in contexts where it was entrusted some very specific functions. It was expected to implement policies geared toward the modernisation of society, and catching up with the advanced North. All this happened within an atmosphere dominated by a specific ideology: nationalism and voluntarist attitudes related to it. It led to a dismembering of traditional society and to the dismantling of its main institutions – including those that performed social functions and defined what we called 'proto-civil society'. At the same time, it did not achieve any substantial progress in changing durably the conceptions and value-systems linked to them. Traditional conceptions of political legitimacy kept their influence on prevailing attitudes, even as formulations for new expectations made their way to the consciousness of the multitudes.

After a few decades, it became clear that nation states in most Muslim contexts were not to be allowed to mature, in contrast to what happened in southern Europe, for example. The end of what we may call the 'modernising', 'reforming' or 'upgrading' state was brought by external factors: globalisation and the constraints imposed on young states by the rapid networking of economies throughout the world. Sudden paralysis caught these institutions before they had put in place structures able to sustain active societies and economies, and allow real modernisation and participation in world competition.

However, these states, through their education programmes, had achieved a genuine success at least in one area: they brought the traditional high culture of small elites within reach of the masses. Public education policies, as Mohamed Charfi has shown, disseminated a culture where religion, political power and legitimacy are viewed through traditional concepts, especially through ideas elaborated within the classical, 'high' tradition. Ironically, modern states diffused, through their educational institutions, trends opposed to their very own fundamental principles. Arabisation, for example, allowed a return to traditional culture and views embedded in it, because it was conceived, planned and implemented as a return to 'authentic' ideas uncontaminated by the West – as a departure from, and rejection of, modern culture. Says Charfi:

> Il est paradoxal d'enseigner dans les écoles de l'Etat de vieilles traditions qui sont contraires au droit et à la pratique officielle du pays. Si les règles charaūques étaient enseignées et en même temps placées dans leur contexte historique et soumises à une appréciation critique pour justifier l'attitude du législateur contemporain qui les a abandonnées, cela aurait été très utile pour favoriser l'intégration de l'élève dans son milieu social et lui faire accepter la modernité sans rejeter sa culture originelle. Mais ce n'est pas le cas. Au contraire, il est clairement affirmé que la liberté n'est permise qu'à la condition que la charia ne soit pas remise en cause et que la raison ou l'esprit critique ont pour limite les règles de la charia qui ne doivent pas être critiquées. ... Le feu traditionaliste était éteint. Il a fallu la toute-puissance de l'Etat pour le rallumer de ses cendres et le rôle 'multiplicateur' de l'école pour lui donner de l'ampleur.[20]

Instead of being mobilised for liberation from pre-modern

world views and attitudes, modern education thus became a source
of resistance to modernisation. This helped the return of, or nostalgia for, traditional forms of political practice, what Jabri called
'making politics *within* religion'. As the management of public
affairs within pre-modern societies was not an autonomous field
and was not recognised as a legitimate practice, political views
and actions had to adopt religious concepts and symbols as forms
of expression. It is in this sense that we can say that religion has
still an instrumental role in mediating relations in the political
sphere.

An Ambivalent Role for Civil Society?

The modern state in the Maghreb certainly did not become strong,
like the ones it was modelled on in the North. It failed to provide
the infrastructures required for economic development or to build
the national culture required for a modern national community.
Before finishing those foundational tasks, it has been attracted to
and governed by the paradigm of the minimal, 'regulator' state.
During its short historical experience, it was driven by two different trends:

1. On the international scene, nationalist and voluntarist notions
   of the state were replaced by the minimal, regulatory state,
   before expectations relating to economic and cultural services
   to the population had been satisfied, or even received the beginnings of satisfaction.
2. Within almost all societies of Muslims, a new cycle of intense
   polarisation between the self and the 'Other' began, gained
   momentum and gave unexpected strength to seemingly pre-
   modern views and attitudes.

The state in contemporary Muslim environments is therefore
weak, but not in the same way as the traditional or sultanian state.
It controls the whole territory and the whole population, but it
remains fearful of society, which it views as a kind of unpredictable force. It was compelled to abandon its ambitions of
modernisng the economy and society through authoritarian

methods. It withdrew hastily from areas and operations such as public education and health, and concentrated on the defence of its own security. Its recent policies contributed to a new fragmentation of society. As seen by Desrues and Moyano, with particular regard to Morocco:

> [T]he state's withdrawal from certain social and economic commitments is a fact. Thus, the state looks to relief being provided by private non-profit associations, to limit the negative effects of withdrawal, while at the same time meeting the demands of supranational organisations, such as the World Bank and IMF, for reductions in the public deficit. For example, the integration of a positive discourse by the state on the non-profit sector, and this sector's collaboration with the public administration, contribute to the development of associative initiatives in this area. The state does not, however, relinquish the control it exercises through restrictive legislation governing the setting up and funding of these associations.
>
> Secondly, it is also a fact that the demands for respect of human rights made chiefly by the beneficiaries of social change since the 1980s (the literate urban population) are having an influence on the development of civil society. These demands have been tolerated by the *makhzen* because of the need for Morocco to improve its international image. Particularly active within this sphere are the associations for the defense of human rights and those for the advancement of women, which belong to a very sensitive area given its direct political repercussions on the fundamental pillars of traditional Moroccan society.[21]

Since the modern state was born during what we regard now as the 'nationalist' era, it was opposed to all forms of spontaneous, free, autonomous social organisation, be they political, cultural or otherwise. Nationalism and its ideology made their way to Maghrebi societies, although they rested on ambiguous foundations. The national identity was viewed in altogether ethnic, religious and regional terms and its content varied in time and context. Yet the idea of the nation-state was effective, and legitimised newly-born entities with modern expectations. The state *atomised* society in the sense given to this word by Gellner and did everything to prevent the birth or development of effective civil society organisations. When the reversal began, many associations and organisations were born.

The most striking fact is that associative life has flourished as former leftist militants shifted their activism from politics to humanitarianism. They were shortly followed, and surpassed, by other activists from the opposite side, the 'fundamentalists'. It is as if, once convinced that no real change can happen within the political realm, all those who dreamed of achieving change went to the social field and adopted associative systems and approaches in order to serve their ideals.

Most scholars have offered negative judgements on this particular strain of nascent civil society. In their view, it is artificial, its role marginal and often manipulated by state (secret) services. It is, for most of them, either an elite operation, a kind of fashion, or an outcome, a product of foreign influence. Elite strata are seen to continue manipulating society to serve their interests. Even if most of these accusations are exaggerated or lack foundation, the 'outburst' of civil society activity does not appear to have imparted durable and dependable strength, or meaningful autonomy, to society.

Other scholars have stressed the specificity of such evolutions. Once again, Brandell was among those who pointed to the particular sets of questions raised by these configurations, and the inflections that need to be introduced into the concept of civil society. 'Modern' civil society was put under stress with the rolling back of the colonial state, which meant that once independence had been achieved modern organisations were tied to the would-be state that in its 'nation-building' did not admit autonomous spaces or organisations. 'A party-state, mass organisations linked to it and no independent organisation was the rule, sometimes achieved at a high price of repression.' Moreover, it is important to distinguish between limiting and 'rolling back' an authoritarian state, and the establishment of democracy on the other. Fusing the two harms the evaluation of civil society organisations, as well as a proper appreciation of Islamism. Brandell therefore calls for a reconsideration – even a rebuilding – of civil society in order to distance our views from the contexts, the issues and expectations to which it was intimately linked at the beginning:

> [C]lassical formulations of the civil society-democracy nexus turn around the forms taken first by political centralization under absolutist monarchies and their counter-forces consti- tuted by corporations and representation of stander, then by their successive weakening and replacement by modern limits to central power, in the form of parliaments and a modern pub- lic space: newspapers, clubs, coffee houses, etc. In non-Western and colonized parts of the world the approach will have to take into account, firstly, the replacement of an indigenous or local state with a modern state imposed either directly or indirectly from the outside, and, secondly, its replacement with an inde- pendent state. Political parties, newspapers, coffee houses, even chorals, evolved differently under those circumstances, and in relationship to the pre-colonial, colonial and post-colonial po- litical systems and states.[22]

The challenges faced by civil society in Muslim environments, then, have no common measure with those already known in the West, especially in the wake of economic and cultural globalisation and the burdens of a prolonged debt-crisis for so many states of the South.

These realities are graphically illustrated in a recent episode of Moroccan history, notably the polemics around what was called the Plan for the Integration of Women in Development.[23] The initial moment was a project proposed by the government of Abderrahman Youssoufi, composed mainly by a leftist and nation- alist coalition, aimed at offering women better access to some basic services in health, education and, to a lesser degree, in legal sta- tus. This sparked a profound division in society: pros and cons engaged in great confrontations, through which they mobilised supporters in street demonstrations and launched press cam- paigns. Those who were in favour of the governmental programme included mainly modern, educated elites, and in general all 'pro- gressivists' open to modern ideals and universalist views. Those who were against the programme included fundamentalist and conservative elements, and in general elements keen to defend the local identity and oppose its weakening through 'Westernisation'. The latter, who adopted the discourse of pre-modern politics, could eventually mobilise, in street demonstrations, larger numbers against their opponents and, in fact, against the very ideals of civil society as they are conceptualised from a traditional perspective. The mood was of contestation of the very foundations of modern polities and their agendas, of the 'social contract' that defines the new national communities.

The idea of an entrenched, eternal, God-given constitution has been invoked, successfully in cases like this, to oppose and block an ambitious programme for modernising social relations and improving the status of women and their economic and social integration. Was it an attempt to move back to pre-modern practices and views, or a way of grounding modern approaches in religious views deeply entrenched in public consciousness? Some authors stressed that these pro-tradition movements were in fact not hostile to women's rights as such, but rather to the secular rationales for them. We then have alternative approaches to modernisation: one based on the rejection of tradition, and the other on the transformation of tradition 'from within'. Which prompts us to question the mode of presence, the function (and the strength) of religious faith in these societies.

What we can conclude from these observations is that the state and society are, manifestly, weak. Manipulator and manipulated, they stand in mutual defiance. And what of creed? Is it really strengthening – or even maintaining its hold on minds, and on the social order? Does its strength explain the apparent resistance to modernisation? If this is true of societies where Islam prevails, can a civil society exist there – and, if it does, can it accomplish anything? Would it not turn against itself or be mobilised against its own conditions of existence, as seemed to happen in the case of the battle over the Plan for the Integration of Women in Development? In fact, what can be seen is that civil society organisations may turn against the very principles of civil society when the feeling predominates that basic threats are directed toward the 'fundamentals' of society, that is, to symbols that define the historical continuity and life of the community. Democracy and freedom of expression mobilise the masses as intensely as the defence of integrity only when two conditions are met: that the symbols of collective identity (sublimated in religion) are respected, and that a minimum of solidarity is shown within the social fabric. The threats (real or imagined) lead to intense polarisations, to a rejection of the slogans and the ideals expressed through the notions of democracy, human rights, and so on. When these threats are lost sight of, the defence of the opposite ideals – of authenticity and defence of identity, among others – is championed only by active minority groups. In these cases, a determined minority obstructs changes desired by a large but inarticulate majority.

Are we witnessing here a return of medieval forms and attitudes, of the censorship of a whole society by a minority of its members? In fact, it is not a simple attempt to revive pre-modern attitudes. Through modern education and mass communication, large strata of the population have taken hold (or attempted to take hold) of religious symbols in order to endow them with modern vindications, to use them as means to defend 'new expectations'. Religious discourse, as noted by many scholars, is no longer the exclusive domain of traditional clerics.[24] Societies where the modern state has not developed infrastructures and services able to sustain modern economies, where systems of basic social solidarity (in public health, education) are lacking, where the state remains alien (or is felt to be alien), seem to be forced back to pre-modern solidarities and 'basic' vindications. It is at a later stage, when the state has recuperated – and when, in the public opinion, it is not felt to be confiscated by a hostile elite – that views and attitudes of civil society shift towards modern vindications. When that happens they voice expectations of the type that conform to the pattern of civil society activism known in other settings.

Iran shows plainly, on the political stage, the kind of evolution that occurs in other societies of Muslims: an overwhelming majority (including progressivist forces) sided with religious clerics, and adopted religious symbols, in order to face down a regime regarded as alienating and hostile. An agenda calling for the return of an Islamic state and the negation of all modern political forms was thrown up. But once the *ancien régime* was toppled, views, attitudes and vindications altered. Today, a conservative minority faces and successfully (temporarily) resists an overwhelming (but subdued) majority. Does this not show a different mode of action of civil society? The fact that the masses seek to take back religion from the sultan (the state) and from the ulama or *mullah*s (clerics) in some cases does create a situation without precedent in Muslim contexts. The struggle is not of 'politics within religion', but about the status of religion and its role in the social order. The key question is: who will have the final say? Who will take control of the religious discourse? Will it be used as a weapon against the majority? We witness not a modern incarnation of the 'Khaldunian cycle', whereby every reforming or opposition group would be constrained to adopt religious doctrines to defend its agenda, but an episode where attempts are made to replace that cycle by other forms or 'pulsations' of political life.

This leads to the (provisional) remark that far from strengthening creed at the expense of society, society may be facing a new challenge. Taking control of the creed, or rather extracting the creed from the control of the clerics and the state and extremist minorities, is arguably the hallmark of the present phase in the evolution of societies of Muslims. This turn may be better described as an attempt to build a new social contract, *where religion cannot be played against society*. The illegitimate character of non-democratic modern states creates a situation where, apparently, traditional forms of opposition may prevail over modern forms at earlier stages, and thence either relegate or spawn civil society of a modern type. If this seems to impose varied tasks upon emerging social forces, it is because society is caught between varying forms of socio-political action.

This may explain why, if we go back to the concept of civil society in the sense given to it in the literature, we are led to express some doubts about its pertinence in present conditions. What seems to be at stake in contemporary Muslim environments is really a search for the rule of law, of making and enforcing the law, where the law is not of sacred origins. The main concern in these contexts seems to be to understand how the law prevails upon the will and the power of the powerful, even though it is not religious law. Gellner explains this turn in European societies by a mechanical device: a stalemate among different powers (the economic, the symbolic or religious and the political/military) where none can eliminate its rivals. This helped enforce the prevalence of rules over specific actors. What occurs today in Muslim societies is chiefly a struggle for the appropriation of these three powers. The contestation takes place among limited elites (military, economic), new modern states, still of the *makhzen* type,[25] and popular strata, now 'massified', urbanised and impoverished. 'Civil society' – if we want to retain the expression – is not of a different type but, since historical situations vary, has a different agenda. In the contemporary Maghreb, it is called on to contribute to the building of a new 'social contract' that would arrange for the withdrawal of religion from political usage (and from mediation of relations in the public sphere) and, at the same time, maintain impetus for enforcement of the rule of law, where law-making and enforcement occur outside the religious sphere and are rescued from self-imposed elites. It is to help obtain what Desrues and Moyano call an 'elite pact', given the reality of entrenched, overpowering elites.[26] In effect, this refers to a much more fundamental evolution that involves nothing less than the design and implementation of a new 'social contract'.

Conclusion: The Case for Normative Invocation of Civil Society

The instance of the Maghreb shows that while civil society may seek a modern distribution of roles, actors and practices, it is deterred by a global context of polarisation, of confrontation between the self and the 'Other', and by views and attitudes disseminated through traditionalist education. Hence, the descriptive value of the concept is sharply constrained. It makes the naive use of civil society create and give credibility to ambiguous views and evaluations about the current state of affairs within these settings. If a more cautious use of the concept is sought, one must continuously introduce readjustments in the content of the concept itself. We came to observe that:

1. When used as a key to the essential features of particular forms of social order, 'civil society' can lead to the build-up of grand and facile schemes that abet pre-established views on cultural identities, and lead to support of prejudices on supposedly unbridgeable differences between 'Western' and 'non-Western' societies. The idea may be used, as in the work of Kawtharani, as an historical referent for different processes and provide a tool to better understand social forms that existed in the past. This remains, however, a 'negative' use and leaves the observer in the position of applying external, arbitrary standards to living forms of collective behaviour (or showing that they are not applicable).

2. When used as a tool to interpret recent phenomena in Muslim societies, we found again that 'civil society' had to be relativised or at least 'situated'. This meant either that it was not pertinent to describe what was happening in these contexts, or that it had to be substantially redefined to be able to take into account apparently paradoxical or contradictory trends. In both situations, we found ourselves in 'familiar territory': societies of Muslims being defined by 'clusters of absence'. Analytical tools taken from other contexts are applied mechanically, leading to further confusion rather than clarity in the understanding of particular living forms. Not surprisingly, much social research in recent decades has looked for ways and means to attenuate, and sometimes to oppose, the effects entailed by the use of such tools on the knowledge generated about societies of Muslims.

These difficulties with the concept lead some scholars to seek alternatives. We found, for example, that the notion of *mujtama' ahli* refers to a 'sultanian' paradigm conceived, in Muslim environments, as an alternative to the 'caliphal' paradigm. This may be just another formulation of the Khaldunian theory of 'cycles' through which public life evolved in pre-modern Muslim societies. *Flux and reflux in the faith of men*, to take an expression from David Hume popularised by Gellner, visualised communities going back and forth between states of intense mobilisation (leading to strife and civil war) and moments of peaceful compromise.

Modern societies have known also their forms of *flux and reflux*. If their faith was more political than religious, it was nevertheless faith. Between the 'revolutionary' moments where transformation was sought by violent means, and the peaceful ones where democracy and the normal life of established institutions prevailed, they have gone through comparable cycles of 'enthusiasm' and 'compromise'. Nowadays, 'civil society' appears to be the setting where social mobilisation takes the form of peaceable attitudes, based on lobbying, persuasion, bargaining, rational debate, political action and the like – all being different means to promote interests in ways opposed to 'revolutionary', violent and truth-founded approaches. Practising 'cool' forms of mobilisation rather than violent ones has become a criterion of political success and proved that, in contrast to its 'rivals', it delivers the best outcome for all concerned.

Thus, even if the concept of 'civil society' is problematic when used analytically – or because it is so problematic in such usage – it is most valuable normatively. One can only disagree with Göran Therborn in his claim that this robust normative quality means 'the notion of civil society has little to offer people concerned with prospects and strategies of democratisation'.[27] On the contrary, the most appropriate use is one that makes of it an ideal, yet an attainable and relative one. As long as we confine ourselves to considering real situations as they present themselves through the plurality of their forms and evolutions, we can measure the distance between our real states of affairs and what they could be. The question would then be: if the ideal expressed through the concept of a living and active 'civil society' is to be attained, what conditions should be fulfilled? How should we proceed to replace Khaldunian cycles, be they pre-modern or modern, by the institutional interplay of various social and political actors and movements?

Notes

1. B. Beckman, 'Explaining Democracy: Notes on the Concept of Civil Society', in E. Özdalga and S. Persson, ed., *Civil Society, Democracy and the*

Muslim World (Istanbul, 1997), p.1.

2. Ibid.

3. E. Gellner, *Conditions of Liberty: Civil Society and its Rivals* (London, 1994), pp.1, 2 and 12.

4. M. Hodgson, *The Venture of Islam: Conscience and History in a World Civilization* (Chicago, 1974), p.57.

5. Gellner, *Conditions of Liberty*, p.5.

6. Ibid., p.28.

7. Ibid., p.92.

8. Ibid., p.199.

9. Ibid., p.209.

10. A review on this subject was proposed in my article, 'Histoire universelle et exception islamique', *Prologues: revue maghrébine du livre*, Hors Série No.1 (Casablanca, 1997), pp.66–70.

11. İlkay Sunar, 'Civil Society and Islam', in *Civil Society, Democracy and the Muslim World*, p.11.

12. Ibid., p.13.

13. Ibid., p.15.

14. Ibid.

15. W. Kawtharani, 'In Relation to Our History: Civil Society or Communal Society?", *Al Hayat* (No.11731), 4 April 1995, p.17.

16. See L. Binder, 'Area Studies: A Critical Reassessment', in L. Binder, ed., *The Study of the Middle East: Research and Scholarship in the Humanities and Social Sciences* (New York, 1976), pp.1–28.

17. I. Brandell, 'Labour, Civil Society and Democratisation in North Africa', in *Civil Society, Democracy and the Muslim World* (Istanbul, 1997), pp.102–8.

18. Quoted in Gellner, *Conditions of Liberty*, p.28.

19. M.A. Jabri, *Arab Political Reason: Determinants and Expressions (Al-'aql al-siyasi al-arabi: muhaddidatuh wa tajalliyatuh)* (Casablanca, 1990), p.17.

20. M. Charfi, *Islam et liberté, le malentendu historique* (Paris, 1999), pp.225, 228.

21. T. Desrues and E. Moyano, 'Social Change and Political Transition in Morocco', *Mediterranean Politics*, 6 (2001), p.36.

22. Brandell, 'Labour, Civil Society and Democratisation in North Africa', pp.102–8.

23. 'The National Program for Integration of Women in Development: Supporters and Opponents', Collected Papers. (Rabat, Tariq Ibn Ziyad Centre), 2001.

24. J. Piscatori, *Islam, Islamists, and the Electoral Principle in the Middle East* (Leiden, 2000), p.3.

25. 'In consolidated Western democracies there usually exists a formal separation between both branches of the state: while the first (the administrative apparatus) is characterised by its permanence and is subject to bureaucratic procedures guided by objective norms of a universal nature, the second (represented by the government) is contingent and subject to the political logic of those who exercise power, while its continuity depends upon results obtained at the ballot box. To use Weberian terminology, it can be said that the legitimacy of both branches is a rational-legal one. In Morocco, the presence of the *makhzen* means that the two branches of state are not clearly separated but confused, producing the subordination of a rational-legal legitimacy (dominant in Western governments) to a tradition-oriented legitimacy. Hence, the elite that controls the *makhzen* system ... [controls] the bureaucratic-administrative and infrastructural power and consequently the state's capacity to truly penetrate civil society and take political decisions within national territory.' Desrues and Moyano, 'Social Change and Political Transition in Morocco', pp.27–8.

26. 'We have discussed the issue of governability within this context, highlighting the difficulties that the Moroccan state has to institutionally channel conflicts that emerge in the process of double transition. In accordance with our analysis, it can be said that these difficulties are not only a result of the magnitude of the conflicts in Morocco's deeply fragmented society, but also of the incapacity of the political system – a multi-party system which is divided and weakened by the patrimonialist practices and clientele favoritism of the *makhzen* – to provide mediators and assimilate the demands of its people. The situation described here places Morocco's double transition in the framework of an elite pact. If this pact is incapable of broadening the scope of opportunities to include the population as a whole, it runs the risk of becoming deadlocked and widening the gap between the official and the real society. This, in turn, would accentuate the conflicts in a process that, if it is to advance, requires stability for the necessary reforms to be undertaken successfully'. Desrues and Moyano, 'Social Change and Political Transition in Morocco', p.43.

27. G. Therborn, 'Beyond Civil Society: Democratic Experiences and Their Relevance to the "Middle East"', in *Civil Society, Democracy and the Muslim World*, p.45.

Bibliography

Abdullaev, K. and C. Barnes, ed. *Politics of Compromise: The Tajikistan Peace Process*. London, 2001.

Abdullaev, K. *Exiles of Bolshevism*. London, 2002.

Abu-Lughod, J. 'The Islamic City', *International Journal of Middle East Studies*, 19 (1987), pp.155–76.

Ahmad, Aziz. *Islamic Modernism in India and Pakistan, 1857–1947*. Oxford, 1967.

Akarlı, Engin D. 'The State as a Socio-Cultural Phenomenon and Political Participation in Turkey' in Engin D. Akarlı and Gabriel Ben-Dor, ed., *Political Participation in Turkey: Historical Background and Present Problems*. Istanbul:1975, pp. 135–55.

Akiner, Shirin. 'Between Tradition and Modernity: the Dilemma Facing Contemporary Central Asian Women', in Mary Buckley, ed., *Post-Soviet Women: From the Baltic to Central Asia*. Cambridge, 1997, pp.261–304.

—— 'Ethnicity, Nationality and Citizenship as Expressions of Self-Determination in Central Asia' in D. Clark and R. Williamson, ed., *Self-Determination: International Perspectives*. London, 1996, pp.249–74.

—— 'Islam, the State and Ethnicity in Central Asia in Historical Perspective', *Religion, State and Society: The Keston Journal*, 24 (1996), pp.91–132.

319

—— 'Social and Political Reorganisation in Central Asia: Transition from Pre-Colonial to Post-Colonial Society', in T. Atabaki and J. O'Kane, ed., *Post-Soviet Central Asia*. London, 1998, pp. 1–34.

—— *Tajikistan: Reconciliation or Disintegration?* London, 2001.

Alexander, J.C., ed. *Real Civil Societies: Dilemmas of Institutionalization*. London, 1998.

Almond, Gabriel A. and G. Bingham Powell, Jr. *Comparative Politics: System, Process, and Policy*, (2nd ed.). Boston, 1978.

Amin, Camron Michael. 'Selling and Saving "Mother Iran": Gender and the Iranian Press in the 1940s', *International Journal of Middle Eastern Studies*, 33 (2001), pp. 335–61.

Anderson, Benedict. *Imagined Communities: Reflections on the Origin and Spread of Nationalism*. London, 1991.

Anderson, John. 'Creating a Framework for Civil Society in Kyrgyzstan' *Europe-Asia Studies*, 52 (2000), pp.73–93.

Anheier, H., M. Glasius and M. Kaldor, ed. *Global Civil Society 2001*. Oxford and New York, 2001.

Antoun, Richard. 'Civil Society, Tribal Process, and Change in Jordan', *International Journal of Middle Eastern Studies*, 32 (2000), pp.441–63.

Arat, Yesim. 'Feminist Institutions and Democratic Aspirations: The Case of the Purple Roof Women's Shelter Foundation', in Zehra F. Arat (ed.), *Deconstructing Images of 'The Turkish Women'* New York, NY: 1999, pp. 295–309.

Arkoun, Mohammed. *The Unthought in Contemporary Islamic Thought*. London, 2002

—— *Rethinking Islam: Common Questions, Uncommon Answers*, tr. Robert D. Lee. Boulder, Colorado and Oxford, 1994.

Askari-Rizvi, Hasan. *Military and Politics in Pakistan*. Karachi, 1998.

Babadjanov, Bakhtyar. 'Muhammadjan Hindustani and the Beginning of the "Great Schism" among Muslims in Uzbekistan', in Stéphane A. Dudoignon and Hisao Komatsu, ed., *Islam and Politics in Russia and Central Asia (Early 18th-Late 20th Centuries)*. London, forthcoming.

Bellah, R. N., ed. *Beyond Belief: Essays on Religion in a Post-Traditionalist World*. Berkeley, California, 1991.

Bellah, R.N., R. Madsen and W.M. Sullivan. *The Good Society*. New York, 1992.

Berlin, Isaiah. *The Sense of Reality: Studies in Ideas and their History*. London, 1996.

Berrada, M. *The Game of Forgetting*, tr. I.J. Boullata. Austin, TX, 1996, p.128, original title, *Lu'bat al-Nisyan*. Rabat, 1987.

Binder, Leonard. *Religion and Politics in Pakistan*. Berkeley, CA, 1961.

Boroujerdi, M. 'The Paradoxes of Politics in Postrevolutionary Iran', in J.L. Esposito and R.K. Ramazani, ed., *Iran at the Crossroads*. New York, 2001, pp.13–27.

Bunt, G. *Virtually Islamic*. (Cardiff, 2000), pp.13–27.

Carkoglu, A. 'Religion and Public Policy in Turkey', *Institute for the Study of Islam in the Modern World (ISIM) Newsletter*, 8 (September 2001), p.29.

Carothers, T. 'The Rule of Law Revival', *Foreign Affairs* (1998), pp.95–106.

Carter, Stephen. *Civility*. New York and London, 1999.

—— *The Culture of Disbelief: How American Law and Politics Trivializes Religious Devotion*. New York, 1993.

Castoriadis, C. *The Imaginary Institution of Society*, tr. K. Blamey. Cambridge, Mass., 1998.

Castoriadis, C. *World in Fragments*, ed. D. A. Curtis. Palo Alto, Calif., 1997.

Causse, Maurice. 'Theologie de rupture et theologie de la communaute', *Revue d'histoire et de philosophie religieuse*, 44 (1964), pp. 60–80.

Chandoke, N. *State and Civil Society: Explorations in Political Theory*. New Delhi, 1995.

Charfi, Mohamed. *Islam et Liberté, le malentendu historique*. Paris, 1999.

Cloughley, Brian. *The Pakistan Army*. Karachi, 1999.

Cohen J., and A. Arato, *Civil Society and Political Theory*. Cambridge, MA, 1992.

Cole, D.H. 'An Unqualified Human Good: E.P.Thompson and the Rule of Law', *Journal of Law and Society*, 28, 2 (2001), pp.177–203.

Coles, R. *The Secular Mind*. Princeton, NJ, 1999.

Cox, Eva. *A Truly Civil Society*. Sydney, 2001.

Dabashi, Hamid. *Theology of Discontent*. New York, 1993.

Dagger, R. *Civic Virtues: Rights, Citizenship, and Republican Liberalism*. Oxford and New York, 1997.

Desrues, Thierry and Moyano, Eduardo. 'Social Change and Political Transition in Morocco', *Mediterranean Politics*, 6 (2001), pp.21–47.

Diamond, Larry. 'Rethinking Civil Society: Toward Democratic Consolidation' *Journal of Democracy*, 5 (1994).), pp.4–17.

Dudoignon, S. 'Political Parties and Forces in Tajikistan, 1989–1993', in M-R. Djalili, F. Grare and S. Akiner, ed., *Tajikistan: The Trials of Independence*. London, 1998, pp. 52–85.

Dupret, Baudouin. *Au nom de quell droit*. Cairo, 2000.

Durkheim, Emile. *De la division du travail social.* 4th ed., Paris, 1922.

Dworkin, Ronald. *Sovereign Virtue: The Theory and Practice of Equality.* Cambridge, MA, 2000.

Eickelman, D. and J. Anderson, ed. '*New Media in the Muslim World: The Emerging Public Sphere.* Bloomington and Indianapolis, IN, 1999.

Enayat, Hamid. 'Iran: Khumayni's concept of the "Guardianship of the Juriconsult"', in James Piscatori, ed., *Islam and the Political Process.*Cambridge, 1982, pp. 160–80.

Esmer, Yılmaz. *Devrim, Evrim ve Statüko: Türkiye'de Sosyal, Siyasal, Ekonomik Değerler.* Istanbul: 1999.

Esposito, J.L. *Unholy War: Terror in the Name of Islam.* New York, 2002.

Esposito, J.L. and J.O. Voll. *Islam and Democracy.* New York and Oxford, 1996.

Etzioni, A. 'Law in Civil Society, Good Society, and the Prescriptive State', *Chicago-Kent Law Review,* 75 (2000), p.355.

—— *The Spirit of Community.* New York, 1994.

Faier, Elizabeth. 'Making "Civil Society" in Divided Communities', *Workshop for Homegrown Models of Civil Society in the Muslim World,* Watson Institute for International Studies, Brown University, March 12–13, 1999.

Fakhry, M. *Ethical Theories in Islam.* Leiden, 1994.

Falk, R. *Religion and Humane Governance.* New York and Basingstoke, UK, 2001.

Fandy, M. *Saudi Arabia and the Politics of Dissent.* New York, 2001.

Farhi, Farideh. 'Fifty Years Later', *India Today* (New Delhi), vol. 22:21 (18 August 1997), pp.66–71.

—— 'Fifty Years, Fifty Questions', *The Herald* (Karachi), vol. 28:1 (January 1997), pp.139–92.

—— 'Religious Intellectuals, the "Woman Question" and the Struggle for the Creation of a Democratic Public Sphere in Iran', in Ahmed Ashraf, ed., *Intellectual Discourse in Post-Revolutionary Iran,* special issue of *International Journal of Politics, Culture and Society.* 2001, pp.315–39.

Filaly-Ansari, A. 'Can Modern Rationality Shape a New Religiosity? Mohamed Abed Jabri and the Paradox of Islam and Modernity', in J. Cooper et al., ed., *Islam and Modernity.* London and New York, 1998, pp.156–71.

—— 'The Challenge of Secularization', in *Journal of Democracy,* 7 (1996), pp.76–80.

Fukuyama, Francis. *Trust: The Social Virtues and the Creation of Prosperity.*

London and New York, 1995.

Gellner, Ernest. *Conditions of Liberty: Civil Society and its Rivals.* London, 1994.

Gerber, H. *Islamic Law and Culture, 1600–1840.* Leiden and Boston, 1999.

Geyushev, A. 'Peculiarities of the Process of Revival of Islam in Azerbaijan', *Pole*, 1 (2000), pp.32–7.

al-Ghannouchi, Rachid. 'Traditional Muslim Society is a Model of Civil Society', in Azzam Tamimi and John Esposito, ed., *Islam and Secularism in the Middle East.* London, 2000, pp.97–123.

Giddens, A, ed. *The Global Third Way Debate.* Cambridge, 2001.

Glendon, Mary Ann. 'Introduction: Forgotten Questions', in Glendon, Mary Ann and D. Blankenhorn, ed., *Seedbeds of Virtue: Sources of Competence, Character, and Citizenship in American Society.* Lanham, MD, 1995.

Goldberg, E. 'Private Goods, Public Wrongs and Civil Society in Some Medieval Arab Theory and Practice', in E. Goldberg, R. Kasaba and J. Migdal, ed., *Rules and Rights in the Middle East.* London and Seattle, 1993, pp.248–71.

Göle, Nilüfer. 'Toward an Autonomization of Politics and Civil Society in Turkey', in Metin Heper and Ahmet Evin, ed., *Politics in the Third Turkish Republic.* Oxford, 1994, pp. 213–22.

—— 'Authoritarian Secularism and Islamist Politics: The Case of Turkey', in Augustus Richard Norton (ed.) *Civil Society in the Middle East.* New York and Koln:1996, pp. 17–43.

Gretsky, S. 'Profile: Qadi Akbar Turajonzoda', *Central Asia Monitor*, 1 (1994), p.20.

Habermas, J. *Between Facts and Norms: Contributions to a Discourse Theory of Law and Democracy,* tr. W. Rehg. Cambridge, MA and Cambridge, UK, 1996, pp.329–87.

—— *Moral Consciousness and Communicative Action,* tr. C. Lenhardt and S.W. Nicholson. Cambridge, UK, 1992.

Haddad, Y, ed., *Muslims in the West: From Sojourners to Citizens.* New York, 2002.

Hall, J.A., ed. *Civil Society: Theory, History, Comparison.* Cambridge, MA and Cambridge, UK, 1995.

Halliday, F. *Two Hours That Shook the World – September 11, 2001: Causes and Consequences.* London, 2002.

Hammoudi, Abdellah. *Master and Disciple: The Cultural Foundations of Moroccan Authoritarianism.* London, 1997

Hann, Chris and Elizabeth Dunn, ed. *Civil Society: Challenging Western Models.* London and New York, 1996.

Harrison, L.E. and Samuel P. Huntington, ed. *Culture Matters: How Values Shape Human Progress.* New York, 2000.

Hasan, Mushirul. *Legacy of a Divided Nation: India's Muslims since Independence.* London, 1997.

Hashmi, Taj-ul-Islam. *Pakistan as a Peasant Utopia: The Communalization of Class Politics in East Bengal.* Boulder, 1992.

Havel, V. *Summer Meditations.* New York, 1992.

Heper, Metin. *The State Tradition in Turkey.* Walkington, 1985.

Hesse, C. and R. Post, ed., *Human Rights and Political Transitions: Gettysburg to Bosnia.* New York, 1999.

Himmelfarb, G. *The De-Moralization of Society: From Victorian Virtues to Modern Values.* New York, 1995.

Hodgson, Marshall G.S. *The Venture of Islam: Conscience and History in a World Civilization.* Chicago, 1974.

Hovannisian, R.G., ed. *Ethics in Islam.* Malibu, CA, 1985.

Howard, M.M. 'The Weakness of Postcommunist Civil Society', *Journal of Democracy,* 13 (2002), pp.157–69.

Huband, M. , J. Dempsey and R. Khalaf. 'Middle Eastern NGOs Strain at the Bonds of Authoritarian Government'. *The Financial Times* (London, 10 June 1999), p.7.

Human Rights Watch, *World Report 2002.* New York and London, 2002.

Humphrey, Benedict. *Marx Went Away but Karl Stayed Behind: Economy, Society and Religion in a Siberian Collective Farm.* Ann Arbor, MI, 1998.

Huntington, Samuel P. *The Clash of Civilizations and the Remaking of World Order.* New York, 1996.

Ibn al-Jawzi. *Talbis Iblis.* Cairo, 1928.

Ibrahim, Saad Eddin. 'From Taliban to Erbakan: The Case of Islam, Civil Society and Democracy', in Elisabeth Özdalga and Sune Persson, ed., *Civil Society, Democracy and the Muslim World.* Istanbul, 1997, pp.33–44.

Inglehart, Ronald. *Modernization and Postmodernization: Cultural, Economic, and Political Change in 43 Countries.* Princeton, NJ, 1997.

Iqbal, M. *The Reconstruction of Religious Thought in Islam.* Lahore, 1962.

Izutsu, T. *God and Man in the Koran: Semantics of the Koranic Weltanschauung.* Tokyo, 1964.

Jabri, Mohamed Abed. *Arab Political Reason: Determinants and Expressions (al-'aql al-siyasi al-arabi: muhaddidatuh wa tajalliyatuh).* Casablanca, 1990.

Jabri, V. *Discourses on Violence: Conflict Analysis Reconsidered.* New York, 1996.

Jalaeipour, Hamidreza. 'Religious Intellectuals and Political Action in the Reform Movement', paper presented at a conference on 'Intellectual Trends in 20th Century Iran', Princeton University, 21 Oct. 2000; available at <www.seraj.org>.

Kalaycıoğlu, Ersin. 'Civil Society in Turkey: Continuity and Change?' in Brian W. Beely, ed., *Turkish Transformation: New Century, New Challenges.* Walkington, 2001.

—— 'The Shaping of Party Preferences in Turkey: Coping with the Post-Cold War Era', *New Perspectives on Turkey,* 20 (1999), pp. 47–76.

—— 'Türkiye'de Siyasal Kültür ve Demokrasi' in Ergun Özbudun, Ersin Kalaycıoğlu, Levent Köker, ed., *Türkiye'de Demokratik Siyasal Kültür.* Ankara,1995, pp. 43–69.

Kamali, M. *Revolutionary Iran: Civil Society and the State in the Modernization Process.* Aldershot, UK, 1998.

Kamrava, M. 'The Civil Society Discourse in Iran', *British Journal of Middle Eastern Studies,* 28 (2001), pp.165–85.

Kandiyoti, D. 'Rural Livelihoods and Social Networks in Uzbekistan', 17 *Central Asian Survey* (1998), pp.561–78.

Karatnycky, A. 'The 2001 Freedom House Survey: Muslim Countries and the Democracy Gap', *Journal of Democracy,* 13 (2002), pp.99–112.

Kaviraj S. and S. Khilnani, ed. *Civil Society: History and Possibilities.* Cambridge, UK, 2001.

Kawtharani, Wajih. *The Arab Renaissance Project or the Crisis of Evolution from Sultanian to National Society.* Beirut, 1995.

Keane, John, ed., *Civil Society and the State: New European Perspectives.* New York and London, 1988.

Keane, John. *Civil Society: Old Images, New Visions.* Cambridge, UK, 1998.

Kepel, Gilles. *Expansion et déclin de l'islamisme.* Paris, 2000.

—— *Jihad: The Trail of Political Islam.* London and Cambridge, MA, 2002.

Khan, Gulfishan. *Indian Muslim Perceptions of the West during the Eighteenth Century.* Karachi, 1998.

Khiabany, Gholam and Annabelle Sreberny, 'The Iranian Press and the Continuing Struggle over Civil Society 1998–2000', *Gazette: International Journal for Communication Studies,* 63 (2001), pp. 203–23.

Lewis, Bernard. *What Went Wrong? Western Impact and Middle Eastern Response.* New York, 2002.

Maalouf, Amin. *In the Name of Identity: Violence and the Need to Belong,* tr. B. Bray. New York, 2000.

Madjid, N. 'Potential Islamic Doctrinal Resources for the Establishment and Appreciation of the Modern Concept of Civil Society', in N. Mitsuo et al., ed., *Islam and Civil Society in Southeast Asia.* Singapore, 2001.

Makarova, Ekaterina. 'The Mahalla, Civil Society and the Domestication of the State in Soviet and Post-Soviet Uzbekistan', *Workshop for Homegrown Models of Civil Society in the Muslim World,* Watson Institute for International Studies, Brown University, March 12–13, 1999.

Makdisi, G. 'The Marriage of Tughril Beg', *International Journal of Middle East Studies* (1970), pp.259–75.

Maleshenko, A. and M.B. Olcott. *Islam in the Post-Soviet Newly Independent States: The View from Within.* New York, 2001.

Malik, Iftikhar. *Islam, Nationalism and the West: Issues of Identity in Pakistan.* Oxford, 1999.

—— *State and Civil Society in Pakistan: Politics of Authority, Ideology and Ethnicity.* Oxford, 1997.

Martinez, Luis. *La guerre civile en Algérie.* Karthala, 1998.

Mardin, Şerif. 'Center-Periphery Relations: A Key to Turkish Politics?' in E. Akarlı and G. Ben-Dor (ed.), *Political Participation in Turkey: Historical Background and Present Problems.* Istanbul, 1975, pp.7–32.

Mayer, Anne Elizabeth. *Islam and Human Rights: Tradition and Politics.* 2nd ed., London, 1995.

Merchant, Liaquat H., ed. *The Jinnah Anthology.* Karachi, 1999.

Migdal, Joel S. *Strong Societies and Weak States: State-Society Relations and State Capabilities in the Third World.* Princeton, NJ, 1988.

Mir-Hosseini, Ziba. *Islam and Gender: The Religious Debate in Contemporary Iran.* London, 2000.

Miskawayh. *The Refinement of Character,* tr. C.K. Zurayk. Beirut, 1968.

Mitra, Subrata, ed. *Sub-national Movements in South Asia.* Boulder and Oxford, 1996.

Monshipouri, M. 'State Prerogatives, Civil Society, and Liberalization: The Paradoxes of the Late Twentieth Century in the Third World'. *Ethics and International Affairs,* 11 (1997), pp.232–51.

Mumtaz, Khawar. 'NGOs in Pakistan: An Overview', in Tariq Banuri, et al. ed., *Just Development: Beyond Adjustment with a Human Face.* Karachi, 1997, pp.171–90.

Murshid, Tazeen. 'Nations Imagined and Fragmented: Bengali Ethnicity and the Break up of Pakistan', in W. van Schendel and E.J. Zurcher, ed., *Identity Politics in Central Asia and the Muslim World: Nationalism, Ethnicity and Labour in the Twentieth Century.* London, 2001, pp.85–105.

Muzaffar, C. 'Ethnicity, Ethnic Conflict and Human Rights in Malaysia', in C.E. Welch and V.A. Leary, ed., *Asian Perspectives on Human Rights.* Boulder, Colorado, 1990, pp.107–41.

Najmabadi, Afsaneh. 'Feminism in an Islamic Republic: Years of Hardship, Years of Growth', in Yvonne Yazbeck Haddad and John L. Esposito, ed., *Islam, Gender and Social Change.* Oxford, 1998, pp.59–84.

Neuhaus, Richard, John. *The Naked Public Square: Religion and Democracy in America.* Grand Rapids, MI, 1984.

Newberg, Paula. *Judging the State: Courts and Constitutional Politics in Pakistan.* Cambridge, 1995.

Norton, Richard, Augustus, ed. *Civil Society in the Middle East.* Leiden and New York, 1994, vol.1, and 1995, vol.2.

Olcott Martha B. and N. Udalova. *Drug Trafficking on the Great Silk Road: The Security Environment in Central Asia.* Working Papers, Carnegie Endowment for International Peace, 11 (March, 2000). *Opinion Analysis,* Office of Research Department of State, Washington DC (July 6, 2000).

Owusu, M. 'Domesticating Democracy: Culture, Civil Society and Constitutionalism in Africa', *Comparative Studies in Society and History,* 39 (1997), pp.120–52.

Özdalga, Elisabeth. 'Civil Society and Its Enemies', in Elisabeth Özdalga and Sune Persson, ed., *Civil Society, Democracy, and the Muslim World.* Istanbul, 1997.

Pasha-zade, A.S. *Islam in the Caucasus.* Baku, 1991.

Pippin, R.B. 'The Ethical Status of Civility?', in L.S. Rouner, ed., *Civility.* Notre Dame, Indiana, 2000, pp.103–17.

Piscatori, James. *Islam, Islamists, and the Electoral Principle in the Middle East.* Leiden, 2000.

Plagemann, Gottfried. 'Human Rights Organizations: Defending the Particular or the Universal?' in Stefanos Yerasimos et al., ed., *Civil Society in the Grip of Nationalism: Studies on Political Culture in Contemporary Turkey.* Istanbul, 2000, pp.433–73.

Popper, Karl. *The Open Society and its Enemies,* vol.1. London, 1945; repr. London, 1999.

Pusch, Barbara. 'Stepping into the Public Sphere: The Rise of Islamist and Religious-Conservative Women's Non-Governmental Organizations' in Stefanos Yerasimos et al., ed., *Civil Society in the Grip of Nationalism: Studies on Political Culture in Contemporary Turkey.* Istanbul, 2000, pp.475–505.

Putnam, R. D. *Bowling Alone: The Collapse and Revival of American Community*. New York, 2000.

Pye, L. *Asian Power and Politics: The Cultural Dimensions of Authority*, Cambridge, MA, 1985.

Rahnema, Ali. *An Islamic Utopian: A Political Biography of Ali Shari'ati*. London and New York, 1998.

Rashid, Ahmed. *Jihad: The Rise of Militant Islam in Central Asia*. New Haven, CT, 2002.

Rawls, John. *A Theory of Justice*. Rev. ed. Cambridge, MA, 1999.

Ro'i, Y. *Islam in the Soviet Union: From World War II to Perestroika*. London, 2000. 'Rowshan-fekri-ye dini va mas'aleh-ye zanan', ('Religious Intellectualism and the Woman Question') *Rah-e Now* 1 (16), 17 Mordad 1377, pp. 32–3.

Rorty, Richard. 'The Priority of Democracy to Philosophy', in *Objectivity, Relativism, and Truth: Philosophical Papers*. Cambridge, UK, 1991, vol.1.

Roy, Olivier. 'Kolkhoz and Civil Society in the Independent States of Central Asia' in M.H. Ruffin and D. Waugh, ed., *Civil Society in Central Asia*. Baltimore and Seattle, 1999, pp. 109–21.

—— *The Failure of Political Islam*. Cambridge, Mass., 1994.

—— *The New Central Asia*. London, 2000.

Ruffin, Holt and Daniel Waugh, ed. *Civil Society in Central Asia*. Baltimore and Seattle, 1999.

Rzayeva, L. 'Azerbaijani Intellectuals during the Transition', *Central Eurasian Studies Review*, 1 (2002) pp.13–14.

Sadri, M. and A. Sadri, ed. *Reason, Freedom, and Democracy in Islam: Essential Writings of 'Abdolkarim Soroush*. Oxford, 2000.

Saghafi, Morad. 'Crossing the Deserts: Iranian Intellectuals after the Islamic Republic', *Critique: Journal for Critical Studies of the Middle East*, 18 (2001), pp.15–46.

Said, Edward. 'Impossible Histories: Why the many Islams cannot be simplified', *Harper's Magazine*, July 2002, pp.69–74.

Sajoo, Amyn B. 'The Islamic Ethos and the Spirit of Humanism', *International Journal of Politics, Culture and Society*, 8 (1995), pp.579–96.

—— *Pluralism in Old Societies and New States*. Singapore, 1994.

—— Review of Ernest Gellner, *Conditions of Liberty:Civil Society and its Rivals*, *Canadian Journal of Law and Society*, 11 (1996), pp.307–10.

Sandel, M. *Liberalism and the Limits of Justice*. Cambridge, 1998.

Saul, J.R. *On Equilibrium*. Toronto, New York, London, 2001, pp.86, 65–7.

Schirazi, Asghar. *The Constitution of Iran: Politics and the State in the Islamic*

Republic, tr. John O'Kane. London, 1998.

Seligman, Adam B. *The Idea of Civil Society*. Princeton, NJ, 1992.

Shahrani, Nazif. 'Re-building Communities of Trust in Muslim Central Asia: Past Legacies and Future Prospects', *Workshop for Home-grown Models of Civil Society in the Muslim World* (Watson Institute for International Studies, Brown University, March 12–13, 1999).

Shaikh, Farzana. *Community and Consensus in Islam: Muslim Representation in Colonial India, 1860–1947*. Cambridge, 1989.

Sharabi, Hicham. *Neopatriarchy: A Theory of Distorted Change in Arab Society*. Oxford, 1988.

Smith, J. *Moralities: Sex, Money and Power in the Twenty-first Century*. London, 2001.

Smith-Christopher, D.L. "That was Then ...': Debating Nonviolence within the Textual Traditions of Judaism, Christianity, and Islam', in J. Runzo and N.M. Martin, ed., *Ethics in the world religions*. New York and Oxford, 2001, pp.256–9.

Soroush, Abdolkarim, 'Reforming the Revolution', tr. Nilou Mobasser, *Index on Censorship* (London), January 2002, pp.64–77.

Sunar, İlkay. 'Politics of Citizenship in the Middle East: An Agenda for Research', in *Suna Kili'ye Armagan: Cumhuriyet'e Adanan bir Yaşam*. Istanbul, 1998, pp. 365–71.

Tajikistan: Refugee Reintegration and Conflict Prevention, Forced Migration Projects of the Open Society Institute. New York, 1998.

Talaqani, Azam. 'Fa'aliyat-ha-ye dah saleh-ye mo'assaseh-ye eslami-ye zanan-e Iran', *Daftar-e Dovvom: Masa'el-e Zanan* (Second Volume: Women's Issues). Tehran, 1991, pp.1–10.

Tarock, Adam. 'The Muzzling of the Liberal Press in Iran', *Third World Quarterly*, 22 (2001), pp. 585–602.

Taylor, C. *Philosophical Arguments*. Cambridge, MA and London, 1995.

—— *The Ethics of Authenticity*. Cambridge, MA, 1992.

Teitelbaum, J. *Holier Than Thou: Saudi Arabia's Islamic Opposition*. Washington, DC, 2000.

Thiemann, R. *Religion in Public Life: A Dilemma for Democracy*. Washington, DC, 1996.

Tibi, B. *Islam between Culture and Politics*. New York, 2001.

Tohidi, N. 'Soviet in Public, Azeri in Private: Gender, Islam, and Nationalism in Soviet and Post-Soviet Azerbaijan' (Hoover Institution Working Paper). Stanford, Calif., 1995.

Toprak, Binnaz. 'Civil Society in Turkey' in Norton, ed. *Civil Society in the Middle East*. Leiden, New York, Koln, 1996, pp.87–118.

Tornquist, Olle. *Tajikistan: Human Development Report 2000*. New York, 2000.

Turner, B.S. *Orientalism, Post-modernism and Globalism*. London and New York, 1994.

Tusi, Nasir al-Din. *The Nasirean Ethics*, tr. G.M. Wickens. London, 1964.

United Nations Development Programme's Annual *Human Development Report*, New York and Oxford.

Viswanathan, G. éd. *Power, Politics, and Culture: Interviews with Edward Said*. New York, 2001.

Walzer, Michael. *The Revolution of the Saints*. Cambridge, Mass., 1965.

Walzer, R. *al-Farabi on the Perfect State*. Oxford, 1985.

Weiss, B. 'Interpretation in Islamic Law: The Process of Ijtihad', *American Journal of Comparative Law*, 26 (1978), p.199.

Wiktorowicz, Q. and S. Taji-Farouki. 'Islamic NGOs and Muslim Politics: A Case from Jordan'. *Third World Quarterly*, 21 (2000), pp.685–99.

Wright, R. 'Two Visions of Reformation' (on Soroush and Ghannouchi), *Journal of Democracy*, 7 (1996), pp.64–75.

—— *The Last Great Revolution: Turmoil and Transformation in Iran*. New York, 2000.

Yalman, Nur. 'Some Observations on Secularism in Islam: The Cultural Revolution in Turkey', *Daedalus*, 102 (1973), pp. 139–67.

Yamamoto, T., ed. *Emerging Civil Society in the Asia Pacific Community*. Singapore, 1995.

Yavuzyiğit, Hikmet. 'Derneklerin Demokratik Toplumsal Yapıya Katkısı' *Mülkiyeliler Birliği Dergisi*, vol. XXII No. 210–12, (1998), 62–9.

Zeghal, Malika. *Gardiens de l'Islam: Les oulémas d'al-Azhar dans l'Egypte contemporaine*. Paris, 1996.

Index